# The Road to Confrontation

# The Road to

# CONFRONTATION

## American Policy
## toward China and
## Korea, 1947–1950

William Whitney Stueck, Jr.

The University of North Carolina Press *Chapel Hill*

© 1981 The University of North Carolina Press
All rights reserved
Manufactured in the United States of America
ISBN 0-8078-1445-8
Library of Congress Catalog Card Number 80-11818

Library of Congress Cataloging in Publication Data

Stueck, William Whitney, 1945–
   The road to confrontation.

  Bibliography: p.
  Includes index.
   1.  United States—Foreign relations—Korea.
2.  Korea—Foreign relations—United States.
3.  United States—Foreign relations—China.
4.  China—Foreign relations—United States.
5.  United States—Foreign relations—1945–1953.
6.  Truman, Harry S., Pres. U.S., 1884–1972.
I.  Title.
E183.8.K7S88 · 327.73051 80-11818
ISBN 0-8078-1445-8
ISBN 0-8078-4080-7 pbk.

*To* JAMES T. PATTERSON

*and* JOHN L. THOMAS

# Contents

Acknowledgments      ix

Introduction      3

**Part I**    **The Decline of China and the Rise of Korea in**    9
**American Foreign Policy**

1. The American Relationship with China and    11
Korea: World War II and Its Aftermath

**Part II**    **China and Korea Policy under Marshall's**    31
**Stewardship**

2. The China Problem: To Contain    33
Communism or to Contain a Commitment

3. The Korean Dilemma: How to Arrange a    75
Graceful Withdrawal from an Awkward
Entanglement

**Part III**    **China and Korea Policy on the Eve of War**    111

4. Letting the Dust Settle: China Policy on the    113
Eve of War

5. Hoping the Worst Won't Happen: Korea    153
Policy on the Eve of War

**Part IV**    **Containment, Liberation, and Confrontation:**    173
**American Policy in the Early Months of the**
**Korean War**

6. The Attack and the Response    177

7. The Adventure      223

Conclusion      251

Notes      259

Bibliography      299

Index      313

## Maps

1. The Communist Advance in China, 1945–  34–35
  1949

2. The War in Korea, 25 June–4 August 1950  176

3. The Defeat of the North Korean Forces  224

4. U.N. Forces Advance to the Yalu, 11 October–  242
  1 November 1950

5. The Communist Chinese Offensive, 25–28  252
  November 1950

# Acknowledgments

I began the study of American policy toward China and Korea during the Truman period in 1970 under the supervision of Alan D. Harper at Queens College. He has provided encouragement and useful criticism to me at virtually every stage of this book's development. At Brown University, I benefited greatly from the advice of Charles E. Neu. His incisive comments on chapters three and six were especially useful. James T. Patterson and John L. Thomas, also of Brown, have offered beneficial criticism. Their efforts on my behalf have gone far beyond the call of duty. To repay my debt to them would be impossible, but I hope that the dedication page expresses the depth of my appreciation.

I have also profited from the criticism of Thomas G. Paterson of the University of Connecticut, O. Edmund Clubb of Columbia University, Justus D. Doenecke of New College of the University of South Florida, and especially Lloyd C. Gardner of Rutgers University and Bruce Cumings of the University of Washington.

These scholars represent a broad range of opinion on the issues discussed herein. I should emphasize, therefore, that I alone am responsible for the interpretations that follow and that they are sometimes at odds with the views of those mentioned above.

Grants from the Liberty Fund of Indianapolis, Indiana, and the Harry S. Truman Library Institute of Independence, Missouri, provided me with income that enabled me to pursue research and writing at crucial times.

Several archivists and librarians deserve special mention for the pleasant and efficient service they provided me in tracking down relevant materials. Dennis Bilger, Philip Lagerquist, and Elizabeth Safly of the Harry S. Truman Library belong at the top of the list. William Cunliffe and Edward Reese of the Modern Military Branch and Milton Gustafson of the Diplomatic Branch at the National Archives were always helpful and patient with me in my often fumbling efforts to work through the prodigious collections of their branches. The same may be said of Jack Saunders of the Federal Records Center and Ron Bulatoff of the Hoover Institution Library.

Finally, I want to thank my wife, Pat, who has not typed, criticized, or even read the manuscript, but who has, over thirteen years of marriage, sacrificed far more for me than I have for her. Without that sacrifice, this book would never have been written.

# The Road to Confrontation

# Introduction

On 28 November 1950, General Douglas MacArthur wrote despondently to his superiors in Washington that United Nations forces in Korea faced "an entirely new war."[1] Although prone to overstatement, the irrepressible general was not exaggerating this time. In the previous forty-eight hours, Chinese Communist forces had launched a massive counteroffensive south of the Yalu River. Instead of completing the military unification of the entire peninsula under non-Communist leadership, United Nations troops now reeled from an attack by numerically superior forces. The situation, at best, was uncertain, at worst disastrous.

Communist Chinese intervention in the Korean War had a momentous impact on American politics and foreign policy. Shortly after the end of his tenure as secretary of state in 1953, Dean Acheson correctly observed that

> this Chinese Communist advance into North Korea . . . was one of the most terrific disasters that has occurred to American foreign policy, and certainly . . . the greatest disaster which occurred to the Truman administration. It did more to destroy and undermine American foreign policy than anything that I know about—the whole Communists-in-government business, the whole corruption outcry, was really just window-dressing put upon this great disaster.[2]

After the first year of the Truman administration, to be sure, the "Communists-in-government business" was never far below the surface of American politics. In early 1950, with Senator Joseph R. McCarthy's charges of widespread Communist infiltration into the State Department, the issue moved to center stage. Yet the Sino-American confrontation in Korea gave tremendous momentum to the "Red Scare" at home.[3] McCarthy's attacks centered on American China policy, and the extended conflict in Korea could only add weight to his charge that Chiang Kai-shek had been "sold down the river." Although many Americans continued to reject domestic "treason" as the source of their nation's trials in Asia, developments in Korea in November 1950 made the Truman administration's earlier failure to prevent a Communist victory in China look all the more catastrophic.

The Sino-American collision led directly to the clash over Asian strategy between the president and General MacArthur, which, in turn, bolstered Republican efforts to undermine public confidence in Democratic leadership. Chinese intervention turned what promised to be a badly needed American victory in Asia into a defeat from which the Truman administration never recovered, even after United Nations forces halted the Chinese advance and largely reestablished the prewar boundary in Korea. In the spring of 1952, despite economic prosperity at home, the president's popularity in a national public opinion poll reached a low of 26 percent.[4] The Republican party approached the presidential election of 1952 in an enviable position.

The Sino-American engagement in Korea also had substantial long-term consequences. Prior to November 1950, the Truman administration had demonstrated some flexibility in its attitude toward Communist China. Despite Acheson's assertion that "Communist leaders have foresworn their Chinese heritage and have publicly announced their subservience to . . . Russia,"[5] uncertainty remained in Washington as to the nature of the relationship between Peking and Moscow and the degree to which the United States could influence it. On 17 November 1949, the secretary of state proposed to the president a policy aimed at detaching Peking from Moscow's orbit.[6] For the next seven months, Acheson opposed any major American effort to defend Taiwan from Communism, in part because such action might distract the new mainland regime's attention from Soviet domination of the northern provinces of China.[7]

Even after the outbreak of war in Korea in June 1950, the administration remained hopeful that China and Russia were not necessarily close allies. On 10 September, Acheson, in discussing the prospect of Communist Chinese intervention in Korea, asserted that a Sino-American confrontation on the peninsula would assist the Soviet Union in its imperialist designs in northern China and that Peking, recognizing this fact, was unlikely to intervene.[8]

But, as historian John Lewis Gaddis has noted, when Communist China did move into Korea, the assumption that "there existed significant differences between varieties of Communism, and that these could be turned to the advantage of the United States" largely disappeared from high government circles in Washington.[9] Secretary of Defense George C. Marshall, testifying at the Senate hearings that followed General MacArthur's dismissal in April 1951, asserted that China was acting "literally under the direction of the Soviet Union."[10] When asked if, in effect, China had been "conquered by Russia," Marshall replied, "I think that is generally a fact."[11] Increasingly, the United States perceived international relations as a zero sum game, in which each Communist victory constituted a proportionate setback to "the Free World."[12] American intervention abroad to prevent such victories seemed to become more necessary than ever before.

The path to American globalism, of course, was to be long and winding. No single event was decisive in itself. Numerous developments between 1946 and 1950 might be regarded as turning points in the direction of American policy.[13] And, despite the universalistic rhetoric of Secretary of State John Foster Dulles, the Eisenhower administration at times exercised restraint on the issue of committing American forces abroad. The decision to accept a partial Communist victory in Indochina in 1954 rather than give the French massive air support at Dienbienphu reflected a foreign policy that fell short of global containment.

Still, Communist Chinese intervention in Korea had a decisive impact on the evolution of American policy. The Seventh Fleet had moved into the Taiwan Strait after the North Korean attack in June 1950, but an American victory in Korea later in the year might have brought an end to the policy of protecting Generalissimo Chiang Kai-shek.[14] The Sino-American confrontation made a retreat by the United States on the Taiwan issue impossible politically and undesirable strategically. The issue, in turn, became a major impediment to improved relations between the United States and Communist China for more than two decades. In the United States, the prolonged encounter in Korea left a legacy of frustration and bitterness toward China that continued into the 1960s, even after the surfacing of the Sino-Soviet split.

The Democratic administrations of John F. Kennedy and Lyndon B. Johnson never forgot the success with which Republicans had used the China issue in the early 1950s.[15] And the memory of Chinese hordes storming United Nations forces in Korea bolstered the image of Communist China as an aggressive revolutionary power. As United States military involvement in Vietnam increased rapidly after 1964, American leaders constantly warned of the "shadow of Communist China" that threatened Southeast Asia and the entire underdeveloped world.[16] "Moving Peking to peaceful coexistence," Secretary of State Dean Rusk asserted in January 1966, was "the No. 1 problem in the world today."[17] More than a decade after the truce had been reached in Korea, therefore, the containment of China remained a central objective of American foreign policy.

How did the United States become engaged in this unwanted conflict with China in Korea? This study seeks to answer that question by analyzing American policy toward China and Korea from 1947 through November 1950. At the beginning of 1947, explosive conditions prevailed in both countries. In China, General George C. Marshall had just ended his mission in disgust after failing to unite the Nationalists and the Communists in a coalition government. The renewal of full-scale civil war appeared inevitable. Such a conflict promised to create serious dilemmas for American decision makers. As Soviet-American relations deteriorated, the containment of Communism became a primary goal of the United States. In China, however, there was no attractive alternative to the Communists. The National government of Chiang Kai-shek was corrupt, reactionary, and inefficient, and no viable third force appeared on the horizon.

Moreover, American resources were finite. In 1947, they became increasingly committed to the European theater. Because Congress and the public had limited tolerance for costly programs abroad, leaders in Washington were forced to make difficult choices as to how much of the resources at their disposal should be allotted to particular areas of the world. At a time of revolutionary developments in China, Washington's continuing Europe-first strategy severely restricted possibilities for the exertion of American influence.

Prospects in Korea were hardly more encouraging. Unlike China, Korea had never been an area of substantial interest to the United States. When Japanese rule ended in 1945 and the peninsula was divided into Soviet and American occupation zones, however, Korea became an area of confrontation between the two superpowers. As cold war tensions grew, the chances for Soviet-American agreement on a framework for a unified Korea declined. At the same time, unrest in the American zone south of the thirty-eighth parallel intensified. Impatient at the lack of progress toward unification and independence, South Koreans took out their frustrations on American occupation officials and on each other. Washington, in turn, grew increasingly impatient with the sizable commitment of men and resources to an area of limited strategic significance. Yet, given the Soviet-American confrontation there, the possibility of abandoning Korea to Communism seemed politically hazardous. Action had to be taken to halt the drift toward chaos and the continuing drain on scarce resources, but no easy solutions beckoned.

Thus, 1947 was a year of crucial decisions regarding both China and Korea that would exert a major impact on the future of the United States in East Asia. It is a logical starting point for an analysis of the process by which the United States became embroiled with Communist China in November 1950.

The present is an especially apt time for new studies of American China and Korea policy during the period 1947–50. Since the early 1970s, a tremendous volume of source material has for the first time become available to students of this era. It is now possible to move well beyond the path-breaking works of the 1960s by Tang Tsou on China and Soon Sung Cho on Korea, which depended on very limited documentation.[18] Tsou and Cho labored at a time when the State Department's foreign-relations series had not even reached the post-World War II era. Their efforts were far from fruitless, yet newly available evidence suggests that some of their conclusions merit revision.

On China, it now appears that sentimentality and idealism played a lesser role in American decision making than Tsou believed. So too did domestic politics. Although American ethnocentrism, as well as political pressures in Washington, receive considerable attention in the pages that follow, they often play secondary roles where Tsou saw them as central.

A new element in the story is the Truman administration's concern for American credibility abroad. In his recent study of the Nixon years, Jonathan Schell traces credibility as a key aspect of United States foreign policy back to the late 1950s, when the Soviet Union acquired the capacity to inflict rapid and extensive damage on the American homeland. For that reason, he argues, decision makers increasingly questioned the effectiveness of America's atomic weapons as a deterrent to Soviet expansionism. Because an atomic strike on the Soviet Union could now result in an immediate counterstrike on the United States, the reasoning went, leaders in the Kremlin might doubt Washington's readiness to use its nuclear weapons in response to a Russian move into Western Europe or elsewhere. To discourage Soviet adventurism, therefore, the United States must demonstrate its will and its capacity to act militarily by means other than strategic air power.[19]

My research also indicates that America's quest for credibility deserves a major place in analyses of the early cold war. As historian Gaddis Smith has noted, most American officials first played significant roles in foreign affairs "when Hitler was at the peak of his terrible power."[20] From this experience, they gained many attitudes, including a wariness toward negotiations and a sense of the importance of military strength. First and foremost, they came to believe that the United States must play a central part in the world—politically, economically, militarily. The disastrous events of the 1930s, it seemed, had occurred because the United States failed to exert itself sufficiently beyond its shores. To obtain a measure of peace and order in the postwar world, the United States must demonstrate to other nations—friends and foes alike—that it would act with more force and reliability than it had in the past. In short, Washington must build American credibility abroad.

This perspective did not always lead to massive American intervention in foreign lands. In China, it actually dictated caution regarding expanded American involvement. Such involvement would commit American prestige to a possibly unwinnable venture. On the other hand, concern for American credibility encouraged the continuation of some aid to the National government and increased difficulties in building a constructive relationship with the Communists.

Fears about American credibility were also central to United States policy in Korea, first in 1948 in the creation of an independent government below the thirty-eighth parallel, then two years later in the commitment of American military forces to the peninsula. Although prior to June 1950 the United States failed to protect its position in Korea adequately, the Soviet-American confrontation there after 1945 had led State Department officials to connect the United States position below the thirty-eighth parallel to American credibility worldwide. And this fact suggests a measure of continuity to American policy before and after the North Korean attack that heretofore has been largely ignored.

Finally, the concept of credibility adds a major dimension to American policy in Korea between July and November 1950. It helps explain why the Truman administration, which had previously been content with *containing* Communism abroad, now sought to *liberate* the entire peninsula from enemy control. American credibility was seen as resting not only on the containment of "aggression," but on its punishment as well. Late in the fall, after considerable evidence surfaced of major Chinese intervention in Korea, Washington failed to halt offensive operations, in part because decision makers feared that any show of weakness or hesitation would embolden Peking. Credibility again made its mark on policy.

Still, too much should not be claimed for a single concept. New evidence has made it possible to identify an important theme, but it has also served to reemphasize that decision making is a complex process, one in which a variety of forces operate. Although credibility was of concern to all American leaders, its significance varied from person to person, from moment to moment. Sometimes, it even tugged people in different directions. The same can be said for domestic politics and institutional forces within the executive branch. Thus a complicated picture emerges, and science often gives way to art in its rendition. Documents tell much but not all. The historian's judgment and imagination frequently stand as the final arbiters.

# PART I
The Decline of China
and the Rise of Korea in
American Foreign Policy

For the first forty-five years of the twentieth century, American concerns about China and Korea followed a neatly reversed pattern. As the century began, the United States was in the midst of a diplomatic struggle to prevent the division of China into European spheres of influence. Yet, when Japan expanded into Korea soon thereafter, Washington scarcely bothered to protest. Again, in the 1930s, Japanese aggression, this time against China, led to rapidly mounting tensions in relations with the United States. In 1941, it was a major source of the diplomatic impasse leading to the attack on Pearl Harbor. In contrast, Japan's continued subjugation of Korea attracted little American attention. During World War II, China remained a constant topic of Allied discussions, and, despite limited American military operations in the China theater, Chiang Kai-shek's government received massive amounts of aid to support its struggle against Japan. Korea, on the other hand, rarely appeared on the agenda of wartime conferences: its fate simply did not much concern Allied wartime planners.

America's lack of interest in Korea, in stark contrast to China, is easily explained. Whether missionaries, businessmen, concession-hunters or diplomats, interested Americans agreed enthusiastically on the potential significance of China. Its size and population alone commanded respect. Korea, hardly larger than the state of Minnesota, remained chiefly of regional importance. The great powers of northern Asia—Japan and Russia—viewed the peninsula as a convenient east-west stepping-stone of considerable strategic value. But, to a nation located thousands of miles eastward across the Pacific, the "Land of the Morning Calm" was never of serious concern.

By 1947, however, some forty thousand American troops were stationed in Korea. Meanwhile, American forces in China, which had numbered more than a hundred thousand immediately following the Japanese surrender, had dwindled to a mere ten thousand. The dispatch of forces to Korea resulted in a new American commitment to that country, one that departed sharply from the traditional pattern of non-involvement. Although the Truman administration never cut off aid to the Chinese National government, a fact of far-reaching consequences for the United States in East Asia, the gradual withdrawal of American troops from China during 1946 did aim at limiting

American commitments there. Whereas the United States studiously avoided large-scale intervention in China as the Communists marched to victory between 1947 and 1949, in June 1950 American troops were rushed to Korea when the Communists suddenly invaded the southern half of the peninsula. A brief examination of United States relations with China and Korea prior to 1947 helps explain this sudden reversal.

# 1

## The American Relationship with China and Korea: World War II and Its Aftermath

### The Internal Struggle in China: America Leans to One Side

Chiang Kai-shek was angry. It was January 1947 and, in meetings at Nanking with General George C. Marshall, he lambasted the Yalta accords of February 1945. The United States had made major concessions to the Soviet Union regarding postwar Manchuria. The Russians gained a naval base at Port Arthur, recognition of their "preeminent interests" at the port of Dairen, and joint operation with the Chinese of the South Manchurian and Chinese-Eastern railroads. His countrymen, Chiang asserted, "bitterly resented" not being consulted about agreements affecting their future.

Then, as was characteristic of his dealings with "barbarians," Chiang abruptly altered his tone and invited Marshall to stay on in China as his "Supreme Adviser." According to Ambassador John Leighton Stuart, the generalissimo pleaded "with great earnestness," and offered Marshall "all the power which he himself possessed." The foreigner would command both the U.S. Army Advisory Group and a powerful consultative body in civil affairs. Marshall politely rejected the offer.[1] He was returning to Washington to replace James F. Byrnes as secretary of state. Appointment as a top adviser to Chiang would entail a level of American participation in Chinese affairs unacceptable to Washington.

The incident was at once revealing and misleading. It reflected the determination of Chiang to pursue a military solution to the internal divisions in China and his desire to commit the United States to this endeavor. Since the 1920s, he had always put much stock in the use of force. But, after 1937, outside pressures had led him to downplay somewhat the military struggle with the Communists. The Japanese invasion of China necessitated a united front between the Nationalists and the Communists. Although the alliance was always uneasy, especially after 1940, the continuing struggle against Japan prevented either of the domestic contestants from devoting full attention to their conflict. When the war against Japan ended in victory in August 1945, one deterrent to full-scale civil war disappeared.

Yet both parties continued to exercise a degree of restraint. Although Communist forces had multiplied rapidly during the past decade, Chiang's still outnumbered them five to one. The Nationalists held a clear advantage in light arms, artillery, and transportation facilities. Unlike the Nationalists, the Communists had no air force.[2] Their potential ally, the Soviet Union, sent troops into Manchuria on 8 August 1945, but six days later Joseph Stalin concluded a Treaty of Friendship and Alliance with Chiang pledging "moral support and military aid" exclusively to the National government.[3] The Chinese Communists, uncertain of the intentions of their ideological comrades in the Kremlin, had good reason to avoid war with the Nationalists.[4]

Chiang also had cause for restraint. His military superiority depended largely on American aid. If his troops were to beat the Communists in the race to liberate Manchuria and North China from Japanese occupation, they would need American ships and planes to transport them. Despite Soviet guarantees to support only the National government, he feared that Russian forces would assist the Communists in areas he did not occupy quickly.[5]

For the long term, Chiang hoped for American military assistance to train and equip ninety divisions of his army. During the war, he claimed, President Franklin D. Roosevelt had committed the United States to this project, which was essential to Nationalist prospects.[6] China had little capacity for producing modern arms. A balance-of-payments deficit and rampant inflation limited the ability of the Nationalists to pay for arms imports. And their armies were often poorly trained and led. An American military mission would help solve these problems.

Chiang also hoped for continued American economic aid. He had been receiving such help since 1938, when the Export-Import Bank had extended him a $25 million commodity credit. The largest lump sum came in 1942 in the form of a $500 million loan. Yet this assistance constantly aggravated Sino-American relations. Washington wanted to supervise disbursement of the funds to prevent waste and corruption. Chiang resisted, not only because of his intense nationalism but also because his influence within China rested in part on his ability to confer financial rewards on loyalists among the landlord, merchant, and military classes.[7]

Although the generalissimo usually had his way, most American officials deeply resented his use of their nation's largess. For instance, he allotted much of the 1942 loan to an issue of Chinese bonds and certificates, allegedly to combat inflation. He confined the purchase of these instruments, however, to high government functionaries and wealthy private citizens. Through currency manipulation that actually sparked inflation, speculators made windfall profits. The wives of Chiang and his finance minister, H. H. Kung, as well as T. V. Soong, the generalissimo's brother-in-law and the chief negotiator of the loan, were among the profiteers.[8] Three years later, Soong, now the minister of foreign affairs, concluded a deal for trucks, cotton textiles, and gold. Again, Chiang's use of United States aid—especially the gold—did not meet American expectations.[9] Such incidents depleted his political capital in Washington. Given his urgent need for ongoing assistance, he could not afford to reject out of hand American pressure to negotiate with the Communists. Their willingness to talk further induced the Nationalists to adopt a moderate course.[10]

By 1947, the circumstances had changed considerably. Chiang still needed American aid, as his offer to Marshall suggests. Yet, despite Marshall's refusal to become the generalissimo's "Supreme Adviser," the United States was in many ways in a weaker position to deny assistance to the Nationalists than it had been two years earlier. After more than a year of intense diplomatic activity, American attempts to bring Communists into the National government had failed. Although Marshall's efforts during 1946 had started auspiciously, by April heavy fighting had broken out in Manchuria, and Communist leader Mao Tse-tung had renounced an earlier cease-fire order. Only with great difficulty over a two-month span was Marshall able to patch together another truce, and it did nothing to foster a permanent settlement. The Communists understandably refused to give up their independent army without receiving in return more than token power in a coalition government. Their earlier experiment in cooperation with the Nationalists had ended in Chiang's ruthless purge of 1926–27, which had nearly proved disastrous to the Communists. They were determined to avoid a repeat performance.

For their part, the Nationalists showed slight disposition to accommodate their foe. Even an American embargo on arms shipments to China and an accelerated withdrawal of American forces had little impact on Chiang. Fighting resumed on a large scale. Negotiations dragged on for several months, only to end permanently in November, when Chou En-lai, the top Communist diplomat in Nanking, departed for his Yenan headquarters.[11] This move turned out to be the beginning of a long-term adversary relationship between the United States and the Chinese Communists.

Actually, the Communists had long displayed patience with Washington. For much of World War II, their press had applauded the United States as a forward-looking ally struggling gallantly against fascism.[12] In 1944, as Roosevelt became increasingly aware of Chiang's ineffectual leadership against Japan, Washington had considered funneling aid to the Communists. American "observers" traveled to Yenan, and were warmly received by their Communist hosts. After living for years amidst the squalor and official venality of Nationalist-controlled areas, the visitors were fascinated by what they saw. John Stewart Service, a young and talented foreign service officer, reported that "We have come into a different country and are meeting a different people."[13] Energy, efficiency, and optimism characterized the populace of Yenan, in sharp contrast with the oppressive atmosphere of cynicism and decay prevalent in Chungking, the Nationalists' wartime capital.[14]

The honeymoon did not last. In August 1944, Roosevelt appointed Patrick J. Hurley as a special emissary to China. Although Hurley had grown up in poverty in Oklahoma, his industry, an engaging personality, and a fair dose of luck brought him wealth as an oil-company lawyer and land speculator as well as political prominence in the Republican party. After serving as secretary of war in the Hoover administration, he became a defender of many New Deal programs and cultivated a personal relationship with Roosevelt. During World War II, Hurley emerged as a presidential trouble-shooter in foreign affairs, and traveled to New Zealand, the Middle East, Russia, and China.

When an impasse arose between Chiang and General Joseph W. Stilwell, commander of American forces in the China-India-Burma theater, Hurley was rushed to Chungking to reconcile their differences. Unfortunately, he knew little about Chinese politics or culture. Even worse, his vanity and crusading temperament blinded him to his own ignorance. The astute gener-alissimo soon held Hurley in his pocket. The emissary pressed for Stilwell's recall and obtained it. Hurley also opposed American assistance to the Com-munists, and supported the Nationalist plan for uniting the rival Chinese armies. Mao Tse-tung became "Moose Dung"; the Communist leader re-ciprocated by labeling Hurley "the Clown." The staunch anti-Communist General Albert C. Wedemeyer replaced Stilwell, and, at the end of the year, Hurley became ambassador to China.[15]

These developments did not halt Communist efforts to work with the United States. Rather, Yenan sought to bypass the American ambassador by appealing directly to Roosevelt. Mao and Chou offered to visit Washington and meet with him.[16] Hurley learned of the ploy, however, and helped con-vince the president to reject the overture and continue pressure on the Com-munists by persuading Moscow to support Chiang. Foreign service, military, and intelligence officers who attempted to circumvent Hurley were removed from Yenan and replaced by strict anti-Communists. Hurley and Wede-meyer asserted rigid control over American reporting out of China. Ameri-can military assistance to the Nationalists increased. In the six months fol-lowing Japan's surrender in August 1945, the United States transported between 400,000 and 500,000 Nationalist troops to North China and Man-churia to help the central government establish its authority over the entire country. Although angered, the Communists remained too insecure in their own position to break completely with the United States.[17]

At the end of 1945, Yenan even hoped that American policy would turn toward neutrality. In late November, Hurley, perhaps sensing the hopeless-ness of his mission, resigned in a huff and President Truman appointed Mar-shall to mediate in China.[18] During World War II, Marshall, as Army chief of staff, had usually backed Stilwell in his frequent squabbles with Chiang.[19] Certainly Marshall would be easier to deal with than Hurley. Initially, this seemed to be the case. Marshall and Chou got along well.

Yet American aid to Chiang continued. The Nationalist armed forces re-ceived substantial quantities of American matériel through Lend-Lease and surplus property programs.[20] The Export-Import Bank approved $66.8 mil-lion in credits for the Chinese government. Hundreds of tons of food and medical supplies flowed into China through the United Nations Relief and Rehabilitation Administration (UNRRA). The bulk of the goods went to Nationalist-controlled areas.[21] Marshall's alleged impartial mediation was revealed as a fraud. In June 1946, major Communist verbal attacks on the United States began. Three months later, following the conclusion of a surplus-property agreement between Washington and Nanking, the anti-American propaganda campaign intensified.[22]

To most American officials, growing Communist hostility was not a response to their government's actions. Rather, Soviet moves encouraged the belief that a close connection existed between the Communists of Russia and China, and that this presumed relationship explained the antagonism. On several occasions between the fall of 1945 and the following spring, the Soviet Union obstructed Nationalist plans in Manchuria and North China.[23] First, Moscow prevented Chiang's forces from landing at Dairen and other ports. Then, after the generalissimo had requested a postponement of Soviet troop withdrawals from Manchuria until 1 February 1946 to give his armies time to reach key areas, Moscow suddenly demanded new concessions. Simultaneously, the Russians increased their diplomatic presence in Yenan and stalled their military evacuation of Manchuria. It was not until 3 May that Moscow announced the final departure of Soviet forces.[24] Meanwhile, Soviet maneuvers had assisted the Chinese Communists, albeit indirectly, in occupying new territory and in capturing arms and ammunition.

Great power tensions elsewhere gave particular significance to these developments. A diplomatic confrontation occurred over Iran when the Soviet Union refused to remove its troops from the northern province of Azerbaijan while encouraging separatist forces there to revolt against the central government. Although the withdrawal of Russian military personnel ended the impasse, the incident seriously divided the superpowers. Problems over Turkey arose when the Kremlin pressed for territorial concessions along the Russo-Turkish border and a revision of the Montreux Convention regarding the passage of warships through the Dardanelles. The United States supported Turkish resistance to these pressures. By the beginning of 1947, Washington feared that either the Soviet Union would resort to force or that the Turks, discouraged by the increasing economic burden of military preparedness, would give in. In Europe, the problems of Germany and Eastern Europe continued to embitter Soviet-American relations. Americans also watched with growing apprehension the situation in Greece, where a Communist-led rebellion against the established government persisted. In Korea, Soviet and American diplomats and occupation officials labored without success to end the artificial division of that country. From Washington, Soviet behavior looked increasingly like an aggressive and disruptive force in international affairs that must be resisted to achieve a stable and peaceful world order compatible with American interests.

The deterioration of Soviet-American relations, the apparent ideological affinity of the Chinese Communists and Moscow,[25] the growing hostility of Mao Tse-tung and his followers toward the United States, and the removal of Soviet forces from Manchuria—all encouraged Chiang to pursue a military solution to China's disunity. General Marshall advised him against this course. The cost of military action, the general argued, would lead to financial chaos. He warned that, if full-scale civil war resumed, the United States would stand aside.[26] But Chiang was confident that he could destroy the Communist armies in eight to ten months. Because its forces were out of Manchuria and its attention directed toward Europe, the Soviet Union was not likely to intervene, and Chiang refused to believe the United States would disengage.[27] The World War II experience suggested the emptiness of American threats to withdraw aid.[28] Circumstances in 1947, he concluded, were not unlike those between 1941 and 1945, when the United States had depended on China to tie down large numbers of Japanese troops. In 1947, the United States once again needed the National government, this time to contain Russia and Communism.

Chiang also counted on support from the many Americans who possessed a deep sentimental attachment to China and to his "Christian" leadership. They felt that the United States enjoyed a "special relationship" with the country. Since the 1930s, they believed, American policy had often undermined its quest for independence, unity, and modernization; now the United States was obligated to assist the National government. Ambassador Stuart, a longtime educator in China, and Congressman Walter Judd (Republican-Minnesota), a former medical missionary there, were only two of the prominent public officials harboring such thoughts.[29] Henry Luce, who had been born in China to American missionaries, used dozens of radio stations and his widely circulated magazines *Time, Life,* and *Fortune* to keep such views before the public.[30] Stuart, Judd, and Luce combined sentimentalism with militant anti-Communism in actively espousing Chiang's cause.

For other Americans, economic interests encouraged a strong pro-Nationalist stance. During 1946, for example, Alfred Kohlberg, an importer of Chinese textiles, helped found the American China Policy Association, which feverishly pressed the Truman administration and Congress for increased aid to Chiang.[31] Thus, the generalissimo could count on a steady flow of pro-Nationalist opinion to the American public and to high channels within the government. America had leaned to his side for nearly a decade, and he had much reason to believe that attitude would continue.

## The Limits of American Involvement in China

Still, the potential for misunderstanding between the United States and China was great. Intent on maintaining his position as head of the

National government, Chiang had come to depend on those whose loyalty to him was unquestioned. Many of his supporters were both inept and corrupt, yet he continued to base his estimates of the military situation on their reports.[32] Official American estimates, on the other hand, rested upon the more solid evaluations of well-trained foreign service officers who enjoyed long experience in China. Two such men were O. Edmund Clubb, the consul general at Mukden and later Changchun and Peiping, and Raymond P. Ludden, the first secretary in the American embassy at Nanking. Clubb's experience in China reached back to 1929; Ludden's to 1932. A studious man of humble Midwestern beginnings, Clubb had a deep knowledge of Chinese culture and was an astute analyst of affairs in Manchuria and North China. Ludden was a bluff character who had been educated at Georgetown University and in the public schools of Fall River, Massachusetts. During the war, he had served under Stilwell and later in the American observer group at Yenan. One evening in 1946, he told Marshall that "the only time we ever got anything out of Chiang Kai-shek was when we backed him in a corner and beat it out of him."[33]

Back in Washington, the State Department was well staffed with China experts. Heading the Office of Far Eastern Affairs was John Carter Vincent, a courtly southerner who had served for fourteen years in China. His chief assistant was James K. Penfield, a Stanford graduate whose assignments in China had extended from Mukden in the north to Canton in the south. Arthur Ringwalt, son of an Omaha insurance salesman, manned the China desk after holding assignments in the Orient from 1928 to 1945.[34] Often ignored during the Roosevelt years, the professional diplomats enjoyed a temporary renaissance after Truman entered the White House and Hurley resigned. Because of the expertise on China available in the State Department, American perceptions and prescriptions for action inevitably strayed from those of the Nationalist leadership.

The varied cultural and political traditions of the two nations also led to disagreement. Marshall, in typical American fashion, found the solution to China's problems in the adoption of democratic procedures. Minority parties should function freely and be fully represented in the government. The development of a democratic system would create an open, nonviolent contest for power that would root out Nationalist corruption and inefficiency. Instead of relying on force to maintain authority, parties would need to appeal directly to the needs and wants of the Chinese people.[35]

This sanguine outlook conflicted with the deep-seated traditions to which Chiang was rigidly committed. For nearly two decades, he had openly celebrated Confucianism. In his eyes, it emphasized "complete loyalty to the state and ... filial piety toward the nation." In the hierarchy of China's needs, psychological and ethical reconstruction ranked ahead of political and economic reform.[36] In contrast to the American system of free enterprise, as John King Fairbank notes, Chiang planned an economy of "anti-

Marxian totalitarianism"—state-controlled industrialization aimed at the formation of "a defense state, rather than toward mass welfare."[37]

When the Sino-Japanese War had broken out in 1937 and the Nationalist government retreated from coastal areas to the interior, Chiang's base of support shifted somewhat from urban mercantilists and bankers, who accepted modernization and moderate reform in the countryside, to conservative landlords who adhered strongly to the standards of an older China.[38] By 1947, his dependence on this group was complete. Domestic political perceptions and needs had become mutually reinforcing.

The different lessons learned by China and the United States from World War II provided still another source of misunderstanding. Although Chiang concluded from American concessions between 1941 and 1945 that the United States would not abandon his government, most American observers had come to doubt the Nationalists' ability to unite and rule the country. At the beginning of 1947, Americans watched carefully as Chiang adopted a new Constitution more liberal than those of the past. They hoped it would prove to be a first step in broadening the popular base of his rule, and that possibly Communists and liberals would enter the government. Despite these hopes, most American officials were now convinced that seeing was believing. Too often in the past, Chiang had instituted paper reforms that resulted in no real change. Concrete results, not empty promises, were needed if the United States was to help bring about a unified, non-Communist China.[39]

The frequently incompatible objectives of the two sides brought about another misunderstanding. Chiang's primary goal was to sustain his own rule. Although the United States did not contest this goal, it saw his rule as a means to the higher end of peace and stability in Asia. As Acting Secretary of State Dean Acheson explained in November 1946, the United States desired that China "not become an unstabilizing influence" in Asia or "a serious irritant in our relations with Russia."[40] The escalation of civil war in China would compromise these two objectives.

Chiang was correct in concluding that the United States would not abandon him in the event of an extended civil conflict. Although decision makers in Washington frequently took issue with him on the extent of America's obligations to the National government, they admitted that certain American commitments made during World War II must be kept, especially those to equip the armed forces. This admission, together with the perception of a close affinity between the Chinese Communists and the Soviet Union and political pressures at home, sufficed to keep U.S. aid flowing into Nationalist coffers. Such aid severely reduced the chance for a productive relationship between the United States and the Communists, and thus it was to play a major role in the process leading to Sino-American confrontation in Korea in late 1950.

Yet Chiang ignored a central aspect of American foreign policy that had its roots in the early years of the twentieth century, namely the priority of Europe over Asia. In 1941, the United States had risked conflict in Asia by taking a hard line against Japanese hegemony in Manchuria and north China, but only after concluding that Japan threatened the British and Dutch empires in Southeast Asia, the loss of which might weaken European resistance to Hitler.[41] For the next four years, China took a back seat not only to Europe but to the Pacific theater as well. After the war, Washington saw China as a difficult area to influence, especially in light of Russian proximity. More important, its industrial backwardness and limited natural resources kept it well down on the list of priorities for American attention. It was important, but not sufficiently so to risk American objectives in Europe. Chiang's mistaken belief that the United States would never permit his decline on the Chinese mainland would cost him dearly in future years.

## Korea and the "Lessons" of World War II

Conditions in Korea in early 1947 were no more reassuring to American leaders than were those in China. As in China, political forces were polarized. Although initially supporting rightist groups, the United States had tried during 1946 to move toward the political center. Unlike China, however, Korea possessed no internationally recognized government at the time of the Japanese surrender. Part of Japan since 1910, Korea had spawned several independence movements, plus an exiled provisional government situated in Chungking.[42] Shortly after Japan's surrender, a People's Republic emerged in Seoul and promptly claimed jurisdiction over the entire country. Korean leaders who had remained in their homeland to fight for independence dominated this body. But the provisional government had shallow roots in Korea itself, and the People's Republic, though enjoying substantial indigenous support, appeared only after foreign powers had determined the country's immediate fate.[43]

The "lessons" of World War II figured prominently in American intervention in this unstable setting. Decision makers assumed first that, if a stable and peaceful world order was to emerge from the war, the United States must play a central role in its creation; and, second, that the great powers must work together, especially where prewar arrangements were to be overturned.[44] Japan's empire, of course, fit into this category. When a territory appeared too immature politically to manage the problems of immediate independence, trusteeships could teach "backward" peoples the art of self rule. Great power interests, in turn, would be protected through multipower participation in the process of tutelage.[45]

This preconceived framework fit the Korean situation neatly. Using the American experience in the Philippines as his model, President Roosevelt saw that Korea was undergoing "a period of training after the war for ultimate independent sovereignty."[46] At the Cairo Conference of November 1943, China and Great Britain, following an American initiative, agreed that Japan should be stripped of its colonies and that "in due course Korea shall become free and independent." Shortly thereafter, at Teheran, Joseph Stalin concurred with the American president that Korea would "need some period of apprenticeship before full independence, . . . perhaps forty years."[47] In early 1945, at Yalta, Roosevelt proposed a multipower trusteeship for the country to include the United States, the Soviet Union, China, and Great Britain. Stalin orally approved.[48]

State Department planners had also anticipated multipower involvement in Korean affairs.[49] Recognizing that rivalry over the peninsula had played an unsettling role in Sino-Japanese relations in the early 1890s, and again in Russo-Japanese relations in the ensuing decade, American officials now sought to avoid its occupation by a single nation. The Soviet Union would resent exclusive Chinese occupation, and China feared that Soviet control would lead to expanded Communist influence in Manchuria and north China. Moreover, a sovietized Korea might well threaten the American position in the Pacific. On the other hand, until the summer of 1945, Washington viewed unilateral American occupation as an undesirable responsibility.[50] Multipower participation was thus the logical formula. As a long standing power in Asia, Great Britain was included as a likely member of the group.

The changing balance of power in Asia also encouraged expectations of American involvement in Korea in a multipower context. Japan's projected defeat might result in a power vacuum in Northeast Asia. Some Americans, including Roosevelt, hoped that China would emerge as a major force for stability, but its worsening internal divisions, along with its technological backwardness, diminished such hopes. This realization coincided with the growing likelihood of Soviet intervention in the Pacific war. Policymakers in Washington, intent on achieving victory at the lowest cost possible in American lives and resources, were eager for Soviet participation. Yet that would greatly enhance Soviet prospects in Northeast Asia at a time when Japan, the traditional counterweight to Russia there, was removed. This reality became even more pressing because of Roosevelt's extensive concessions to Stalin at Yalta.[51]

In retrospect, the United States would have been wiser to let Russia occupy the Korea vacuum uncontested. The Asian peoples, so numerous and so nationalistic, were poor prospects for long-term exploitation by a foreign power, no matter how strong. Realizing this, American leaders could have settled for an island defense perimeter in the western Pacific. But American officials were determined to avoid the mistakes of the 1930s, when the United States had watched from the sidelines while Japan ran rampant in Asia and Germany seized control of Central Europe. Washington preoccupied itself less with the dangers of overcommitment than with the reverse.

Multipower occupation of Korea was certain to produce trouble, particularly because the two powers destined to play the largest roles, the United States and the Soviet Union, differed so widely in outlook. The United States generally envisioned a postwar world in which small nations would maintain a degree of freedom in relations with their stronger neighbors or more distant imperial powers; the Soviet Union preferred the traditional spheres-of-influence approach, especially regarding territories on its borders. At home, the United States adhered to a liberal capitalist ideology, and the Soviet Union espoused communism. Compounding the potential for conflict was the absence of detailed agreements among the great powers on the nature of the occupation.

Several reasons account for this oversight. Many Americans had learned the lesson from World War I that secret commitments made during wartime usually created severe problems afterward.[52] Reinforcing this consideration was Roosevelt's own inclination to postpone the solution of difficult problems.[53] In contrast to China, moreover, few American officials knew much about Korea, and, because it had not been involved in wartime planning, there was no pressing reason to focus attention on it. In any event, Roosevelt had little confidence in State Department professionals, and usually did not encourage initiatives on their part.

Yet the State Department did not ignore Korea entirely.[54] In a memorandum of 29 March 1944, the Inter-Divisional Area Committee on the Far East recommended that zonal military governments be avoided, that Korea be occupied "on the principle of centralized administration," and that such administration "be established as early as possible with all participating countries bearing a joint responsibility." The next fifteen months, however, saw little movement beyond these general points.[55] By late July 1945, the United States was probably even avoiding negotiations regarding the peninsula because Washington hoped that the atomic bomb would force Japan's surrender before Russia entered the war. Much of whatever trust had existed in Soviet-American relations had disappeared as a result of disagreements over Eastern Europe, and President Truman contemplated excluding Russia entirely from the occupation of Korea.[56]

But the Soviet Union entered the war on 8 August, well in advance of the anticipated date, and thus it already had troops in Korea when Japan surrendered. American forces did not arrive until 8 September, so the United States suffered from the lack of concrete agreements. With few precise commitments to carry out, the Soviet Union was in a strong position to establish a sphere of influence. Whether or not detailed wartime agreements on a joint occupation were possible is an open question, but it is hard to imagine that an intensive effort in that direction could have led to anything worse than the situation that eventually developed. At best, talks prior to August 1945 might have produced a neutralization of the peninsula.

The establishment of occupation zones awaited the end of the war. By that time, the dispersal of forces in Asia made the Soviet Union and the United States the only nations capable of participating in the occupation, and agreement between these two powers sufficed.[57] As it had before, the United States once more took the initiative. On 10 and 11 August 1945, the State-War-Navy Coordinating Committee in Washington proposed the thirty-eighth parallel as the dividing line between Soviet and American occupation forces.[58] The proposal placed almost two-thirds of the Korean population and Seoul, the nation's capital, in the American zone. Stalin accepted these terms, even though Soviet troops had a clear lead in occupying Korea.

His motives remain uncertain: perhaps he still hoped for meaningful participation in the occupation of Japan and saw a concession to the United States on Korea as a means of achieving this objective. In addition, he probably interpreted the line as a permanent boundary designating spheres of influence on the peninsula. At the turn of the century, Russia and Japan had discussed the thirty-eighth parallel as a possible point of division between their spheres. American leaders, unaware of this fact, regarded the line merely as delineating responsibilities for the surrender of Japanese forces.[59] Thus, by August 1945, the bases of future disagreements over Korea were firmly established.

## The Process of Polarization in Korea

Soviet occupation authorities soon grasped the political initiative. Two factors were crucial. First, although Japan had been successful in suppressing resistance movements in Korea, past efforts to sustain an indigenous Communist party had left a foundation on which to build once the foreign master departed. Second, hundreds of Koreans with Communist backgrounds and sympathies, who in the 1930s and early 1940s had fled to the Soviet Union and Manchuria, accompanied the Russians.[60] As Korean nationals, they were more readily accepted by the population than Russians or Japanese, yet, as people with training in and sympathy for the Soviet Union, they at least initially accepted the advice of Russian occupation authorities.

These circumstances contrasted sharply with the position of the United States below the thirty-eighth parallel. When its forces belatedly entered Korea on 8 September 1945, they were greeted as liberators. Jubilant crowds lined the road from Inchon to Seoul to welcome the soldiers who were making their way to the capital city.[61] But no Korean nationals accompanied them. The commander of the occupation was Lieutenant General John R. Hodge, a down-to-earth Midwesterner, whose main qualification for the position was his geographical proximity to Korea when Japan surrendered.[62] In mid-August, he and his XXIV Army Corps, though 600 miles away in Okinawa, were closer than any other American unit of comparable size. Hodge and his immediate subordinate, Major General A. V. Arnold, were competent field commanders, but they lacked knowledge of Korea and had little administrative experience or political sophistication.[63] To assist the military authorities, the State Department sent H. Merrell Benninghoff, a class three foreign service officer. His assignments in Japan and China between 1927 and 1941, and his work in the Office of Far Eastern Affairs in Washington during the war, had given him some familiarity with the peninsula. Nevertheless, he was a low-ranking, rather unimaginative official to place in such a challenging position.[64] His appointment reflected the low priority of Korea to American planners.

English-speaking Koreans and Japanese soon became influential with the American command. Unfortunately, they were often unpopular with the bulk of the Korean population—the Japanese because they had been imperial masters, and the educated, upper-class Koreans because they frequently had collaborated with those masters. Lyuh Woon-hyung, a popular figure, spoke English, but was a leader of the People's Republic. Hodge refused to conduct relations with that government or accept its assistance in managing the volatile situation. In part, his position rested on orders from Washington not to recognize an indigenous Korean government; in part it was an outgrowth of his rigid interpretation of those orders and his early—and false—suspicion that the republic was Communist-dominated.[65] Anxious above all to maintain order, he initially favored those who accepted American authority without question and possessed some language or technical skill that could be of immediate use. The result was early backing of conservative forces. Combined with Soviet policies in the north, this made the polarization of Korean politics inevitable. Prospects for national unification rapidly declined.

Hodge pleaded to Washington for an initiative at the governmental level to end the zonal division of Korea, but until December 1945 no major action took place.[66] By that time, Hodge and State Department representatives in Korea had concluded that indigenous opposition to trusteeship made that approach unwise.[67] Yet top officials in the United States, far removed from the pressures encountered by occupation leaders and preoccupied with Soviet-American relations in more crucial areas, made no effort to reevaluate the trusteeship approach.

In December 1945, at the Moscow meeting of the foreign ministers of the Soviet Union, the United States, and Great Britain, Secretary of State Byrnes recommended the immediate end of the military division of Korea as a preliminary to establishing a four-power trusteeship under the United Nations. Rather than a lengthy period of tutelage, however, he suggested that independence might be granted within five years.[68] Expanding on this proposal, the Russians suggested the establishment of a joint commission to bring about economic unification, a Korean provisional government, and a four-power trusteeship.

The final agreement followed closely the above outline. Representatives of the two occupation commands were to meet as a joint commission "to assist in the formation of a provisional Korean government." The commission, in turn, would confer with "Korean democratic parties and social organizations." Recommendations of the commission were to be presented to the governments of the four trustees—the Soviet Union, the United States, Great Britain, and China—before the nations on the joint commission made a final decision. The commission would also submit proposals for a five-year, four-power trusteeship. A preliminary conference of representatives of the two commands would convene within two weeks.[69]

These agreements resolved little of a substantive nature. The first step to Korean unification, the breakdown of the barrier at the thirty-eighth parallel, remained to be worked out by a joint commission. Byrnes undoubtedly understood the limitations of the accords. His primary objective, however, may have been to satisfy the thirst at home for smooth relations with the Russians.[70] To have pushed for more meaningful arrangements regarding Korea might have compromised this goal. Preoccupied with such issues as the international control of atomic energy and the composition of governments in Rumania and Bulgaria, Byrnes was not inclined to take risks on peripheral matters.

For their part, the Russians stood to gain nothing by pushing negotiations on Korea to an immediate standoff. The northern half of the country already was solidly under Soviet control; American authority in the south was less secure. In time, the United States even might abandon its foothold on the peninsula. To the Kremlin, a waiting game surely appeared prudent.

The prospect of delaying independence left most Koreans disappointed and angry. In the south, civil disorder spread rapidly. Hodge worsened matters when, upon hearing of the Moscow accord, he assured Korean leaders that, if the populace cooperated with the American command, trusteeship might be avoided. Because Hodge had advised Washington against the trusteeship approach, he assumed that the Moscow agreement was Soviet inspired.[71] This assumption gained force when the Communist party followed the Soviet lead in supporting the Moscow agreement. When the Korean Right charged the Russians alone with delaying independence, however, the Soviet Union released an account of the Moscow conference showing that the United States had initiated the trusteeship proposal. This revelation seriously undermined America's standing with the Korean people.[72]

In January 1946, at Seoul, the preliminary conference on interzonal problems convened in a volatile atmosphere. Agreements emerged in some areas, but on such major questions as the movement of Koreans between zones, the circulation of newspapers, and the development of a uniform currency and telecommunication system there was little progress.[73] Establishment of a joint commission to create a provisional Korean government represented the most significant achievement. The commission, consisting of five representatives from each of the occupation commands, was to meet in Seoul no later than a month after the preliminary conference.[74]

Despite this agreement, the prospects for establishing a united provisional government were never good. From the beginning, the Soviet Union closed off its zone to outside influences.[75] And, by February 1946, relations between the United States and the Soviet Union, both at the governmental and occupational command levels, had deteriorated to a point where settlement of difficult matters was almost impossible to achieve. In a policy paper of 11 February, the State-War-Navy Coordinating Committee expressed pessimism regarding prospects for agreement by the Joint Commission. After outlining the measures to be pursued in upcoming commission meetings, the Washington-based committee stated that, if a deadlock emerged, the American command was to proceed on its own and appoint an advisory group for the South "in matters relating to the creation of a provisional Korean government."[76]

Events soon justified American pessimism. The Joint Commission convened on 20 March and rapidly became deadlocked on the question of consulting Korean groups. The Russians insisted on consulting only groups supporting the Moscow agreements. The Americans objected, not only because such a criterion restricted freedom of speech—which the Truman administration sought to export to the peninsula—but because acceptance of the Russian demand would eliminate from consultation all except the leftist groups under Soviet influence. An agreement was eventually reached requiring "a reasonable degree of cooperation on the part of democratic parties and social organizations . . . to be consulted," but this vague settlement did little to eradicate the barrier of the thirty-eighth parallel or to create a provisional government. On 6 May, the Joint Commission adjourned.[77] The stalemate reflected an unwillingness on both sides to accept procedures for unification that might lead to an unfriendly Korea.

Under pressure from the State Department in Washington, the American occupation command launched a spring political campaign aimed at establishing a coalition of moderate groups in South Korea. This effort had several objectives, one of which was to end American dependence on the extreme Right. At the forefront of this element was Syngman Rhee, who had spent the war in Washington making a nuisance of himself through persistent efforts to gain recognition of the provisional government. Now he pressed for immediate independence, aggressively opposed any form of trusteeship, and appeared hostile to a program of progressive land and fiscal reform, which most Koreans favored.[78] A broadening of Korean participation in governmental functions was to accompany the American campaign. Elections were to be held for local offices, and eventually for an interim legislative assembly. Such a program, it was thought, would enhance the American position and undermine the Communists in South Korea. Combined with strict U.S. observance of the Moscow agreements, the election of a group more moderate and representative than the Rhee faction might facilitate progress in the Joint Commission.[79]

During the summer and fall of 1946, American efforts to court moderate rightist Kimm Kiu-sic and moderate leftist Lyuh Woon-hyung met with some success. Middle-of-the-road political parties merged into a Coalition Committee and agreed on basic principles, including the establishment of an interim legislative assembly.[80] But many problems remained. Lyuh, a charismatic but unpredictable man, frequently traveled between the two zones to maintain friendly relations with northern leaders. As a result, Hodge remained suspicious of his sincerity in working with the American occupation.[81] On the other hand, continued rightist control of the police and most administrative posts irritated the moderate Left. The problem surfaced when October elections produced a rightist victory. When the Coalition Committee complained about unfair balloting procedures, Hodge declared the elections void in two districts.[82] This incident laid bare the inherent difficulty for the American command of courting a centrist coalition and enhancing its strength while tolerating an inevitably partisan police force in Rhee's hands. The dualism in American policy paralleled somewhat Marshall's efforts in China.

In a Joint Korean-American Conference during the fall of 1946, members of the coalition pressed for the dismissal of top police officials. Although conceding police excesses in certain instances, Hodge defended their overall performance and refused to make major changes. Pressure from the non-Communist Left placed the occupation commander in a serious dilemma. He was in sympathy with the coalition movement, but did not trust some of its leaders. In particular, he feared that some members of the Coalition Committee wanted to seize control of the police force for the Left.[83] In September and October, a series of strikes broke out among railroad, factory, and electrical workers that ushered in a period characterized by numerous demonstrations and extensive rioting. In the city of Taegu, for example, in October forty-four policemen were killed and one hundred fifty-three injured. Casualties among the rioters were only slightly lower. Uprisings quickly spread to the countryside, where landlords frequently came under attack and many bridges and communication lines were put out of service.[84] To Hodge, the unrest was Communist inspired. Under such circumstances, leftist control of the police could jeopardize the authority of the occupation command. His dilemma emphasizes the long-term problems created by decisions made during the first months of the occupation. The initial support given to the Right culminated in an estrangement of the occupation authorities and the moderate Left, which made the construction of a workable partnership later on a difficult task.

As 1946 drew to a close, therefore, the United States faced an uncertain situation in Korea. Below the thirty-eighth parallel, Hodge's attempts to befriend and maintain a centrist coalition had produced indefinite results. Although strong repressive action from August onward had begun to weaken the Communist party, the social and economic problems that bred unrest remained unsolved. The situation might improve if a centrist coalition grasped political control from Rhee's extreme rightist forces and carried out broad reforms. (In March, a massive program of redistributing land to the peasants had begun in the north. Three months later, a labor law was proclaimed, aimed at improving the lot of the North Korean workers. These actions received widespread support above the thirty-eighth parallel.)[85] But the unwillingness of the occupation command to initiate reform on its own served only to perpetuate a system of land ownership that had long been in need of change.

Compounding American problems was the growing agitation of Rhee's forces. Angered by Hodge's encouragement of the centrist coalition—his appointment of forty-five members to the interim legislative assembly had added substantially to the strength of the moderate Right and Left within that body—and by his suggestion that a four-power trusteeship might be the only means of unifying the peninsula, the extreme Right acted aggressively. When the new assembly convened on 12 December, thirty-eight rightist members boycotted it. Demonstrations against trusteeship increased in intensity. Rhee, whom Hodge labeled "a worse pain in the neck every day," departed for the United States to press for the creation of an independent government for South Korea.[86] Hodge, in turn, urged Washington to take the initiative at the governmental level to end the division of Korea. The State Department, however, argued against such a move. Unless conditions in South Korea stabilized in favor of non-Communist elements, it warned, the Russians would interpret an American approach as a sign of weakness.

Thus Hodge remained burdened with a task for which he was ill suited by both training and temperament. Without help from home, his best hope rested in continued suppression of the Communists, combined with cautious encouragement for the moderate parties in the interim legislative assembly. Although circumstances were less than ideal, they were not hopeless. The Central Intelligence Group even suggested that the worst might be over, that as long as the occupation command maintained order and moved toward the establishment of a provisional Korean government, the Communists would continue to lose ground. The Soviet Union might then make concessions "in an effort to reconvene the Joint Commission and carry out the Moscow Decision before a democratic regime in South Korea gained a firm foothold."[87] Such concessions might be the first step toward the creation of an independent, unified peninsula friendly to the United States. Few people on the American side were so optimistic, but no one had yet suggested an easy way for the United States to disentangle itself from the troubled land.

## China, Korea, and American Credibility

America's course in China and Korea following World War II rested on the desire for a stable world order characterized by peace and prosperity. Initially, American leaders viewed cooperation with the Soviet Union as a prerequisite for achieving this goal. Given Russia's interest in Manchuria and its apparent ideological affinity to the Chinese Communists on the one hand and given American ties to the Nationalists on the other, civil war in China would threaten this cooperation. And disorder in China would create instability throughout Asia. Moreover, State Department observers regarded Chiang as being too weak economically and militarily to sustain a victorious military offensive against the Communists, even with large-scale American aid. Thus, the United States sought to show the way toward a Nationalist-dominated coalition government in China that would resolve internal divisions peacefully.

The situation in Korea was different primarily because at the end of World War II no internationally recognized authority existed there to replace the Japanese. The Soviet-American occupation of the peninsula, therefore, had broader political significance than the presence of foreign troops in China. Russia's apparent intention to establish a sphere of influence above the thirty-eighth parallel jeopardized the fulfillment of the American objective of a united independent Korea. The United States, however, did not immediately abandon efforts to reach agreement with the Soviet Union. Although by December 1946 American efforts to prevent a conflict in China had failed, the United States had not given up hope of achieving its goals in Korea. At the same time, in Korea as in China, a preoccupation with order and a distrust of Soviet designs inclined the United States toward dependence on the political Right.

The feeling that the United States must play a major role in constructing a stable world led most American officials to acknowledge a commitment to both countries. Convinced that the retreat of the United States from international responsibility in the 1920s and 1930s had been a prime cause of World War II, aware that foreign governments and peoples questioned America's determination to exert itself consistently beyond its shores, and certain that American credibility abroad was essential for the achievement of national purposes, most decision makers rejected total U.S. withdrawal from China and Korea.[88]

Unfortunately, the United States often regarded the exporting of its political institutions as the major means for achieving its purposes. This approach rested on the assumption of the universal applicability of liberal democracy.[89] Time that could have been used in pressing Chiang to institute social and economic reforms was frequently taken up in lobbying for procedural measures alien to centuries of Chinese practice. The effort to unite the Nationalists and the Communists in a coalition government, though in large part the result of an absence of attractive alternatives, reflected considerable misunderstanding on the American side of the internal conflict in China. Such endeavors merely reinforced the generalissimo's belief that Americans must be manipulated, not heeded. In Korea, Hodge's conviction that reforms should await the creation of an indigenous government reduced his capacity to meet the needs of a majority of the population. And the American failure to deal more firmly with disruptive forces on both the extreme Right and Left simply helped perpetuate disorder. Soviet actions in North Korea contrasted sharply with the American approach and produced an early advantage for Russia in the contest for influence on the peninsula.

As earlier, during 1946 American decision makers linked the status of China and Korea. According to a State Department policy paper of 6 June, Korea's independence was important: Soviet domination of the peninsula "would further endanger Chinese control of Manchuria and would thus lessen the prospect [for] . . . a strong and stable China, without which there [could] . . . be no permanent political stability in the Far East."[90] Two weeks later, Edwin Pauley, whose trip through Manchuria to study the reparations issue had been followed by a visit to Korea, reported to President Truman that the Russians might be trying to encircle China through the sovietization of the peninsula and Outer Mongolia.[91]

Ultimately, however, Korea possessed a broader significance for American planners. Pauley labeled the country "an ideological battleground." "It is here," he asserted, "where a test will be made of whether a democratic competitive system can be adopted to meet the challenge of defeated feudalism, or whether some other system, i.e., Communism will become stronger."[92] President Truman agreed.[93] The direct involvement of the superpowers in Korea and Russia's apparent determination to communize the North—and possibly the entire peninsula—had led the Truman administration to perceive a substantial American stake in the country. A show of weakness there might undermine the credibility of the United States worldwide.

Soviet and American roles in China were less dominant than in Korea. Chiang did not owe his position of power to American sponsorship any more than Mao owed his to Soviet support. Neither the United States nor the Soviet Union had any control over a major portion of the country. During 1946, in fact, the limited nature of American influence in China had become more and more apparent; and, though Americans increasingly linked the Communist Chinese to Moscow, the tie was far more subtle than that between the North Korean Communists and the Russians. Thus, despite America's traditionally deeper involvement in China and that country's strategic significance, Korea now had a claim on the United States that, in some ways, exceeded that of China.

# PART II

## China and Korea Policy under Marshall's Stewardship

During 1947 and 1948, the differing U.S. perceptions regarding involvement in China and Korea manifested themselves in concrete policy decisions. In China, the United States scrupulously avoided an expanded commitment to the National government, but aid did continue at a substantial level. Army and navy advisory groups remained in the country, and shipments of American goods continued to flow into Nationalist-controlled areas. In the spring of 1947, arms sales were resumed, and the transfer to Nationalist forces of American ammunition dumps began. Late in the year, the Truman administration increased arms shipments, broadened its responsibilities for training Chiang's forces, and decided to present to Congress an economic assistance program for China. In March 1948, the lawmakers authorized funds for both economic and military aid.

These moves perpetuated Washington's ties to a decaying regime. A decisive disengagement that might have widened American options later on never occurred. Still, aid to the Nationalists fell short of large-scale military intervention in the civil war. The United States refused to assume the responsibilities of advising Nationalist units in the field or of operating the central government. Unlike the pattern in Western Europe, assistance was rendered on a short-term basis and in a piecemeal fashion.

In Korea, on the other hand, the United States expanded its stake. The initial step leading to massive American military intervention in June 1950 had occurred at the end of World War II, when the United States occupied half the peninsula. Now, between the fall of 1947 and the summer of 1948, a second giant step was taken. First, the United States pushed through the United Nations General Assembly its own plan for the unification of Korea. Then, after the Russians refused to cooperate in implementing the scheme, the Americans moved forward with United Nations-sponsored elections in the southern zone. On 15 August 1948, the process culminated in the creation of the Republic of Korea below the thirty-eighth parallel. In part, United Nations involvement was to serve as a cloak for American troop withdrawals from the peninsula. But friendly nations supported United States designs in Korea only under considerable pressure from Washington. As a result, the process of constructing an indigenous authority within South Korea more than ever before tied American credibility abroad to the maintenance of an anti-Communist government in a divided and polarized nation.

The divergent choices regarding China and Korea grew out of complex pressures, both foreign and domestic. At home, an expanded commitment to China in the fall of 1947 would involve a significant expenditure of scarce manpower and financial resources. If made, this commitment would reduce America's capacity to respond effectively to the crisis in Europe. In contrast, an increased commitment in Korea required no immediate allocation of material resources. Moreover, in both land and population, China was massive; Korea was microscopic in comparison. In the first case, therefore, the cost of resolving crucial problems defied precise calculation; in the second, problems, though difficult, seemed more manageable. In the end, however, there was a more compelling reason to defend the American position in Korea but not in China. Neither area was crucial to America's physical security, yet State Department officials regarded Korea as of substantial importance to U.S. political standing abroad. While guarding against a deepening commitment to a non-Communist China, the diplomats pushed forward on Korea with a policy that seemed merely the necessary fulfillment of an existing obligation.

# 2 The China Problem: To Contain Communism or to Contain a Commitment

## The State Department Perspective

The year 1947 was one of momentous initiatives in American foreign policy that significantly expanded the nation's commitments abroad. Yet, early in the year, the United States actually reduced its diplomatic and military presence in China. The State Department announced America's withdrawal from the Committee of Three and Executive Headquarters, two groups created to mediate between the Nationalists and the Communists.[1] U.S. Marines began to depart from Peiping, Tientsin, and Tangku.[2] These moves reflected Washington's frustration with efforts to prevent civil war as well as the desire to avoid direct American involvement in such a conflict.

General Marshall took a central role in directing China policy. Although not a specialist on that country, the new secretary of state had substantial experience with it. In the mid-1920s, as a lieutenant colonel in the army, he had spent nearly three years at Tientsin helping to protect American privileges amidst the turmoil of a proud people searching for their modern identity. He had even made a fumbling effort to learn the language. The experience had taught him that China was a complex and mysterious land, to which the proper Western approach was far from certain. As army chief of staff during World War II, he had devoted considerable time to studying military developments in China, despite its secondary importance to the overall war effort. During 1946, Marshall had returned there and devoted all his energies to resolving peacefully the tense situation. His wartime and postwar encounters had fostered deep apprehensions regarding the National government. During the Pacific war, his friend and colleague, General Joseph Stilwell, had tried without success to mold Nationalist armies into an efficient fighting machine against the Japanese. In the process, Stilwell acquired an intense and poorly concealed dislike for Chiang. Marshall had confidence in Stilwell's judgment, and, though fear of Soviet penetration had led him in late 1945 to support aid to the Nationalists, his stay in China bolstered his negative preconceptions regarding Chiang's leadership.[3] Because Marshall possessed strong views on the matter, he was determined to have a major input in formulating China policy.

President Truman was happy to give Marshall a central policymaking role.

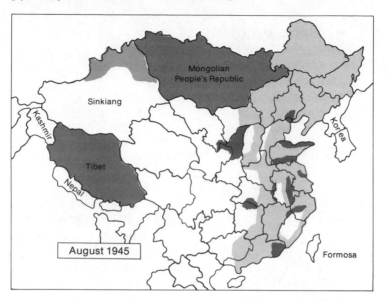

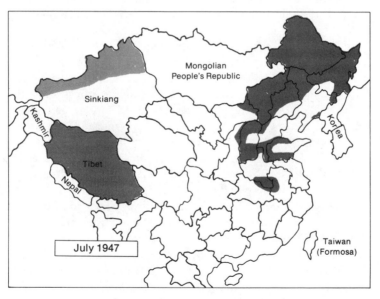

MAP I. The Communist Advance in China, 1945–1949

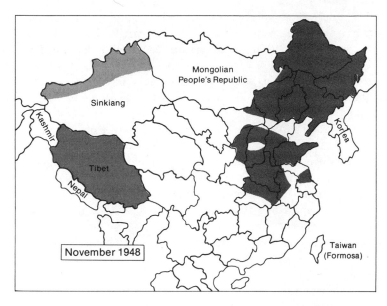

November 1948

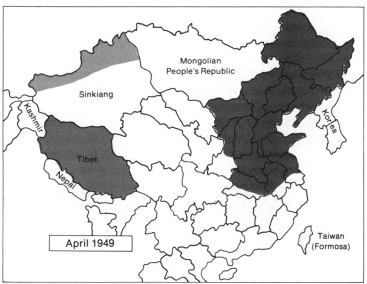

April 1949

The chief executive believed that policy should evolve through his direct contact with department heads. No elaborate White House staff served as a barrier between the president and the Department of State. Truman's White House advisers were generalists who often discussed world politics with their boss, but the secretary of state always enjoyed direct access to Truman, and, in most cases, could expect to have the pivotal voice in presidential decisions on foreign policy.[4]

Marshall's appointment as secretary of state emphasized Truman's attitude. The general had emerged from World War II with a standing second to none in Washington. As a central figure in devising and directing the strategy for American victory, he had achieved the virtually unanimous respect and admiration of the American public as well as of its military and political leaders. Despite his rather cold and formal demeanor, he impressed most of his contemporaries as one of the great Americans of his generation. The president not only shared this feeling, but also viewed him as a man with a breadth of vision and competence far exceeding those of other professional soldiers. Never flamboyant or pretentious, always dignified, Marshall worked smoothly if not intimately with Truman.[5]

Marshall was an ideal leader to raise State Department morale. For some time, the professionals there had labored under adverse conditions. President Roosevelt constantly bypassed them. James Byrnes, Truman's first appointee as secretary of state, depended on a few officers at the head of the department rather than consulting the regional specialists. In contrast, Marshall's military background had taught him to follow clearly delineated lines of authority and responsibility. The head of the Office of Far Eastern Affairs should serve as the secretary's top adviser concerning East Asian policy. Advice from office heads might not always be heeded, but it should certainly be sought and given careful consideration. Charles E. Bohlen, a longtime foreign service officer, later noted that

> [it] did not take Marshall long to win over every important member of the State Department. He gave a sense of purpose and direction. His personality infected the whole Foreign Service. Under him . . . the department functioned with as much efficiency as I was to note in my nearly forty years in the Foreign Service. . . . [All] senior officers were consulted, and when policy was decided, there was no question what it was.[6]

The department's China experts concurred with Marshall's attitude toward the Nationalist regime. John Carter Vincent, James K. Penfield, and Arthur Ringwalt, as well as Philip Sprouse and Edward Rice, Ringwalt's leading assistants in the Division of Chinese Affairs, agreed on the wisdom of a wait-and-see policy. Nationalist armies were not short of arms and ammunition. Withholding new aid, especially that of a military nature, might discourage Chiang from pursuing the civil war and encourage him to institute needed reforms. Such a policy also would prevent a worsening of superpower relations over the China issue.[7]

Yet Marshall and his subordinates viewed as inevitable an eventual expansion of aid to the Nationalists.[8] A sense of obligation, assiduously cultivated by Chiang, was important in this respect. Most of the Nationalist armies had been equipped with American weapons during the war against Japan. Because the United States was the only source of ammunition for these weapons, the embargo on military material, if continued indefinitely, would result in the disarming of hundreds of thousands of government troops. If Nationalist military strength declined, Communist influence would grow. The Communists, according to prevailing State Department opinion, "drew their inspiration from Russian sources and on most questions they . . . react in accordance with the Marxist line."[9] Continuing anti-American statements emanating from Yenan reinforced this outlook.[10] Thus, total abandonment of the Nationalists would not only require renunciation of former obligations; it would be contrary to concrete American interests.

In early April 1947, the Office of Far Eastern Affairs finally recommended a slackening of the arms embargo, a move that would permit the National government to purchase rifle ammunition. The proposal grew out of two events. First, in late March Ambassador Stuart had reported that American-trained units in the Nationalist army had only a three-month supply of ammunition.[11] Second, on 2 April the chairman of the Chinese Supply Commission saw Ringwalt and asked to purchase the ammunition. The chairman claimed it had been procured by the American army during World War II "for shipment to China as military Lend-Lease but [had] never left the [United States]." Upon checking with the War Department, Ringwalt found this assertion to be substantially correct.[12]

But Marshall objected. The president, he argued, had ended American obligations under Lend-Lease, the National government had shown no sign of improvement, and the sale could not be kept secret. It would be widely interpreted as an alteration of American policy.[13] Preoccupied with other matters at the allied foreign ministers' meeting in Moscow, Marshall clearly did not want to make a major decision on China.

Marshall, however, did order the transfer from American to Nationalist troops of responsibility for guarding an ammunition dump at Tangku. Precipitating this move was a Communist attack on the dump, which resulted in the death of five United States marines. In retaliation, Marshall believed that the United States could abandon the ammunition to the Nationalists without giving the Communists strong grounds for charging that Washington was supporting the civil war. On 21 April 1947, the transfer was completed.[14] By October, such transfers had provided the Nationalists with 6,500 tons of ammunition.[15] Marshall soon became less intent on finding excuses for such action than with removing American marines and insuring that nationalist forces possessed an adequate supply of ammunition. The knowledge that Soviet forces had left behind large quantities of Japanese military equipment when they withdrew from Manchuria served to allay doubts about the propriety of assistance through abandonment.

In May 1947, the administration took further action on arms aid. On the fifth, Ringwalt renewed the recommendation to sell rifle ammunition to Chiang. Ringwalt also suggested that the National government be allowed to purchase military supplies from American industry.[16] Three weeks later, the secretary of state complied by ordering the ban removed on the issuance of export licenses covering the shipment of arms and ammunition.[17]

## Pressures within the Executive Branch

China policy, however, involved more than a few experts in the State Department and the issue of arms assistance to the Nationalists. By May 1947, other aid for Nationalist armies had been under consideration for some time. On 25 April, President Truman had issued an executive order giving the secretary of the navy, with the concurrence of the secretary of state, authority to transfer to China certain naval equipment and related spare parts. Although Marshall did not approve the transfer until June, the executive order reflected the president's responsiveness to pressures within the administration.[18]

In military circles, discontent with American China policy had existed at least since the fall of 1945.[19] The end of the Marshall mission brought this discontent to the surface. On 7 February 1947, Major General Lauris Norstad, the army's director of plans and operations, wrote to the secretary of war regarding five uncompleted American military programs in China.[20] "The deterioration of stockpiled items," he noted, made impossible War Department completion of the programs. As funds and personnel to service American materials in the Pacific became more scarce, War Department capabilities would decrease further. Moreover, the current reorganization of Nationalist armies would be "very difficult without the [American] material required to increase Chinese military efficiency." With good reason, Norstad argued, the Chinese regarded the programs as firm American commitments. Their termination prior to completion might lead Chiang to reject American military advice. Withdrawal of the United States military groups might become necessary, "with possible far reaching political and strategic results." Norstad conceded that decisions on American military aid must rest upon "political factors," but he wanted the State Department to understand the consequences of continued delay.

Norstad's concern had two sources. First, since mid-1945 the prevailing view within the army regarding the Chinese Communists was that they were "supported and guided by Moscow."[21] Thus, when Communist offensives in Manchuria in January 1947 forced Nationalist retreats to their fortified towns, Norstad became disturbed. Second, the army would suffer a major public relations defeat if unused American matériel was wasted because of inadequate servicing.[22] Because the shortages in funds and personnel precluded proper care of most of the ammunition and equipment in the Pacific, their transfer to the Chinese was the only way to avoid embarrassment. Both strategic and bureaucratic factors, therefore, inclined top army officials toward ending the embargo on American arms shipments to China.

Secretary of War Robert P. Patterson sympathized with Norstad. The former had little experience with China and no history of rabid support for the Nationalists. But he was under constant pressure from his friend, the well-connected and persistent columnist Joseph Alsop, who had served in China during World War II, had been a harsh critic of Stilwell, and now lobbied for stepped-up aid to Chiang. Influenced by Alsop and by his leading subordinates in the army, including Major General John P. Lucas, chief of the Army Advisory Group in China, Patterson contacted Marshall and presented Norstad's arguments.[23]

Secretary of the Navy James Forrestal already had approached Marshall on naval assistance to China. The Seventy-ninth Congress had provided for such aid. Forrestal now pressed for an executive order to implement the legislation.[24] Although the navy secretary knew little about China, he had toured East Asia during the previous July and talked with leading American officials there. Walter S. Robertson, a State Department officer in Peiping, Admiral Charles Cooke, commander of United States Naval Forces, Western Pacific, and General MacArthur, in Tokyo, made the biggest impression. Robertson, like Forrestal, was an investment banker by trade. As such, he held an advantage over career foreign service officers in dealing with the secretary. Robertson spoke of Communist atrocities and predicted that if the United States "withdrew from China, the Russians would surge in and flood Manchuria and North China."[25] To MacArthur, the National government was "not the best in the world," but it was "on our side" and "should be supported."[26] Deeply concerned about Communist expansion and pressed by Cooke, who was eager to proceed with helping Chiang unite the country, Forrestal became a leader within the administration for expanded aid to Nationalist China.[27]

In mid-February, two significant interdepartmental meetings occurred. The first, held on the twelfth, included the secretaries of state, war, and navy and their chief assistants. Marshall pushed the State Department view aggressively. Chiang, he argued, had overestimated his ability to solve the Communist problem and remained unconvinced that his government "could only be saved by drastic political and military reforms." To Forrestal, however, the United States "must face the fact that termination of American support would invariably lead to increased Russian influence in China." Although he did not advocate an immediate extension of American material assistance, he thought the Truman administration should send General MacArthur on "a financial and economic mission" to China to demonstrate American concern. The discussion ended with Marshall's comment that John Blandford, an American currently employed as a financial adviser by the National government, would soon return from China and that the State Department could keep the secretaries apprised of any information he submitted.[28]

Eight days later, another meeting took place. This time only top State and Navy department officials attended. Forrestal, Admirals Chester Nimitz and Forrest Sherman, the chief and deputy of naval operations respectively, and Admiral Cooke, who was on a visit to the United States, represented the navy. Marshall approved its earlier request to permit the Naval Advisory Group to implement its limited program of aid to Chiang.[29] The secretary of state adopted a tougher line on the continued presence of American marines in China. Despite Cooke's desire to maintain between 4,300 and 4,800 men in Tsingtao alone—allegedly to protect American civilians, the naval installation, and the air field—Marshall advocated the reduction of marines in all China to 3,500. "The whole concept of stationing American armed forces in China to protect Americans and their interests was outmoded," he claimed, and added that such an endeavor might involve the United States in difficulties with the Soviet Union, which would be most pleasing to "the reactionary Chinese clique."[30] Cooke also pressed for the transfer of ammunition dumps to the Nationalists. Marshall saw the proposed action as contrary to American policy and as risking undesirable publicity; yet he proposed that the ammunition be "left on the spot" when the American marines withdrew, that the Nationalists be so informed, and that the action be explained publicly as a result of the necessity to withdraw American troops earlier than previously planned.[31]

Interdepartmental pressures on the secretary of state did not end with these meetings. On 26 February, the secretary of war wrote Marshall taking issue with several aspects of American China policy. His primary concern was the advance of the Moscow-oriented Communists. He feared that the secretary of state expected too much in the way of Nationalist purification before increasing American aid. An end to the arms embargo and the dispatch of an "Economic Advisory Group" seemed advisable. The State-War-Navy Coordinating Committee (SWNCC)—or a special interdepartmental committee similar to one recently created to deal with Korea—should study the entire China question and make specific policy recommendations, after which the Joint Chiefs of Staff would evaluate the military aspects of the problem.[32]

A day later, Forrestal renewed his proposal for a mission to China to advise Chiang on economic and technological matters.[33] On the same day, the president asked Marshall if the United States should now give ammunition to the National government.[34] In the midst of preparations to save Greece and Turkey from Communism, Truman showed deep concern about reports of the continuing decline of Nationalist strength in China.

Still, Marshall resisted an abrupt change of policy. Although expansion of American advice and material aid appeared necessary for the long term, he felt that the United States must await a more propitious time to make adjustments. On objectives, he differed little with Forrestal and Patterson. His firsthand experience with Nationalist inefficiency and corruption, however, had taught him that American aid would serve no useful purpose unless Chiang instituted extensive reforms. Convinced of American weakness on the mainland of Asia, the secretary of state favored a cautious policy that would result in neither a deepening and irreversible commitment to the Nationalists nor an irrepressible conflict with the Soviet Union. Nevertheless, he encouraged the Joint Chiefs to study the military aspects of the problem.[35] He also urged Vincent to give new attention to both military and economic aid to Chiang.[36]

Actually, on the question of economic assistance, Vincent had already taken the lead within the State Department. On 3 February 1947, he suggested that a grant of at least $40 million to China be proposed to Congress.[37] Later, he recommended that the administration present a program of credits for China to the Export-Import Bank.[38] As a particularly unobtrusive method of aiding the Nationalists, such an approach held special appeal for Marshall.

The proposal immediately ran into difficulty. During August 1946, a Democratic Congress had earmarked $500 million in credits to China through the Export-Import Bank. The bank, however, retained authority to decide when and for what purpose they should be extended. The bank's charter stipulated that loans could be granted when there was a "reasonable assurance of repayment" and when such assistance could serve as an impetus to international trade.[39] When in March Vincent approached bank director William McChesney Martin regarding reconstruction and improvement loans, Martin replied that the money should come from the International Bank. Prospects for repayment were poor, and, because the director soon would appear before Congress regarding recharter legislation for his bank, approval of credits to China "might seriously embarrass him."[40] Despite Martin's negative response, Vincent continued to press for a loan to enable China to purchase foreign cotton. China needed raw cotton to keep its mills busy, and the export of finished cotton products could help pay off the loan.[41] But the view of the bank's directors made movement painfully slow, slower in fact than in the highly sensitive area of military assistance.

## Pressures from Congress

Ironically, congressional pressures pushed the Office of Far Eastern Affairs toward advocacy of increased support for Chiang. Chiang could depend on backing from influential people in both houses of Congress. In the lower chamber, John Vorys, an Ohio Republican who had spent three years with Yale-in-China, joined Walter Judd in supporting the Nationalists. Central to Vorys's thought on China was a fear of the "universal danger of Communist expansion." Although initially tolerant of Marshall's efforts during 1946, Vorys and Judd became increasingly impatient as the year progressed. By early 1947, they urged stepped-up aid to Chiang. The defeat of several anti-Chiang congressmen in the November 1946 elections, together with the absence of strong leadership by the senior members of the Foreign Affairs Committee, created a vacuum on the China issue in the lower house that Judd and Vorys rushed to fill.[42]

Republicans Arthur H. Vandenberg (Michigan) and Styles Bridges (New Hampshire) played prominent roles in the Senate. Although neither man had direct experience in China, both advocated increased support to Chiang. Vandenberg was a self-made man, an ardent conservative on domestic issues, and a past opponent of Roosevelt's foreign policies on the eve of American intervention in World War II. He was affable but vain, a person who, one commentator asserted, "could strut sitting down."[43] As a recent convert to internationalism, he paid particular attention to honoring American commitments abroad.

A correspondence with General Claire L. Chennault strengthened Vandenberg's attitude toward China. Following the defeat of Japan, Chennault, the commander of American air forces in China during World War II, had become involved in stimulating commercial air traffic in East Asia.[44] An enterprising businessman, whose exploits in the Flying Tigers made him a folk hero in the United States, he cultivated powerful contacts in Washington. On 17 January, he outlined his views to Vandenberg. The American effort to create a coalition government in China, the general asserted, had aided the Communists. The United States must abandon negotiations and give full support to Chiang. Otherwise, China would fall to the Communists. This would strengthen the Soviet position immeasurably, for—with its Asian flank secure—Russia could adopt a more aggressive policy in Europe. Vandenberg replied that the letter brought "great encouragement in my viewpoint"; the general's arguments were "entirely invincible." The senator hoped to read the letter aloud before an executive session of the Senate Foreign Relations Committee, which he chaired.[45]

A member of the upper chamber's "inner circle," Vandenberg had become, by the spring of 1947, the central cog in the Truman administration's bipartisan strategy in Congress. As the number of Chiang's supporters in Re-

publican ranks swelled, the senator increasingly pressed for aid to China—
not only to assist Chiang, but to muster support for more crucial programs
to contain Communism in Europe. His relationship with both the largely
Republican China bloc in Congress and the Democratic administration
made him a broker on the question of aid to the National government.[46]

The motives of Bridges are more obscure. His support for Chiang became
visible in December 1945 during Senate hearings on the resignation of
Patrick Hurley as ambassador to China. Hurley charged that American foreign service officers had undermined his negotiations for unity in China by
being overly sympathetic to the Communists. He substantiated his charges
with little evidence, but the hearings took place in the aftermath of the
*Amerasia* affair, in which Philip Jaffe, a known sympathizer with the Left,
had published almost verbatim a classified document regarding American
China policy. One source of the leaks was allegedly foreign service officer
John Stewart Service. Service also appeared on Hurley's list of officials who
had subverted his endeavors. Bridges considered the two incidents as indica-
tions that something was rotten in the State Department. A staunch, conservative critic of the New Deal and a highly partisan politician, Bridges
more and more came to see sinister motives in Chiang's critics.[47] As chairman of the powerful Senate Appropriations Committee in the Eightieth
Congress, he presented a threat to administration foreign policy that could
not be ignored.

Although in early 1947 China policy was not yet a major issue in American politics, Vincent in the State Department showed much sensitivity to
congressional opinion. In his proposal to include China in any program to
extend the United Nations Relief and Rehabilitation Administration, he argued that a "pro-China lobby in Congress" would raise a storm if that nation
was not among the recipients.[48] In pursuing credits for China from the
Export-Import Bank, Vincent noted that this effort would strengthen the administration's position "vis-à-vis [both] China and those in this country impatient to aid China."[49]

A sense of personal vulnerability probably increased Vincent's wariness of
congressional opinion—and perhaps Ringwalt's as well. In 1945 Hurley had
attacked both men. A year later, Vincent drew strong criticism from pro-
Chiang forces after he publicly warned the American Foreign Trade Council
againt the investment of public or private capital in China.[50] Early in 1947,
Vincent's nomination to the rank of career minister went to the Senate Foreign Relations Committee. Bridges immediately sent information to Vandenberg that allegedly called into question Vincent's judgment and loyalty.[51]
The nomination passed the Senate, but only after a delay of several months.
Vincent's transfer in the summer from the Office of Far Eastern Affairs to the
position of ambassador to Switzerland was a result of pressure on the administration by congressional Republicans.

In March 1947, when the Greek-Turkish aid bill was presented to Congress, China received increased attention on Capitol Hill. Republican Senators Owen Brewster (Maine), Joseph Ball (Minnesota), Homer Ferguson (Michigan), and Kenneth Wherry (Nebraska) all expressed concern about China.[52] If Communism was to be resisted in Greece and Turkey, why not in East Asia as well? The universalistic rhetoric of Truman's presentation to Congress of 12 March—the talk of assisting "free peoples who are resisting attempted subjugation by armed minorities or outside pressures"—encouraged this query. In hearings before the Foreign Affairs Committee, Representatives Judd and James G. Fulton (Republican-Pennsylvania) pursued the matter with Under Secretary of State Acheson. Acheson first noted that the National government already had received considerable aid from the United States. He then drew a sharp distinction between nations "approaching collapse" like Greece and Turkey and a nation, such as China, which was some way from this condition.[53] The Greek-Turkish aid bill passed both houses in May with the support—except of Wherry—of those who had raised the China question. Because a broader program of aid was in the works for Europe and because of the continuing deterioration of the situation in China, however, the administration could not ignore the mounting pressure for increased support of Chiang.

## The Issue Drawn

At the same time, administration officials were genuinely concerned with the growing military strength of the Communists and the worsening financial crisis in the National government. Communist offensives in Manchuria in February and April 1947 underscored the generalissimo's inability to bring the armed conflict to a quick and favorable conclusion. And, as Marshall and other Americans had predicted during the previous fall, the escalation of civil war had pushed his regime to the brink of economic collapse.

In June, the Joint Chiefs of Staff completed a major paper on the military aspects of American China policy. This paper, based primarily on arguments made by subordinate agencies during the previous fall but blocked at that time by military leaders, dramatized the conflict over China policy within the executive branch. The Joint Chiefs put China into a global context. Although it lacked "a united national government on which effective resistance to Soviet expansionist policy may be based," the fundamental problem there—the spread of Russian influence—was the same as elsewhere. The Soviets sought the economic separation of China and Manchuria and the latter's integration "into the economy of Eastern Siberia." This outcome would move the Soviet far eastern provinces toward economic and military self-sufficiency. Eventually it would lead to either the National government's "economic collapse [or] its ultimate submission to Soviet and Chinese communist pressure." Soviet power might then move southward through China, into Southeast Asia, and even India.

Concluding that such occurrences would threaten U.S. security, the Joint Chiefs suggested preventive action. Anticipating a State Department rebuttal, they admitted that the extensive American aid since the defeat of Japan had not been put to good use. But this fact could be partly explained, they insisted, by its "piecemeal and uncoordinated" nature. The absence of clear goals—other than a peaceful solution to the "irreconcilable differences" between the leading political contestants—was as much a factor in the effectiveness of aid as the inefficiency and corruption of the National government. "[C]arefully planned, selective and well-supervised assistance," they asserted, would "definitely contribute to the United States' security interests." Because the morale factor was of such significance, an expression of American support and the intention to grant additional aid to the National government might exert a substantial impact on the course of the civil conflict. In such circumstances, the Communists might even accept terms offered by Chiang for an end to the fighting. If this did not occur, "a relatively small amount of military assistance, in large part merely ammunition and replacement parts for American equipment" should enable the Nationalists to defeat the Communists by force.[54]

State Department officials disagreed with much of this analysis. They doubted America's capacity to shape events in China. Chiang refused to institute reforms that would enable his government to make good use of American aid. Furthermore, increased help to the Nationalists probably would lead the Soviets to assist the Communists. Even if such a process of action and reaction did not materialize, effective American intervention on the side of an unreformed National government would require directing "Chinese military operations and administration" over an indefinite period. The Chinese people would offer "formidable opposition" to such action, which would also necessitate "a strategic commitment" inconsistent with the conclusion of the Joint Chiefs that China belonged "very low" on the list of priorities for military aid.[55]

Vincent doubted that Russia could dominate China after an American withdrawal. Although he and others saw a strong ideological bond between Moscow and the Chinese Communists, they believed several factors dictated against Soviet influence over the entire country. These included "the administrative inefficiencies of the Chinese" and "the magnitude of the task of dominating China," both of which were impediments to effective centralized rule; and "the easily aroused Chinese resentment at foreign interference, the lack of industrial development and material resources, and the inability of the Russians to give the material assistance necessary to make

China a going concern." In sum, the Office of Far Eastern Affairs viewed a Russian-dominated China as "a danger of [in]sufficient immediacy or probability" to merit greatly expanded American involvement in the civil war.[56]

The State Department was more realistic than the Joint Chiefs in assessing United States capabilities and interests in China. Yet certain tendencies in the Office of Far Eastern Affairs—to extend Nationalist inefficiency to the Chinese people as a whole, to view extensive foreign assistance as necessary, under any circumstances, to make China "a going concern," and to perceive China as a geographical entity of unmanageable size—turned out to be wide of the mark. Unfortunately, they soon become guiding assumptions in the formation of American policy.[57]

Despite State Department opposition to direct American participation in the civil war, Marshall conceded that the United States should insure that Chiang's armies were supplied with adequate ammunition. Because the civil war was raging on and no end was in sight, this goal required more than the mere abandonment of American ammunition dumps on the Chinese mainland and an end to the arms embargo.[58] A search began on the Pacific islands for additional surplus ammunition that might be turned over to the Nationalists at a nominal cost. Army officials sought out American companies that could manufacture the ammunition rapidly and sell it to the Chinese government. To expedite delivery to China, the War and Navy departments even offered to relinquish temporarily their existing contracts.[59] The secretary of state, under continuing pressure from both inside and outside the administration, encouraged the submittal of "constructive" proposals. He refused, however, to accept American intervention beyond limited arms assistance and credits through the Export-Import Bank. Direct American supervision of aid and Nationalist military operations soon became the central issue within the Truman administration.

## Marshall Buys Time: The Wedemeyer Mission

As often happens in the face of divisions within the administration and pressures from without, the idea of an American mission to the center of events came to the fore. In early July 1947, Marshall decided to send such a mission, headed by Lieutenant General Albert Wedemeyer, to survey both the China scene and the increasingly unsettled situation in South Korea. The successor to Stilwell and a leading figure in China from the fall of 1944 to the spring of 1946, Wedemeyer was an avid proponent of expanded American aid to Chiang.

Why Marshall allowed such a man to head a survey group remains somewhat of a mystery. Pressure from Capitol Hill, especially in the person of Congressman Judd, played some role.[60] The secretary of state noted on 2 July that, in the past three days, Wedemeyer had been suggested as the leader of a mission by three people outside the department, but he also stated that he had been considering "the probable desirability" of sending Wedemeyer to China "for about two weeks."[61]

Certainly Wedemeyer's past experience in China and his cordial relations with Chiang and other Nationalist officials were basic considerations in Marshall's choice. In June, James K. Penfield had made a brief, on-the-spot survey of the China situation, but his position in the State Department made him suspect as a source to some observers. An undercurrent of suspicion toward anti-Chiang elements in the American embassy in Nanking, and in the State Department's Office of Far Eastern Affairs, already circulated in the military branches and in Congress.[62] Given Wedemeyer's solid reputation among Chiang's more vociferous defenders in Washington, his appointment might serve to take some heat off those diplomats. Still, to send a man of Wedemeyer's sentiments was risky. If he returned with proposals for an expanded American role, pressure would increase for Marshall to alter his policy.

Apparently overriding this negative consideration were the personal relationship between the secretary of state and Wedemeyer as well as the complex pressures that confronted Marshall in the summer of 1947. Marshall took pride in his ability to pick out the most promising young officers in army ranks. As chief of war plans in the late 1930s, he had come into close contact with Wedemeyer following the latter's return from two years at the German War College. The intense young major immediately impressed his superior. Partially as a result of Marshall's favor, Wedemeyer progressed rapidly in army ranks and emerged from World War II as a lieutenant general.[63] Despite the differences over China policy, the older man had considerable respect for his protégé's judgment. Because Wedemeyer had not been in China for more than a year, Marshall may have believed that a firsthand look at the deteriorating situation there would lead him to adjust his opinions.

In any event, the appointment of Wedemeyer would give Marshall a breathing spell on the China issue. In May and June 1947, as Chiang's prospects worsened in Manchuria and North China, his agents—both official and otherwise—had increased their activities in Washington.[64] At a time when the secretary of state strained to promote and create a program for European recovery, therefore, he was under constant pressure on China. Although he sought to contain Communism there, he had uncovered no positive program that took into account the limits of American capabilities. In such circumstances, Marshall probably looked more closely at the immediate respite the Wedemeyer mission would provide than at its possible long-term consequences.

The mission arrived in Nanking in late July, during a sweltering heat wave that would actually make Wedemeyer "physically ill" during some of the

trying days ahead.[65] The political and military situation did nothing to ame-
liorate the climatic discomforts. Wedemeyer found the Nationalists in a
state of "apathy and bewilderment." Their forces had "lost confidence in
their leadership"; the soldiers foresaw "complete collapse"; and their superiors strove "corruptly" to enrich themselves before this occurred. Rather than
attempt to effect improvements, most Nationalist officials blamed their
woes on an American sellout at Yalta. In contrast, reports indicated "an excellent spirit, almost a fanatical fervor" in Communist ranks.[66] Clearly,
Wedemeyer did not miss the unpleasant realities that foreign service officials had been reporting to the State Department for months.

Wedemeyer's last meetings with the generalissimo were extremely tense,
and his statement upon leaving China on 24 August even implied a reorientation in his thinking. He asserted that, despite the lengthy civil and military strife, China possessed "most of the physical resources needed for her
own rehabilitation." Inspirational leadership and a "moral and spiritual re-
surgence" were the main prerequisites for recovery, and they could come
only from within China. "Drastic and far-reaching political and economic
reforms" had to be made, Wedemeyer concluded, if the National government was to regain popular support.[67]

Chiang and his cronies, who originally had interpreted Wedemeyer's mission as reflecting an American decision to increase aid, finally realized that,
as American diplomat John F. Melby put it, "this was no free lunch wagon
that had descended on them."[68] In the face of this sudden awakening, the
Chinese government's policy shifted slightly. During September, the Nationalist-controlled press became more critical of the United States while
attacks on the Soviet Union "perceptibly decreased."[69] Senior Chinese officials made "thinly-veiled suggestions" that, unless additional aid came soon,
it might "become necessary to seek assistance from the Soviet Union."[70]
Rather than responding to Wedemeyer's lecture by instituting reforms, the
Nationalists expanded their own tactics of pressure on the United States.

American officials did not take the new tactics seriously. The perceived
ideological bond between the Russians and the Chinese Communists made
agreement between Nanking and Moscow appear most unlikely. Although
the tendency had existed for some time in the State Department to view an
expansion of Communist power in China as advantageous to Moscow, during the summer of 1947 a hardening in this position occurred.

American decision makers devoted considerable attention to this issue at
the time of the Wedemeyer mission. In early July, the minister-counselor at
the American embassy in Nanking, W. Walton Butterworth, directed the
staff there to analyze the options open to the United States. He was a talented, hard-nosed foreign service officer. Prior to mid-1946, his primary experience had been in Europe. He was a quick learner, however, and soon
grasped many of the essentials of the Chinese scene. In early 1947, one foreign service officer in Nanking wrote that

Butterworth's toughness is most disturbing to the Chinese, especially to [T. V.] Soong, . . . who hates him because he is tough too and does not like competition. Soong is still trying to bamboozle us out of some kind of stopgap but is making no impression on Butterworth, who has decided that Shanghai needs to do some sweating—and that is what it is going to do.[71]

Because Ambassador Stuart was inclined toward a strongly pro-Chiang position, Butterworth's dominant position in operating the embassy was a godsend from the standpoint of effective policy implementation. Stuart had been a leading American in China for decades, but was seventy-one years old, beset by physical ailments, and inexperienced in the art of diplomacy. He depended heavily on the minister-counselor.

By July, however, Butterworth and his staff had altered their views on American aid. Although aware of continued Nationalist inefficiency and corruption, the staff proposed "a reasoned and coordinated program of conditional aid." Although the word "conditional" stood out, the proposal represented a significant shift away from Butterworth's smug position at the beginning of the year. The rationale for an aid program was the need to engage "in a holding operation against the progressive spread of indigenous communism *and its corollary, Soviet political expansionism.*" (emphasis added)[72]

Admiral Cooke, stationed at Tsingtao, in North China, drew an even more disturbing picture for the Wedemeyer team. The naval commander argued that Chinese Communist actions in Manchuria and North China appeared "to be moving in accord with a definite plan approved and supported from Moscow." Like Chennault in his earlier letter to Vandenberg, Cooke believed a Communist victory in Manchuria, parts of North China, and all Korea— where America's hold was increasingly precarious—would have dangerous military consequences.

If the Soviet position in the maritime provinces is not integrated to the industrial and agricultural support of Manchuria, not supported by the strategic reinforcement of the warmwater ports of Port Arthur, Dairen, and northern Korea, and is forced to continue to be dependent upon a line of supplies over the trans-Siberian railway, . . . [the area] continues to be a source of . . . vulnerability to Russia. . . . Soviet aggressive action to exploit favorable prospects in central Europe would tend to be restrained by the comparatively weak position in eastern Asia. . . . If, however, Soviet eastern Asia becomes self-sufficient by the addition and development of Manchuria, Korea, and parts of north China, Soviet Asia can then become an element of strength in the overall Soviet power structure.[73]

China hand Philip Sprouse, the State Department representative on the Wedemeyer mission, never subscribed fully to Cooke's analysis. By the end of the trip, however, Sprouse had reached conclusions identical to those of the foreign service officers in Nanking. Calling for a program of "conditional aid," he suggested that the United States give moral and material support "to any groups or combination of groups [able] to consolidate its control over sizable portions of the country and which would be receptive to U.S. ideas of government." The United States, he argued, should reach precise agreement with the Nationalists on the conditions for granting aid. If the National government then violated the agreement, the United States "should be prepared to withdraw completely from China."[74]

Wedemeyer agonized over his recommendations to President Truman.[75] The general's final report, submitted to the White House on 19 September 1947, bore some resemblance to Sprouse's memorandum. Wedemeyer viewed the Communists as closely tied to Moscow, and he recognized that extensive reform within the National government was essential to make American aid effective. Both men saw the need for close American supervision of any aid program. Such a program, they agreed, should include both economic and military support.[76]

Yet the Wedemeyer and Sprouse analyses differed in major respects. True, the State Department official feared the consequences of a Nationalist collapse and believed a Communist victory in Manchuria and North China would lead to such a result; however, he was less certain than Wedemeyer that the Soviets would thereby reap immediate and substantial rewards. To Sprouse, the Communists would have some of the same problems in uniting and ruling the country that the Nationalists were now experiencing. In contrast, Wedemeyer saw that concrete Soviet gains would emanate from a Communist conquest of Manchuria and North China. Warm water ports and airbases within easy reach of American installations in Japan, the Ryukyus, and the Philippines would become available to Russia. Manchuria and North China, combined with Siberia, would form "an industrial crescent" of considerable value to the Soviet economy. Unlike Sprouse, Wedemeyer was unwilling to withdraw all support for Chiang. His estimate of the immediate strategic advantages to the Soviet Union of a continued Communist advance in China, as well as his belief that the United States was at least partially to blame for the plight of the Nationalists, produced this difference. Although the general talked of specific reforms that should be effected before the influx of American aid, he did not advocate a quid pro quo policy. To do so, he told Sprouse, would mean that no assistance would ever be sent.[77]

Wedemeyer also went beyond Sprouse in advocating United Nations involvement in China. Pointing to the criticism by some member nations of American "circumvention" of the international body in launching an aid program for Greece and Turkey, Wedemeyer suggested that China inform the United Nations "officially of her request to the United States for material assistance and advisory aid." Furthermore, the United States should press China to seek United Nations intervention in Manchuria "to bring about a cessation of hostilities [there] . . . as a prelude to the establishment of a Guardianship or Trusteeship." A guardianship, Wedemeyer said, "might consist of China, Soviet Russia, the United States, Great Britain, and France." If one of these nations resisted, China might turn to the General Assembly and seek the establishment of a trusteeship. Wedemeyer conceded that Chiang initially might view this course as an "infringement" of China's sovereignty, but, given the urgency of the situation, the American believed, realism ultimately would prevail. Otherwise, Manchuria might "be drawn into the Soviet Orbit, despite United States aid, and lost perhaps permanently to China."[78]

The trusteeship proposal brought immediate controversy, and led the administration to withhold the report from public scrutiny for almost two years. Because of the suggested infringement of China's sovereignty and the implication that the National government was incapable of ruling the entire country, State Department officials argued that revelation of the proposal "would be highly offensive to [the] Chinese."[79] Unfortunately, influential voices outside the executive branch, unaware of this reasoning and looking for issues on which to attack those in power, used the suppression of the report as evidence of administration perfidy.

Wedemeyer later claimed—probably correctly—that Marshall never intended his mission to serve as a basis for a "fundamental change" in American China policy.[80] His report, however, was not ignored. The State Department studied his Manchurian proposal carefully, but rejected it not only because it infringed upon China's sovereignty, but also because the Communists and the Soviet Union would almost certainly resist it. In such circumstances, the plan could be imposed only by force. Because the United States could not provide a sizable number of ground troops, the proposal was unworkable.[81] In any event, the fate of trusteeship in Korea did not encourage the diplomats to adopt similar plans for other areas.

Wedemeyer had contemplated the trusteeship idea for two years.[82] During the second half of 1946, the Plans and Operations Division of the army had studied its feasibility for Manchuria, expressed reservations about it, and concluded that the time was not propitious for its initiation by the United States.[83] Although Wedemeyer had discussed the matter with Secretary of State Byrnes, he requested that the State Department not be informed of the army's interest in the idea.[84] It may not have been broached to a State Department official—other than on a casual basis to Byrnes—until 7 September 1947, when Wedemeyer told the members of his mission that he intended to recommend a United Nations trusteeship for Manchuria in his final report.[85] Thus, the general probably recognized the controversial nature of the plan and sought to gain a tactical advantage by presenting it directly to the president, rather than discussing it first with all interested executive agencies. Here Wedemeyer appears to have had a pet idea, one that smoldered in his mind for some time until the opportunity arose to bring it forth in a forceful manner. In its manner of presentation, the proposal revealed Wedemeyer's adeptness at the game of interdepartmental politics; in substance, however, it, along with his public remarks to nationalist officials upon his departure from China in late August, disclosed his failure to grasp the importance of "face" in Chinese politics and culture.[86] Surely the American experience with trusteeship in Korea should have steered Wedemeyer away from a similar scheme in China.

Wedemeyer's other recommendations followed more closely the lines of recent discussion within the administration. Nevertheless, the State Department discarded his proposals for direct American participation in civilian administration and in planning tactical military operations. In both cases, Marshall judged that the American involvement would be too great so long as the Nationalists refused to institute meaningful reforms and increasingly blamed all their troubles on the United States.[87] He also rejected Wedemeyer's proposal for a five-year recovery program. Conditions in China were too uncertain to warrant long-term projections regarding that nation's needs and its government's capacity to use American aid effectively.[88] Unlike the problems in Western Europe, those in China stretched beyond the economic and social dislocation emanating from a recent war to the more fundamental issue of the quality of its ruling elites.

Despite these rebuffs, the State Department did follow some of Wedemeyer's proposals. In mid-October, the Army Advisory Group received permission to assist the National government in organizing a more efficient military supply system and in training new recruits at a base on Taiwan.[89] At the beginning of November, material support increased when Marshall approved surplus-property procedures for the transfer of American munitions in the Marianas.[90] He also announced plans to submit to Congress an economic aid program for China early in 1948. The fifteen-month program would cost $400 million.[91] Two weeks earlier, the administration had granted $27.7 million to the National government through a congressional foreign-relief appropriation of the previous spring.[92]

## The China Bloc on the Offensive

These moves were as much a response to domestic political pressures as to the Wedemeyer report. During the fall recess of Congress, four members of the House Military Affairs Committee visited China. In a meeting with Chiang, they received a stern lecture on American responsibilities there.[93] The congressmen then wired President Truman urging the "extension of immediate aid to the Chinese government."[94] Soon afterward, Judd, who had just returned from China, held a private meeting with Walton Butterworth, the new director of the State Department's Office of Far Eastern Affairs. Judd emphasized the urgent need for American aid to Chiang and queried Butterworth as to why the administration sought to help Europe but hesitated on assistance to China.[95] House Speaker Joseph W. Martin, a Republican from Massachusetts, followed with a public call for a worldwide battle against Communism. He surmised that Congress would want to add China to any foreign assistance program for Europe.[96] Senator Vandenberg held similar views.[97]

An article in the 13 October issue of *Life* magazine reinforced the trend on Capitol Hill. The author of the piece, William C. Bullitt, was an eccentric man from a wealthy and well-connected family. Under Roosevelt, he had served as American ambassador to Russia and later to France. In the summer of 1947, he visited China and returned to the United States with a proposal for a three-year, $1.35 billion program of American military and economic aid to Chiang.[98] To insure the widest possible readership, Henry Luce ran a preview article in his news weekly *Time*, and placed full-page ads in several eastern newspapers.[99] In the face of such pressures, George F. Kennan, the influential head of the State Department's Policy Planning Staff and an advocate of concentrating American attention on Europe, advised Marshall "to extend the minimum aid necessary to satisfy American public opinion and, if possible, to prevent any sudden and total collapse of the Chinese government."[100]

Despite the new aid to Chiang and Marshall's promise of more help in the near future, many members of Congress remained dissatisfied with the administration's China policy. The discontent manifested itself in an effort to include assistance to the National government in the interim aid bill for Europe sent to Capitol Hill in early November. Vandenberg, whom the State Department had kept informed on China for several months, initially prevented such a move in the Senate, though he voiced regret that China was not included in the bill.[101] In the House, Judd and Vorys pushed through an authorization calling for $60 million to China. This act threatened to reduce funds available for Western Europe, but Vandenberg came to the rescue in the conference committee.[102] Under his guidance a State Department plan passed the interhouse group providing Chiang with $18 million of unexpended funds from previous foreign relief legislation.[103] Thus, although China remained an aid recipient, the amount of funds available for Europe was not affected. Appropriations bills still had to be passed. At the behest of Styles Bridges, several of Chiang's strongest supporters—Wedemeyer, Judd, Bullitt, and Alfred Kohlberg of the aggressively pro-Nationalist American China Policy Association—testified before the Senate Appropriations Committee. Despite the maneuvering of Bridges and the efforts of many others outside the government (in perhaps a slight overstatement, newsman Robert S. Allen asserted that Washington "literally swarmed with Chinese lobbyists"), the State Department compromise held up.[104] The administration, therefore, won a temporary victory in its efforts for Western European recovery.

Nevertheless, the experience with interim aid indicated that pro-Chiang forces in Congress might prevent passage of a long-range program for European recovery unless it was accompanied by a sizable allotment for China.[105] In addition to Vandenberg's adept maneuvering, the administration's success in the fall of 1947 depended in part on the belief of most in the China bloc that aid was urgently needed in Western Europe, but also on Marshall's assurance that he would soon present a program for China.[106] This assurance reflected the impact of congressional pressure on administration policy. The move could not help but undermine the State Department tactic of withholding aid from Chiang for as long as possible in order to pressure the Chinese leader to institute reforms.

In retrospect, some warning signals of what was to come on the China question were apparent by the end of 1947. James Reston, Washington correspondent for the *New York Times*, noted in late November that China was "the first issue in postwar foreign policy in which the Republicans had the opportunity to lead the Democrats, rather than the reverse."[107] Although congressional Republicans remained divided over large-scale aid to China, the number of those advocating that course had increased since early in the year. Republican interest in the issue also surfaced outside Congress. In late November, Thomas E. Dewey, the leading candidate for the Republican presidential nomination in 1948, advocated an immediate increase in aid to Chiang.[108]

Administration leaders confronted far more pressing issues, however, that made the China problem only a minor annoyance on the domestic political scene. Admittedly, its relationship to the task of obtaining congressional approval for a European recovery program contributed significantly to several administration moves. Yet these were short-term tactical maneuvers. The Truman administration showed little concern at this point that the China issue would eventually move to center stage in a Republican scramble to seize political leadership from the Democrats.

## The Truman Administration's Options in China

Scholars have often wondered why, in late 1947, the Truman administration did not take its case on the China issue to the American people. Surely, the scholars reason, an informed public would have recognized the implications of a deepening commitment to Chiang and supported administration policy. The Democrats might thereby have avoided the repercussions they endured after China's fall to Communism in 1949.[109] A careful analysis of the domestic climate belies this argument.

Marshall faced a dilemma. Informing the American people on China would undermine Chiang's prestige, both at home and abroad, thus expediting his fall. Although the State Department regarded his survival as unlikely, it viewed a slow decline as preferable to a precipitous collapse. The chance remained that he would institute reforms in time to save himself, or that a viable alternative to Chiang and Mao would emerge. Yet, if the American public was not given a realistic view of the rottenness of the National government, Chiang's eventual fall might have serious political consequences in the United States.[110]

Understandably, the administration adopted the course that presented the fewest immediate risks. An increase in aid to Chiang short of direct American participation in the civil war would help prevent his abrupt collapse. It would also serve to avoid a political confrontation with the China bloc that would have jeopardized the European recovery program in Congress. Granted, an effort to withhold further aid to Chiang would have had considerable support in the nation. State Department studies of newspaper, periodical, and radio opinion indicated that, though an increasing number of commentators advocated expanded assistance to the Nationalists, a majority—including such China specialists as John King Fairbank, Nathaniel Peffer, and Lawrence Rosinger—continued to oppose such a course unless the Chinese government instituted large-scale reforms. Many journalists also expressed concern that programs for China would cut into those for Western Europe, which deserved priority.[111] Furthermore, there was no evidence of a ground swell of popular opinion in favor of deeper involvement in the Chinese civil war. In a nationwide poll of March 1947, those interviewed split evenly on the question of a loan to Chiang.[112] Had surveys been taken later in the year, they probably would have shown somewhat of a shift in favor of immediate help for the generalissimo. It is unlikely, however, that any decisive change occurred in either direction. Certainly, the administration could have manipulated public sentiment on the matter.[113]

To a considerable extent, however, these facts were irrelevant. Congress, not the news media or the public at large, had the final say on the crucial issue of emergency aid to Europe. Because individual congressional constituencies often did not conform to national patterns of opinion, pivotal senators and representatives might have remained insistent on at least a promise of future assistance to Chiang as a quid pro quo for their support of a program for Western Europe. Given the powerful positions on key committees of such pro-Chiang legislators as Vandenberg, Bridges, Judd, and Vorys, the interim aid bill was seriously threatened by amendment and delay. A battle over China would have exacerbated national divisions on foreign policy and destroyed the atmosphere of bipartisan cooperation. At a time of deep economic and psychological infirmity in Western Europe, American delay and a show of internal divisiveness in responding to the crisis there could only have weakened the prospects for containing Soviet influence. To the Truman administration, therefore, an effort to abandon Chiang simply risked too much in the area most critical to American security.

Although domestic political considerations loomed large in administration calculations regarding China, anxiety about the Nationalist decline also carried considerable weight. Administration moves in the fall of 1947 probably would have been different if the China bloc had not endangered plans for Western Europe. Surely no announcement would have been made of the intended submittal of a China aid program to Congress. Indeed, such a program might not have been presented in 1948. Yet pro-Chiang forces in Congress did not prevent a total withdrawal from China. Perhaps they helped to speed up the transfer of American munitions to Nationalist armies, but a sense of long-standing commitment to Chiang, and a related desire not to undermine his chances to halt the Communist advance, in the end would have led the United States to provide surplus matériels to the National government.

The accumulated effect of long involvement in Chinese affairs reinforced the belief that the United States had some minimal commitment to insure American-armed Nationalist soldiers adequate spare parts and ammunition. Most State Department officials saw through Nationalist appeals to American sentimentality. They were aware of the Chinese perception of them as representatives of "Uncle Chump from over the Hump." Still, they found it difficult to conceive of a total withdrawal of United States influence from the country, and, unless such a withdrawal was to be carried out, some aid to Chiang appeared essential.

The pressure put on Marshall by military leaders in Washington reinforced his disinclination to abandon Chiang. Despite the secretary of state's strength within the executive branch and his own strong opinions on China, this pressure from men he had known and worked with for many years may have influenced him. Certainly, the existence of internal divisions emphasized to Truman and Marshall the risks of a confrontation with the China bloc.

Given the pressures from both inside and outside the executive branch, and the feeling within the State Department that the Chinese Communists were under the influence of Moscow, the question remains as to why the United States did not intervene in China on a broader scale. Although a lack of confidence in Chiang and the reactionary clique around him was a basic consideration, it is inadequate as a sole explanation. The rulers of Greece, after all, hardly represented the epitome of the American ideals of democracy and efficiency. Yet the United States did not reject large-scale intervention in that country.

In China, however, another component—the size of the country—served to emphasize the seriousness of its government's inadequacies. Whereas Greece was a land of some fifty thousand square miles and less than eight million people, China was more than fifty times as large in both respects. The magnitude of the tasks of establishing order and of repulsing the Communist challenge was far greater there than in Greece. Most State Department specialists had grown so accustomed to disorder in China that they were beginning to view it as permanent. In addition to the country's lack of an industrial base, its unsettled condition would make it of limited significance as an ally of the Soviet Union.[114]

The scant resources available to the Truman administration added gravity to the problem of China's manageability. By the time a clear choice appeared in China between direct American involvement in the civil war and the collapse of the National government, extensive military aid was on the way to Greece and Turkey. American decision makers were sufficiently experienced with Greece to know the difficulties of propping up corrupt, inefficient regimes.[115] Moreover, a massive program of economic aid was contemplated for Western Europe, and sizable congressional cuts of an already tight military budget appeared inevitable.[116] Concern regarding congressional treatment of the European program was a crucial factor in Marshall's desire to postpone an economic aid program for China. Recently expanded military commitments in the Mediterranean, combined with the slashing of the defense budget by Congress, were pivotal in the rejection of proposals by the Joint Chiefs and Wedemeyer for the use of American officers in advising Nationalist combat units. As Acheson later noted, such proposals required an additional commitment of some ten thousand officers and enlisted men, who were not readily available.[117]

Military leaders may have seen a decision to expand American involvement as a selling point to Congress for reversing the dangerous trend in defense expenditures, but to Marshall such a decision promised to engage American credibility in an extremely uncertain situation. Although the China bloc held an influential position in Congress, countervailing forces dictated against opening the way to a possibly never-ending spiral of involvement in the civil war. Even Chief of Naval Operations Chester Nimitz conceded that prevailing sentiment in the United States made a commitment of American combat troops impossible.[118] Yet, if ten thousand United States advisers turned out to be unable to guide the Nationalist armies to victory, or even perhaps to stave off defeat, the Truman administration would face the unenviable choice of cutting its losses in an area of substantial commitment or of attempting to sell deeper intervention to the American people.

Sprouse's proposal of a strict quid pro quo strategy did not provide adequate safeguards against deeper embroilment in the Chinese morass. In theory, the United States could withdraw completely if Chiang did not accept its terms and carry them out in good faith. In reality, however, politics in the United States made a total withdrawal virtually impossible, and, unless the threat of such a move appeared viable, the chance of success for the strategy disappeared.[119] Furthermore, past experiences with Chiang indicated that it would be difficult to hold him to his promises. The danger remained that he would concede enough to deepen American involvement, but that, as before, reforms would turn out to be a mirage. Even with his complete cooperation, it was questionable if he had sufficient control over his subordinates in the field to insure that American advice would be followed. Thus the limits of recognized obligations led to a refusal to increase American entanglement significantly.

Marshall's influence was central in the Truman administration's refusal to become more deeply committed to Chiang. In the president's eyes, no other man surpassed his capacity for sound judgment. On China, the secretary of state had more extensive recent experience than any of the top military men. Although he held a diplomatic post, his position as a military expert remained second to none. Had a man of lesser standing been in his office in 1947, the chances of a gradual but dangerous increase of America's involvement in the Chinese civil war would have grown immeasurably. This fact is demonstrated by the shakiness of the State Department's Office of Far Eastern Affairs—by Vincent's sensitivity to congressional pressure and Sprouse's ultimate willingness to accept American aid to Chiang on a level contemplated by Wedemeyer.

## The Marshall Plan, the China Aid Act, and the Election of 1948

Marshall's battle to resist direct American intervention in the civil war by no means ended with the passage of the interim aid bill for Europe. During 1948, pro-Chiang forces in the United States continued their attack on official policy. This offensive gained impetus from events in China, where Nationalist strength deteriorated rapidly. The National government's decline was reflected most palpably in its failure to halt runaway inflation and in the retreat or surrender of its armies in the face of Communist military pressure. Between January and March, wholesale prices in principal Chinese cities more than doubled; between March and June, they tripled; between June and August, they rose more than 500 percent. Currency reform late in the summer did little to stem this long-term trend.[120] In the military sphere, Nationalist forces in Manchuria and North China at times inflicted heavy casualties on their foes, but the end result of battle was virtually always a Communist advance.[121] Although such critical cities as Tsinan, Changchun, and Mukden did not fall until autumn, American officials had long anticipated a Nationalist collapse in the north.[122]

Yet the State Department held fast in resisting deeper American involvement in China. Early in the year, it even stalled on sending to Congress an economic aid bill for Chiang, hoping to avoid its association and completion with the program for Europe.[123] By mid-February, however, the administration was under heavy pressure from Bridges, Vandenberg, Judd, and others to present a relief and recovery bill for China.[124] Further delay threatened to hold up passage of the Marshall Plan. Because interim aid would end on 1 April and a national election would take place in Italy eighteen days later, serious consequences might result if Congress did not soon authorize new funds for Europe. Thus on 18 February 1948 the White House sent a China aid program to Capitol Hill that called for $570 million in economic assistance to the National government over fifteen months.

Even so, State Department officials continued to fear harmful delays in the passage of enabling legislation for European aid.[125] House Speaker Joseph Martin opined that his body might not finish with the Marshall Plan until 10 April, which appeared all the more ominous because powerful forces in the lower house pressed for adoption of a bill substantially different from that in the Senate.[126] Congressmen Judd and Vorys persuaded the House Foreign Affairs Committee to combine in one omnibus bill the Marshall Plan, the Greek-Turkish aid program, which was up for renewal, and the China aid legislation. Despite criticism in the Senate, House Republican leaders backed the committee's decision.[127] Worse still, the committee presented legislation to the entire house providing for $150 million in military aid. The United States was to have direct responsibility for programming, procuring, and delivering matériel for Nationalist China, as well as for supervising its use through advice to tactical units in the field.[128] Because the Senate showed no inclination to support such commitments to China, passage of this measure by Congress appeared unlikely. Yet its adoption by the House might result in additional delays in conference committee.

On 31 March 1948, more than a week earlier than expected, the House approved the Foreign Affairs Committee's package. Fortunately, Vandenberg had anticipated this action and had sought to narrow the differences between Senate and House measures. This effort was complicated because several members of his Foreign Relations Committee lacked enthusiasm for any aid to Chiang.[129] Nevertheless, the Michigan senator steered a bill through the upper chamber that provided $463 million for the National government over twelve months, $100 million of which could be used for the purchase of military supplies. At the same time, the Senate refused to combine military aid to China with that to Greece and Turkey. The Foreign Relations Committee report stated explicitly that the bill did not commit the United States to underwrite or guide the Nationalist military effort.[130]

The conference committee assigned to reconcile the House and Senate bills accomplished its task in one day. Senators accepted the foreign aid measures in a single omnibus package. Representatives were conceded $125 million for China that could be used for military purposes, but the United States was not obligated to participate in its dispensation or to become directly involved in the Chinese civil war. On 2 April, the compromise passed both chambers.[131]

Passage of the authorization for European recovery virtually on schedule, and without a major reorientation of American China policy, represented a substantial victory for the Truman administration. The success again owed much to Vandenberg's tactical skills, to persistent pressure from the executive branch, and to the commitment of most members of the China bloc to the containment of Communism in Europe. Yet events abroad—especially Communist consolidation of power in Czechoslovakia during February and March 1948—were essential to the growing climate of urgency in both Washington and the nation at large.

Given the State Department's unwillingness to educate the public on China policy, the increasing commitment of the American people to the containment of Communism could not help but influence attitudes toward the Chinese civil war. This was especially true because of the intensifying campaign in certain elements of the press for military aid to Chiang. In mid-February, the *New York Times* called for stepped-up military assistance to the National government.[132] Luce and Scripps-Howard publications continued to express dissatisfaction with the administration's limited support for the anti-Communist cause in China. In March and April, Scripps-Howard newspapers carried a series of articles by General Chennault on America's past mistakes and current obligations there.[133] Although some commentators remained strong critics of the generalissimo, the testimony before open sessions of the House Foreign Affairs Committee of Chennault, Wedemeyer, and Bullitt—all of whom favored extensive military aid to China—gained wide press coverage.[134]

These developments in the United States and abroad brought a marked shift in public attitudes regarding China. In February 1948, a private poll revealed a 60-32 split among those questioned *against aid to Chiang*. A month later, a national survey indicated only a 46-41 split against *military* aid to the Nationalists. A similar poll in April showed a continuation of the trend; 55 percent were in favor of military aid to China and only 32 percent were opposed.[135] A study by the American Institute of Public Opinion indicated that 39 percent of the group "informed" on China favored sending "more military supplies, goods, and money" to Chiang, and 23 percent were opposed.[136]

At the same time, considerable sentiment remained within the executive branch in favor of extensive military aid to Chiang. The State Department, fearful that new assistance in this area would imply an expanded American obligation to the Nationalist government, preferred to restrict such support to the sale of surplus matériels and limited advice in general planning and the training of Nationalist forces. The Joint Chiefs, on the other hand, favored both substantial arms aid and deep American participation in its dispensation.[137] On the second matter, they received support from the Budget Bureau, which, as a watchdog over government operations, sought to protect against wastage of American dollars.[138] The military leaders gained backing from China in the person of Vice Admiral Oscar C. Badger, who in February had replaced Admiral Cooke as commander of United States naval forces in the western Pacific.[139] Because the Truman administration was divided, the American people increasingly receptive to aid to China, and powerful members of Congress intent on containing Communism in Asia as well as Europe, China policy was destined to remain an issue even after passage of the Marshall Plan and the China Aid Act.

Throughout the spring, summer, and much of the fall of 1948 congressional critics centered their attention on the procurement of military supplies for China in the United States and their distribution in the field. Only vague guidelines existed for administering the $125 million in grants: the president could dispense this sum to the National government "on such terms [as he might] . . . determine." [140] Controversy arose over the administration's handling of part of the $50 million to be advanced to the Nationalists prior to the passage by Congress of an appropriation act. The State Department decided immediately that $36.5 million of the sum should be applied to economic aid, to be administered by the Economic Cooperation Administration (ECA), and that the remainder would go for special grants (matériels). [141] But the Budget Bureau argued against a State Department plan in which the United States would take only a minor part in administering military aid. Specific procedures were not agreed upon until 18 May 1948. [142]

Then, members of the House Appropriations Committee expressed dissatisfaction with the minimal level of American supervision of the grant program. [143] The committee sent the bill to the House floor stipulating that the China aid program adhere to the objectives of that for Greece and Turkey. On 4 June, the House passed legislation that followed the Appropriations Committee recommendation and included no mention of funds for special grants. [144] This action brought to a standstill administration efforts to begin dispensing the $13.5 million in advance grants. The Senate reinstated the $125 million in grants, but removed the clause referring to the program for Greece and Turkey. The legislative process was not completed until 14 June, when both houses passed a conference bill that followed the Senate version, except on the total amount of aid, which was cut to $400 million. [145]

Yet, pressures on the administration did not abate. On 28 June, Senator Bridges wrote to Marshall complaining of State Department laxity in furnishing arms to China through the $13.5 million in advance grants. [146] Three days later, Congressman John Taber, the chairman of the House Appropriations Committee, joined Bridges in reminding the president that congressional conferees desired careful checks on expenditure of the $125 million. They requested adherence on this matter to the proposal of Secretary of the Army Kenneth Royall and General Wedemeyer. [147] Fortunately, the Royall-Wedemeyer proposal, made to the Senate Appropriations Committee in mid-June, had grown out of a meeting with top State Department officials. Wedemeyer, who earlier in the year had become the army's director of plans and operations, was no longer anxious to embroil the United States more deeply in the Chinese civil war. The authority of Chiang had so declined in recent months that Wedemeyer doubted his ability to compel commanders in the field to follow American advice. Thus, he agreed that the Army Advisory Group in China should merely "check on the delivery of the military supplies from that end."[148]

Congressman Judd pressed the State Department regarding another aspect of the grants. He urged that the army assist the Chinese in procuring military items in a manner similar to the procedures applied to Greece and Turkey. Elimination of "the Greek-Turkey proviso" from both the authorizing and appropriation bills, Judd claimed, did not rule out his proposal.[149] The State Department cooperated with Judd, but it took until 28 July for State Department lawyers to grant legal clearance, for the armed services and the Budget Bureau to approve their approach, and for the president to revise his orders for disbursing the grants.[150]

One further difficulty remained. Personnel and munitions shortages within the army threatened to hold up shipments to China. The problem of munitions shortages was partially overcome by going ahead with the foreign programs prior to completion of a study of the army's own expanding needs.[151] Marshall sidestepped civilian personnel ceilings established by Congress in 1946 by pointing to a section of the Economic Cooperation Act that permitted the employment of the manpower necessary for its implementation.[152] Finally, in mid-August, seven weeks after Congress approved an appropriation bill and more than four months after the legislators advanced funds that could be used for military assistance, the Truman administration was ready to begin meeting China's requests for munitions. The China bloc had pressured the executive branch into participating in the procurement process, but it had failed to expedite deliveries of military supplies to Chiang's forces.

After all the pressure from Republicans on aid to Chiang, it is surprising perhaps that GOP presidential candidate Thomas E. Dewey did not make China a central issue in his campaign for office. The Republican national platform stated only that "We shall foster and cherish our historic policy of friendship for China and assert our deep interest in the maintenance of the integrity and freedom of China."[153] Dewey attacked Democratic policy only occasionally, and then merely by referring to America's "tragic neglect" of China.[154] This cautious approach rested on three assumptions: first, the Republicans did not need the issue to win the White House and thus should not create unnecessary obligations for a new regime by making extensive campaign promises; second, because Republicans were far from united on what should be done in China, dwelling on the issue might breed disunity in GOP ranks;[155] and, third, a Republican offensive on China would bring a Democratic rebuttal which, in turn, would emphasize Chiang's shortcomings. At home, a partisan exchange would produce uncertain results; in China, it certainly would undermine the prestige of the National government.[156]

Nevertheless, the executive branch understood the potential explosiveness of the China issue. Even though General Wedemeyer had lost his earlier confidence that aid short of American combat troops could save Chiang, he continued to push for the rapid implementation of existing arms programs for China. Otherwise, he feared, the army would become an object of attack in the partisan recriminations that would follow Chiang's demise.[157] When in October 1948 presidential assistant John R. Steelman relayed to Wedemeyer Truman's concern regarding the grant program, even the White House demonstrated an awareness of the possible impact of the China issue in American politics.[158]

Although the Nationalists surrendered Mukden, which signified the Communist conquest of Manchuria, before Americans went to the polls, election eve brought no new Republican offensive on China. Rumblings in Washington, however, indicated that China policy was unlikely to remain in the background in American politics. At the end of October, William Bullitt, a long-time Democrat, officially ended his support for the Truman candidacy, and announced that he would soon leave for China as a special representative of the congressional "watchdog" committee on foreign aid.[159] On 1 November, Roger D. Lapham, the chief administrator of the Economic Cooperation Administration in China, urged that the United States "stick our neck out" and "take full responsibility" for supervising and controlling military and economic aid to the National government.[160] Republican Congressmen Judd and Charles Eaton (New Jersey) called for immediate action on a massive scale.[161] Senator Bridges requested a special session of Congress to consider new aid for China.[162] His colleague, Alexander Wiley (Republican-Wisconsin), wanted a "joint and secret" investigation of the problem in the Senate and the House.[163] Some observers, to be sure, agreed with columnist Louis Bromfield, who suggested that the United States give China to Russia "on a platter to bring on stomach ulcers."[164] Yet, when Representative Mike Mansfield (Democrat-Montana), long a defender of administration policy, predicted that China would become "a strong issue" in the Eighty-first Congress, he merely stated the obvious.[165]

One of the charges that was certain to arise concerned administration of military assistance under the China Aid Act. Despite Wedemeyer's and Truman's sensitivity to possible repercussions in this area, between mid-August and mid-November only $10 million worth of matériel left for China under the grant program. An incident in China during the summer of 1948 reveals much of the cause for delay.

The central figure in the incident on the American side was Admiral Badger. An energetic, willful man who had little prior experience in China, he was an aggressive advocate of concerted American action to contain the Communists. In July, he began a campaign from his base in Tsingtao to obtain military supplies for General Fu Tso-yi, the commander of most anti-Communist forces in North China. Americans in China regarded the general as one of the most competent of Nationalist officers. Edmund Clubb, for example, had approvingly sent to Washington an analysis by Lang Wei-hsu, a translator in the American consulate general in Peiping, that labeled Fu and General Yen Hsi-shan the only effective government leaders in all of north China. These two men, Lang noted, recognized "the need of equalizing living in urban areas and ameliorating the lot of the peasantry." They had instituted "a mild agrarian reform" in areas under their control, and appeared to be holding their own against the Communists among the poor farmers. Their "frugality, integrity and high zeal in service" had helped them rally much support to the anti-Communist cause. Lang thought they might "prove a hard nut to crack for the Communists." [166] Badger believed that Fu, if properly supplied, could hold North China almost indefinitely. [167]

Unfortunately, as a close friend of Li Tsung-jen, Fu was not trusted by Chiang. Thus Badger commenced a drive to persuade the generalissimo to use a substantial portion of the $125 million in American grants for shipments to North China. The admiral suggested to Chiang that supplies going to Fu might be transported in American navy bottoms at no cost to the National government and sold by the United States at procurement rather than replacement costs. [168] Badger had no authority from Washington to make these suggestions, and Stuart's staff warned the ambassador that Badger was acting contrary to U.S. policy. Major General David Barr, head of the Army Advisory Group, questioned the prudence of disrupting the balanced distribution plan already established. Yet the ambassador supported the naval commander's efforts. [169] A former president of Yenching University in Peiping, Stuart's sentimental ties to North China may have influenced his judgment. [170] Given Fu's capabilities and the region's resources and location, however, the Badger approach had some merit.

In late August, Badger appeared to make headway. Not only did Chiang seem to agree that shipments for north China and Shantung deserved first priority; he apparently wanted to go beyond the admiral's recommendation to meet the ordnance requirements of four of Fu's armies and insisted on equipment for seven armies. Clearly, the generalissimo sought to make the most of Badger's suggestion that free transportation and lower prices might be applied to this matériel. [171] On 9 September, the Joint Chiefs of Staff approved the deal, and eight days later the State Department went along. [172] But the plan necessitated that the Chinese submit new lists of their requirements. The army had already spent several weeks doing price and availability studies. [173] Now much of the work needed to be redone, a process that lasted well into October. It was November before major shipments of matériel left for China from the continental United States. [174]

This delay might have been worthwhile had most of the aid gone to Fu's armies. Yet the Chinese embassy in Washington called for the shipment of 60 percent of the ordnance items to Shanghai and only 40 percent to North China. Although this irritated the State Department, it dropped the matter after Secretary of Defense Forrestal assured Under Secretary of State

Robert A. Lovett that, strictly speaking, the generalissimo had lived up to his end of the agreement.[175]

This incident demonstrated the inability of the United States to influence the behavior of Chiang. To some extent, American impotence rested on his refusal to bolster the anti-Communist cause at the risk of undermining his own position in the National government, and on the State Department's unwillingness to bypass him in dispensing aid. Yet his anticipation of political trends in the United States encouraged his stubbornness. After the United States failed during late 1947 and early 1948 to grant massive aid to the Nationalists, he probably grasped the fact that the Truman administration would accept a Communist victory in China rather than become more deeply embroiled in the civil war.

This realization did not push him toward reform, however, in part because some members of the China bloc in the United States encouraged him to believe that all he need do was hold his regime together until the end of the year. William Bullitt and others implied that after the Republicans captured the White House in November—as virtually all informed observers believed they would—the Nationalists could depend on massive American intervention to save the country from Communism.[176] Ironically, therefore, many of those Americans most concerned about the Communist advance in China strengthened Chiang's resolve to persist in a course that could only result in a Communist victory. As representatives of what was, for all practical purposes, a lame-duck government, American officials in China had little hope of swaying Chiang.

Political scientist H. Bradford Westerfield asserts that, had the Truman administration furnished military aid under the China Aid Act with more efficiency, "the paralyzing effects of rigidly partisan recrimination when Chiang fell" might have been minimized.[177] This argument overestimates the Republican commitment to administration China policy in early 1948. A substantial number of prominent Republicans, especially in the Senate, did support the Marshall policy through the spring, but others pressed for more extensive aid to Chiang. Robert A. Taft of Ohio, a GOP leader in the Senate, was prominent in this category.[178] A third group, including Senators H. Alexander Smith of New Jersey and William Knowland of California, said little or nothing on the China question until later. During 1949, Taft, Smith, and Knowland all would become sharp critics of American China policy.[179]

Dean Acheson offers a more convincing view than Westerfield. Despite "endless consultation" with top executive officials, Acheson argues, many Republicans refused to commit themselves to administration policy because it appeared inadequate to halt the Communist advance. Thus the GOP anticipated an opportunity to use the issue to undermine the Democrats.[180] The virtual collapse of Nationalist forces in Manchuria and much of North China before the arrival of military aid previously authorized by Congress increased the Truman administration's vulnerability, but it was not the primary basis for later Republican attacks. In fact, the Yalta accords of February 1945 and the Marshall mission of the following year were more prominent in the ensuing barrage against Democratic China policy.

The simple fact is that an administration is bound to be criticized extensively by the opposition party whenever a policy does not attain its stated objectives. The passions of the time made the emergence of the China issue inevitable. In March 1947, the administration commenced an offensive to gain congressional and public support for the containment of Communism abroad. This venture accelerated tensions that encouraged polemics in the political arena. The surprise victory of Truman over Dewey in November 1948 insured that a frustrated and bitter Republican party would exploit to the fullest any issue that promised to bring political advantage.

It is also unlikely that the slow dispensation of the $125 million in grants had a major impact on the outcome of the civil war in China. On 16 November 1948, after the fall of Manchuria and of Tsinan, a key city in North China, General Barr reported that "no battle has been lost since my arrival due to lack of ammunition or equipment." The main cause of Nationalist defeats, he asserted, was "the world's worst leadership and many other morale destroying factors that lead to a complete loss of will to fight."[181] Admiral Badger, on the other hand, placed more responsibility on American shoulders. A lack of sufficient ammunition, he argued, discouraged the Nationalists from taking offensive actions that might have cleared important areas from Communist control.[182] This assertion may have some validity, especially with regard to the armies of General Fu Tso-Yi in North China. Yet Nationalist leaders shared responsibility with the United States. Not only did Chiang avoid sending adequate supplies to generals who might weaken his hold on the National government, but also his representatives in Washington, intent on receiving military supplies at the lowest possible cost, sometimes delayed in making firm orders and wasted time dickering with American officials.[183] Moreover, by mid-1948 most American officials in China believed that expanding the United States role to advising principal Nationalist commanders in the field was a minimum prerequisite for arresting Chiang's rapid decline.[184] As Tang Tsou notes, the military supply problem was, at best, "a relatively minor factor in one of the most profound social and political revolutions in world history."[185]

The administration of military aid to China does not provide the key to understanding either the intense Republican attacks on Democratic policy beginning in 1949 or the collapse of Chiang's forces on the mainland. It does emphasize, however, the degree of division that existed within the American government over how to arrest the Nationalist decline. The absence of a consensus in either the legislative or executive branches seriously hindered policy formulation and execution. Although Marshall prevailed in his view that the United States must not become irrevocably committed to the generalissimo, the secretary of state gave in to his opponents on several occasions. Contrary to his desire, Congress combined the programs for China and Europe in a single bill. The legislators then provided funds that the National government could use to purchase military supplies. Finally, under pressure from Capitol Hill, the State Department accepted a bigger American role in the administration of military grants than it originally intended.

The anti-Communist zeal of some American representatives in China, combined with the intense rivalries between army and navy advisers in Nanking and Tsingtao—which mirrored interservice squabbles at home— also complicated the fulfillment of policy. In May 1948, a potentially dangerous situation arose when the headstrong Badger wired to the Joint Chiefs his plans to use American forces in the defense of Tsingtao against the Communists. The military leaders, perhaps as a result of their dissatisfaction with U.S. China policy, gave the naval commander a temporary go-ahead. Long before the Communists approached Tsingtao, the State Department succeeded in rescinding Badger's orders, but, with a man of Badger's inclinations in such a sensitive post, a chance remained that a pretext would be found—such as the protection of American lives and property—to embroil American forces in hostilities with the Communists.[186]

Finally, the record on military aid to China revealed the physical inadequacies of the defense establishment in implementing aspects of the Truman administration's recent departures in foreign policy. Although congressional indecision and Nationalist dallying produced some delays in getting matériel to China, other delays stemmed from American unpreparedness, a result of the rapid demobilization of United States armed forces following World War II. By mid-1948, personnel and material shortages in the army made it impossible to carry out expeditiously all the military assistance programs passed by Congress. At times, orders had to be filled by private firms which had converted to peacetime production and took months to turn out arms and ammunition.[187] When needs in Greece, Turkey, and Iran conflicted with those for China, American strategy dictated a delay in aid to China. Although these circumstances were not decisive in the decline of the National government, they would appear again in relation to other areas—most notably Korea—and perhaps with more profound results.

## Diplomatic Alternatives to Chiang

As 1948 drew to a close, most policymakers in Washington viewed as inevitable Chiang's fall from power on the mainland. Since the beginning of the year, in fact, the Nationalist decline had sparked efforts among American diplomats in China to prepare for the day when the generalissimo had passed from the scene. Three maneuvers were proposed at different times and by different people and were discussed in the State Department, but were ultimately rejected. The first move was suggested by O. Edmund Clubb, the consul general at Peiping. On 3 January 1948, he reported to Ambassador Stuart on the recent experiences of a UNRRA employee, Marcy Ditmanson, in Communist-held territory. Ditmanson stated that, though anti-American feeling was growing in these areas, Communist officials generally conceded the desirability of friendly relations with the United States once the civil war ended. This desire, they said, rested in their need for "American financial and technical assistance in reconstruction of communications and utilities." Ditmanson believed the Communists might even accept an American consular official in areas they controlled. Clubb, who for weeks had pondered the idea of sending an information-gathering mission into Communist territory, raised the possibility with Stuart. Not only was the time ripe for such a venture, Clubb argued; if postponed, and if American assistance to the Nationalists increased in future months, it might become impossible to carry out.[188]

Stuart took no immediate action on the proposal. On 9 February, three days after receiving an inquiry on the matter from Secretary of State Marshall, the ambassador finally outlined the embassy's position. He and his staff noted that the mission could not be kept secret, that rumors were rife of impending peace talks between the Nationalists and the Communists, and that an American venture into Communist-controlled territory could only increase widespread speculation of an impending shift in U.S. policy. This result, Stuart asserted, would have a detrimental effect on the National government and "would thus be unwise at this time."[189]

Upon receipt of Stuart's telegram, the State Department dropped Clubb's idea. Perhaps the most crucial point in the ambassador's argument was that the mission could not be kept secret. Although State Department planners had already resigned themselves to the possibility of Chiang's demise, they surely did not want to hasten its occurrence. More important still, the European Recovery Program was now before Congress and State Department officials were already "in a state of melancholy decline" over the poor prospects for its rapid passage.[190] In such circumstances, and with Senator Bridges blasting the administration for failing to submit an assistance program for China, the Clubb project surely looked risky.[191]

By July, when the second proposed maneuver reached the State Department, the European Recovery Program had passed Congress. This time, the American embassy in Nanking took the initiative. Ambassador Stuart had been in a state of near panic for many months. Although fully cognizant of the National government's shortcomings, his emotional ties to a China of bygone days made Chiang's decline especially painful to him. In January 1948, Stuart had recommended an extensive broadening of American aid to the Nationalists on a quid pro quo basis.[192] Marshall sharply rejected this course, but the ambassador continued to seek other methods to prevent further Communist gains.

Increasingly, Stuart's search forced him to reassess Chiang's leadership. Particularly important in this agonizing process was the generalissimo's appointment in May 1948 of Ku Chu-tung as army chief of staff and of Yu Han-móu as commander of ground forces. Stuart described them as having "long and distinguished records for accomplishing nothing and for avoiding battle under any circumstances."[193] From this point onward, Stuart and his top assistant, Minister-Counselor Lewis Clark, actively sought out non-Communist alternatives to Chiang. Prospects in this area seemed good to many observers, especially after events of late April, when the National Assembly elected Li Tsung-jen as vice-president of the National government over the generalissimo's active opposition.[194]

On 14 July, Stuart finally wired Marshall and suggested that in the near future an American official arrange a conversation with Marshal Li Chi-shen, the head of the Kuomintang Revolutionary Committee, which was based in Hong Kong. In the previous year, Li had been ejected from the Kuomintang for antigovernment activities. The American embassy had followed his movements for several months and was convinced he was about to establish a provisional government. He appeared to have considerable popular support, including the private backing of Li Tsung-jen. The ambassador proposed that an embassy official go to Hong Kong to talk with Li Chi-shen and persuade him to openly oppose Communist aims in his statement upon the formation of a government. This ploy, Stuart thought, might help to rally anti-Communists to his side.[195]

Again, Washington squelched the initiative. To Marshall, American recognition and support for the National government made the proposal "improper and undesirable." Furthermore, the move probably could not be kept secret and, therefore, might "seriously embarrass" the United States. As Walton Butterworth noted in late May, "we are in the year 1948," a presidential election campaign was on the horizon, and any even implied attack on Chiang might produce a "storm" in the United States that would "damage . . . our relations with China."[196] On the other hand, the secretary of state noted that Washington would determine its future attitude toward Li in accordance with his government's strength and especially the status of the National government.[197]

Marshall's course was a prudent one. Nothing came of Li's reported plans. Even had the Kuomintang Revolutionary Committee been a viable third force, it is unlikely it would have adopted a strong anti-Communist line.[198] And American encouragement of the movement almost certainly would have become public and possibly produced serious domestic repercussions for the Truman administration. The Stuart initiative simply risked too much and promised too little in return. Nevertheless, the incident demonstrated the continuing limits imposed on American diplomats by domestic politics and by the policy of support for the National government.

Yet domestic politics are inadequate either to explain or to justify a more promising maneuver that was proposed later in 1948 by Roger Lapham. In early November, the ECA administrator broached the idea of continuing economic aid to the rapidly expanding Communist-controlled areas of north China.[199] Such a move, he said, would follow the premises of the "original Marshall Plan"—that is, irrespective of ideology, the economic recovery of peoples was important to the United States and the world. Continuing economic assistance would be the "most effective counterpropaganda" that could be employed in China. Many Chinese under Communist rule, Lapham contended, had accepted their circumstances "by force of arms" rather than by choice. Many who had actually joined Communist ranks had done so out of distaste for the National government, "not from love of communism." By perpetuating contacts with "non-Communist groups and persons," the ECA mission could encourage resistance to the efforts of "international communism"—which Lapham carefully distinguished from "communism"—to dominate China.[200]

Clubb and Paul G. Hoffman, the overall head of ECA, supported Lapham's proposal, but State Department officials in Washington demurred.[201] Butterworth, Kennan, and Lovett all gave the question careful consideration—Marshall was in Paris attending a meeting of the General Assembly of the United Nations—but concluded that the legislative intent of the China Aid Act dictated against Lapham's plan unless Chiang gave his approval.[202] In early December, Stuart, who originally appeared to favor the initiative, wired his and his staff's objection to it. Supplying food, fertilizer, cotton, and petroleum products to Communist-held areas, they reasoned, would merely assist the Communists in surviving "the critical early days of take-over."[203] The Communists might not be able to govern China effectively, and the United States should avoid any action that might ease their task. President Truman approved the State Department view. American goods already in Chinese ports need not be redirected, but all supplies en route to destinations overcome by the Communists would be diverted to other locations.[204]

This decision reflected the administration's cautious wait-and-see policy, which was encouraged but not in large part determined by the China issue at home. In early December, Hoffman even went some distance in preparing the way politically for the Lapham maneuver. He discussed the plan with the congressional "watchdog" committee on foreign aid. Several committee members believed he had adequate authority to decide the issue himself. Senators Henry Cabot Lodge and Tom Connally viewed the Lapham policy as worthwhile. Congressmen Vorys and Fulton voiced no objection, and Representative Taber thought no advice should be given the ECA director. Senator Smith and Representatives Sol Bloom and Clarence Cannon were noncommittal.[205] Thus Hoffman did not gain legislative approval of the move, but his consultations indicated that some key members of both houses were not adverse to the Lapham plan. Because Hoffman was a prominent Republican, his initiation of the idea with the lawmakers lessened the risks of a State Department follow-up. Yet no such effort occurred.

State Department perceptions played a pivotal role in the demise of Lapham's idea. First, to American officials, Communist statements indicated a deep hostility to the United States. This conclusion was hardly new, though in October and November 1948 Stuart believed that Communist propaganda shifted to the left. Mao called for "third forces" in China to choose between revolution and counterrevolution. He exhibited "much greater enthusiasm [than before] for the primacy of the Soviet Union in international communism." The Communist leader enjoined revolutionary groups in China "to drive out aggressive forces of American imperialism."[206] Certainly, the United States should avoid any action that might strengthen an antagonistic party that was friendly to Russia.

This reasoning was particularly compelling because American analysts did not regard Communist control of China as inevitable. The Communists, in fact, were now likely to have many of the same problems in governing that vast territory as the Nationalists had experienced before them. Those problems would be difficult to resolve without substantial economic and technical assistance from outside, which only the United States could afford to provide.[207] It followed, therefore, that if the United States was going to help the Communists it should be only after using leverage to achieve concessions.

These views represented an extension of those that had played such a key role in the formulation of American policy in the summer and fall of 1947. Then, the perception of Communist antagonism had encouraged continuing aid to Chiang, while doubts regarding the Communist and/or Soviet capacity to dominate China had discouraged a total commitment to the Nationalists. Now, as the central issue became that of possible relations with the Communists, the two perceptions joined to pull American policymakers away from making positive overtures to the prevailing force in China.

This was unfortunate. Surely, it was wishful thinking to believe that the Communists, hat in hand, might eventually approach the United States for aid. Such a hope greatly underestimated Communist organizational and political capabilities. Moreover, as Communists, Mao and his subordinates were likely to regard the capitalist West as needing intercourse with China to maintain economic prosperity rather than the reverse.[208] Besides, national pride dictated against their making any move toward the United States that gave even the slightest sign of dependence.

There is no certainty, of course, that the Lapham maneuver—or any other for that matter—would have turned Communist behavior in a direction favorable to the United States. The Communists, after all, had a substantial ideological bond with the Soviet Union, and the Russian presence in Manchuria resulting from the Yalta accords and the Sino-Soviet treaty of August

1945 dictated against a precipitous shift away from the Moscow connection.

On the other hand, Soviet penetration in the north, along with the prospect of receiving aid from the United States, might have discouraged the Communists from burning all bridges with the capitalist world. Scholar James Reardon-Anderson argues persuasively that Communist Chinese foreign policy was rooted less in a "global and ideological division between East and West" than in the "necessity for the Chinese to make their own way between these rival camps." [209] Although close American friendship with the Communists was not possible, neither was a Sino-Soviet alliance or a sharply antagonistic relationship between China and the United States inevitable.

Despite the uncertainties involved, Lapham's proposal had merit. Even had it not proved to be the first step toward a constructive liaison with the Communists, it stood to do little harm. A few million dollars worth of food was unlikely to make a significant impact on Communist prospects in China. Back home, the presidential election was over, the European Recovery Program was well underway, and the North Atlantic Treaty was not yet before the Senate. If there was to be any chance of the Communists moderating their pro-Soviet, anti-American line, the United States would have to alter its relationship to the National government. As a move in that direction, the Lapham initiative would have served to probe Communist attitudes. [210] Reports from ECA officials in the Communist-held countryside might have added significantly to American knowledge and understanding of events in China. And, if the Lapham plan turned out to be the first move toward an accommodation with the Communists, it could help the Truman administration parry Republican charges that it had "lost" China. Late 1948, therefore, was an opportune moment for the United States to explore new approaches to China, ones designed to adapt to the onrush of events there. Tragically, long-standing attitudes produced a stance that would help to poison Sino-American relations for a generation to come.

## American Perceptions of the Chinese Communists: The Sources

The question remains as to the roots of American perceptions of the Communists. In fairness to the policymakers, it is appropriate to note that we today have a distinct advantage over those three decades ago who tried to anticipate the ultimate outcome of the civil war in China. That land had been in chaos for generations, and it was far from obvious that the Communists could alter that situation in the near future. Moreover, it remains uncertain even in the present what kind of relationship the Communists were willing to accept with the United States as they consolidated their hold on the mainland. And American diplomats were by no means unbending in their views. They recognized that China was in a state of flux and that their conclusions were based on incomplete and sometimes contradictory evidence. That said, however, it is still a fact that they seriously underestimated the ability of the Communists to unite the mainland and probably overestimated inherent Communist hostility to the United States.

Those grappling with China policy during 1947 and 1948 were a varied group, ranging in experience in the country from Stuart's nearly five decades to Butterworth's matter of months. Ironically, the American ambassador was among the least in tune with realities. His view of Sino-American relations was highly sentimental. To him, the Chinese were pliant and backward with a deep "sympathy to our history and principles."[211] The people were highly individualistic and profoundly committed to "inherited social patterns and cultural attachments," to which Communism was totally alien.[212] The Communists' "fanatical dogmatism" in propounding foreign and anti-American ideas was bound to meet resistance from the masses, and the absence of sufficient technological and managerial skills in the society dictated against the smooth operation of the country without American assistance. In a word, Stuart perceived a "special relationship" between the United States and China, in which the latter nation would be willingly and rightfully in the position of junior partner. The Communists challenged this conception and, therefore, were so out of tune with Chinese life that they were unlikely to prevail. The ambassador was a gentle and sensitive man in personal relations, but, as a public official and long-time educator in China, he was a cultural chauvinist of the kind that was all too common in Western relations with the "underdeveloped" world.

Although most American foreign service officers lacked Stuart's extreme sentimentalism, their thought often ran parallel to his. Indeed, a Policy Planning Staff analysis of 7 September 1948, the product of consultation with several State Department China specialists, included a number of attitudes expressed in the ambassador's dispatches. The memorandum concluded that the Communists and the nation as a whole lacked sufficient "personnel experienced in national, provincial and urban administration." Even more critical were "the complex problems" growing out of the clash between Communist "ideology and Chinese realities." If Mao followed his "intellectual compulsion" as a Marxist to "collectivize and industrialize," he would "encounter at minimum the passive drag and sly resistance of Chinese individualism and at a maximum disruptive social revolt." If, on the other hand, he chose the road of gradualism and socialized the country at a slow pace, his crusade "would run the risk of losing the vitality [that accompanies]...ideological zeal, ... of becoming another Kuomintang baffled and bogged down in China's troubles." Finally, the Communists, in pursuing close ties with the Kremlin, might have difficulty accommodating Chinese nationalism.[213]

These views were not totally without foundation. The Communists initially did experience some serious problems in bringing stability to China. Yet American experts failed early on to grasp the degree to which the Communists might use Chinese nationalism against the United States in the final drive for power. American observers also overestimated the need for Western technological and managerial skills in establishing control over an essentially rural and agricultural nation, and underestimated Mao's ability to balance ideology and tradition without losing the revolution's sense of purpose.

These failures of perception had three sources. First, since 1946, American officials had had no direct contact with Communist-held areas, and thus they lacked the opportunities to study closely Communist practices and attitudes. Second, although the "China hands" were talented, dedicated men whose knowledge of their area was often impressive, they approached the nation through American standards and values. In so doing, they could not fully appreciate the depth of resentment felt by most Chinese over the West's incursion into their society over the last century, and the diplomats were perhaps a trifle susceptible to the myth of a special Sino-American relationship. Nor could they wholly comprehend the different requirements of preindustrial China, however vast, from those of the United States. As believers in liberal democracy, they found it hard to accept a Communist victory in a place where considerable effort had been expended to stop it.

This leads to a third source of misperception, namely the rapidly escalating cold war, which encouraged emphasis on revolutionary fanaticism as the root of tough Communist rhetoric rather than American aid to the Nationalists. Early in 1948, to be sure, John Paton Davies, the brilliant if somewhat erratic China specialist on the Policy Planning Staff, noted that only a total American withdrawal from China could provide the ultimate test of the possibility that Communist policy derived from "external pressure."[214] This insight would emerge again in 1949 and 1950 and would have some impact in high administration circles, but, in the prevailing climate of international tension, it was not one on which officials were often inclined to base significant initiatives. Although the cold war did not totally dominate Sino-American relations until late 1950, its impact on the Truman administration's China policy was considerable during 1947 and 1948, and it would continue to increase in the months ahead. In resisting an escalation of United States involvement in the civil war, the State Department had served the nation well, but as that war drew to a close the diplomats carried some weighty baggage that seriously limited American flexibility in responding to the march of revolution in Asia.

# 3 The Korean Dilemma: How to Arrange a Graceful Withdrawal from an Awkward Entanglement

American policy toward Korea during 1947 and 1948 also fell victim to the growing rigidity engendered by cold war tensions. Interestingly enough, however, those tensions joined with other forces to nudge Korea policy along divergent paths. On the one hand, there was the view, prevalent in the State Department and the army, that American credibility was engaged on the peninsula. As General Dwight D. Eisenhower, the army chief of staff, put it in late January 1947, "in the long run the costs of our retreat from Korea would be far, far greater than any present or contemplated appropriations to maintain ourselves there." [1]

On the other hand, there was the reality of a budget-conscious legislative branch in Washington that sought to hold down government expenditures. The Truman administration's offensive, beginning in March, to persuade Congress of the need for expensive programs abroad achieved a large measure of success. But that success had limits that forced a reduction of America's presence in Korea. Although cold war perceptions made the prospect of a Communist victory on the peninsula highly distasteful, the limited resources available made its prevention ever more difficult. Thus, policy became an increasingly desperate juggling act between conflicting pressures.

## The War Department Besieged and Divided

Like China, Korea during 1947 and 1948 was in a state of considerable turmoil, a condition that was disturbing to both State and War department officials in Washington. Predictably, American authorities experienced plenty of trouble containing the extreme Left, but the militance of the Right against trusteeship and the American occupation was just as thorny a problem. During January 1947, General Hodge's reports became increasingly alarmist. He had encouraged Syngman Rhee to visit the United States to press for Korean independence, and had even coached him on how best to accomplish this end. After the seventy-one year old patriot departed on his trip, however, Hodge discovered that Rhee sought primarily to discredit the occupation and push for a separate South Korean government. Rhee left behind plans for a massive uprising and the establishment of a provisional government below the thirty-eighth parallel. In mid-January, American officials prevented a major outbreak of violence, but Hodge suspected that Rhee and Kim Koo, another conservative nationalist, soon would stir up more trouble.[2]

To make matters worse, on 20 January the interim legislative assembly passed a resolution condemning Hodge's policies and trusteeship in Korea. The occupation commander believed that, with Rhee's cooperation, a strong coalition of non-Communist political groups might emerge, but the activities of the rightist leader in the United States and of his cronies in the new assembly indicated that this eventuality was not likely to occur.[3] After months of courting the Right and moderate Left, therefore, Hodge had failed to construct a dominant centrist coalition sympathetic to American policy.

Economic conditions aggravated the unrest. The assimilation of hundreds of thousands of Korean nationals, who fled the north after Soviet entry, placed a severe strain on the economy of South Korea.[4] Cut off from traditional commercial ties with the north and Japan, it had difficulty sustaining its growing population. By January, the military government's civilian supply program had been halted because of a lack of funds, and the distribution of rice to the general populace became more difficult. Shortages in fertilizer impeded the production of a rice crop equal to those of prewar years. Railroads deteriorated from a lack of spare parts, and electricity, the source of which was largely in the north, declined in availability.

Although State Department officials deeply feared the political repercussions of an American debacle in Korea, the War Department, as the agency chiefly responsible for the occupation, had suffered most of the day-to-day headaches relating to the peninsula. During 1946, a shipping strike in the United States adversely affected the food-relief program for South Korea. When the strikes ended, a shortage of boxcars held up the transport of food to American ports for shipment to Korea. Added to this problem of logistics, which also appeared in the occupations of Japan and Germany, was that of fielding complaints from American troops unhappy with life in an alien land lacking the amenities to which they were accustomed.[5]

Compared to the problems emerging in Washington, these difficulties were relatively minor. In the fall of 1946, the Budget Bureau, in preparing the budget for the next fiscal year and faced with the usual contest for limited funds between the army and navy—the air force was then under the former—split up the projected military allotment on what to Secretary of War Patterson was "an arbitrary 60-40 basis." The army was on the upper end of this breakdown, but the War Department took a cut of $2.5 billion from the $8.4 billion it requested. To Patterson, this reduction was unreasonable in view of army occupation duties in Japan, Germany, and Korea, but Budget Director James E. Webb, an aggressive and energetic official who had the president's confidence, stood his ground.[6]

The election of a Republican Congress in November 1946 further complicated matters. Government spending had been a leading issue in the campaign. In a general assault on expensive New Deal programs and the alleged proclivity of Democratic administrations for managing resources inefficiently, Republican candidates asked the voters, "Had enough?" Election returns indicated that the answer was "yes." Thus the Eightieth Congress convened in January 1947 determined to hold a right rein on expenditures. In February, there was talk of cutting the president's military budget by $1 billion. Among the areas of most concern to legislators were the high ratios in the army of officers to enlisted men and of civilians to military personnel, both of which were closely related to occupation duties. Patterson noted that a sizable cut in the proposed budget "would render the continuance of occupations impossible."[7]

Since the fall of 1946, the activities of Rhee and his supporters in the United States had increased the possibility of budget cuts affecting the occupation of Korea. In October, the forces of Rhee opened a press campaign for Korea's immediate independence. His arrival in the United States at the end of the year reinforced this enterprise. Fluent in English, holder of a Ph.D. from Princeton University, and, prior to 1945, a long-time resident of Washington, "the old man," as Hodge called him, was far from a neophyte in American politics. He had no embassy in the United States and lacked the extensive and persistent support on Capitol Hill enjoyed by Chiang Kai-shek, but he did possess a small group of aggressive backers in New York and Washington.

In the former city, Korean-born Louise Yim led Rhee's allies in pressing to get the Korean issue before the United Nations General Assembly. She cultivated many wealthy and influential friends, including Eleanor Roosevelt and several journalists in the McCormick and Hearst newspaper chains. Colonel M. Preston Goodfellow, formerly a deputy director of the Office of Strategic Services and in 1947 the publisher of the *Brooklyn Eagle*; Ben. C. Limb, a Washington-based importer of Japanese products; John S. Staggers, a successful attorney in the nation's capital; Jay Williams, a retired public-relations man; and Dr. Robert T. Oliver of Syracuse University—all pressed Rhee's cause in various high circles in the United States. When the Eightieth Congress convened in January 1947, Rhee put great effort into persuading lawmakers that the American occupation of South Korea was a failure.[8]

As a result, the War Department received a growing number of inquiries from the legislative branch on conditions in Korea, which led General Eisenhower to conclude that "the Congress may require a formal investigation by the Secretary of War or by a Congressional Committee."[9] To Rhee, the primary fact of the occupation was that it impeded Korean independence; to budget-conscious congressmen, it was that the occupation cost money. The perspectives were different, but the outcome was the same: Rhee gained some support on Capitol Hill for his view that America's role in Korea should be reduced.

Despite these problems, the army was not ready to abandon South Korea to Communism. In January 1947, Major General Lauris Norstad, the army's director of plans and operations, offered two primary reasons for maintaining the American position in Korea, at least until agreement could be reached with Russia: first, to do otherwise would exert a negative impact on the military occupation in Japan; second, the peninsula was of "considerable strategic importance" to the Soviet Union. Russian domination of Korea would bring it "measurably closer to a capability of outflanking Japan both on the south and on the north, and of dominating Manchuria and the China coast as far south as Shanghai." To Norstad, an American abandonment of Korea would also produce negative political repercussions worldwide, especially in Japan and China.[10] The director of army intelligence, Major General S. J. Chamberlin, agreed. He emphasized Norstad's unstated assumption that the Communists in North Korea, who possessed the military capability to overrun the peninsula if American forces withdrew, were under the tight control of Moscow.[11]

Secretary of War Patterson disagreed with Norstad. The secretary had long been upset by Washington's lack of initiative on Korea. In January 1946, on a trip to the western Pacific, he visited the peninsula and met with representatives of discontented American occupation troops. To him, Korea was "a strange land, with strange-looking people."[12] American interests there were never clear to him. In contrast to top army officers, he was not inclined to link the U.S. position on the peninsula with that in nearby areas. In early 1947, therefore, while pushing for increased American involvement in China, he concluded that the United States must soon withdraw from the peninsula.

## The Emergence of a Policy

Although the professional soldiers disagreed with their civilian chief regarding American interests in Korea, both acknowledged that some American initiative there was essential.[13] Until February 1947, however, the State Department's Office of Far Eastern Affairs opposed a fundamental aspect of the War Department's conception of an American initiative, namely, an approach to the Soviet Union at the governmental level. As in the previous fall, John Carter Vincent argued that such a move might "be interpreted and taken advantage of by the Russians as an indication of over-anxiety to ... [liquidate] our responsibilities in Korea." Vincent also believed that three other possibilities suggested recently by General MacArthur—United Nations intervention, the "formation of a commission ... of disinterested nations" to recommend a solution, and a meeting of the Soviet, American, British, and Chinese governments to seek clarification of the Moscow agreement—were unlikely to result in progress satisfactory to the United States. Vincent agreed only that the United States should pick up on any Soviet initiative. In such an event, the United States might propose "the immediate setting up of a 4-power trusteeship." The tasks of establishing a provisional government and writing a constitution could be temporarily postponed. While awaiting a Russian initiative, Vincent concluded, the State Department should support War Department efforts to obtain increased funds for relief and rehabilitation on the peninsula.[14]

This last proposal reflected the continued hope that Russia would become more receptive to an agreement for Korean unification once the United States demonstrated its intention to carry out a long-term program in the south.[15] Still, Secretary of War Patterson was not about to allow the Korean issue to lie dormant in the executive branch as it had during much of 1946, and Secretary of State Marshall was of a similar mind.[16] Thus, they created a special interdepartmental committee, including members from the State and War departments and the Bureau of the Budget, and charged it with recommending American action in Korea.

In late February 1947, the committee made concrete proposals.[17] They represented a compromise between the views of Patterson and Vincent. Both military and diplomatic planners agreed that South Korea should not be abandoned.[18] The challenge was to obtain a favorable Soviet response to an American initiative, and, at the same time, prepare for the possibility that ultimately the United States could reach no satisfactory agreement with Russia. The committee decided to combine an approach to the Soviet Union at the upcoming conference of allied foreign ministers in Moscow with the presentation to Congress of "an aggressive, positive long-term program" for the political, cultural, and economic development of South Korea.[19] The estimated cost of the three-year program was $600 million, $250 million of which would be spent in fiscal year 1948. This sum was $113 million more than that allocated to Korea in the proposed War Department budget. Acceptance by the War Department and the Budget Bureau representative of a plan for large-scale assistance went some distance in accommodating Vincent's outlook, though he still urged Marshall to postpone discussion on Korea at Moscow for as long as possible in order to give the Soviets ample opportunity to make the first move.[20]

Vincent could hardly resist further. The State Department had prevented an initiative at the governmental level for many months in an area for which the War Department held the major administrative responsibility. The War Department also wanted to end military government and to turn over the remaining civilian responsibilities in Korea to the State Department. The diplomats, in turn, shied away from such a thankless task. Pressure for adjustments in American policy increased with the approach of a visit to Washington by General Hodge, who had long pleaded for an initiative at the governmental level.

Yet Patterson and a top assistant, Howard C. Petersen, were dubious about the prospects either of strengthening the American position in South Korea or of pushing the proposed aid program through Congress. "[B]ecause of our withdrawal from China and because of the political immaturity of the Korean people, their economic situation, etc.," Peterson argued, Russian domination of the peninsula was virtually inevitable following America's departure. Because the United States must leave eventually, it should seek to do so now, provided the move did not entail "too great a loss of prestige." Petersen noted the likelihood of a Russian proposal for joint withdrawal. In the face of such a plan, he concluded, the Truman administration should not "hold on tenaciously to what is essentially a weak position which [it] . . . will be forced to abandon at some later date."[21]

The interdepartmental committee's report appeared only days after the Truman administration learned that, in six weeks, British aid to Greece and Turkey would end. London estimated Greece's immediate foreign exchange needs at more than $200 million, and large additional sums would be required for years to come. Turkey also wanted help with its burden of financing both economic development and military strength to counter Russian pressure. On 26 February 1947, the president approved a recommendation for extensive American aid to both nations, and a day later administration leaders met with their "congressional masters" in the White House. Senator Vandenberg gave his conditional approval to an aid program, and speculated that most of the Congress would follow.[22] Yet Truman and his advisers recognized that a battle lay ahead. Even if a Greek-Turkish aid bill passed, Congress's receptivity to expensive foreign programs was certain to have limits. The chief executive needed to exercise extreme care, not only in determining where aid was necessary but how necessary it was in each area. Petersen doubted that Congress would approve $600 million for Korea, and he considered such an expenditure inadvisable in light of impending needs in more important theaters.

Patterson agreed essentially with Petersen's analysis, but he did not openly oppose the Korean aid program. Instead, he used his reservations as an instrument to gain concessions from the State Department on other aspects of Korean policy. First, he sought to transfer to the State Department responsibility for operations in Korea. Second, he continued to push for early withdrawal from the peninsula.

Major General John H. Hilldring mediated between Vincent and the secretary of war. A career officer, Hilldring had worked on occupation matters for the army at the end of the war until his transfer to the State Department in early 1946 as assistant secretary of state for occupied areas. A forceful man and a protégé of General Marshall, he was in an excellent position to resolve conflicts between the War and State Departments.[23] By early April 1947, he had narrowed the differences between Vincent and Patterson.

The diplomat agreed that a political adviser should be appointed to negotiate with the Soviet Union as well as eventually to take over a civilian administration. As soon as the interim legislative assembly passed a general election law, a new legislative body should be elected. Rapid progress could then be made toward transferring authority for domestic affairs from the military government to an indigenous provisional government for South Korea. If no agreement with the Soviet Union emerged for national unification, the United States might refer the problem to the United Nations, or an independent government might be established below the thirty-eighth parallel. In any event, the United States would withdraw from the peninsula within three years. Finally, Vincent agreed that the State Department would assume responsibility for administering relief and reconstruction funds in the War Department budget then before Congress.[24]

## Congress Takes a Hand

Despite the consensus within the Truman administration on a Korean aid program, political realities at home combined with developments abroad to force postponement of its presentation to Congress. In March 1947, the project took a cut from $600 million to $540 million. Two months later, the State Department decided to present a one- rather than a three-year program to Congress. The new scheme called for an additional request of merely $78 million over the War Department budget. In early August, notwithstanding pleas from American officials in Korea, policymakers in Washington shelved the program until 1948.[25]

Pressures from Congress explain these retreats. In a reversal of the trend with regard to China, the unveiling of the Greek-Turkish aid program triggered sentiment in the legislative branch against increased aid for Korea. In the midst of growing apprehension in Congress that America's expanding commitments abroad had no bounds, word leaked out of an impending $600 million request for Korea.[26] Senator Vandenberg, already the congressional guardian of administration programs abroad, argued on the Senate floor "that there is an inescapable obligation in Korea which is totally unrelated to the question we are here discussing, and which we shall confront regardless of what we do in Greece and Turkey."[27] As with China, Vandenberg viewed American commitments to Korea as irreversible. To many of Vandenberg's colleagues, however, the central fact in foreign aid programs was their cost. Senator Harry F. Byrd (Democrat-Virginia) warned that "new foreign burdens" would result in "increased taxation on an already overburdened people." Communism's most potent weapon, he asserted, was "an American internal collapse" engendered by reckless spending abroad.[28] Private State Department talks with congressional leaders led to further discouragement.

After the legislature passed the Greek-Turkish aid program in May 1947, Vandenberg insisted that the Foreign Relations Committee not be asked to sponsor any further requests for funds in the current session. Moreover, the War Department appropriation for civilian relief was already in "a log jam" in Congress, and its overall budget request also faced serious problems. From the army's perspective, the moment was not opportune to present a new request to committees dealing with the armed forces in either house.[29] In July, when the Wedemeyer mission received instructions to visit the peninsula and report on conditions there with special attention to the projected economic aid program, the State Department tacitly conceded defeat of its earlier plans.[30]

The story would be incomplete without mention of the major initiative of the Truman administration in Europe in mid-1947. When the Greek-Turkish aid program was presented to Congress, administration leaders had considered combining assistance for those nations with that to other countries resisting Communist penetration. Concern centered on the obvious political repercussions that would accompany the continued economic stagnation and human misery pervading war-torn Western Europe. The administration decided against broadening the aid requests—an expansion of the package might delay its approval, thus increasing the chance of a total collapse in Greece—but an intensive study began of deteriorating conditions in Europe. On 1 May, in a speech at Cleveland, Mississippi, Under Secretary of State Dean Acheson asserted that, if non-Communist nations were to remain "free," Congress must appropriate new funds to make available essential commodities and services that were in short supply. A month later, Secretary of State Marshall expanded on this theme in a Harvard commencement address. The clear message was that billions of dollars would soon be required for European recovery. Obtaining such funds from Congress promised to be a difficult task. Given America's traditional orientation toward Europe, Korea retreated further into the background of priorities for aid.

## Soviet-American Deadlock

The postponement in sending a Korean aid program to Congress, however, did not result in delay in approaching the Soviet government. In early April 1947, as the Moscow meeting of foreign ministers drew to a close, Marshall proposed to his Russian counterpart, V. M. Molotov, that the Joint Commission reconvene under the guiding principle of respect for the right of freedom of opinion among Koreans.[31] Molotov sidestepped the question of ground rules for conferring with Korean groups, but he agreed that the commission should reconvene.[32]

An ensuing exchange of letters led to a mutually satisfactory framework for consultation. The signing of Communiqué No. 5, a statement of willingness to uphold the Moscow agreement, would be "'accepted as a declaration of good faith' entitling the signatory to initial consultation by the Joint Commission." Korean parties or individuals *could* be excluded from this procedure only by agreement between the Soviet and American delegations, and "only on the ground of fomenting or instigating active opposition to the work of the Joint Commission, the fulfillment of the Moscow decision, or one of the two powers."[33] Later, however, the American delegation agreed that groups actively opposing the Moscow decision *would not* be consulted.[34]

For most of June, progress continued. On 25 June more than four hundred representatives of the political parties and social organizations of South Korea, some two hundred guests, and the press attended the thirty-fifth meeting of the commission, held in Seoul. According to Joseph E. Jacobs, the recently arrived political adviser to the American command, "much cordiality" existed between the Soviet delegates and the Korean representatives.[35]

This auspicious beginning did not last. On 27 June, Soviet officials identified eight parties, which had a declared membership of three million, as ineligible for consultation. All were "rightists or with rightist leanings." A day later, Soviet delegates declared that members of an antitrusteeship committee formed in January 1946 to protest the Moscow agreement should be consulted only if they abandoned membership in the committee. Approximately thirty-five groups were in the antitrusteeship body, and all were rightist.[36]

These demands put the American negotiators in a difficult position. If accepted, they would lead to leftist domination of the consultative process. Rightist groups were already lukewarm toward the Joint Commission. Rhee even claimed that the reconvening of that commission contradicted official American policy.[37] He hoped that the commission would fail to unify the peninsula, for such a failure probably would result in referral of the Korean problem to the United Nations and eventually to the creation of an indigenous regime below the thirty-eighth parallel.[38] Rhee's chances of dominating a regime in the south were excellent.[39] American acceptance of the Soviet position would give Rhee an excuse to launch a mass campaign against the Joint Commission.

The United States countered the Soviet stance by suggesting that the Joint Commission proceed with consultation and consider specific cases "on their merits" along the way. Ultimately, American officials insisted, the commission could exclude groups only with the approval of both its members.[40] In early July, the area of disagreement widened; the Soviets offered a plan for consultation that excluded rightist groups affiliated with the antitrusteeship committee and all groups that had a claimed membership of under ten thousand. This plan would give extreme leftists a further advantage in the procedures for creating a provisional government.[41]

During July and August, the American delegation tried hard to break the impasse in the Joint Commission. First, it suggested that Soviet delegates consult with groups above the thirty-eighth parallel and American representatives approach those to the south. When Russia rejected this plan, the

Americans proposed that the two delegations consult with those acceptable to both and the United States confer with those unacceptable to the Soviets. When Russia again demurred, the American delegation proposed acceptance of the written replies to Joint Commission questionnaires, which were already on file, as adequate consultation on the future provisional government. This proposal also called for the preparation of "a provisional charter and political platform" by a subcommittee of the Joint Commission. The charter would provide for "a general election to elect a national legislature." Another subcommittee would construct a plan "for the integration of the existing governmental functions of North and South Korea."[42]

On 26 August, the Soviet delegation offered counterproposals. Agreeing to dispense with oral consultations, it suggested the creation of a provisional assembly. The body was to include members of democratic parties, "half from North and half from South Korea," which represented at least ten thousand people and "fully support[ed] the Moscow agreement."[43] This plan merely pushed the question of acceptable Korean groups from the consultative to the assembly level.

By this time, the United States had decided upon an approach at the governmental level. A day after Russia presented its counterproposals, Acting Secretary of State Robert A. Lovett addressed a letter to Molotov suggesting that on 8 September the four powers adhering to the Moscow agreement meet in Washington "to consider how that agreement may be speedily carried out." Lovett proposed that each zone hold early elections to choose provisional legislatures. The zonal legislatures would then select representatives in numbers reflecting the "proportion between the populations of the two zones." These representatives would constitute a national provisional government. Next, the four powers would meet with the provisional government to discuss further aid needed for the establishment of a stable, independent Korea. United Nations officials would observe all these stages. The provisional government and the occupying powers together would eventually set a date for the withdrawal of foreign forces.[44]

The Soviet Union rejected the American plan and the proposal for a four-power meeting.[45] The Truman administration then decided to submit the Korean question to the United Nations. On 23 September, over the objections of the Soviet bloc, the General Assembly agreed to deliberate on "The Problem of the Independence of Korea." The debate between the United States and the Soviet Union now shifted from the Joint Commission to the United Nations.[46]

## Korea Policy Reappraised

American officials in Washington had discussed a move to the United Nations since February 1947, but the proposal emerged as policy only late in the summer, when postwar trends crystallized in both Korea and the United States. In Korea, the Joint Commission remained deadlocked, while the political situation in the south continued to deteriorate.[47] Communist strength there increased steadily, in part because of the "well-trained and well-indoctrinated assistance infiltrating from North Korea."[48] To American representatives on the scene, the ninety-member Soviet delegation in Seoul appeared to be assisting leftist-directed disruptive activities.[49] Rightist leaders added to the unrest. Rhee continued his efforts to prevent Soviet-American agreement. As desertions to the far Right and Left became more and more common, moderates who had cooperated with the United States became increasingly concerned about being "crushed" between the two extremes.[50]

Back in Washington, Congress passed an appropriations bill for fiscal year 1948 that reduced the army's civilian employees by 58,371 from the administration's request and also cut 12,500 officers.[51] Because the Budget Bureau had already slashed the original War Department requests, these further reductions jeopardized the continued fulfillment of army occupation functions. Inasmuch as Korea ranked well below Japan and Germany in strategic significance, military leaders naturally contemplated reducing Korean occupation costs more than others. If this was to be done without simply abandoning the peninsula to Communism, new initiatives had to be taken, either to end the Soviet-American deadlock or to establish an independent government in South Korea capable of survival without a major American military presence.

On 4 August 1947, an ad hoc committee of the State-War-Navy Coordinating Committee (SWNCC) proposed initiatives outside the Joint Commission, and responsible officials in each department quickly approved them. Their implementation resulted in Lovett's approach to Molotov later in the month and finally to an American presentation to the United Nations in mid-September. By this time, decision makers in Washington had abandoned all hope for the bilateral and four-power approaches. Because the long-standing State Department view was that the Soviet Union would not accept a reasonable agreement unless conditions in South Korea stabilized—an unlikely occurrence—there was little reason to expect such approaches to bear fruit. With the issue before the United Nations, Soviet intransigence would be revealed for all the world to see. One of two results might ensue: either the Soviet Union would back down under pressure of world opinion and accept the plan for unification of the peninsula, or, more likely, Soviet stubbornness would become apparent and prepare the way for establishing an independent South Korea.[52]

These initiatives did not alter the basic premises of American policy. Like the interdepartmental committee of February 1947, the ad hoc committee concluded that the United States could not "withdraw from Korea under circumstances which would inevitably lead to Communist domination of the entire country" without suffering "severe political repercussions." America would forfeit prestige—or credibility—throughout the world. "Those small nations now relying upon the U.S. to support them in resisting internal or external Communist pressure" might lose hope. Although the United States should make "every effort . . . to liquidate or reduce the U.S. commitment of men and money in Korea as soon as possible," this should be done "without abandoning Korea to Soviet domination."[53]

In the following years, this analysis continued to carry weight in the Truman administration. Certain adjustments took shape in September 1947, however, that were to be crucial in determining American decisions prior to 25 June 1950. First, the Joint Chiefs of Staff concluded that the United States had "little strategic interest" in maintaining troops in Korea. In the event of war, they asserted, the United States would bypass the peninsula in any offensive operation. The extension of Soviet control over the entire country would increase that nation's capacity "to interfere with United States communications and operations in East China, Manchuria, the Yellow Sea, Sea of Japan and adjacent islands," but the neutralization of such a threat "by air action would be more feasible and less costly than large-scale ground operations."[54]

This judgment represented no sudden reversal of military-strategic thinking. It was more a reflection of growing American responsibilities in other areas of the world, the continuing disorder in South Korea, and recent cuts in the army budget. Despite its desire to withdraw, the army continued to view the salvaging of South Korea as worth some effort. A study by its Plans and Operations Division, which served as the basis for the conclusions of the Joint Chiefs, emphasized that political initiatives had to be taken immediately, for continued delays in the granting of independence would result in further disruption in South Korea. Under such circumstances, only a doubling of American expenditures there could assure the maintenance of the status quo. Yet the lack of public interest in Korea was more likely to result in a decrease, not an increase, in funds available. If the Truman administration failed to move on the political front, a forced American withdrawal might result that would compromise "the prestige of the United States." Submission of the Korean problem to the United Nations offered "the greatest chance of bringing about the most favorable conditions for early U.S. withdrawal . . . without serious damage to the military security position of the United States in the Far East."[55]

In his report of September on Korea, General Wedemeyer ignored the problem of funding a firm Korea policy, but, like the army's Plans and Operations Division, he emphasized the cost to American prestige of a simple withdrawal from the peninsula. Such a move would certainly lead to Soviet domination of "all Korea." America would suffer "an immense loss in moral prestige among the peoples of Asia." On the other hand, Russia would gain in prestige, which would enhance its prospects for expansion in other areas near its borders. Surely, Communist control of Korea would make easier the infiltration of subversive agents into Japan. It also would undermine Chiang Kai-shek's efforts to halt the Communist advance in Manchuria and North China.[56]

Still, army planners now conceded that the United States might eventually have to accept Communist domination of Korea, and the State Department agreed. In an intradepartmental meeting late in September, Marshall, Lovett, John Allison, the head of the Division of Northeast Asian Affairs, Walton Butterworth, Dean Rusk, director of the Office of Special Political Affairs, and George F. Kennan of the recently formed Policy Planning Staff agreed that "ultimately the U.S. position in Korea is untenable even with expenditure of considerable . . . money and effort." The United States, however, could not merely " 'scuttle' and run." The Truman administration should seek "a settlement . . . which would enable the U.S. to withdraw . . . as soon as possible with the minimum of bad effects."[57]

These officials probably recognized that an independent Korean government established through the procedures outlined in the Lovett letter to Molotov of late August 1947 might lead to Communist domination of the peninsula. W. Bedell Smith, the American ambassador in Moscow, argued this point forcefully.[58] This prospect had continued relevance even after referral of the Korean issue to the United Nations, because a unification plan somewhat similar to that in the Lovett letter remained a possible solution.[59]

During September, accounts from South Korea added substance to Smith's appraisal. The Wedemeyer mission reported a leftist trend in political thinking below the thirty-eighth parallel.[60] Jacobs, in Seoul, agreeing, noted that "at least thirty percent of the people in South Korea are leftists, following Comintern Communist leaders who would support the Soviets behind United States lines." The feisty Jacobs was a veteran foreign service officer with wide experience in Asia. On the verge of promotion to the rank of career minister, he was, to date, the highest ranking State Department official to serve in Korea. (He was also the first American diplomat there who worked well with Hodge, in part because Jacob's bluntness appealed to the military commander. Thirty years later a former colleague recalled—perhaps with a trifle of overstatement—that the two men had identical solutions to the cold war: to drop a few atomic bombs on the Kremlin.)[61] Jacobs estimated that, if unification efforts failed and the United States proceeded to sponsor the creation of an independent South Korea, American armed forces in Korea probably would have to be increased. "At least one division of well-trained American troops" would have to be stationed along the thirty-eighth parallel "more or less permanently."[62] The requirements for maintaining an independent South Korea had never been stated quite so baldly. Jacobs's estimate carried considerable weight because American intelligence sources estimated the size of North Korean armed forces at between 150,000 and 200,000 men, not to mention the 50,000 Russian troops that remained in the northern zone.[63]

By late September, therefore, a consensus had emerged among State and Defense planners in favor of a graceful withdrawal from Korea. On 26 September, an opportunity arose, for the Russians proposed that early in 1948 all foreign troops leave the peninsula.[64] A major drawback to such a course was the existence of a North Korean army far stronger than the South Korean constabulary. Yet a careful weighing of American options suggests that the proposal deserved serious consideration.

## American Policy in the United Nations: An Evaluation

An evaluation of American policy toward Korea in the fall of 1947 rightfully begins with the move to the United Nations. Scholar Leland Goodrich has criticized the action as the unloading of a "hot potato" on the international organization prior to giving other approaches a fair trial.[65] A realistic appraisal requires not only a judgment on the truth of the charge—there is little doubt that neither the bilateral approach at the governmental level nor the four-power alternative had been pursued with any persistence—but also consideration of three additional questions: Were the other approaches as or more likely to produce results than an effort in the United Nations? Could the United States afford to exhaust all possibilities before going to the General Assembly? Were there drawbacks to this move that outweighed any advantages?

An answer to the first question depends largely on one's perception of the Soviet position. American leaders saw the United Nations as more likely to handle the problem effectively because it would receive wider publicity there. The Russians, therefore, would be under more pressure to make concessions. A precedent may have been seen in the Iranian case of the previous year in which a withdrawal of Soviet troops from the northern province of Azerbaijan followed pressure within the Security Council. On the other hand, the Soviet Union had always shown sensitivity regarding the jurisdiction of the United Nations. Ever careful to guard its sovereignty, and well aware of American domination of the General Assembly, Russia defined the role of the organization narrowly. From a legal standpoint, the Korean issue was appropriate for United Nations consideration, though resolutions passing the General Assembly had the force of recommendations only.[66] Yet there was no provision in the Moscow agreement for referral of the question to the United Nations, and in the past the Kremlin had been insistent on following this accord to the letter. Still, efforts in the Joint Commission had proven fruitless. Because the Soviet delegation undoubtedly operated under orders from Moscow, negotiations at the governmental level were no more likely to bring positive results than the Joint Commission—unless, of course, the United States offered substantive proposals different from those previously advanced. Moreover, prior to submittal of the problem to the General Assembly, the United States did suggest a four-power meeting in Washington, and Russia demurred.

The time factor adds weight to these last two points. Jacobs and Hodge both emphasized that the American position in South Korea became more and more precarious without concrete progress toward the establishment of an independent government. While Soviet forces remained in Korea, the chances of an invasion from the north appeared remote, but, if Russian troops withdrew, an attack would no longer result in direct confrontation between Soviet and American troops. Thus, the possibility of large-scale hostilities would increase. Intelligence reports in early October 1947 indicated that renewed recruiting for the North Korean army was under way and that, for the first time, several of its units had moved to provinces bordering on the thirty-eighth parallel.[67] Given the numerical advantage of North Korean forces, the poor condition of American and South Korean soldiers, and the unstable situation below the thirty-eighth parallel, an attack from the north might prove disastrous for the United States.

Even if an invasion did not occur, army personnel shortages soon would force the scaling down of American strength in South Korea. This process would reduce the capacity of the American occupation to fulfill its responsibilities. More tasks were being turned over to the South Koreans, but their general lack of technical skills remained a problem. The effectiveness of the national police suffered because of its unpopularity with the public, a condition rooted in that group's partisanship and the presence in its ranks of many former collaborators with the Japanese. Again, the difficulty of finding dependable replacements remained an impediment to solving the problem. Limited training, small size, and poor coordination with the police force hindered the performance of the South Korean constabulary. Such weaknesses could lead to catastrophe if the lack of progress toward independence resulted in further unrest.

In this situation, a move to the United Nations presented at least one advantage: Rhee favored the action.[68] As head of the strongest group in South Korea, with the possible exception of the Communists, he was in a position to make matters easier or more difficult for the occupation command. With the Korean question before the international organization, the United States could anticipate a temporary decline in Rhee's agitation against American policy. As a result, precious time might be gained in the race to solve the Korean problem before circumstances in the south worsened.

In one respect, there was also an advantage in launching an independent government for South Korea through the United Nations, rather than unilaterally. Sponsorship of such a government by the largest organization of states in the world would add legitimacy to the project. Because time was a major factor, because a failure of the United States and the Soviet Union to reach agreement on unification was a distinct possibility, and because Washington regarded a simple American withdrawal as inadvisable, submittal of the Korean problem to the United Nations prior to the exhaustion of other approaches appeared attractive.

An effort through the United Nations, however, entailed serious risks. If the United States sponsored the creation of an independent South Korea, the American stake in its survival would be substantial no matter what the approach. Yet sponsorship through the United Nations would compound the American obligation. The General Assembly, after all, would act only in response to an American initiative. In the eyes of member nations, therefore, the United States would assume the primary responsibility for the success of the venture. A failure to live up to this responsibility would undermine both the prestige of the international body and the confidence of friendly nations in the United States. At a time when State Department officials had concluded that the American position in Korea was "untenable" and had little hope of containing the Communist advance in nearby Manchuria, an expansion of commitments on the peninsula was of dubious wisdom.

Yet American policy in the fall of 1947 moved precisely in this direction. Despite the apparent desire to avoid burning all bridges with the Russians, Americans pushed their program through the General Assembly in the face of staunch Soviet opposition.[69] On 17 October, the American representatives submitted a draft resolution in the First Committee of the General Assembly calling for elections by 31 March 1948 to select a national assembly in Korea. The occupying power in each zone would conduct elections, but a United Nations Temporary Commission responsible to the General Assembly would supervise. Population would determine representation on the new legislative body, which would give South Korea roughly twice the membership of the north. The national assembly would harbor responsibility for creating a government and establishing a security force. Foreign troops would withdraw "at the earliest practicable date."[70]

Russia countered with a draft resolution providing for simultaneous withdrawal of all foreign forces by the beginning of 1948. Soviet representative Andrei Gromyko also suggested that the United Nations invite elected delegates from North and South Korea to participate in discussions on the Korean problem.[71] The United States, which in the early postwar years consistently mustered huge majorities against the Soviet Union in the General Assembly and its various committees, lobbied aggressively for the American resolution.[72] On 14 November, the General Assembly passed a revised measure satisfactory to the United States, the only major change providing for elections on a national not a zonal basis.[73] All major Soviet resolutions and amendments were defeated. Two weeks before the resolution passed, the Soviets announced that they would not participate in the work of the Temporary Commission if the General Assembly acted without hearing Korean representatives.[74] This position suggested that the commission would not be permitted to carry out its tasks above the thirty-eighth parallel. Thus, by mid-November, the United States had taken a major step toward a total impasse with the Soviet Union. Under these circumstances, the creation of an independent South Korea became all but inevitable.

The rapid emergence of a Soviet-American impasse in the General Assembly suggests that planners in Washington failed to coordinate actions with premises. When Gromyko threatened to break up unification efforts if the General Assembly did not hear Korean representatives, the United States was in a weak position to call his bluff. Arguments existed, to be sure, against halting consideration of the general problem to invite Korean participation. As American delegate John Foster Dulles noted in First Committee debates, the Russians offered no method for choosing representatives for consultation.[75] The question had been central in the deadlock of the Joint Commission. Some five hundred political and social organizations claimed to represent at least a portion of the Korean populace. Clearly, the issue would be difficult to resolve in the General Assembly. American officials especially wanted to avoid appointment of Korean representatives by the occupying powers, for such a method would place the United States in a serious dilemma. If appointments for the south went to Rhee and other individuals sympathetic to his cause, the non-Communist leader most distasteful to the United States would be strengthened. In the General Assembly, Rhee might further disrupt efforts for unification. Yet if he did not dominate a South Korean delegation, he would be likely to cause additional trouble for the American occupation.[76] Given the liabilities involved in the establishment of an independent government below the thirty-eighth parallel, however, a more concerted effort should have been made to reach agreement with the Soviets on consultation.

Rhee might have been influenced by a threat of total American withdrawal from the peninsula.[77] A reduction in occupation personnel could have lent credibility to the threat. Ultimately, the option existed of forcefully removing Rhee from the scene. In July 1947, Jacobs had come close to advocating such a course when he stated that the United States might "eventually be compelled to arrange somehow" that the Right choose leaders other than Rhee and Kim Koo.[78] Rent by factionalism even in Rhee's dynamic presence, the extreme Right surely would have suffered tremendously from his loss. But a level of cynicism—or realism—adequate to permit serious consideration of such action had not yet emerged among top American officials. The United States continued to shy away from a decisive course in relation to South Korean political groups. As in China, America's effort to nudge domestic politics in a moderate direction failed.

In a society lacking a liberal tradition and a social and economic structure conducive to the short-term growth of pluralistic democracy, the American occupation's refusal to commit itself forcefully to one group or leader could only increase the overall confusion. After the fall of 1945, effective support for any group other than the extreme Right would have involved a major overturning of official Korean personnel. In view of Rhee's character—his deviousness, his erratic and seemingly irrational behavior, and his ties to radical elements on the Right—such a move might well have been worthwhile. By the fall of 1947, however, the best alternative to Rhee, Lyuh Woonhyung, had fallen victim to an assassin's bullet. Although American officials in South Korea and in Washington generally refused to admit the unpleasant fact, the creation of an independent government below the thirty-eighth parallel could lead only to a major political victory for Rhee. And, despite Rhee's impressive capacity for self-promotion, his disinterest in social and economic reform made it unlikely that he could garner the kind of mass support necessary for the long term to sustain a regime.

The United States simply lacked attractive alternatives in Korea. Again, the fateful character of decisions made at the end of World War II come to mind: once made, political factors joined the relatively minor military ones in American calculations. In the absence of some concrete agreement for peaceful unification, a withdrawal from the peninsula took on serious implications. Nevertheless, the Soviet proposal for simultaneous withdrawal had merit. Such action would have led to civil war in Korea and probably to a Communist victory, but it is not clear that this outcome would have enabled the Soviet Union to dominate the country.

The Communist movement among Koreans had been seriously divided virtually since its inception at the end of World War I. In 1945, there were several major factions in the Korean Communist party. Kim Il-sung was thirty-three years old, a member of the "Kapsan faction," and largely unknown in the country. Two years later, he was a central and increasingly powerful figure in North Korean politics. Yet his position was far from secure, and his influence over the Communist party in the south certainly was limited.[79] Below the thirty-eighth parallel, Pak Hon-yong, whose experience in party affairs dated back to the early 1920s, probably carried greater weight than Kim right up to the outbreak of war on the peninsula in June 1950. Had Russian and American troops left Korea in early 1948, the Kremlin surely would have sought to control ensuing events through material assistance to groups receptive to its direction. Although that aid undoubtedly would have strengthened Kim, it is not certain that he would have emerged victorious, or that, with the civil war over, he or any other governing faction would have remained an ally of Moscow. The Russian occupation of the north, though far more effective in maintaining control of its zone than its American counterpart in the south, was often harsh, arbitrary, and exploitative. This created much indigenous resentment that might have surfaced after Soviet withdrawal.[80] As in China, the evolution of Communist relations with the Soviet Union may have rested in part on the attitude of the United States.

This is not to deny that a withdrawal of foreign troops from Korea would have been an American setback. Surely, it would have raised doubts in Japan regarding U.S. determination to defend that island nation in the face of possible Soviet pressure. The communization of Korea might also have served to increase the Soviet military threat to Japan. Yet political losses could have been minimized by bolstering the American commitment to Japan through verbal reassurances and the maintenance of occupation forces there at full strength. The withdrawal from Korea would have helped make such a presence feasible, even with the cuts in the army budget. The continuation of resourceful action on the European front could have discouraged U.S. allies—and the Russians—from interpreting events in Korea as a reflection of American weakness in other theaters.[81] Military repercussions might have been avoided through a prior agreement with the Soviet Union against the establishment of foreign bases on the peninsula. In sum, American losses would have been limited in scope and duration and they should have been accepted as an alternative to risking possibly greater problems later on.

The American move to the United Nations was not inherently flawed. The failure of that organization to achieve a solution could do no irreparable harm. Few people regarded the United Nations as a remedy for all conflicts among nations. Furthermore, a continuing deadlock with the Russians would not necessitate the establishment of an independent South Korea. The inability of foreign powers to unify the peninsula could serve as a pretext for allowing the Koreans to determine their own future.

Yet negotiations with the Russians on the mechanics of withdrawal might have been more productive at the bilateral level than in the United Nations. With good reason, the Kremlin has always preferred diplomacy behind closed doors, and, in the charged atmosphere of the times, that approach was better served through government-to-government talks than through the General Assembly or the Joint Commission. The most promising tactic involved a direct approach to the Soviets for mutual withdrawal together with placement of the Korean issue on the General Assembly agenda shortly thereafter.[82] Such a ploy satisfied the need for private diplomacy while simultaneously applying pressure on Moscow for speedy negotiations at the bilateral level. Still, the most questionable aspect of American policy toward Korea arose after the problem arrived at the General Assembly. The flexibility that should have stemmed from recognition of American weakness never appeared.

Why did the United States fail to coordinate its strategy more closely with its perception of American weakness? A comparison with China policy is instructive here. In the fall of 1947, expanding America's stake in China necessitated a large and almost immediate expenditure of funds, a substantial consumption of scarce resources, and the dispatch of government personnel, especially military. In contrast, increasing America's commitment to South Korea required no such action. Eventually, American economic and military aid would be needed to sustain a government below the thirty-eighth parallel, but such a program could wait. When it did become essential, it would be accompanied by a reduction—and ultimately an elimination—of American occupation duties. Granted, this action would make South Korea vulnerable to attack from the north, but American planners were not deterred by this fact.

This was because they thought in terms of the already existing commitment to South Korea rather than a possible expansion of that commitment. Direct United States involvement on the peninsula, accompanied by a similar presence of the Soviet Union, led American diplomats to perceive a substantial political stake in containing Communism. This stake exceeded that in China, even though obligations to the National government made inconceivable a total American withdrawal from the country.

Thus, in late 1947, concern in Washington for America's credibility abroad pushed China and Korea policy in opposite directions. In a physical sense, neither country was critical to the United States. Their location denied them a significance equal to Greece and Turkey. Their limited industrial potential made them of less concern than Western Europe or Japan. American diplomats, therefore, viewed China and Korea largely in terms of their possible impact on efforts to protect more vital territories from Communist domination. Deeper involvement in China might compromise other endeavors, first by spreading American resources too thin, and second by engaging American prestige in a possibly losing enterprise. Because the Truman administration was most anxious to convey to the world an image of strength and determination—both to keep its friends and to deter its enemies—such a development was potentially disastrous. In Korea, on the other hand, American prestige was already extensively committed. For the United States to acquiesce in a Communist victory below the thirty-eighth parallel would call into question American reliability. At a time of deep insecurity in Western Europe and of growing American concern about economic conditions in Japan, this prospect evoked nightmares in Washington.[83] It might encourage adventurism in the Kremlin, undermine the will of America's friends to resist Communist penetration, and thereby imperil the entire strategy of containing Soviet expansionism.

A final consideration was Korea's size. While massive China tended to intimidate American diplomats, tiny South Korea beckoned a salvaging effort. The possibilities for survival of an independent government in the south were poor, but they were far from nonexistent. Communist forces in the north would be stronger than in the south following termination of the foreign occupation; thus an all out attack from the north would be a danger. Nevertheless, Communist tactics in the past, in Korea and elsewhere, had been directed toward infiltration and subversion rather than large-scale, overt military operations.[84] And United Nations sponsorship of South Korea might make the Kremlin hesitate to support a military venture below the thirty-eighth parallel. A chance remained, however slim, that with the inauguration of an independent government, the implementation of land reforms, and the launching of a small program of American economic aid, the south would survive as an independent, non-Communist state.

Certainly the program for a national government below the thirty-eighth parallel came closest to synthesizing the conflicting desires of halting Communism and withdrawing American troops from the peninsula. As the fall of 1947 progressed and the Soviet Union seemed less willing than ever to accept open, democratic procedures for unification, it became preferable to risk integrating Korea into the prevailing containment strategy rather than to face up to the fact of American weakness. Ultimately, a sense of past commitment that had to be met as fully as possible overcame any fear of increasing obligations in the process of reducing America's physical presence in the troubled land.

## The American Occupation, the United Nations, and Elections in South Korea

The American political offensive on Korea did not end on 14 November when the General Assembly passed a resolution outlining a process for unifying the country. Because the Truman administration hoped to withdraw American troops from the peninsula during 1948, State Department officials labored hard to create conditions that would make this action feasible. The first goal was to assist the United Nations Temporary Commission on Korea (UNTCOK) in conducting elections throughout the country. If, as a result of Communist opposition, nationwide elections were not possible, UNTCOK should be pressed to implement the General Assembly resolution in South Korea alone.[85] Delays in holding elections would place hardships on the army in meeting its commitments elsewhere and create further dissatisfaction within South Korea, especially among groups controlled by Rhee.

In January 1948, when UNTCOK personnel arrived in Seoul, the United States had reason to believe that its wishes would be followed. Australia, Canada, China, El Salvador, France, India, the Philippines, and Syria were represented on the commission (the Ukraine was chosen to serve but refused). Six of these countries had close relations with the United States. Only India, a newly independent nation which sought to play a leading role in Asian affairs, and Syria, whose hostility toward the American position on Palestine would surely influence its stance on Korea, appeared to be unmanageable.

From the start, however, the Australian, Canadian, Indian, and Syrian members of UNTCOK tended to oppose any election that was not national in character. Only the representatives from China and the Philippines leaned

toward the American position, and those from France and El Salvador vac-
illated. Thus, when the Soviet Union refused to respond to UNTCOK's
overtures regarding its entry into the north, the commission did not move
immediately toward organizing an election below the thirty-eighth parallel. S. H. Jackson of Australia suggested that, because the Soviets had not
explicitly repudiated UNTCOK's advances, the body should make a physical attempt to enter the northern zone.[86] This proposal was never adopted,
for the other delegates interpreted the Russian refusal to receive letters from
the commission as representing an unwillingness to cooperate. On 5 February, UNTCOK voted to consult the Interim Committee of the General
Assembly.[87]

The United States, led by a prominent expert on international law, Philip
C. Jessup, worked hard to sell its view to the Interim Committee.[88] As a result, on 26 February, that body voted 31-2 (with 11 abstentions) in favor of an
American resolution envisioning an UNTCOK-supervised election in South
Korea. India, France, and El Salvador, as well as the Philippines and China,
supported the United States. Only Canada and Australia opposed the resolution. Syria abstained.[89]

Yet America's difficulties did not end here. Canadian and Australian opposition continued in UNTCOK and threatened to block establishment of a
United Nations-sponsored government in South Korea. Jackson and his Canadian colleague on the commission, George S. Patterson, proved to be persistent adversaries. Their ongoing argument that UNTCOK should refuse to
observe an election in the south rested on the view that the Interim Committee resolution had the standing of advice only.

Canadian and Australian opposition to the United States reflected several
concerns. Canada, led by Prime Minister W. L. Mackenzie King, had not desired membership on the commission; he agreed to his country's participation only after a direct appeal from President Truman.[90] But Canadian reluc-
tance to become involved in precipitating a new crisis in Soviet relations
with the West continued. Initially, both Canada and Australia were influenced by their commonwealth partner, Great Britain. London suspected that
the United States was using the United Nations as an instrument for American withdrawal from Korea, and that the Truman administration had written off the peninsula. To British leaders, preventing the creation of an independent government below the thirty-eighth parallel might serve to keep the
United States "tied up in Korea." In so doing, it would prevent a serious debacle for the international organization and a victory for the Soviet Union.[91]

Furthermore, Jackson and Patterson believed that possibilities for unifying
Korea were not exhausted. These men were committed liberals less cynical
than American officials regarding Soviet intentions. They objected to many
of the activities of the Rhee-controlled police in South Korea. Their hopes
for unification rested to a considerable extent on the efforts of moderate

Kimm Kiu-sic, who in late January 1948 proposed a conference of northern and southern leaders under UNTCOK's observation.[92] In mid-February, Rhee and Kim Koo agreed with Kimm to contact Korean officials in Pyongyang to propose a meeting on national elections, thereby encouraging hopes in the south of forestalling a divided Korea.[93]

Jackson and Patterson were encouraged in their position by the response in South Korea to the Interim Committee resolution. After the South Korean interim legislative assembly voted in favor of separate elections below the thirty-eighth parallel, Kimm resigned from the body, of which he had been chairman. On 12 March, he, Kim Koo, and five other prominent South Korean political figures—but not Rhee—wrote to North Korean leaders Kim Il-sung and Kim Tu-bong and proposed a conference on unification.[94] Thirteen days later, North Korea invited South Korean groups opposing separate elections to a conference in Pyongyang on 14 April.[95] In the meantime, leftists in the south, bolstered by infiltrators from the north, intensified their disruptive tactics. Among top politicians on the peninsula, only Rhee favored the Interim Committee action. In March, therefore, it was reasonable to believe that support for an election below the thirty-eighth parallel would come only from organizations on the extreme Right, that such an event could not be held in a peaceful setting, and that it would eliminate whatever chance might remain for national unity.

A majority of UNTCOK disagreed with Jackson and Patterson. In meetings at the end of February 1948, which were not attended by Patterson or K. P. S. Menon, the Indian representative, the commission voted to hold an election in South Korea on 9 May. The full commission soon reconsidered the matter, but on 11 March, despite the opposition of Canada and Australia and the abstention of France and Syria, UNTCOK decided to observe elections in two months, provided there existed a "reasonable degree of free atmosphere" in the south.[96]

American officials in South Korea proceeded to launch a registration and election campaign among the populace. In meetings with provincial governors and police chiefs, Hodge stressed the need for a free electoral process.[97] On 31 March, Major General William F. Dean, the American military governor, signed pardons for 3,140 Koreans who were either awaiting trial, serving prison terms, or on parole. This move represented an attempt by the military command to meet Australian, Canadian, and Syrian complaints regarding alleged political prisoners.[98] During the following week, Hodge issued a proclamation outlining the rights of all South Koreans in the upcoming elections.[99] By the middle of the month, the registration process had been completed, with 91.7 percent of the eligible voters enrolled.[100] In response to these developments, UNTCOK decided that, because the appropriate conditions existed, it would observe elections on 10 May.[101] Patterson, the Syrian delegate, Yasin Mughir, and the Frenchman Jean-Louis Paul-Boncour abstained from the vote; the others favored the measure. Paul-Boncour's position was really pro-American, however, for he believed that *more* than a "reasonable degree of free atmosphere" prevailed.[102]

Serious problems still remained for American officials. Patterson and Jackson apparently had persuaded a wavering Kimm to attend the conference in Pyongyang in the hope that, if sensible terms for unification emerged, the commission might postpone elections in the south.[103] When Kimm and Kim returned from the north in early May, they were cautiously optimistic about North Korean intentions to avoid civil war after the withdrawal of foreign troops, to continue to supply electricity to the south, to refrain from establishing a separate government above the thirty-eighth parallel, and to release Cho Man-sik, a prominent Christian leader of prewar days. By keeping alive hopes for unification, the report of the two men threatened to undermine the legitimacy of the upcoming election.[104]

A second hindrance was the continuing unrest in South Korea. From February 1948 onward, leftist attempts at disrupting official activities in the south increased. State Department representative Joseph Jacobs reported that the military government had evidence of the infiltration from North Korea of propagandists, assassins, and saboteurs.[105] Yet, with UNTCOK representatives on hand to observe electoral procedures, Hodge had to give some leeway to subversive efforts. Considerable fear existed that widespread Communist-inspired disorders would compromise the elections.[106]

For the most part, however, American officials were pleased with events on 10 May. More than 95 percent of the registered voters cast ballots. Although unrest resulted in forty-four deaths, injury to sixty-two others, and attacks on sixty-eight of the 13,407 election booths, Jacobs reported that proceedings went "better than most expected."[107] As anticipated, Rhee's followers were numerous among the successful candidates, but people of widely varied political affiliation were elected. Eighty-five of the 198 representatives to the "National Assembly" were labeled as independents.[108] If the results did not represent the birth of Western-style pluralistic democracy, they did represent a tactical victory for United States policy.[109]

## Coordinating Means and Ends

In the two months before the election, the State Department had become more aggressive than previously in seeking to sustain a strong Korea policy. On 4 March 1948, Butterworth had written to Marshall that "the spirit as well as the letter" of the General Assembly resolution of the previous November "committed the United States . . . to withdraw only after the creation of reasonably adequate native security forces, and under circumstances which will bequeath to the newly established government at least an even chance of survival." This commitment, he asserted, was "very real in the minds of most other members of the United Nations." He concluded that the Department of the Army should "maintain flexibility in its plans for the withdrawal of occupation forces" and should "expedite to the fullest extent possible" the training and equipping of an enlarged South Korean defense establishment.[110]

This position emerged after the army had delayed for several months a decision on augmenting South Korea's armed forces. In October 1947, in the face of a projected American troop withdrawal by the end of the following year, the army asked Hodge and MacArthur for their opinions on strengthening indigenous military units. Hodge recommended the establishment of a South Korean army of six divisions. He believed that American personnel could train and equip such a force in one year. MacArthur, however, thought such a step premature while the Korean problem was before the United Nations.[111] In Washington, MacArthur's view prevailed over Hodge's, though the question remained divisive within the executive branch.

The army was split between the Plans and Operations Division, which favored the equipping of a South Korean army, and the Service, Supply and Procurement Division, which argued that such a course would involve obligations that the United States could not satisfy. The latter division regarded maintenance as the major problem. Recent experience with the Chinese taught that peoples lacking modern technical skills could not adequately service American arms and ammunition. An effective program, therefore, "would entail establishment of U.S. technical maintenance schools in Korea and the training of Korean personnel in the operation of U.S. equipment on a continuing basis." Because current shortages in army personnel and equipment made impossible the effective execution of such a program, its initiation probably would lead to further "loss of face" for the United States.[112] The only way to launch a program without risking this outcome was to obtain new funds from Congress.[113] Not until February 1948 did the army reach a final decision on the proper course. By that time, the Service, Supply and Procurement Division had gained allies in MacArthur and Lieutenant General G. P. Hall, director of the Division of Organization and Training. The Far Eastern commander argued that, at most, the constabulary could be increased to 50,000 soldiers.[114] In the midst of carrying out manpower reductions necessitated by congressional decisions of the previous year, General Omar N. Bradley, the new army chief of staff, concurred.

As a result of these deliberations, the National Security Council concluded in a major policy paper of 2 April 1948 (NSC 8) that South Korean forces should be built up "as a means of providing, *so far as practicable*, effective protection for *the security of South Korea against any but an overt act of aggression*." (emphasis added)[115] Because the Central Intelligence Agency estimated that the "People's Army" of the north had more than five times the manpower of the South Korean constabulary and was equipped "with adequate infantry and infantry-support weapons of Soviet manufacture," a larger goal seemed totally unrealistic.[116]

Still, NSC 8 also incorporated much of Butterworth's thinking. The document mentioned 31 December 1948 as the projected date for the final departure of American occupation forces, but that was contingent upon both the bolstering of indigenous security organizations to enable them to maintain internal order and the establishment of a relief and rehabilitation program to forestall South Korea's economic collapse. A victory "by Soviet-dominated forces" below the thirty-eighth parallel, the report noted, would have a major psychological impact on both East Asia and the United Nations. Despite America's inability to guarantee South Korea against outside attack, every effort should be made short of such a guarantee to prevent Communist control of the area.[117]

When President Truman approved NSC 8 on 8 April, the State Department gained considerable leverage in opposing army efforts to establish a firm timetable for withdrawal. Initially, top military officials did not fully grasp the implications of the paper. Within a month, Under Secretary of the Army William H. Draper wrote Under Secretary of State Lovett and asked that the United States make no specific requests for United Nations action following the upcoming elections. Such an initiative, he feared, would lead the international organization to request a postponement of the American departure from the peninsula. Yet NSC 8 stated that the United States "should encourage continued UN interest and participation in the Korean problem and should continue to cooperate with the UN in the solution of that problem."[118] Lovett referred Draper to this declaration, noting that "the possible ill effects" of American withdrawal might be minimized by associating the United Nations with the act.[119]

State Department hopes for a strong Korea policy rested on more than a strict interpretation of a National Security Council paper. In March 1948, in response to the Communist coup in Czechoslovakia and growing tension in Berlin, President Truman proposed the resumption of the military draft and suggested that a substantial increase in American armed force might be necessary. A month later, he permitted Secretary of Defense Forrestal to present to Congress a supplemental appropriations bill that projected an increase in army manpower of 240,000. Although the chief executive soon hedged on the matter by placing a $15 billion ceiling on the defense budget for fiscal year 1950, prospects remained brighter than before that the United States soon would reduce the incongruity between its foreign obligations and its military strength.[120] And such an endeavor was likely to strengthen the case for flexibility in completing projected troop withdrawals from Korea.

The State Department also had some grounds for optimism regarding its plans for South Korea's economic recovery. In early May, the administration sent to Capitol Hill a bill that included funds not only for relief supplies for

South Korea, but for economic rehabilitation as well. Congressional action on the European Recovery Program already had indicated that lawmakers increasingly accepted America's growing responsibilities abroad. Although the bill for the South Koreans had not yet passed when they went to the polls on 10 May, its mere presentation to Congress represented an advancement over the previous summer, when pressures from the legislative branch succeeded in bottling up an economic aid program in executive departments. When an appropriation for Korea did clear both houses in late June, it provided nearly $150 million in economic aid, an increase of more than $30 million over the relief allocation of the preceeding year.[121] This would have been a paltry sum for a massive area like China, but for tiny South Korea it provided for, among other things, larger shipments of fertilizer, which would pave the way to a resolution of the severe food problem. More aid would be needed in the future; however, a small start had been made toward making South Korea a viable economic unit.

Although by May 1948 the prospects for keeping South Korea out of Communist hands were somewhat brighter than they had been eight months before, the United States also had substantially increased its political stake on the peninsula. American pressure on the United Nations to move forward rapidly with separate elections in South Korea tied United States prestige to the development of a functioning non-Communist state below the thirty-eighth parallel. Despite hopeful signs in the political, military, and economic spheres, circumstances in Korea and the United States continued to place in serious doubt the feasibility of such an enterprise.

Yet it is difficult to prescribe a workable alternative to the course followed by the United States after the fall of 1947. Once the General Assembly had explicitly rejected the Soviet proposal for the simultaneous withdrawal of foreign forces, the adoption of such a course in the face of North Korea's clear military superiority over the south would have represented a major political setback for the United States. American diplomats, to be sure, never probed Russia on the possibility of disbanding North Korea's army prior to a foreign withdrawal. A delay in the implementation of procedures for an election in South Korea, however, entailed serious hazards. American troop strength on the peninsula had declined to 21,000, and, though Rhee was willing to cooperate with efforts at further negotiations, he opposed holding up plans for an election in the south while such attempts were being made. Had his forces resumed their disruptive activities against the American command, instability below the thirty-eighth parallel might have turned into chaos.

Although the United States held the ultimate weapon over Rhee—the threat of a total American withdrawal from Korea—the general discontent of the populace with outside rule made delay of the process toward self-government a risky course. American officials on the scene argued that further indecisiveness would result in a total loss of the occupation's ability to control events. The most that can be said is that negotiations might have been pursued with the Russians and North Koreans at the same time that preparations were being made to create an independent South Korea. But this approach left open the danger that unification talks would be inconclusive in their initial stages. Such a condition would leave the United States with the unenviable choice of holding separate elections in an atmosphere in which some hope remained that national unity could be achieved, or of postponing the balloting to give negotiations a longer trial.

Although the option of a simultaneous foreign withdrawal had become less plausible than during the previous fall, the viability of an independent South Korea had increased somewhat. Whereas in September 1947 the Communists in South Korea had appeared to have the support of at least a third of the population, five months later, largely as a result of police efforts and a counter-propaganda campaign by General Hodge, this figure had dwindled substantially.[122] Although the extreme Left still could produce sizable disruption within the American zone, a decline in its popular following improved the prospects for survival of an independent government below the thirty-eighth parallel. Moreover, the shift in the political climate in the United States during the winter and spring of 1948 reflected an increased ability on the part of American institutions to respond effectively to the Communist challenge abroad.[123] Thus, although the course pursued in Korea during the fall of 1947 seems, in retrospect, to have risked too much for too little, the policy followed a few months later was both a trifle less adventurous and more necessary.

## Continuing Trouble in South Korea

Whatever the options available to American diplomats in early 1948, after 10 May there was no turning away from Korea. Because the election in South Korea was over, plans for the creation of an independent government advanced rapidly. At the end of the month, the National Assembly convened and elected Rhee chairman. A special committee then drafted a Constitution, which was adopted by the main body on 12 July. Eight days later, the legislative body chose Rhee as the first president of the Republic of Korea. Within three weeks, the United States, China, and the Philippines granted de facto recognition to the new government. On 15 August, amid much fanfare and in the presence of General MacArthur, formal inauguration ceremonies took place in Seoul. American military government thus came to an end. John J. Muccio, as special representative of President Truman with the rank of ambassador, replaced Hodge as the top American official in Korea.[124]

By this time, UNTCOK had rendered its judgment on the 10 May election. As in the past, the United Nations body acted only after considerable internal debate. Controversy arose almost immediately when, on 13 May, commission chairman Yasin Mughir of Syria told the press that some members of UNTCOK felt violations of election laws had occurred. Members of the police, rightist youth organizations, and the National Defense Corps had been observed "in and around some polling places." This situation, Mughir asserted, "may have constituted a certain degree of restriction on the freedom of voters." In addition, the high level of efficiency with which the balloting had been administered caused suspicion.[125] In early June, the commission remained divided over a variety of substantive and procedural issues.[126] Apparently as a result of pressure from Americans and South Koreans, and S. H. Jackson's departure for Australia on the call of his government, UNTCOK finally voted unanimously late in the month to accept a report describing the elections as "valid expressions of the free will of the electorate in those parts of Korea which were accessible to the Commission."[127] The often tense relationship between American occupation authorities and the United Nations body thus ended in a significant victory for the United States. A solid foundation had been constructed for General Assembly recognition of the republic as a legitimate government.

Yet the establishment of an independent South Korea with United Nations backing did not guarantee the long-term success of American policy toward the peninsula. A variety of dangers threatened the very existence of the new government, the most obvious being the political and military strength of the emergent regime north of the thirty-eighth parallel.

The Russians and North Koreans followed the lead of their adversaries in the south regarding the construction of an independent government. In July, the People's Assembly, which had been created in Pyongyang during 1947, announced plans for a national election on 25 August to choose a new Supreme People's Assembly. This institution was to decree a Constitution, already drafted, and proclaim a formal government.[128] The "election" took place on schedule. North Korea claimed, obviously falsely, that 77.8 percent of the eligible voters in the south had cast ballots. When the assembly convened a week later, 360 of the 572 delegates held seats designated to the area below the thirty-eighth parallel. On 9 September, the Democratic People's Republic of Korea was established, with Kim Il-sung as premier.[129]

Information on North Korea is limited, but it is safe to say that the new government there was far more stable than its South Korean counterpart. This fact derived from the greater decisiveness with which affairs had been conducted in the northern zone since World War II. The contrast appeared not only in the military sphere, but in the area of internal security as well. Although there is no evidence that violence in the northern half of the peninsula threatened the North Korean regime, revolts below the thirty-eighth parallel endangered the Rhee government almost immediately. For some time, a Communist-dominated "People's Liberation Army" had been active below the thirty-eighth parallel. The group engaged in a variety of subversive activities, including infiltration into the South Korean police force and constabulary.

As 1948 progressed, the Communists, encouraged by but not dependent upon North Korea, which had established an institute near Pyongyang to train men in guerrilla techniques for use in the south, directed their activities increasingly toward armed disruption.[130] In April, a major revolt began on Cheju Island located off the southern coast of the peninsula. The revolt received substantial popular support at the local level, and led to temporary Communist control of the island. Six months later, when the rebellion was still out of control, Rhee ordered the Fourteenth Regiment of the South Korean Constabulary to proceed to Cheju. Rather than comply, the soldiers, stationed at the southern port of Yosu, revolted. The uprising soon spread to the Fifteenth Regiment as well. On 2 November, at Taegu, more constabulary personnel rose against the government. Rooted in the widespread discontent with conditions in the south, these were only two among many incidents that occurred throughout island and mountainous regions. In mid-November, Rhee declared martial law over one-fourth of South Korea.[131]

For the long term, these episodes served to strengthen South Korea's armed forces. Troops loyal to the regime gained valuable fighting experience while large numbers of subversives were identified and weeded out. For the moment, however, the Republic of Korea was in serious jeopardy. Not only did the revolts themselves threaten the government; if they continued, North Korea might use them as a pretext to march south to restore order.[132]

Much of the problem in South Korea was Rhee himself. His appointment to the cabinet of personal friends of dubious qualifications raised widespread dissension in the press and among prominent Koreans. As the fall progressed, it became clear that one key to the republic's survival was the ability of Rhee to build a coalition of rightist forces in the National Assembly. Yet his stubbornness, in addition to the extreme factionalism of South Korean politics, made the prospect of such a development appear slim.

Muccio grew increasingly disgusted. The Italian-born diplomat, who had grown up in a working-class family in Rhode Island and been educated at Brown University, was far from an impatient man. After joining the foreign service in 1924, he had served in several areas, including China, Latin America, and Europe. In November 1947, at the age of forty-seven, he had attained the rank of career minister, thus reaching the top of his profession. His assignment to Korea reflected the State Department's confidence in his ability to thrive in difficult circumstances. By the end of 1948, however, his patience with Rhee had worn thin. He reported to Washington that the new government was "incompetent" and "without strong public support."[133]

In fairness to Rhee, his trials were partially a result of forces beyond his control. Although he had emerged as the leading political figure below the thirty-eighth parallel, the support given him by such key groups as the state bureaucracy, the police force, various youth corps, and the large landholders was far from consistent. According to scholar Joungwon A. Kim, the Korea Democratic party (KDP), which held 80 percent of the 198 seats in the National Assembly, viewed the president merely as a "convenient figurehead." As the representative of the landholding elite, this party was frequently at odds with government workers, including the police. This factionalism helped Rhee maintain his regime, but it also made the passage of legislation—and later its efficient implementation—extremely difficult. Against Rhee's wishes, for example, the KDP was sometimes able to obtain National Assembly approval of bills that conflicted palpably with the interests of the police and the government bureaucracy, which bore major responsibility for their execution. The result often bordered on open warfare within the right wing of the political spectrum at a time when the very existence of the republic was seriously threatened by left-wing guerrilla activity.[134]

Despite Muccio's irritation with South Korean politics, he argued that the presence of American troops for "several [additional] months" *might* provide a "period of grace," in which conditions in South Korea could be "stabilized."[135] On the heels of this judgment came pleas from Rhee and the National Assembly for the temporary retention of American forces on the peninsula.[136] Thus, a total U.S. withdrawal would constitute abandonment of a government by the country that was largely responsible for its creation.

## A Reappraisal of Policy Begins

The State Department had already won a postponement of the withdrawal of some 7,500 American soldiers. Early in the fall, the army had set 15 January 1949 as the final departure date. By mid-November, however, the General Assembly still had not made new recommendations on Korea. Because NSC 8 stated that the United States should cooperate with the United Nations and because the army needed two months' notice to make arrangements for the movement of soldiers either to Japan or to America, the January deadline could not be met. But this circumstance provided only a short-term reprieve. On 12 December, the General Assembly finally passed a resolution advising "that the occupying powers withdraw their armed forces from Korea as early as practicable."[137] The Russians had previously announced their intention to leave by the end of the year.[138]

Now, however, the State Department marshaled new arguments for delay. On 17 December, Max W. Bishop, who six weeks earlier had replaced John M. Allison as chief of the State Department's Division of Northeast Asian Affairs, recommended that the National Security Council reconsider the policy of American withdrawal.[139] Bishop's memorandum, drafted by his assistant Niles Bond, represented the culmination of thought processes within the State Department extending back at least to early 1947. Bishop could have argued that continued unrest below the thirty-eighth parallel provided a solid basis within the framework of NSC 8 for postponement of American withdrawal. But he went further and proposed a reexamination of the broad question of Korea's significance to American security in the Pacific area.

In the hope of gaining support from the Joint Chiefs, Bishop centered on the impact of Communist domination of the peninsula on the United States position in Japan, and he began his analysis with military considerations.[140] He asserted that a Communist conquest of South Korea would bring "the Japanese archipelago virtually within gunshot range of the Soviet position in Sakhalin, the Kuriles in the northeast and Communist positions in southern Korea to the southwest." Furthermore, the Communists would make "full use of the enticement value of the economic resources at their command, of the political persuasiveness of the increasing number of communist governments in Asia and Europe, and of the familiar psychological appeal to 'brother Asiatic and comrade.'" Northeast Asia, Bishop asserted, was "one of the four or five significant power centers of the world," and Japan was "the industrial heart of the area." Thus "control of Japan would for the foreseeable future be the greatest prize which the communist power system could obtain in Asia."

Although Bishop made no mention of the impending victory of the Communists in China, the strategic and political repercussions of this event helped shape his analysis. At a time when the problems of economic recovery and political growth in Japan were far from being resolved, a second defeat for American policy in Northeast Asia might have a momentous impact.[141] Events in Europe over the past eight months, most notably the Russian blockade of Berlin, also may have influenced Bishop's perspective. Clearly, he desired to make an American withdrawal from Korea conditional on South Korea's ability to resist Communist encroachment, from both within and without, on its own.[142]

Bishop's arguments surfaced during a transitional period in the leadership of the State Department. Tired and in poor health, Marshall had already arranged with the president to retire in January 1949. Lovett, his top assistant, also planned to return to private life. The making of hard decisions on Korea policy would have to await a new regime.[143] Nevertheless, Butterworth regarded the question of American withdrawal as of sufficient magnitude to merit renewed attention by the National Security Council.[144] Thus the stage was set for another round of bargaining between the diplomats and the military.

Although the Bishop memorandum stands out as a bold statement of State Department opinion on South Korea, by the end of 1948 substantial momentum had built up for a total American troop withdrawal. This fact reflected the ever-present tension in policy development between desirable objectives and the means available for their accomplishment. In early 1948, as more and more soldiers departed from Korea, this tension mounted. By March a series of events—the passage by the General Assembly of an American-sponsored resolution, the arrival in Seoul of the United Nations Temporary Commission on Korea, the refusal of Russia to cooperate with that body, and the increase of Communist-inspired violence below the thirty-eighth parallel—had made a retreat from the policy of creating an independent South Korea unthinkable. The task remained, however, to make that policy a viable one within the structure of American priorities and capabilities.

Despite State Department efforts, long-term prospects for the survival of South Korea were poor. On the positive side, the United Nations had recognized the Republic of Korea as a legitimate government in the territory accessible to its representatives.[145] The economic picture was more hopeful than before, largely as a result of an increase in assistance from the United States. The shortage of electricity had become more acute after 14 May 1948 when, in response to the election four days earlier, the Russians shut off South Korea's access to its traditional sources of power in the north. If the south was ever to produce electricity sufficient for its needs, the United States would have to supply coal in far greater quantities than it had in the past. To meet this requirement, the administration intended to present a sizeable Korean aid program to the next session of Congress.[146] Because the Democrats then would control both houses, there was reason to believe the venture would receive a sympathetic hearing.

The negative factors still outweighed the positive. Although the containment of unrest in South Korea by indigenous forces was not necessarily beyond reach, little hope existed that the thirty-eighth parallel could be made secure against outside attack. Muccio noted that "a determined move south by Soviet forces or by the still unknown number of Korean Communist forces in North China, in Manchuria and in North Korea" might not be stopped by all the troops in South Korea and the United States combined.[147] Direct Russian participation in military operations was unlikely, especially while American soldiers remained on the peninsula, but an attack by North Korea, bolstered by the many thousands of Koreans who had fought alongside the Communists in China for several years, was now a distinct possibility.[148] In such an event, a small contingent from the United States Army would make little difference. This fact serves to emphasize the significance of the Truman administration's failure in the fall of 1947 to closely coordinate its long-term policies toward China and Korea. The American forces remaining in the latter country at the end of 1948 could only hope to assist the Rhee government in maintaining internal order, and, by conveying to the enemy Washington's commitment to South Korea's defense, discourage a strategic offensive from the North.

Yet the Truman administration's policy on military spending gave the army an advantage in combating any State Department effort to keep even a token American force in Korea. In the fall of 1948, pressed by congressional determination to lower taxes in an election year, imbued with the traditional economic wisdom that budgets should be balanced—especially in inflationary periods—and irritated with squabbling among the armed services over their respective missions, President Truman lowered previously projected manpower levels of the armed forces from 1,734,000, including an army of 790,000 men, to 1,616,000 and an army of 667,000 men. Thus, in a period of expanding commitments abroad, the United States pursued a dangerously frugal course in the area of defense expenditures. Budgetary considerations had brought into vogue, on both Capitol Hill and in the White House, the concept of strength through air power. Only the outbreak of war in Korea in June 1950 would alter this situation decisively, and then only temporarily.[149]

A possible alternative to stationing American troops in South Korea indefinitely was a U.S. guarantee of that nation's security. This move could be accomplished through a treaty with the Rhee government, or through a warning to the North Koreans or the Russians that the United States would not tolerate an invasion. Both approaches, however, had serious drawbacks. For one thing, no certainty existed that American forces in Japan could respond effectively to an offensive from north of the thirty-eighth parallel. For another, an American buildup in Korea would leave Japan exposed to a Soviet assault. A guarantee to South Korea might encourage Moscow to use an attack on that territory as a diversion for a move in another more important theater, such as the Middle East or Western Europe. In the event of all-out war, Korea was not a good place, either from an offensive or a defensive standpoint, to tie up American forces.

A final negative consideration was the effect an American guarantee might have on Rhee. He already displayed many of the characteristics of Chiang Kai-shek. He was arrogant, extremely sensitive about American advice, and surrounded by officials of dubious efficiency and integrity. If the United States was to maintain any influence over Rhee, it must keep him in a state of some uncertainty regarding American support. An assurance that the United States would defend South Korea against outside aggression might also encourage him to move against the north. This approach simply left the United States with insufficient flexibility in dealing with the Korean problem.

The best hope of avoiding a major setback rested in conveying to Moscow and Pyongyang, without an explicit guarantee, the seriousness with which Washington would regard an attack on South Korea. One method of imparting this impression was to develop sizable military and economic aid programs for the republic. Progress in the economic arena had already begun. Military assistance had also commenced through a United States Provisional Army Advisory Group that remained in the country to help train the indigenous forces, and through transfers of small arms and ammunition to the South Koreans by departing American soldiers. Yet munitions were left for only 50,000 troops. If Rhee's forces were to be strengthened, the United States surely would have to do more. In December 1948, South Korea transformed its constabulary into an army and launched an expansion program to increase its size from 50,000 to 65,000 men by the following spring.[150] This move was a first step in an attempt to narrow the gap between North and South Korean armed strength. Further legislation from Congress was necessary to enable the Truman administration to support this effort. Certainly the verve with which the United States assisted in meeting South Korea's most pressing material needs would have some impact on Communist perceptions of the American commitment to the new nation.

As historian Adam Ulam has pointed out, however, Washington's failure to intervene on a massive scale to resist the Communist advance in China made it difficult to impart an image of American determination in Korea.[151] To a degree, this problem could be overcome by maintaining a strong position in Japan. American forces there could be kept up to strength and put through maneuvers to demonstrate their readiness for more than occupation duties. MacArthur could be ordered to take an active public interest in events in Korea. Top American military and diplomatic officials could periodically visit the country.

In some respects, the United States did not follow the above course in the year and a half prior to the outbreak of war on the peninsula. Its potential effectiveness, therefore, is difficult to judge. Nevertheless, former Soviet premier Nikita Khrushchev's retrospective account of the origins of the North Korean attack of June 1950 suggests that more extensive symbolic acts by the United States might well have deterred Stalin from giving Kim Il-sung the go-ahead for an invasion of the south.[152] Unfortunately, the pursuit by the Truman administration of a consistently attentive, well-coordinated strategy was simply out of character with the past course of American policy toward Korea.

## Looking Backward—and Forward

In the less than three and a half years since the end of the war in the Pacific, America's historic relationship with China and Korea had undergone a transformation. Although the United States continued to take a major interest in China, its prospects for shaping events there had declined sharply. American influence in the country had never been predominant, but at times it had been considerable. It peaked during World War II, only to fall off after 1946. In Korea, on the other hand, the American role was either inconsequential or nonexistent until the war's end, only to become central shortly afterward. Despite the reduction of foreign military personnel there during 1947 and 1948, the United States remained a major influence below the thirty-eighth parallel. As in China, a reduction in America's ability to mold events had occurred. Yet two facts combined to give the United States considerable sway in South Korean affairs: the Rhee regime clearly was dependent on American aid for its survival, and the example of China indicated that America's patience with corrupt and reactionary governments had limits. Thus pressure from Washington had an impact in Seoul that it had rarely exerted in Nanking.

Responsibility accompanied influence. Bishop's memorandum to the contrary notwithstanding, the prevailing American argument for involvement on the peninsula had shifted between 1945 and 1948 from physical considerations (Korea's strategic location as a possible launching pad for Soviet domination of Japan and China) to political concerns (Korea's importance as a symbol of American reliability worldwide). Rationale aside, a perceptive observer within the government at the end of 1948 might well have anticipated the response of American diplomats a year and a half later when North Korea moved en masse across the thirty-eighth parallel. At the same time, divisions within the executive branch and higher priorities in other areas of the world made it unlikely that the United States would cultivate deterrence in Korea in a diligent and sophisticated manner. Without such an endeavor, that country, now divided against its will into ideologically antagonistic regimes, was likely to erupt in major violence in the near future.

Evidence also existed that, in such an event, the United States would fail to handle relations with China in an adept fashion. The underestimation of Communist strength there by now impeded the development of a prudent response to emerging realities. Domestic politics reinforced the hesitation to take new initiatives. The Sino-American clash in Korea, to be sure, was nearly two years away. Many opportunities remained to avoid it. Yet, as Marshall stepped down as secretary of state and Truman, with new confidence approached a full term in the White House, several of the forces that brought on the tragedy already had appeared in high government circles in Washington.

# PART III

## China and Korea Policy on the Eve of War

The rapid advance of the Communists in China sparked a major reappraisal of American East Asian policy. In mid-1949, an uneasy balance emerged in Washington between efforts to prevent the Communist victory from exerting a "domino" effect in Asia and tactics aimed at exploiting conflicts of interest between Peking and Moscow. On the one hand, the United States sought to prop up anti-Communist forces in Indochina and moved toward a separate peace treaty with Japan. On the other hand, the Truman administration refused to launch new aid programs to sustain anti-Communist groups on Taiwan or in southwestern China.

Conflicts within the executive branch remained a prominent element of the decision making process. The State and Defense departments clashed over the final withdrawal of troops from Korea and further efforts to contain Communism in China. The disagreements grew out of differing institutional perspectives. In Korea, the diplomats continued to believe that the United States had a major political commitment. In Taiwan and China, they perceived no such stake. Expanded involvement in those two areas promised only ultimate defeat and severe political embarrassment. Less sensitive to political than to physical considerations, and conscious of ever-expanding American obligations abroad in a time of limited defense budgets, some Pentagon officials viewed matters differently. To them, Taiwan was more important than Korea because of the island's logical place in an offshore defense perimeter in the western Pacific. Aid to anti-Communist forces in south and west China was cheap, and it might help block Chinese expansion into Southeast Asia. On Korea, military leaders had their way. American troops withdrew from the peninsula, and the Rhee regime, in the south, had to settle for limited economic and arms assistance. On China, however, the diplomats won out. American aid to Chiang Kai-shek remained token.

Despite the State Department's resistance to Pentagon adventurism in China, the tactic of encouraging Titoism there was never pursued diligently. American aid to Chiang was not terminated completely. United States recognition of his government continued. Communist overtures to American diplomats in China received cool treatment. After January 1950, the State Department was more intent on helping the French fight the Communist-led Vietminh in Indochina, and moving expeditiously toward a peace treaty with Japan, than on undermining a Moscow-Peking axis. By May, even the policy of negligible assistance to Chiang gained critical scrutiny. State Department officials increasingly flirted with military containment in Asia.

In early 1949, domestic political considerations and an underestimation of Communist capabilities in China discouraged full-fledged pursuit of the Titoist strategy. Then, irritation with Communist mistreatment of American diplomats and nonrecognition of alleged treaty obligations came to the forefront of administration calculations. To Dean Acheson, the new secretary of state, these instances of international lawlessness, if condoned, would undermine the very fabric of relations among nations. Thus ideology, reinforced by public and congressional pressures and uncertainties about Communist durability in China, blocked any diplomatic initiative aimed at wresting Mao from Stalin's grasp. The dualism in American Asian policy increasingly became weighted on the side of containing Communism to the east and south of China's borders.

This tendency, however, did not have an immediate impact on conditions in Korea. By June 1950, there was some activity in the State and Defense departments toward increased American military assistance to the Rhee regime. Yet this action came too late to avert the explosion on the peninsula that occurred during the early morning hours of 25 June. Fiscal conservatism in the White House, the preoccupation with events and needs elsewhere, bureaucratic squabbling, and intelligence blunders—all contributed to a failure in American policy that would result in momentous consequences for the United States and the world at large.

# 4

## Letting the Dust Settle: China Policy on the Eve of War

### Old Personalities in New Positions

Although the presidency did not change hands with the inaugural ceremonies in Washington on 20 January 1949, changes did occur in top State Department personnel. Dean Acheson replaced Marshall as secretary of state, and James Webb moved from the Budget Bureau to succeed Robert Lovett as under secretary. The shift brought no modification in the influence of the department in foreign policymaking. Truman had full confidence in both men.

The new secretary, a graduate of Yale and the Harvard Law School, was a dapper man who exuded the self-confident smugness often exhibited by members of the Eastern intellectual establishment. Yet the down-to-earth chief executive, who possessed a traditional Midwestern suspicion of such people, got along well with Acheson. In his capacity as under secretary of state between August 1945 and July 1947, Acheson had worked closely with the president. After the frequent deviousness and condescension of Roosevelt, he found Truman's simple directness refreshing.[1] As acting secretary of state while James Byrnes traveled abroad, Acheson had acquired a clear understanding of Truman's expectations regarding his leading adviser in foreign affairs.[2]

As director of the Bureau of the Budget for more than three years, Webb also had worked closely with the president. Although Acheson respected Webb's abilities, he accepted him as his chief assistant largely at Truman's suggestion.[3] Unlike Lovett, Webb had little prior experience in world politics. His influence was to be less in policymaking than in the areas of reorganizing the department and maintaining communications with the White House while Acheson was out of the country.

If the State Department would work smoothly with the White House during Truman's full term of office, the Acheson regime was not destined to have an amicable relationship with Congress. This was ironic, for in the past both the secretary and his top assistant had enjoyed extensive and largely successful relations with the legislative branch. In 1944 and 1945, Acheson had served effectively as assistant secretary for congressional relations.[4] Webb had spent much time on Capitol Hill during his directorship of the Budget Bureau. Yet a variety of forces made unlikely the continued high level of bipartisanship in foreign affairs that had evolved over the past two years.

The results of the recent elections both embittered the Republicans, who had felt certain of victory in the presidential race, and emboldened the Democrats, whose restraint during the Eightieth Congress had rested in the needs of the moment rather than in any transcendent belief in the virtue of bipartisanship. Whereas the minority party's determination to exploit the China issue became apparent only over a period of months, Democratic independence appeared almost immediately. In early January, the majority party in the Senate increased its own representation on the Foreign Relations Committee from seven to eight and lowered that of the GOP from six to five. This move was aimed at satisfying J. William Fulbright (Democrat-Arkansas), who had long desired membership in that powerful and prestigious group. The act was unnecessary from the standpoint of policy because Vandenberg's choice for the sixth Republican seat would have been Wayne L. Morse of Oregon, a sympathizer with recent administration moves abroad.[5] Republican consternation mounted when Truman announced Acheson's appointment without first consulting GOP leaders. This fact took on added significance because the president's choice was strongly associated with the Democratic party.[6] Vandenberg, who had been on intimate terms with Lovett, accepted the nomination without enthusiasm.[7]

The circumstances surrounding the election campaign of the previous fall already had damaged communications between the executive and legislative branches. Because Congress was not in session and most of its members were away from Washington tending to political chores in their home districts, policy development proceeded without the close interaction of past months between the Democratic administration and leading figures on Capitol Hill. This situation led to particular difficulties with regard to the creation of the North Atlantic Treaty Organization.[8]

Moreover, the Democratic victory in November resulted in a shift in the chairmanship of the Senate Foreign Relations Committee from Vandenberg to Tom Connally of Texas. Connally enjoyed long experience in Washington, but he lacked the Michigan senator's stature in both Congress and the press. The Texan's jealousy of his colleague made collaboration between the two difficult. Connally's mastery in debate of "sarcasm, irony, and ridicule" often left bitter memories, and his natural combativeness inclined him toward partisanship. His qualifications for maintaining unity within the committee were unimpressive.

At the same time, Acheson's personal characteristics were unlikely to smooth over ruffled feelings. The new secretary of state was always deferential to the president, out of respect for both the office and its occupant, but he often showed impatience with other politicians. H. Bradford Westerfield characterizes him as finding it "difficult to restrain himself from demolishing the arguments of congressional opponents with a swift incisiveness which seemed insulting."[9] His ready wit sometimes touched raw nerves among legislators who, as a rule, have limited capacities for laughing at themselves.[10] Acheson was once accused by a friend of an unwillingness to "suffer fools gladly."[11] The charge is a little unfair, yet Acheson's ability to tolerate knavery and stupidity in others certainly was less well developed than that of most others of his station. Unfortunately, he headed the State Department in a period that produced more than its share of fools, or at least of people disinclined to look favorably upon administration foreign policy (Acheson was never adept at distinguishing between the two groups). By the summer of 1950, his prickliness regarding criticism from Congress had reached a point where he would seek retribution via the agency of an "inexpertly aimed and executed swing" of his clenched fist at Senator Kenneth Wherry.[12]

Acheson also occasionally failed, as columnist James Reston suggested, to anticipate how his words would look in the next morning's newspapers.[13] Only a month after taking office, the secretary—in a meeting with several congressional critics of American policy toward China—described the situation in that country as difficult to comprehend "until the dust settles." The comment soon leaked to the press and served as a convenient source for the accusation that the Truman administration had a do-nothing policy toward China.[14]

Yet even the most conciliatory personality and most skillful manipulator of congressional opinion could not have avoided much of what was to come. On the day Acheson took office, Chiang Kai-shek, in a move that was more apparent than real, announced his retirement from the presidency of the National government. The event served to emphasize the Nationalists' plight in China. Despite the warnings in Congress of Judd, Bridges, and a few others, the extensive press coverage of the civil war, and the pessimistic testimony of Marshall before congressional committees in early 1948, Chiang's rapid decline surprised many people. Preoccupied with events in other areas of the world, with domestic issues and, from the spring of 1948 onward, with the Berlin crisis, most politicians devoted little attention to China until the Nationalist collapse in Manchuria in the months immediately preceding Acheson's assumption of office.

Two such men were Republican Senators William F. Knowland of California and H. Alexander Smith of New Jersey. Knowland's concern with China stemmed from a series of letters he had received in the fall of 1948 from Colonel Robert Griffin, an administrator of the economic aid program to the National government.[15] Early the next year, Knowland began to attack American China policy and to advocate new aid to Chiang, eventually acquiring the title "the senator from Formosa." The lateness of his conversion to Chiang's cause and the bitterly partisan nature of his efforts call his sincerity into question.[16] There is little doubt, however, of his influence in the Senate as an advocate of assistance to Nationalist China.

Smith's motives are less suspicious. Although never directing special attention to East Asia prior to late 1948, Smith was a longtime, if nominal, member of the Princeton-Yenching Foundation, which promoted educational and missionary projects in China. On 23 November 1947, in a speech before the Foreign Policy Association, he had advocated the inclusion of China in the Marshall Plan.[17] As a member of the Foreign Relations Committee the next year, however, he expressed no opposition to Marshall's presentation before that group. Smith was preoccupied at the time with the European Recovery Program, the Palestine question, and domestic issues.[18] By December 1948, the critical situation in China had gained his attention. He talked at some length to Lovett and Vandenberg, two men who had largely written off the country.[19] But Smith also consulted Stanley K. Hornbeck, a prominent China specialist and former chief of the Office of Far Eastern Affairs, and William Bullitt, both of whom believed that Chiang could hold off the Communists if given timely American aid.[20] Smith, whose deep religious faith matched his belief that the United States must exert leadership in the quest for international comity, veered in the ensuing weeks toward Hornbeck's analysis.[21] By late January 1949, the New Jersey senator had concluded that the United States must do something to halt the Communist advance in China.[22]

Smith and Knowland had plenty of company. On 7 February, fifty-one House Republicans wrote to Truman demanding the creation of a commission to reexamine American China policy.[23] Less than three weeks later, Senator Pat McCarran, a conservative Democrat from Nevada, introduced a bill calling for $1.5 billion in loans for the National government and for the sending of American officers to direct anti-Communist troops in the field.[24] In mid-March, fifty senators, including twenty-four Democrats, wrote to Connally urging prompt consideration of the bill.[25]

Actually, the McCarran proposal never had a chance for passage in either house, one of its faults being a provision for $500 million to enable the Nationalists to purchase silver in the United States. Purported by McCarran to be aimed at currency stabilization in China, this plan was obviously an effort to furnish some western states—especially Nevada—with a ready market for their large supply of silver.[26] McCarran, who was later appropriately described by Acheson as "a person who in the eighteenth century would not have been termed a man of sensibility," presented the bill without even going over its contents with Senate colleagues interested in China.[27] Yet the note to Connally indicated that the administration could not ignore the China issue.

Truman and Acheson already had shown considerable sensitivity to the domestic political implications of the developing situation in China. On 5 February 1949, the president met with the secretary of state, Vice-President Alben W. Barkley, Senators Connally and Vandenberg, and Representatives Sol Bloom and Charles Eaton. Two days earlier, the National Security Council, aware that in recent weeks large quantities of American arms had fallen into Communist hands, had recommended the suspension of further aid of this kind to the Nationalists.[28] Vandenberg, objecting strongly, argued that such action would eliminate any possibility of a negotiated settlement between the Nationalists, temporarily under the nominal leadership of Li Tsung-jen, and the Communists. This result, the senator asserted, would make it impossible for the United States "to shake off the charge that *we . . . gave China the final push into disaster.*" "This blood," he concluded dramatically, "must not be on our hands." Apparently, Barkley and the other legislators present agreed.[29] Truman followed their advice, but did order the delay of shipments of matériel whenever possible "without formal action."[30]

Acheson also kept in close contact with Senator Smith. In late January, Smith gave the secretary a memorandum written by a young friend, John Roots, who was the son of missionaries to China. Roots proposed an ideological approach to the China problem. To him, "the controlling fact" about the National government was not its "military incompetency, financial ineptitude, political disintegration, or current unpopularity with the masses." Rather, it was its susceptibility "to the same moral principles as we are." He viewed Chiang as "an Eastern leader who, with all his faults, will in the final count stand like a rock for the traditional values of Christendom and for those moral concepts at the heart of Christian democracy." The most pressing need, Roots claimed, was for the United States to instruct a select group of Chinese "in the elements of our ideology, [to] train them to propagate it in their own country, and [to] teach them how to apply it to the present emergency as well as the long-range future of Asia." This program would follow the Soviet model used successfully in China over the past twenty-five years.[31]

This romantic nonsense was most notable for its attractiveness to some prominent Americans. Smith was so impressed that he passed it along to several friends, both inside and outside the government.[32] Donald C. Stone, a top ECA official in Washington and former assistant director of the Budget Bureau, wrote Webb that "it was so refreshing and appeared to offer the only type of approach possible that I decided to hand it to you."[33] Robert P. Patterson, now practicing law on Wall Street, confessed to Smith his bafflement on the China question, but saw the Roots memorandum as offering "some ground for hope."[34]

## The Evolution of China Policy

The State Department was less impressed. Butterworth attacked Roots's paper on two major points. First, the former questioned the soundness of the Soviet approach. Communist doctrine, he asserted, had failed to attract "widespread Chinese support." Once Mao and his lieutenants had redistributed the nation's riches, they would face the task of creating wealth.

Their revolutionary ideology offered no panaceas in this field. Furthermore, the ultimate Russian objective in China was "the imposition of the alien Lenin-Stalin dogmas." Pursuit of this goal might "eventually conflict with aroused Chinese nationalism." The diplomat also criticized Roots's assertion that Chiang could serve as a rallying point around which anti-Communist forces could gather. An ideological approach, if feasible at all, would have to center on "younger, more progressive and more dynamic Chinese" rather than old Kuomintang leaders.[35]

This response revealed much of the framework for administration China policy, which was already in existence upon Acheson's assumption of office. Despite an appearance of relative simplicity in broad conception, its application to specific problems—the status of Taiwan, trade with the Communists, continuation of economic assistance to the Nationalists, and formal relations with an emergent Communist regime—underscored its basic complexity.

During the fall of 1948, the State Department queried the Joint Chiefs on the strategic significance of Taiwan and the Pescadores. The military leaders replied that the rise of a Kremlin-oriented, Communist government on Taiwan "would be seriously unfavorable" to the United States. American domination of the sea routes between Japan and Malaya would decline, and the "enemy capability of extending his control to the Ryukyus and the Philippines" would "greatly" improve. Japan would lose an important source of food and raw materials, which would make it more of a liability than an asset in the event of war. Economic and diplomatic measures should be undertaken to keep Taiwan and the surrounding islands in friendly hands.[36] In February of the following year, the Joint Chiefs reiterated this opinion, but, in view of the disparity between American military strength and global obligations, they advised against an "overt military commitment" to the defense of the area. They proposed only that the navy station certain fleet units at Taiwanese ports.[37]

The State Department agreed with the Joint Chiefs' appraisal of the strategic importance of Taiwan, and with the recommendation that efforts should be made in the diplomatic and economic spheres to prevent its fall to the Communists. Thus, Acheson proposed that the United States "seek to develop and support a local non-Communist Chinese regime which will provide at least a modicum of decent government for the islands [Pescadores as well as Taiwan]." In pursuit of this goal, he continued, it should be made "discreetly plain" to authorities there that Washington was not "impressed" by Chinese rule on the islands since World War II. The United States disapproved of the increasing influx of Chinese refugees from the mainland and rejected the belief that "an effective barrier to Communist penetration" would emerge merely through a military buildup on Taiwan. American support for those in power would depend upon their overall efficiency and their willingness to respond favorably to indigenous needs and desires. For the present, economic assistance allocated under the China Aid Act should continue, and, if a non-Communist government showed promise of providing stable and efficient rule on the islands, a larger program might eventually be launched.[38]

In late February, Acheson sent Livingston Merchant, the counselor at the American embassy in Nanking, to Taipei to study conditions there and to advise the State Department regarding the possibility of detaching Taiwan from the mainland. Li Tsung-jen, the acting president of the National government, was now negotiating with the Communists in an attempt to end the civil war, and the talks could result in a deal that would rule out American action to keep the island out of hostile hands. The continued presence of Chen Cheng as governor of Taiwan might also prevent a major American move. Chen was loyal to Chiang and had little apparent interest in reform, but the secretary of state wanted to explore all options, including such maneuvers as promoting Taiwanese autonomy in the United Nations, supporting indigenous independence forces on the island, or arranging for the appointment of a competent Nationalist official such as Sun Li-jen, the commander in chief of Chinese Army Training Headquarters, or K. C. Wu, the mayor of Shanghai, as governor of Taiwan.[39]

Acheson opposed the Joint Chiefs' proposal to send American ships to Taiwanese ports, however, and in so doing he revealed a determination to avoid futile action that would reduce American flexibility later on. He argued that, despite the ideological affinity of Mao with the Kremlin, Russian penetration in Manchuria and Sinkiang would eventually lead to a Sino-Soviet rift. Any overt American move aimed at separating Taiwan from the mainland would turn irredentist sentiments in China away from the northern provinces and toward the island. This would compromise efforts to prevent China from becoming "an adjunct of Soviet power." Furthermore, by taking advantage of Taiwanese dissatisfaction with Nationalist rule and the general demoralization of anti-Communist forces, the Communists might capture the island without a massive invasion from the mainland. If American diplomatic and economic maneuvering proved inadequate to keep Taiwan out of hostile hands, only United States occupation of the island and a naval blockade to isolate it from the continent could achieve that purpose.[40]

Economic assistance to Taiwan presented fewer liabilities than overt military action, however limited. Imports of food and fertilizer were less inciting than the movement of battleships, which involved American prestige. American cargoes of a nonmilitary nature had been going to Taiwan for some time. Their continuation in modest numbers was not likely to influence significantly Communist attitudes toward the United States. Moreover, economic aid to Taiwan came under the general program of assistance to China. Abrupt termination of this program would lead to a breakdown of the economies of cities on the central and southern coast of the mainland. This would undermine the National government in its efforts to negotiate an end to the civil war and result in serious hardships for millions of Chinese, hardships that would be blamed on the United States.[41] Thus, shipments to the continent would continue to accompany aid to Taiwan.

Added to these considerations was the political setting in the United States. Pro-Nationalist forces in and outside of Congress already were pressing for expanded aid to China. With the experience of trying to cut off military assistance behind them and that of attempting to push through Congress a framework for Western European defense immediately ahead, administration leaders sought to avoid a confrontation with the China bloc. In March, as the termination date approached for the commitment of funds through the China Aid Act, and more than $100 million of the appropriation remaining unobligated, the president asked Congress to continue the program. He did seek more freedom in dispensing the assistance as well as the separation of funds for China from the legislation to renew the Marshall Plan. Congress extended the deadline for committing money from 3 April 1949 to 5 February 1950, but Senator Knowland successfully led moves to combine the bills for Western Europe and China and to restrict the distribution of aid to areas not in Communist hands.[42]

The question of trade with the Chinese Communists remained outside the realm of domestic politics. In late February 1949, Acheson presented a lengthy paper on commercial relations with China to the National Security Council. The overriding objective of American policy, the State Department argued, was to undermine Soviet influence. In the past, Chinese trade had been largely with Japan and the West, but Moscow probably would seek to alter this "historic pattern." Russia's limited willingness and capacity for meeting China's needs, plus its desire to exploit the resources of Manchuria and Sinkiang, could lead to cracks in the Sino-Soviet relationship. If the United States took a severely restrictive line on trade with the Communists, however, China would become increasingly dependent on its northern neighbor. In any event, the experience of Russia following its revolution indicated that "a determined and ruthless leadership can survive and even consolidate itself in the face of extreme economic hardships aggravated by the imposition of external restrictions and embargoes." Even if economic sanctions could stall or prevent the Communist rise to power in China, little chance existed of creating a Western front of sufficient unity to be effective. Finally, trade between China and Japan was important in the latter's quest for economic self-sufficiency. If Japan failed in this effort, it would remain dependent on large-scale aid from the United States. The United States should attempt to halt only those goods going into China that might be used by the Communists for military purposes.[43]

The issue of political relations with a Chinese Communist regime was closely tied to commercial matters. The Communists might survive a Western economic boycott, but State Department officials believed that the new masters of China would at least temporarily want trade with the capitalist powers.[44] Yet, during late 1948 and early 1949, as the Communists moved into cities of Manchuria and North China in which American consular personnel resided, they refused to acknowledge the official standing of the representatives of foreign governments. Communist leaders also announced their intention to abrogate U.S. treaties with Nationalist China.

American officials deeply resented this attitude. Not only were representatives of the United States accustomed to favored treatment in China, they, as well as top policymakers in Washington, regarded the upholding of treaty obligations as "basic to relations among modern States."[45] This view, together with the belief that, for commercial reasons, the Communists would soon adopt a less extreme course, produced a tough position regarding the formal recognition of Peking. As Ambassador Stuart put it, "the Communists, rather than nations with well-established tradition[s] and accepted international standards," should be placed "on trial."[46] In early May 1949, Acheson decided that the United States should not initiate moves toward recognition, and he instructed American officials to impress upon Western European governments the desirability of developing a "common front" on the issue.[47] Weeks before the secretary, responding to political pressures at home, outlined publicly the criteria for establishing political relations, he privately had adopted the Jeffersonian model. A Communist regime would be judged in three areas: its capacity to control the territory it purported to govern, its "ability and willingness . . . to discharge its international obligations," and the "general acquiescence" of the people of the country under its rule.[48]

This attitude led to rejection of an apparent opportunity for an American official to talk directly to Mao and other top men in Peking. Ironically, just after the United States moved to create a united front among the Western powers on the recognition question, Huang Hua, head of the Communist Alien Affairs Bureau in Nanking, approached Ambassador Stuart. On 13 May, the two men talked for nearly two hours. Raising the matter of recognition, Huang expressed much interest in Communist relations with the United States on a basis of "equality and mutual benefit." Stuart outlined the criteria recently established in Washington. The Chinese official then apologized for a recent incident in which Communist soldiers had trespassed on Stuart's living quarters.[49]

Then, at the end of the month, Chou En-lai, a powerful figure in the Chinese Communist Party, made an indirect approach to the American consulate general at Peking through Michael Keon, an Australian journalist employed by the United Press. Chou talked of a division within the Communist camp between a liberal group, of which he was a leader, and a radical faction, headed by Liu Shao-chi. The liberals desired friendly relations with the Western democracies, especially the United States and Great Britain, as a means of obtaining the assistance necessary for economic reconstruction at home. The radicals demurred, desiring a close alliance with the Soviet

Union.[50] The State Department authorized O. Edmund Clubb, the consul general at Peking, to respond that Washington hoped for amicable relations with the new China on the basis of "mutual respect" and "equality," but was deeply disturbed by Communist treatment of American representatives in the country and propaganda attacks on the United States.[51] President Truman approved this reply, though he emphasized that Clubb must avoid any indication of a "softening" American attitude toward the Communists.[52] When Clubb sought to transmit the message directly to Chou or his secretary, however, the Communist leader abruptly broke off contact.[53]

In the meantime, Stuart's talks with Huang in Nanking had continued. On 28 June, only days after Chou had squelched his own initiative in Peking, Huang told the ambassador that Mao would welcome him in the northern city if he wished to visit Yenching University. This proposal was a response to a query from Philip Fugh, Stuart's secretary and confidant, regarding the feasibility under present circumstances of the ambassador's annual July pilgrimage to his former school. Stuart immediately cabled Washington for instructions. In the State Department, both Butterworth and John Paton Davies considered the invitation to be significant, but they feared the domestic reaction if Stuart accepted. They proposed to skirt this problem. The ambassador could stop in Peking after traveling to Mukden to pick up Angus Ward, the American consul general there, who, along with his staff, was being held under house arrest; or Washington could announce that Stuart had gone to Peking to read Communist leaders "the riot act" regarding mistreatment of American diplomats.[54]

On 1 July, however, Acheson wired Stuart and stated that a decision had been reached at the "highest level" against a journey to Peking.[55] Communist attitudes toward American officials in China, of which the Ward case was only the most extreme expression, and toward treaties concluded by the National government, were foremost in reaching this verdict. On 16 June 1949, President Truman had instructed Webb to be "most careful not to indicate any softening toward the Communists but to insist on judging their intentions by their actions."[56] A trip by Stuart to Peking also might have disrupted American efforts to unite Western governments on a cautious policy regarding recognition, and, to Acheson, a united front was a prerequisite to applying effective pressure on the Communists.[57] Moreover, the Communists had not yet officially proclaimed themselves the government of China. The United States continued to recognize the National government. A trip to Peking by the American ambassador could not be kept secret, and Stuart was known to be inclined to deviate from instructions.[58] His journey would detract from the already diminished prestige of the Nationalists and bolster the Communists at a time when their capacity to rule China remained uncertain.[59] In a narrow legal sense, talks between the United States and a Chinese party, against the wishes of the recognized government, were inappropriate.

From the standpoint of politics in the United States, the trip would add fuel to the already intense attacks from Capitol Hill on Truman administration China policy. On 24 June, twenty-two Senators, including six Democrats, sent a letter to the president urging him to withhold recognition of the Communists.[60] A week later, on the very day that the proposed Stuart trip to Peking was rejected, Acheson wrote to Senator Connally outlining the previously established criteria for recognition; the secretary assured him he would consult the Foreign Relations Committee before acting on the matter.[61] The North Atlantic Treaty was then before the Senate, and the military assistance program, considered essential to give teeth to the pact, had not yet been sent to Congress. The specter, which had been so pervasive in late 1947 and early 1948, of a China bloc on Captol Hill withholding support for critical enterprises in Europe, reappeared.

Yet domestic political concerns probably only reinforced Truman's and Acheson's inclination against the Huang overture. Had they believed that a major opportunity was at hand to advance American interests in China, they surely would have moved with less dispatch to stifle it. Certainly they would have explored the possibility of using Clubb at Peking to initiate talks with Communist leaders, a procedure that stood an excellent chance of remaining secret. If revealed to the public, it could be explained away, both to international lawyers and hostile politicians, far more easily than the Stuart trip. In all likelihood, Acheson advised Truman to reject the Huang initiative, and the president, already inclined in that direction, agreed. To them, a more positive response might encourage the Communists to persist in their aggressive behavior toward American officials in China, and undermine administration efforts to maintain a united Western front on recognition.

Both temperamentally and intellectually, Acheson was poorly suited to deal in an astute manner with the Communists. For one thing, he was preoccupied with the European theater. It was there, he felt, that the great issues of international politics would be played out. Furthermore, as Dean Rusk noted many years later, Acheson never had much respect for Asian peoples.[62] He was a Europeanist not only in American foreign policy, but in culture as well. Finally, he had a passion for order. "In fact, I was always a conservative," he was to declare in 1969: "I sought to meet the Soviet menace and help create some order out of the world. I was seeking stability and never had much use for revolution. As a friend once said, we had plenty of chaos, but not enough to make a world."[63] From this perspective, it was up to Communist China to demonstrate its worthiness to enter into the family of nations. Although the secretary of state was far from inflexible on China policy, neither was he anxious to explore every possible opportunity for constructive relations with the Communists.

Acheson's subordinates in the State Department and in China were little more flexible than their boss. Although Davies strained to find a way of arranging for the Stuart trip to Peking without damaging the Truman administration at home, he regarded the visit primarily as an opportunity for the ambassador to give the Communists a "curtain lecture" on their treatment of American officials in China. Born in that country to American missionary parents, Davies had served there for much of World War II and had urged his superiors in Washington to avoid an alliance with Chiang that would rule out friendly relations with the Communists.[64] To Davies, they were not inherently hostile to the United States and knew that "no government in China can hope to survive without American support."[65] By the summer of 1949, however, it appeared that the Communists would need help in learning this lesson, and Davies was an impatient instructor. In August, he even proposed that the Defense Department consider using "selective" air strikes in China as a means of moderating Communist behavior.[66]

Philip Sprouse, at the head of the Division of Chinese Affairs, was appalled by this suggestion, but he and his colleagues, both in Washington and in the field, were unanimous in their determination to avoid any appearance of weakness in the face of obnoxious Communist conduct.[67] Clubb "recommend[ed] most earnestly" that Stuart go to Peking only if there was a "categorical assurance from [the] Commie side that [a] meeting [is] arranged." Clubb feared that Mao and Chou would decline to receive Stuart and, therefore, that the pilgrimage would be a great blow "to American prestige."[68]

Few American decisions toward China in the postwar period were as unfortunate as the outright rejection of the Huang overture. To be sure, much of Communist behavior in preceding months evinced strong hostility toward the United States. Then, on 1 July—and probably unknown to Truman and Acheson at the time of their decision—Mao published an essay, "On People's Democratic Dictatorship," in which he asserted that the United States was the "one great imperialist power" remaining on earth. Because America sought "to enslave the world," he claimed, China must ally itself "with the Soviet Union, with every New Democratic country, and with the proletariat and broad masses in all other countries."[69]

Such statements, however, do not eliminate the possibility that a careful probing of Peking's position in the summer of 1949 could have been useful to the United States. As John M. Cabot, the outspoken American consul general in Shanghai, observed, "Virulent anti-American propaganda is natural in view of our aid to the Nationalists."[70] That aid was ineffectual in sustaining the Nationalists in China, but it added significantly to the anti-Communist resistance there. Even so, Communist leaders expressed interest in relations with the United States. On 15 June, Mao stated in a speech that his regime was

> willing to discuss with any foreign government the establishment of diplomatic relations on the basis of the principles of equality, mutual benefit and mutual respect for territorial integrity and sovereignty, pro-

vided it is willing to sever relations with the Chinese reactionaries, stops conspiring with them or helping them and adopts an attitude of genuine, and not hypocritical, friendship towards People's China.[71]

Other evidence existed that the Communists were, as Stuart put it, "far from a Soviet Punch and Judy show."[72] Clearly they were not anxious to eliminate the American presence in China. Throughout 1949, the Communist attitude toward American missionaries encouraged them to remain in China.[73] Some American-owned businesses had similar experiences. Relations between the Peking regime and the Shanghai Power Company, for instance, remained smooth for months after the May 1949 Communist takeover of Shanghai.[74]

Talks with Communist leaders could have served a variety of purposes. They could have been used to protest the treatment of American representatives in China. To avoid conveying a sense of American weakness or desperation, the United States could have held to a firm position on this issue. Top officials in Peking might well have demonstrated flexibility on the matter. It was by no means certain, after all, either then or later, that the harassment of American officials represented a centrally coordinated policy of the Communists or merely the independent acts of local forces.[75]

Acheson could have minimized confusion and resentment among Western European nations by keeping their leaders informed of the proceedings. The mere fact of discussions in Peking need not have detracted from caution and unity on the recognition question. In fact, Peking talks might actually have strengthened Western harmony. If they went poorly, tendencies, already apparent in Great Britain and France, to open relations with the Communists once they formed a government, might have been weakened.[76]

On the other hand, conversations in Peking might have been a basic step toward mutual toleration between Communist China and the West. Washington's failure to pursue discussions diminished such prospects. As Cabot noted, the out-and-out rejection of the Huang overture may "have placed those Communists favoring better relations with the West in an impossible situation."[77] The American response was especially damaging because the ambassador's secretary had initiated the idea of a Stuart visit to Peking. The Communists probably viewed the suggestion as a concrete overture by the United States.[78] When Washington squelched it, therefore, Peking was understandably embarrassed and displeased. Indeed, between July and September 1949 there emerged little new evidence that Communist leaders desired a "working relationship with the United States." Even Chou En-lai made strong anti-American speeches.[79] And Communist officials in Mukden, who on 21 June had notified Ward that transportation facilities would be made available for him and his staff to leave the city, hardened their position toward the American diplomat.[80] Although a variety of considerations may have dictated against Stuart traveling to Peking, Acheson should at least have communicated to the Communists that the United States desired talks but wanted, for the present, to pursue them through Clubb.

Direct contacts between the United States and the Communist Chinese were especially desirable in view of continued American aid to Chiang. In the absence of diplomatic exchanges between Peking and Washington, Communist leaders inevitably saw an American plot behind every Nationalist move. In late June, for example, in an effort to impede Communist efforts to rule China, the Nationalists blockaded Shanghai. The action consisted of both air and naval maneuvers to prevent foreign ships from unloading cargoes there.[81] Although the United States did not approve the move, the Communists soon labeled it as American-inspired.[82] This characterization may have been part of a Communist strategy of exploiting popular resentments against foreigners for the purpose of building unity at home. But past American support for the Nationalists—which continued, albeit at a low level—coupled with Washington's rejection of Peking's overtures, made it just as likely that the Communists truly believed that the United States was responsible for the blockade.

In addition to the possibility that talks would have increased Communist understanding of the American position, they also might have added to the Truman administration's grasp of events in China. Washington's perceptions of the Communists already had suffered from insufficient contact. Although the State Department had tentatively concluded—perhaps in part because of the recent example of Yugoslavia—that, in a positive sense, there was little the United States could or need do to influence Communist relations with the Soviet Union, more extensive knowledge might have led to a different judgment.[83] As *New York Times* correspondent Seymour Topping has noted, even if the Truman administration could not have influenced Mao "to adopt a neutral position in the East-West struggle," conversations with the Communist leader might have "led at least to the establishment of a channel of communication between Peking and Washington." "If Americans had continued to talk to the Chinese Communists," Topping maintains, "many of the misunderstandings and much of the agony in Asia over the next two decades might have been averted."[84]

## Chennault Mobilizes the China Bloc

While the Truman administration pondered such issues as the future of Taiwan, continued trade with China, and the recognition of an emerging Communist regime, the China bloc in Congress struggled to unite on, then to push through the legislative branch, a program aimed at keeping part of the mainland out of Communist hands. Although neither the McCarran bill nor the Roots approach gained broad support, General Claire Chennault soon came forth with a plan that would gain widespread attention on Capitol Hill throughout the summer of 1949.

Chennault, of Flying Tiger fame, enjoyed the advantages of a well-known name associated with China and of extensive contacts with congressmen and prominent pro-Nationalist elements in private life. Until returning to the United States in late April 1949, he was in China operating his Civil Air Transport Company. One of the ways his name and ideas were kept before the American public, however, was publication by G. P. Putnam's Sons of his *Way of a Fighter* on 31 January 1949. The volume included a passionate appeal for immediate action by the United States to halt the Communist surge in Asia. Chennault proposed "small, carefully selected military aid" for the Nationalists as well as the commitment of some "technically skilled and imaginative leaders" to advise friendly forces. Such assistance would make possible "a holding action" to keep the lower Yangtze Valley out of enemy hands.[85]

Chennault also kept abreast of renewed efforts to organize pro-Nationalist lobbying groups in Washington. In January, supporters of the Nationalists, led by Frederick C. McKee, a Pittsburgh industrialist, and William J. Goodwin, a paid lobbyist, organized a series of dinners in Washington and New York. Many wealthy and influential businessmen attended these extravaganzas, including several members of the American China Policy Association. The activities led, in early March, to formation of the China Emergency Committee, which advocated new appropriations for the National government, and even suggested that Chennault should receive combat planes for a new Flying Tigers squadron. Americans should be permitted to join such a group, the sponsors argued, without losing their citizenship. Chennault stayed in touch with all these initiatives by corresponding with William Arthur, a Pittsburgh advertising executive. Arthur also was executive vice-president of the Fourteenth Air Force Association, a group that had been formed during 1948 to keep up contacts among fliers who had served under Chennault. When Chennault arrived in Washington in April 1949, therefore, he was enthusiastically supported by many people who were already seeking to alter the so-called "Marshall approach" to American China policy.[86]

Senator Knowland helped Chennault gain access to key congressional bodies. On 3 May, the general testified before the Senate Armed Services Committee and the Joint Committee on Foreign Economic Cooperation and presented a scheme designed to keep Chinese provinces in the west and south out of Communist hands. The plan called for military assistance to several warlords in these regions in the form of weapons, ammunition, and American flyers and advisers. Food and fertilizer also would be provided. Chennault had recently visited these areas and believed that great potential existed for organized resistance to the Communists. Leaders there had armies numbering in the hundreds of thousands. To reach them, the Communists would have to penetrate vast expanses of rugged mountains. An effective program of defense could be established, Chennault believed, "at a cost per year [to the United States] not exceeding the Berlin airlift."[87] Although the latter project had cost approximately $350 million, he later estimated that between $100 and $200 million annually would be adequate.[88]

The Chennault plan received wide press coverage. The *New York Times* reported his testimony on its front page.[89] The Hearst chain also gave his views an extensive airing.[90] In late May and early June, the widely read columnist Stewart Alsop expressed sympathy for Chennault's plan.[91] On 11 July, *Life* magazine published an article by the former "Flying Tiger."[92] Later in the month, he appeared on radio interview shows with Senator Estes Kefauver (Democrat-Tennessee) and Representative F. Edward Hébert (Democrat-Louisiana).[93]

Chennault also expanded his contacts on Capitol Hill. His efforts found reinforcement in those of the China Emergency Committee, which now called itself the Committee to Defend America by Aiding Anti-Communist China. These activities were coordinated with some members of both houses, especially Knowland.[94] On 17 May, the California senator announced his intention to push for an amendment to include China in the forthcoming administration bill for military assistance to Western Europe.[95] Thus began a campaign that would last for more than four months.[96]

The military assistance bill did not reach a congressional committee until late July. In mid-June, however, when the administration nominated Walton Butterworth as assistant secretary of state for Far Eastern affairs, the proponents of aid to non-Communist forces in China had found an issue to which they could temporarily devote their attention. This nomination derived from a recent reorganization of the State Department in which the status of the head of the Office of Far Eastern Affairs rose to that of assistant secretary. Occupants of the position henceforth required confirmation by the upper house. Butterworth's participation in the Marshall mission, and his sympathy for the "Marshall approach" to China policy made him a logical object for attack by the China bloc.

The timing of the Butterworth nomination made a concerted attack on the move inevitable. On 11 May 1949, Chennault had discussed his proposals with State Department officials. Although his project received considerable attention from Deputy Under Secretary Dean Rusk, Philip Sprouse, and the staff of the American embassy in Nanking, they ultimately rejected it. The defense by non-Communist forces of Yunnan, a province that bordered on Indochina, was a key to the scheme, Stuart believed, but this objective was totally unrealistic. Minister-Counselor Lewis Clark contended that Chennault's ideas would help their author's airline business, but be of little use in furthering American interests.[97] Chennault and his backers recognized the State Department as the major stumbling block to the adoption of their views.[98] Preventing Butterworth's confirmation, therefore, became one step in the effort to transform that agency's outlook on China.

Senator Vandenberg's position gave momentum to the anti-Butterworth forces. Despite his failing health, the senior Republican on the Foreign Relations Committee remained critical to the success of administration efforts to preserve extensive bipartisan support for its foreign policies. In committee, Vandenberg voted "present" on the Butterworth nomination.[99] On the Senate floor, he expressed his regret that the administration had not chosen "to bring a fresh point of view" to the new position.[100] He may have been influenced by Senator Smith, also a strong advocate of bipartisanship in international affairs, who opposed Butterworth's confirmation.[101] The China bloc managed to hold up the nomination until late September, when Butterworth was approved in a highly partisan vote.[102]

The China issue also created difficulties for the military assistance program. On 28 July 1949, hearings before the House Foreign Affairs Committee had commenced on the bill. Congressmen Judd and Vorys launched a vicious attack on Acheson for failing to include aid for China in the legislation. Near the close of the proceedings, Frederick McKee testified and strongly criticized administration China policy.[103] Still, by a vote of 11-7, the committee rejected an amendment to provide $200 million in aid to the National government.[104] Representative John Davis Lodge (Republican-Connecticut) took the matter to the floor of the lower house, but it was again defeated, this time 164-94.[105]

Similar efforts also arose in the Senate, where the bill faced hearings before the combined Foreign Relations and Armed Services committees. On 10 August, with Smith of the former group and Knowland of the latter showing the way, an amendment emerged calling for $175 million in military assistance to non-Communist China. Unlike the House Foreign Affairs Committee, however, the joint Senate body passed the measure 13-12. This victory for the China bloc occurred because Democratic Senators Harry Byrd and Richard Russell crossed party lines to vote for the amendment.[106]

The issue remained unresolved well into September. On the ninth, two days after Connally and Knowland had engaged in a bitter debate on the Senate floor, the chairman of the Foreign Relations Committee offered a compromise amendment. The president would be given $75 million to use at his discretion in "China and the Far East." This change passed the joint committee by a straight party vote of 11-9.[107] In a final effort to break up the sharp partisan division, Vandenberg adjusted the wording of the Connally amendment to read "in the general area of China." Despite their continuing dissatisfaction, Republicans on the Foreign Relations and Armed Services committees voted unanimously in favor of the measure.[108] The Vandenberg maneuver also substantially reduced interparty recrimination in both houses over the final passage of the Mutual Defense Assistance Act in early October.[109]

The outcome was a victory for the administration. The executive branch was under no obligation to spend any of the $75 million in China. The sum, in fact, gave the administration the flexibility it desired in its China policy. Despite the State Department's rejection of the Chennault plan, the diplomats viewed a "contingency fund" as desirable for the exploitation of possible opportunities to undermine the Communists.[110] In Senate committee hearings, Acheson had even suggested that the president be given a sum to use at his discretion.[111]

Truman could also spend the appropriated money in areas surrounding China, which would give the administration added latitude in its attempt to halt Communism at China's borders. On 18 July, the secretary of state had instructed Ambassador-at-Large Philip C. Jessup to draft possible programs for the containment of Communism in Asia.[112] American strategists were particularly concerned about the situation in Indochina, where Communist Ho Chi Minh led a rebellion against the French. Nevertheless, the United States had withheld support for non-Communist groups there, and Acheson believed that effective resistance to Ho's movement must be grounded in nationalist elements, not French colonial aspirations. In March 1949, Paris had concluded agreements with Emperor Bao Dai that purported to grant an Indochinese government a degree of autonomy within a French Union. This move stirred some hopes in the State Department, which had no desire to see the old colonial power withdraw completely. Acheson insisted that Bao's regime demonstrate its ability to attract popular support before American aid was extended, but Mao's continuing advance in China made a reevaluation of this posture more and more likely, especially after the French parliament ratified the March agreements.[113]

If the legislative result of the China bloc's campaign actually furthered the administration's desires, the maneuvering and debate within Congress revealed to the White House some bothersome trends. They demonstrated, for instance, the uncertain future of bipartisanship in foreign affairs. For several months, Acheson had personally cultivated Senator Smith. Yet the New Jerseyan took a major role in the campaign to include China in the legislation.[114] The possible alienation of such a staunch advocate of interparty cooperation could not be taken lightly, especially in the face of Vandenberg's uncertain health.

Despite Acheson's herculean efforts to justify American China policy since World War II, committee votes on amendments to the military assistance bill indicated that a growing number of legislators questioned the administration's course. In addition to meeting frequently with congressional leaders to discuss the matter, the secretary of state decided in the spring to have the State Department compose for publication a lengthy treatise on the subject. It was released on 5 August under the title *United States Relations with China with Special Reference to the Period 1944–1949*. The work, which included a narrative of 409 pages and an even longer compilation of documents, sought to demonstrate that, as Acheson asserted in a letter of transmittal, "the ominous result of the civil war in China was beyond the control . . . of the United States."[115] Yet congressional attacks on Truman's China policy only intensified. Acheson, who was characterized by Supreme Court Justice Felix Frankfurter as "a frustrated schoolteacher, persisting against overwhelming evidence to the contrary in the belief that the human mind could be moved by facts and reason," surely came to regard the so-called *China White Paper* as one of his less successful instructional enterprises.[116]

In the final analysis, however, the outcome of the proceedings on the military assistance bill disclosed that the administration was in a stronger position in Congress than it had been in early 1948. Unlike in the earlier period, the State Department avoided sending to Capitol Hill an essentially distasteful aid program for non-Communist forces in China. Despite the growth of the China bloc in size and vocalness, its threat to administration programs in Western Europe had declined. The shift of control in Congress from the Republicans to the Democrats was important in this development, as was the increasingly widespread sense of Western insecurity in Europe— which gained added impetus in mid-September 1949 when the president announced that the Russians had exploded an atomic device. At the same time, a Gallup survey showed that nearly twice as many of those Americans questioned opposed further aid to anti-Communists in China than favored such action.[117]

## The Recognition Issue

In the fall, attention shifted, both inside and outside the administration, to the questions of American recognition of the "People's Republic," which was proclaimed in Peking on 1 October, and to aid for the Nationalists to defend Taiwan. From 6 through 8 October, the State Department held a conference on recognition, an event that grew out of work by a study group that had been created in August to review American policy in Asia. The group included Jessup, Everett Case, the president of Colgate University, and Raymond Fosdick, former president of the Rockefeller Foundation.[118] The last two were outsiders to the State Department and all three were relative neophytes on the problems of the western Pacific, but these facts actually enhanced their status in the eyes of many of those dissatisfied with American China policy. One of the projects recommended by the study group entailed bringing together a number of prominent people in private life to discuss the recognition issue.[119]

Among those in attendance at the conference were General Marshall, Harold Stassen, the president of the University of Pennsylvania and past Republican governor of Minnesota, and Edwin O. Reischauer, a Harvard professor. Although Stassen argued for a delay of a minimum of two years, a majority of the twenty-four guest participants favored the early establishment of relations with the Communist government.[120] The conference made little impact on State Department policy, however, for on 12 October Acheson reiterated to the Senate Foreign Relations Committee the guidelines on recognition that he had adopted five months earlier.[121] As before, the secretary of state regarded the Communist regime's unwillingness to uphold "international obligations" as a major stumbling block to recognition.

The State Department position remained firm, even in the face of urgings to the contrary from the field. Clubb transmitted a letter from Foreign Minister Chou En-lai declaring the formation of a government and expressing a desire to establish relations with all countries.[122] The consul general at Peking recommended that the United States take advantage of this opening to approach the Communists on a variety of issues.[123] "There seems good reason to believe," he observed, that "Communist leaders truly desire American recognition and [the] regularization [of] relations for both political and economic reasons." He also noted that since 1 October little anti-American material had appeared in the local press.[124] Alan G. Kirk, the American ambassador in Moscow, agreed with Clubb that the new government should be approached.[125] But Acheson permitted Clubb to use the Chou letter only as a pretext for reiterating American concern over the welfare of its consul staff at Mukden.[126]

The administration's top priority was to maintain a united front against early recognition. The American effort faced serious difficulties, for the Labor government in Great Britain, in the face of pressures from commercial interests at home, leaned toward the establishment of relations with the Mao government.[127] India's Prime Minister Jawaharlal Nehru also favored quick action.[128] A succession of other Western European and Asian governments undoubtedly would follow the British and Indian lead. Rather than planning to move with the tide, Acheson summoned his persuasive powers in an attempt to reverse it. He failed in the endeavor; India recognized the People's Republic in December, and Great Britain took the same course a week later. By 18 January 1950, nine more non-Communist regimes had taken similar action.[129]

Acheson's stand enjoyed widespread congressional and public support. Gallup polls of the summer and fall of 1949 indicated that Americans with opinions on the matter—only about 60 percent of those questioned—opposed recognition by more than a two to one margin.[130] In late November, the Committee to Defend America by Aiding Anti-Communist China launched a "nationwide drive" against recognition with a rally at Carnegie Hall in New York. Several members of Congress attended the event.[131] On

29 December, Senator Connally, following the overwhelming opinion expressed in letters to him from private citizens, announced his opposition to recognition.[132]

James Reston, Washington correspondent for the *New York Times*, reported that State Department officials conceded in private that the domestic climate alone was delaying American recognition.[133] As earlier, however, this consideration merely reinforced Acheson's inclinations, for Communist China's comportment in international matters genuinely disturbed him. On 24 October 1949, Angus Ward was jailed in Mukden for an alleged assault on a former Chinese servant at the American consulate. The State Department managed to obtain his release a month later, but Communist aggressiveness toward American officials and property in China did not end.[134] On 14 January 1950, the Chinese government seized American consular compounds in Peking.[135] In response to this action, and to the termination two months later of American radio communications with its representatives on the mainland, the United States withdrew completely from China. To the secretary of state, these were only the most overt manifestations of a generally intolerable state of mind that prevailed within the new government. Although he did not desire to slam the door permanently on American recognition, a halt to the "active abuse of us" in Peking was a prerequisite to a reevaluation of his position.[136]

In early 1950, there was little movement on the question. Acheson toyed with the idea of using continued Nationalist air attacks on Shanghai—which often damaged American property—as a pretext for a total break with the Nationalist government, but such a break never occurred.[137] In March, on the eve of Clubb's final departure from Peking, the secretary of state suggested that the consul general seek "an informal discussion with high Commie authorities of outstanding points of friction" between the United States and the new regime. Acheson emphasized, however, that Clubb must avoid "any inference [that] such [a] discussion constituted [a] move toward recognition or is a preliminary to such a move," or that the overture resulted from Communist "pressure" or American "weakness."[138] Concern for American credibility abroad remained a barrier to flexible diplomacy.

In early April, Communist Chinese officials made it clear that termination of United States support for Chiang was a quid pro quo for talks on other issues.[139] For all practical purposes, this exchange closed the matter. Clubb left China before the end of the month. Intent on avoiding any implication that Communist pressure could soften American policy, Acheson held firmly to the view that the Mao regime must submit to generally accepted standards of international conduct before the United States would talk about halting aid to the Nationalists and recognizing Peking. If the domestic political factor was critical, it was so only in an indirect sense: the American failure during 1949 to abandon the Nationalists completely—which was partially a result of pressures at home—influenced the Communist attitude toward the United States which, in turn, shaped the State Department position on relations with the Mao regime.

Another factor early in the fall of 1949 concerned pockets of armed resistance to the Communists in China. Although American officials recognized the probable futility of such activity, they did not want to openly discourage it.[140] The desire remained strong to make the road to power of the Communists as rocky as possible. By mid-November, however, this consideration was no longer a significant impediment to recognition.[141]

Concern for resistance to Communism on China's borders continued to influence Acheson's deliberations.[142] On 16 December, he sent telegrams to his representatives in Southeast Asia requesting their views on the impact of American recognition.[143] In the next two weeks, the secretary received replies from the consul general in Saigon, the chargé in Burma, and the ambassadors to Thailand and the Philippines. All of them emphasized the negative impact early recognition might have on efforts to bolster anti-Communist forces south and east of China's borders.[144] This negative consideration took on decisive weight when combined with the prevailing State Department view that little could be done, in a positive vein, to alter the essentially hostile attitude of the Communists toward the United States.

From a domestic political standpoint, the Truman administration's best opportunity to talk to Peking was in the last months of 1949. The Communist government had been officially established, and the Atlantic pact and the Military Assistance Plan had passed Congress. Public and congressional opinion did not necessitate a negative policy on recognition. In October, for instance, the State Department's Office of Public Opinion Studies reported that "most observers" in the press, while seeing "little need for haste, . . . expected eventual *de facto* recognition as the most 'realistic' course."[145] Even after the Ward case made headlines in late October, most commentators "did not discount the possibility or desirability of recognition at some time in the future."[146] Most Asian experts in the academic community, most Protestant church organizations, and many businessmen with interests in China favored early recognition.[147] Admittedly, Catholic organizations and much of organized labor disagreed, as did large pluralities of those Americans queried by pollsters.[148] The firmness of much of this opposition, however, especially in the general citizenry, may be doubted. Recognizing Peking would not take money or jobs away from many Americans, nor would it lead directly to physical setbacks to the security of the United States. Surely a public-relations offensive by the administration in favor of recognition would have had some impact.

Furthermore, if the hostility of the Chinese Communists toward the United States was related to American hostility toward them, and if the antagonism of many Americans toward recognition derived in part from Peking's antagonism to the United States, then American overtures to Mao might have led ultimately to a decline of public opposition to relations with the new government. In the absence of American initiatives toward Peking, on the other hand, Communist hostility was virtually certain to continue, as was the tendency of the American public to oppose recognition. In fact, much can be said for the argument that the Truman administration's best chance of overcoming the charge that it had "lost" China rested in the cautious but active pursuit of rapprochement with the Communists.

What were the prospects for rapprochement? Although the hostile acts in Mukden in late October 1949 and in Peking in the following January indicated to many the total hostility of the Communists, it remains uncertain that the incidents reflected decisions by a unified national leadership. One plausible explanation of the Ward affair is that Kao Kang, the pro-Russian head of the Northeastern People's Government, which was seated in Mukden—a government that had been established in late August and that temporarily maintained a degree of autonomy—took the action without prior approval from Peking.[149] Clubb believed that the Soviet Union had instigated Ward's arrest in retaliation for the prosecution in the United States of Valentin Gubichev, a Russian citizen who the Kremlin asserted had diplomatic immunity.[150] The State Department's Office of European Affairs suspected a direct connection between the Ward case and the October 1949 arrest in the United States of officials in the Soviet-owned Amtorg Trading Corporation for failing to register as foreign agents.[151] Whatever the reasons for Ward's arrest, its occurrence so soon after Clubb had seen evidence that the Communists genuinely desired to establish relations with the United States suggests that powerful forces were pulling in opposite directions within China. Whether or not the United States could have influenced the situation remains a mystery. It is certain, however, that in October 1949 the State Department rejected an opportunity to explore the possibility.

Initially, Clubb, based on information from a "reliable source," interpreted events in Peking during January 1950 as representing a Communist effort to pressure the United States into recognizing the new regime. British consular property had not been confiscated, he observed, and this fact appeared to be related to London's recognition of the Communists.[152] Years later, Clubb suggested that confiscation of American consular property was the brainstorm of a faction within the Chinese Communist party, rather than the act of a monolithic leadership. The move, after all, came while Mao was in Moscow attempting to negotiate a treaty of alliance with the Russians. The time it took to achieve this purpose—nearly two months—and the meager assistance received by China as a result of the Treaty of Friendship, Alliance, and Mutual Assistance that was signed on 14 February, indicates that all was not smooth in the Sino-Soviet relationship.[153] Prior to the emergence of the pact, the State Department had reliable reports that Mao was seriously dissatisfied with the Soviet position on several points.[154] During the previous fall, Clubb's contacts in Peking had indicated that the Chinese leader was a "moderate" on the question of relations with the United States.[155] It is unlikely that such a man would choose the middle of tough discussions with the Kremlin to intentionally burn all bridges to Washington.

Sino-American talks in Peking in October 1949 would have run into difficulties in two areas: continued American assistance to the Nationalists and the status of treaties between the United States and the Chiang regime. Agreement could have come only through concessions on both sides. The United States undoubtedly would have been expected to end economic and military aid to Taiwan. Past Sino-American agreements would have needed to be renegotiated. Pressures from the pro-Soviet faction in China and the China bloc in the United States made flexibility difficult for either government.

Nevertheless, an exchange of views might have shown compromise to be possible. For instance, the United States might have offered to end all assistance to the Nationalists after 15 February 1950, the termination date for the commitment of funds through the China Aid Act.[156] The United States might also have agreed to revise old pacts between the two countries, provided that changes were more of form than of substance. In a Sino-American agreement of 1943, the United States had renounced the most blatant privileges in the "unequal treaties" of the nineteenth and early twentieth centuries, but dissatisfaction remained among the Communists in certain areas, including the status of part of the United States consular compound in Peking, which had been seized in 1900 as a barracks for American troops in the foreign intervention against the Boxer Rebellion. A protocol of 1901 had given the United States title to this land, and the agreement of 1943, though calling for an end to all rights received in the earlier pact, provided for the continued American use of property allocated for its diplomatic quarters.[157] It may be wondered here if relatively minor concessions by Washington would have satisfied Communist determination to remove all vestiges of "imperialist" domination. A demonstrated willingness on the part of the United States to discuss the matter might at least have prevented precipitous action such as occurred on 14 January 1950.

Perhaps the Communists, fearing the Kremlin's reaction, would have shied away from serious talks with the United States. The Soviets maintained a strong, possibly even dominant, presence in Manchuria, and—in the aftermath of Yugoslavia's revolt against Stalin's direction—were particularly sensitive to any Peking flirtations with the West. Walter McConaughy, who during the previous summer had replaced Cabot as consul general at Shanghai, had information that Mao's trip to Moscow was the result of a "strong and rather sudden . . . pressure" from the Kremlin in response to "moves" by Great Britain and other non-Communist nations toward recognition and an impending visit by Philip Jessup to the western Pacific.[158] On the other hand, McConaughy also reported a "rapidly swelling tide [of] Chinese charges and bitterness re[garding] Soviet greed [and] encroachments" in Manchuria.[159] Had Washington demonstrated greater flexibility toward the new regime, it might have evaluated its options somewhat differently.

But the cold war had so come to dominate Acheson's mentality that common bargaining was unthinkable with a Communist government that repudiated widely accepted standards of international conduct—standards, by the way, that China had had no role in constructing—and showed open allegiance to Moscow. To Acheson, there was little to discuss and nothing to concede. If "keeping a foot in the door" and avoiding the diversion of potential Chinese irredentist sentiments against Russia in the north were of sufficient worth to merit a degree of restraint on the part of the United States, they warranted little in the way of positive effort. And Acheson received little pressure within the administration, from either above or below, to loosen his stance.[160]

## Taiwan Policy in a State of Flux

In late 1949, even the secretary of state's course of restraint regarding Taiwan faced a severe test. The challenge to that policy came from four quarters: the China bloc in Congress, MacArthur in Japan, American officials in Taiwan, and, most importantly, top defense officials in Washington.

As late as September 1949, the Joint Chiefs of Staff advised against sending a military mission to the island to study conditions there.[161] A month earlier, Acheson had asked them to reevaluate their position that American forces should not be committed to the defense of Taiwan. He noted that developments there—the massive influx of "troops and civilian refugees" from the mainland, the "serious inflationary impact of this event on the economy," and the continuing domination of the government by Chiang's often inept and corrupt cronies—had steadily undermined American political and economic actions to keep the island out of Communist hands.[162] The Joint Chiefs quickly reaffirmed their belief that American forces should not occupy it and the Pescadores. They did note, however, that in the event of war, or "some unforeseen contingency," this position might have to be reevaluated.[163]

Yet the trend within the military establishment was toward a more active China policy. Louis A. Johnson, who in March 1949 had replaced James Forrestal as secretary of defense, sympathized with Chennault's strategy.[164] Admiral Badger, who had returned recently from China, pressed for a similar course. On 28 September, the Joint Strategic Survey Committee, a subgroup of the Joint Staff—which was, in turn, the administrative and policy development agency of the Joint Chiefs—recommended a limited program of military assistance to non-Communist forces in western China.[165] The Joint Chiefs set the proposal aside, however, arguing that a National Security

Council paper on Asian policy should precede consideration of the plan.[166] Acheson's views on the matter were well known. Military leaders undoubtedly remembered past defeats on China policy at the hands of the State Department, and were not eager to confront the secretary of state on the issue.[167]

Nevertheless, on 6 October, when Congress passed the military assistance act providing $75 million for "the general area of China," a study began within the Joint Staff on possible uses of the funds. The Joint Munitions Allocations Committee advised against making recommendations until the National Security Council established a concrete policy for Asia. The navy concurred in this view, but the air force and the army demurred.[168]

The army took the lead in pursuing a different course. Chief of Staff J. Lawton Collins ordered the Plans and Operations Division, now headed by Major General Charles L. Bolté, to furnish proposals for the use of the $75 million. They were ready on 10 November. Funds were to be split into two categories: direct support for "the existing legitimate governments or anti-Communist groups" in Burma, Thailand, Indonesia, and China (including Taiwan and Tibet); and "a contingency reserve fund" of $40 million, half for Taiwan and half for Southeast Asia.[169] Army Secretary Gordon Gray contacted Major General Alfred M. Gruenther, the chairman of the Joint Staff, and suggested an exploration of "the military possibilities in connection with Taiwan."[170]

In the meantime, the air force had launched a study of its own. Chief of Staff Hoyt Vandenberg worried about the results of a possible "outright seizure of control" of the island by "Communist agents and sympathizers." The bulk of the Nationalist air force was on Taiwan and, if captured by the Communists, "might well constitute an alteration in the existing balance of military power in South and East Asia."[171] A staff study of 30 November reassured Vandenberg somewhat. It concluded that the "security threat to United States interests" was insufficient to warrant immediate action, such as the occupation of Taiwan or the sabotage of Nationalist aircraft. The study advised, nonetheless, that the "placing of a small United States liaison group on the island would be helpful in improving morale, combatting the defection trend in the Chinese Nationalist Air Force, and collecting intelligence."[172]

The army's International Branch proposed increased "economic and psychological efforts" to save Taiwan, as well as "limited military measures." Specific moves would include the assignment of a military advisory group to Taiwan, the allotment of certain matériel to the Nationalist navy and air force, the stationing of "United States fleet elements" in Taiwanese waters, and a public announcement from Washington that this action was aimed at preventing an attack on the island from the mainland.[173] Gruenther's Joint Strategic Survey Committee, which presented recommendations to the Joint Chiefs on 21 December, followed these proposals closely.[174]

The Joint Chiefs agreed that Taiwan policy needed revision. On 23 December, they proposed to the National Security Council "modest, well-directed, and closely supervised" military assistance and "stepped-up" efforts in the political, economic, and psychological spheres. MacArthur and Admiral Russell S. Berkey, commander of the Seventh Task Fleet, should "make an immediate survey" of the military aid needed by Taiwan and forward their estimates to Secretary Johnson.[175]

The military leaders were responding to a variety of developments, both at home and abroad. Pressures grew on Capitol Hill to increase American efforts to prevent Taiwan from falling under Communist control. In September 1949, Senator Smith left for a lengthy trip to the western Pacific.[176] His first stop was in Tokyo, where he received red-carpet treatment from MacArthur. The commander in chief of United States forces in the Far East, who was now taking a more active interest than before in influencing American China policy, arranged high-level escorts for Smith to Okinawa, the Philippines, and Taiwan. MacArthur and Admiral Turner Joy, commander of American naval forces in the Far East, spoke strongly in favor of aid for the Nationalists on Taiwan. Upon returning to the United States in late October, the New Jersey senator wrote Acheson and asserted that the island must be kept out of Communist hands. Smith argued that the United States, as the occupying power of Japan, could put forces on Taiwan. This course was feasible legally, he claimed, because Taiwan technically remained part of Japan until that nation concluded a peace treaty with the Allied powers of World War II. Thus the United States might occupy the territory and inform the United Nations that the area could temporarily be put under international trusteeship.[177] In late November, Smith presented similar views to the Foreign Relations Committee.[178] On 1 December, he stated his opinions in a news conference and hinted that MacArthur agreed with him.[179]

Senator Knowland also visited East Asia. He was not yet convinced of the futility of military aid to regional authorities in southern and western China. His travels included stops at Chungking and Nanking in Szechwan and Kwangsi provinces respectively, with Chennault as tour guide.[180] Upon Knowland's return to the United States in early December, he was certain to continue pressing for American action on behalf of the Nationalists. With such events in mind, in addition to the widely publicized Ward affair and the surge of activity against American recognition of the Communists, Bolté noted that "the moment is psychologically right for public opinion and the Congress to support positive measures with respect to Taiwan."[181]

Although the army's Plans and Operations Division showed sympathy for an American occupation of the island, Collins demurred.[182] To him, past circumstances dictating against such a course—namely, the sizable American commitments in other areas and the limited forces available for ventures abroad—had not changed. In fact, Johnson was in the midst of an energetic campaign to "cut the fat" from military spending. By October 1949, the army had only ten combat divisions, none of which was close to authorized strength.[183]

Yet both the American military attaché and consul on the island believed that a military assistance group should be sent to assist in the organization of Nationalist defenses.[184] In view of the immediate threat to Taiwan—reports from the field indicated that a Communist assault might come late in the spring of 1950—and the availability of funds for arms aid, the army chief of staff favored a reevaluation of moves other than direct American military involvement.[185]

In early December 1949, a trip to Tokyo by Gruenther and Under Secretary of the Army Tracy S. Voorhees greatly facilitated this process.[186] The precise mission of the two men was kept secret, but they certainly discussed the Taiwan question with MacArthur. The Far Eastern commander's views on the strategic importance of the island were well known in official circles.[187] He likened Taiwan in Communist hands to "an unsinkable aircraft carrier and submarine tender ideally located to accomplish Soviet offensive strategy and at the same time checkmate counteroffensive operations by United States Forces based on Okinawa and the Philippines."[188] On his return to Washington, Voorhees reported that MacArthur believed Taiwan could be held largely through a declaration that the United States would regard an attack on the territory as an act of war and through the use of much of the $75 million congressional appropriation for "the general area of China" to bolster Nationalist defenses.[189] This judgment encouraged the Joint Chiefs to propose an increased American effort to hold Taiwan.

Acheson and President Truman, however, remained to be persuaded. On the morning of 29 December, the secretary of state met with the Joint Chiefs. He dissected brilliantly the call for new action. Repeating State Department conclusions of the previous winter, he asserted that further American moves to separate the island from the mainland would turn Chinese eyes from Soviet imperialism in the north toward American imperialism to the east. Acheson also noted that the Joint Chiefs, despite MacArthur's optimism and K. C. Wu's recent assumption of the governorship of the island—which might increase the competence of Nationalist rule—remained unwilling to predict that the projected American aid could do more than postpone a Communist takeover. State Department officials were uncertain about the impact of Wu's rise, for it seemed possible he was merely being brought forward as "scenery" to draw attention away from Chiang's continued domination of the National government. If the United States became more deeply involved in the attempt to hold the island from the Communists, and, if that attempt failed, American "prestige" would suffer another blow.

The Joint Chiefs weakened their case by differing somewhat with MacArthur's strategic arguments. Collins conceded that airbases on the continent exposed Okinawa to attack just as much as those on Taiwan. He and his colleagues believed that the island in enemy hands would merely hinder American access to sea-lanes from Japan to Malaya; and continued National- ist domination of the island would slow down Communist efforts to con- solidate their regime on the mainland and help deter any plans for expansion into Southeast Asia.

By late December, the secretary of state had no illusions about the pos- sibilities for resistance to the Communists in China, and he believed that American efforts to the south to contain Communism must be directed pri- marily toward raising the general standard of living there and toward allying the United States with nationalist movements. Thus he concluded that the political liabilities of the Joint Chiefs' proposals outweighed the advan- tages.[190] The National Security Council met late on the 29th, and the presi- dent formally approved Acheson's position.

Actually, Truman's mind had been made up for at least forty-eight hours.[191] The secretary of defense, who had vigorously supported the posi- tion of the military leaders, did not even attend the meeting. The incident served to emphasize Acheson's predominant influence at the White House. It also reflected a general tension in relations between Johnson and Acheson that was rooted in broad policy disagreements, but reinforced by a deep per- sonality conflict. The former's ambitions—which may have included a run for the presidency in 1952—along with his abrupt and domineering nature, made for an increasingly strained association with Acheson.[192]

The president's decision did not erase the Taiwan issue from the political landscape because news of the verdict immediately leaked to the press, which led to a sharp Republican counterattack.[193] On 30 December, Knowl- and publicly advocated the assignment of a military mission to Taiwan.[194] Senator Taft proposed naval action to keep the island out of Communist hands.[195] Three days later, Knowland released a letter from former Republi- can President Herbert Hoover asserting that the navy should protect Taiwan, the Pescadores, and perhaps even Hainan Island.[196] Yet Republicans on Capi- tol Hill were far from unanimous in the belief that the United States should act to save Taiwan. Vandenberg refused to make a public statement on the question, and Senator Henry Cabot Lodge, Jr., never an interventionist on China, doubted that the island should be defended by American forces.[197] Knowland found an opening, however, when a State Department informa- tion paper leaked to the press—under suspicious circumstances—through MacArthur's command in Tokyo.[198] On 4 January, the California senator de- nounced the State Department claim that Taiwan was of minor strategic significance.[199] Congressman Charles Eaton, the senior minority member of the Foreign Affairs Committee and not identified with the China bloc, called for American action to hold the area.[200]

Then, perhaps because they overestimated the influence that these pres-

sures exerted on United States policy, the Chinese Communists asserted
that a secret agreement had been reached between Washington and Taipei for
an American occupation of Taiwan.[201]

In this confused and charged atmosphere, the administration sought to
both clarify and defend its position. On 5 January 1950, the president opened
a press conference with a statement on Taiwan. He announced that the
United States had "no desire to obtain special rights or privileges, or to establish military bases on Formosa at this time." The American government
would not extend further "military aid or advice to Chinese forces" there,
but the program of economic assistance would be continued "under existing
legislation."[202] Despite Acheson's recent victory over the Joint Chiefs, General Bradley exerted some influence on the content of the statement. At his
request, the words "at this time" were included, and a disavowal of any
American desire to "detach Formosa from China" was deleted.[203] The military men continued to believe that the United States should maintain the
option of reevaluating its policy in the event of war.

As expected, attacks on the administration continued. Especially discon-
certing to it were suggestions by Senators Vandenberg and Smith that Truman had acted in bad faith by failing to consult the Foreign Relations Committee before making a decision on Taiwan. Actually, the secretary of state
had already planned to meet with that group on 10 January. The confusion
and uproar over American policy, however, had led the president to announce his intentions beforehand.[204] In an attempt to assuage Republican
senators sympathetic to bipartisanship, the administration now sent a number of high officials before the committee.

In the meeting of 10 January, Vandenberg joined Smith in expressing interest in an American move to neutralize Taiwan "pending an appropriate review by . . . the United Nations." Acheson was well prepared to counter this
possibility, for he had investigated it thoroughly during the spring and summer of 1949. In June, Butterworth had even proposed the calling of a special
session of the General Assembly to discuss Taiwan's fate. It was hoped this
ploy would lead to a United Nations plebiscite on the island, which would
prepare the way for an international trusteeship and eventually independence from the mainland.[205] (George Kennan supported a far bolder scheme.
American forces should land on Taiwan, remove the Nationalists, and establish a new regime separate from the mainland.)[206] The secretary of state had
not slammed the door on United Nations action at some future date, but he
realized that the Nationalists would resist any American effort to establish
an indigenous regime among the Taiwanese; that this would make such an
enterprise extremely costly—more costly than anything the Joint Chiefs
wanted to undertake; and that the natives of the island were ill equipped to
construct an orderly, effective government.[207] To Smith and Vandenberg, the
secretary conceded that Taiwan could be separated at least temporarily from
the mainland. He noted, however, that other nations would regard such a

move by the United States "as hypocritical," and that this might undermine America's moral standing throughout the world.[208]

Acheson's efforts to promote administration policy outside the executive branch reached a high point on 12 January 1950, when he spoke before the National Press Club. Entitled "Crisis in Asia—An Examination of United States Policy," the speech advanced an impressive framework for evaluating the problems of that region. Nationalism was the predominant force on the continent, Acheson asserted, and it had two basic ingredients: "a revulsion against the acceptance of misery and poverty as the normal condition of life"; and a "revulsion against foreign domination." The first had played a major role in Chiang's downfall on the mainland, the second would lead to "righteous anger" on the part of the Chinese people if the United States interjected itself deeply into Taiwan's affairs. On the other hand, if the United States exercised restraint, the "wrath" and "hatred" would be directed toward the Russians, who sought to detach "the four northern provinces of China."[209]

In the ensuing weeks, this theme, as Gaddis Smith puts it, of giving "free rein to the natural forces of Asia," dominated Acheson's exposition of American policy.[210] Whatever the impact of his efforts, most observers agreed with him on the Taiwan issue. On 15 January, the *New York Times* reported that recent decisions on the matter were approved by the bulk of informed opinion in all regions of the country.[211] In a survey of leading citizens in twenty-three cities throughout the nation by the Council on Foreign Relations, more than half expressed opposition to further aid to the Nationalists.[212] A Gallup poll indicated that a majority of the public knew little or nothing about Taiwan, but that most of those who did favored a hands-off policy regarding the island. Only 10 percent of those questioned favored the use of American forces to defend it.[213]

## China Policy and the "Red Scare"

Nevertheless, criticism of the Truman administration did not abate. A growing number of Republicans on Capitol Hill viewed Asian policy as a promising issue on which to undermine the Democrats in the upcoming congressional election campaign. Prospects in this area gained a major boost when the dispute over Chiang's fall became connected to that of Communist infiltration into the American government, especially the State Department. The Alger Hiss case directed much attention to the internal subversion question. He was a former State Department officer who, among other things, had attended the Yalta Conference. In late 1948, Whittaker Chambers, a senior editor of *Time* magazine and a former member of the American Communist party, charged him with involvement in espionage activities more than a decade earlier. Hiss denied the charge and sued his accuser for libel. Chambers, however, presented evidence that led a New York grand jury to indict Hiss for perjury. After one trial had resulted in a hung jury, a second ended, on 21 January 1950, in Hiss's conviction. Judith Coplon, a Justice Department aid, had already been arrested for spying on behalf of the Russians. On 3 February, British physicist Klaus Fuchs, who had once worked at Los Alamos, New Mexico, on the Manhattan Project, was charged with espionage. A week later, he made a full confession. The time was ripe for Republican partisans to link "America's failure in China" to Communist penetration of the federal government.

Acheson played into the hands of opposition politicians. In January 1949, during Senate confirmation hearings, he had been questioned about his relationship to Hiss and his brother Donald. The three men had been acquainted for many years. Donald, who also had been accused of Communist activities, had been both Acheson's assistant in the State Department for a time during World War II and a member of his law firm in Washington. Although Acheson's nomination encountered little opposition in the upper house, the press had given extensive attention to his connection with the Hisses.[214] Because of his public position, he had declined to testify as a character witness at Alger's trial. When asked at a press conference about Hiss's conviction, however, Acheson declared, "I do not intend to turn my back on Alger Hiss." The statement was not a proclamation of Hiss's innocence, a plea for leniency, or a condonation of espionage against the United States, but it was widely censured in the press and in Congress.[215] From this point onward, Acheson was a definite political liability to the Democratic administration.

It was in this setting that Joseph R. McCarthy, a little-known Republican senator from Wisconsin, jumped into the limelight. On 9 February, in a speech at Wheeling, West Virginia, he charged that the State Department employed a large number of Communists. They were being protected, he asserted, by Acheson, "this pompous diplomat in striped pants, with a phony British accent."[216] McCarthy had no original evidence to support his allegations, but he soon picked up substantial support from conservative columnists and the Republican Right on Capitol Hill. The Democrats, confident that the absurdity of the charges would become apparent under careful scrutiny, held open hearings on the matter in a subcommittee of the Foreign Relations Committee. These proceedings attracted nationwide press coverage. Although most journalists expressed serious doubts about McCarthy, the attention given him worked to his advantage.[217]

The Senate hearings dealt with people connected, in both the past and present, with American China policy. McCarthy labeled Philip Jessup, who made a lengthy official trip to Asia during the winter, as a man with "an unusual affinity" for Communist causes. The ambassador-at-large was an especially attractive object for attack because he had testified as a character witness for Alger Hiss and because he was active in the formulation of American policy in the Orient.[218] The Wisconsin senator eventually singled out Owen Lattimore, a China scholar at Johns Hopkins University, as "one of the principal architects of our far eastern policy" and a "top Russian espionage agent." Although there was no evidence that Lattimore exerted significant influence in official Washington, the latter assertion temporarily gained an air of authority when, on 20 April, Louis Budenz, a former Communist, testified that the professor had been a party member during the mid-1940s.[219] Finally, McCarthy reopened the *Amerasia* incident of 1945.[220] As a result, foreign service officer and China expert John Stewart Service came under renewed attack. The Tydings committee—the popular name of the Senate subcommittee, which was chaired by Millard E. Tydings, a Maryland Democrat—launched an investigation of the entire case. The outcome was a reaffirmation of the conclusions of a congressional probe of 1946, which had exonerated Service. As Robert Griffith observes, however, "the circumstances surrounding the hearings—the heated partisanship, the various political maneuvers, a whole series of charges and accusations—all contributed to a vague uneasiness which served not the committee's ends but McCarthy's."[221]

In the midst of growing Republican assertiveness, the Truman administration moved to bolster bipartisan cooperation in foreign affairs. In late March 1950, following an appeal by Vandenberg for an "unpartisan" study of European and Asian needs, Acheson named John Sherman Cooper, a former Republican senator from Kentucky, as a top consultant for upcoming meetings in London.[222] Early in April, the secretary of state took on John Foster Dulles as an adviser to the department. Dulles was widely considered to be the leading Republican "expert" on international relations. He had served briefly in the Senate during 1949, and had worked closely with the executive branch on programs for Western Europe. Yet, in the fall of 1949, in New York, when Dulles ran for but failed to win a longer term in the upper house, Truman had intervened on a major scale on behalf of Herbert Lehman. To Democrats, the president's action had been justified in view of Dulles's sharp attacks on the welfare state, but Republicans showed irritation.[223] The April appointment indicated that both Truman and Dulles desired to let bygones be bygones.[224] Dulles's position in the administration became useful almost immediately. For some time, Acheson had desired to move ahead with negotiations for a peace treaty with Japan. Louis Johnson and the Joint Chiefs of Staff objected, however, fearing that the United States would lose its bases in that country. Congressional opposition also appeared likely to arise. To discourage partisanship, the secretary of state put Dulles in charge of preparing a draft agreement with America's former enemy.[225]

To enhance relations with the Senate, the administration sent the Foreign Relations Committee six questions on Asian problems and promised to consult with it prior to making decisions on the issues involved.[226] Acheson spent considerable time cultivating influential senators, even inviting Senator Bridges to his home for sweet talk and bourbon.[227] When, in mid-April,

Senator Connally proposed the establishment of eight subcommittees to talk regularly with high State Department officials, the White House responded enthusiastically.[228] To protect a friend from further attacks, and perhaps to mollify critics on Capitol Hill, Acheson replaced Butterworth as assistant secretary of state for the Far East with Dean Rusk, whose contacts with moderate Republicans and lack of past dealings with China made him—politically at least—an ideal occupant of the sensitive post.[229]

Despite the domestic political climate, the initiative toward Japan indicated that the executive branch remained willing and able to move decisively on certain aspects of Asian policy. Indeed, prior to the outbreak of war in Korea in late June, Truman and Acheson made only marginal concessions in that area. They clung to their position, which had been established in January 1950, that the entry of Communist China into the United Nations was a procedural rather than a substantive matter and, therefore, not subject to an American veto in the Security Council. The secretary of state even took pains to inform friendly governments in the council that the United States did not expect them to follow the American lead in voting against Communist Chinese admission.[230] The Truman administration did permit an extension of the date for sending economic aid through the China Aid Act from 15 February to 30 June, a move largely designed to insure the passage of an economic assistance bill for Korea.[231] In early June, the State Department also agreed to allow the Nationalists to use the remaining $9 million in grants in that legislation for the purchase of military supplies in the United States.[232] Yet Acheson refused to endorse the sale of such goods beyond this small sum.[233] In April 1950, at Dulles's request, he asked the Joint Chiefs if the United States could, *with some assurance*, prevent Taiwan's fall to the Communists, but the military men replied essentially in the negative.[234] A public opinion poll of May indicated that most people did not desire increased aid for Chiang. Fifty-six percent of those questioned believed that the United States had assisted the National government either long enough or too long. Only 27 percent believed that it merited continued support.[235] Congressional votes on foreign aid measures indicated that the China bloc lacked sufficient strength to force increased assistance for the generalissimo in exchange for its support of programs elsewhere.[236] In retrospect, the rise of McCarthy appears ominous. Until the fall of 1950, however, the administration regarded the Communists-in-government issue as a relatively minor irritation.

## Hardening Trends in Asian Policy

But the State Department needed little pressure from the legislative branch to formulate certain policies that could only reinforce Communist China's dependence on the Soviet Union. Official announcements regarding American intentions to move toward a peace treaty with Japan without Soviet or Communist Chinese participation were not made until September. In his National Press Club speech, however, Acheson stated that the United States would assume "the military defense of Japan so long as that is required." There was "no intention of abandoning or weakening the defenses of Japan . . . either through permanent settlement or otherwise."[237] To the Russians this meant, as *Pravda* pointed out, "that the American imperialists have settled down in Japan and have no desire to leave it."[238] The Chinese interpreted Acheson's words in a similar manner.[239] The Sino-Soviet treaty of 14 February 1950 demonstrated the concern of the two Communist powers over American intentions. Article I of that agreement bound the signatories to take steps "for the purpose of preventing aggressive action on the part of Japan or any other state which should unite with Japan, directly or indirectly, in acts of aggression."[240]

Acheson's options on policy toward Japan were limited. The Joint Chiefs and Johnson balked on any move toward a peace treaty. Their minds were changeable only if plans could be worked out insuring a continued American military presence in the islands.[241] In any event, an effort to accommodate the Russians and the Chinese surely would have led to accusations of appeasement from Capitol Hill. Most important was the threat to American security that might have accompanied a withdrawal from Japan. Such a move would have required a complacency regarding Soviet capabilities and designs in Northeast Asia that was difficult to justify. Fortunately, nationalist sentiments in Japan provided no immediate impediment to the continued stationing of American forces there.[242]

Acheson's action in May 1950 regarding Indochina was less justifiable than that toward Japan. The Truman administration had been concerned about that area for many months. In January, when Peking and Moscow recognized Ho Chi Minh's government in Vietnam, a sense of urgency had crept into American policy deliberations.[243] Communist Chinese troops now lurched ominously along Indochina's borders. Although an invasion did not appear imminent, Ho was certain to receive other aid from his new neighbors, which would compound France's difficulties in pacifying the country. In early February, therefore, after the French parliament ratified the Elysée agreements of the previous year, which gave the states of Vietnam, Laos, and Cambodia a degree of autonomy, the United States moved rapidly to bolster anti-Communist forces in those countries. Washington promptly recognized the new governments.[244] At the end of the month, the State Department advised the National Security Council that Indochina was "under [the] immediate threat" of "communist expansion" and that a program must be established quickly for the protection, through "all practicable measures," of American security interests in Indochina.[245] At the beginning of March, an economic survey mission left for Southeast Asia.[246] American deliberations culminated on 8 May, when Acheson announced in Paris that the United States would send economic and military aid to the French in Indochina.[247]

A generation later, Acheson claimed that the French had "blackmailed" the United States into supporting them in Indochina in return for their cooperation in Western Europe.[248] Certainly, the secretary of state gave top priority to European matters and was pressured by Paris to give material aid to maintain its position in Indochina. Certainly, he remained dissatisfied with the limited progress toward Indochinese independence and continued—even in the face of pleas to the contrary from Ambassador David Bruce in Paris and Chargé Edmund Gullion in Saigon—to urge the French to make greater concessions on the matter.[249]

Yet much evidence exists that strategic and psychological considerations played a central role in the fateful decision of May 1950. The divisions that existed between the State and Defense departments over China and Korea policy were totally absent from deliberations on Indochina. The agencies agreed that the area was of great significance to the United States and that, if it fell to Communism, the rest of Southeast Asia would suffer the same fate. The Joint Chiefs regarded this prospect as potentially disastrous to American interests. It would eliminate friendly nations from the Asian continent, threaten Indonesia and the Philippines, deny the United States and Japan access to the raw materials of the region—including tin, rubber and oil—as well as to crucial markets for Japanese goods. It would also give Communist China and the Soviet Union vastly expanded economic and military potential.[250] The diplomats, who held similar views, also feared that the "psychological results of another Communist triumph in Asia, following on the heels of China," would create an impact in India and Pakistan and perhaps even as far away as the Middle East and Western Europe. Effective resistance to Communist expansion southward, on the other hand, "would increase the friction between China and Russia over Manchuria and the northern tier of Chinese provinces."[251] Here a parallel may have been drawn with the rise of Titoism in Yugoslavia, which coincided with increased American opposition to a leftist revolution in nearby Greece.

For the present, limited American capabilities ruled out large-scale intervention in Indochina, but plans were in the works for a general buildup of American military power. In April 1950, the National Security Council approved the famous memorandum NSC 68. It had been in preparation for several months, and was a response to the Communist victory in China and the Soviet explosion of a nuclear device. It was a veritable call to arms, both ideological and military, against the further spread of Soviet-directed Communism. Despite the unprecedented American initiatives in foreign affairs over the last three years, the document concluded that "[a] more rapid buildup of political, economic, and military strength . . . than is now contemplated is the only course which is consistent with progress toward achieving our fundamental purpose." Although offering no specific figures, NSC 68 proposed a huge expansion of United States armed forces, nuclear and conventional alike. This program was not only to protect against a direct attack on the continental United States, but also to support American foreign policy goals elsewhere.[252]

In the face of persistent concerns in Congress over taxes and unbalanced budgets, to be sure, Truman made no immediate move to carry out the new policy. Yet NSC 68 reflected an increasingly alarmist atmosphere in official Washington that encouraged expanded intervention abroad. The diplomatic partner to NSC 68 was the idea, articulated by Acheson in February 1950, of negotiating with the Communists from "situations of strength." Agreements acceptable to the West could be concluded, he suggested, only when threats to national or regional stability, both internal and external, had been eradicated.[253]

Recognition of the problems in selling a vastly enlarged defense budget on Capitol Hill only emphasized the desirability of preventing a precipitate French withdrawal from Indochina, which would add to America's military burdens abroad. Acheson noted in testimony before the Senate Foreign Relations Committee that "[w]e want more effort to contain communism in Indochina but not additional responsibility."[254]

Interestingly enough, most American policymakers ignored the possibility that Ho Chi Minh possessed Titoist inclinations. The State Department had no ready source of expertise on Vietnam as it did on China, and thus was often groping in the dark in evaluating various options.[255] Analysts did recognize, however, that the hunger for independence in Indochina remained unsatisfied, even after the granting of autonomy within a French Union.

Whatever the prospects of Bao Dai, the non-Communist leader of the new state of Vietnam, as an alternative to Ho, they could not be realized until France gave up completely its colonial designs on the country.[256] Acheson conceded the inconsistency of encouraging the French to stay on there while pressing them to play up to nationalist sentiments, but by May 1950 this insight was subordinated to other considerations.[257] If, in arguing against an expanded commitment to Taiwan, the secretary of state could speak with impressive detachment about Asian nationalism, his words lacked sufficient conviction to steer him clear of intervention on the side of France in Indochina.

In fact, by late spring, even Taiwan policy was up for review. In May, Dulles received a report from two friends, who recently had returned from the island, indicating that the National government was carrying out significant reforms.[258] *New York Times* correspondent Burton Crane had already reached that conclusion.[259] The newly created subcommittee on Asia of the

Senate Foreign Relations Committee pressed Dean Rusk for a reexamination of the administration position.[260] Dulles argued that "if we do not act to save Taiwan, it will be everywhere interpreted that we are making another retreat because we do not dare risk war." Such a conclusion abroad might result in "a series of disasters" in the Mediterranean, the Near East, Asia, and the Pacific.[261] Rusk presented this argument to Acheson verbatim. Unlike Butterworth, the new assistant secretary for the Far East, raised in Georgia as the son of a Calvinist preacher, brought to his duties an anti-Communism of religious proportions.[262]

Arguments for a tougher policy regarding Taiwan gained reinforcement from the growing belief in the State Department that a Sino-Soviet split was not likely in the immediate future. In February 1950, a working group preparing recommendations on Indochina concluded that a breach between Moscow and Peking was at least three years away.[263] Before he left Peking, Clubb expressed a similar view.[264] At the beginning of June, McConaughy did likewise. The former consul general at Shanghai, now returned to Washington, labeled the Communist regime's interest in Southeast Asia as "exceptionally strong."[265] As hopes for an early Sino-Soviet split declined, so too did the strength of the argument that the United States should take care to avoid distracting Peking from Russian penetration of its northern provinces.

The Defense Department also revived its effort to alter Taiwan policy. In April 1950, American service attachés in Hong Kong and Taipei urged increased American assistance to the Nationalists, not so much to make Taiwan impregnable but "to direct [greater] Chinese Communist military strength from Southeast Asia."[266] The Joint Chiefs concurred in the view that the dangerous situation in Indochina would be eased "if prompt and continuing measures were undertaken to reduce the pressure from Communist China." They were impressed by "the evidences of renewed vitality and apparent increased effectiveness of the Chinese Nationalist forces."[267] Intelligence reports indicated that Russia was supplying military planes, perhaps even jets, to the mainland government, which underlined the prospect of a hostile Taiwan becoming the "unsinkable aircraft carrier" envisioned by MacArthur.[268] By early May, the military leaders had commenced a systematic reexamination of the American position regarding the island.[269]

Late in the month, in a meeting between State and Defense department officials, it was decided that "every step should be taken within existing United States policy to provide assistance to the Chinese Nationalist government on Formosa." The Nationalists could file new orders for American matériel to be paid for with the remaining grant funds provided in the China Aid Act. The diplomats would approve and expedite requests for export licenses for arms and ammunition bought in the United States. "[C]overt action in support of resistance on Formosa" was to be expanded and the State

Department was to approach the president about releasing a portion of the $75 million for "the general area of China" to support "authorized projects."[270] What was meant by "covert action" remains uncertain. The best guess is that it consisted of air and naval drop-offs of military and propaganda items to sustain anti-Communist guerrilla activities on the Chinese mainland, which Far Eastern Command intelligence reported to be on the upswing.[271] Those activities might not endure over the long term, but they would hopefully undermine any immediate plans in Peking for action against Taiwan—and Indochina as well.

Elements within both departments wanted to go much further. Rusk and Dulles in State favored an effort in the United Nations to create an international trusteeship over the island, with American naval forces preventing an invasion from the continent.[272] In the Pentagon, the army continued to oppose an occupation of Taiwan by United States troops, but not "shows of force" by the navy or air force. Both the army and the navy supported augmented arms and advisory assistance. Only the air force appeared hostile to any new action.[273]

In mid-June, on a trip to Japan, Louis Johnson listened sympathetically to MacArthur's arguments that Taiwan must be defended. Even before war broke out in Korea, the secretary of defense was ready to press for American initiatives to defend it.[274] Acheson, on the other hand, remained dubious.[275] His doubts might have been partially overcome had liberal elements within the Kuomintang removed Chiang from a position of influence. Only days before the outbreak of war in Korea, Rusk received word that an anti-Chiang coup was indeed in the works.[276] Yet, without a crisis in Asia, the secretary of state would still have been hesitant to risk American prestige in such an uncertain enterprise as defending Taiwan from the Communists. Mounting pressures within the executive branch, however, made American intervention in the straits of Taiwan virtually inevitable following North Korea's move across the thirty-eighth parallel.

## Toward Containment in Asia

Thus, on the eve of conflict in Korea, the United States was gradually departing from the Asian strategy outlined in Acheson's impressive January 1950 presentation before the National Press Club. Indeed, elements of panic were already apparent in Washington that would serve to draw the United States more deeply than ever before into conflicts on the Asian mainland. In view of limited U.S. capabilities, policymakers might have concluded that America's resources should be concentrated more and more in Western Europe, the area most crucial to the national interests. As the Central Intelligence Agency concluded in late April,

> Although the member governments [there] and the great majority of
> their peoples are . . . still firmly behind the North Atlantic Treaty as
> the only realistic course available, . . . lingering . . . doubts [remain] as
> to both the firmness of the United States . . . commitment and the con-
> stancy and scale of United States support.[277]

Yet growing fears about the situation in Europe actually encouraged Washington officialdom to stand firm against Communism in Asia. Strategic concerns played a pivotal role, but the psychological factor held equal significance, especially in the State Department. Each potential Communist gain
assumed a global cast, with American credibility in Europe and the Mediterranean the most important prospective loser. The "free" peoples in those regions looked to the United States for leadership, but in the face of recent
events in China and the Soviet acquisition of the atomic bomb, further
Communist victories might have a snowballing effect that ultimately would
destroy their faith in America's will. Whereas in 1947 concern about Europe
had discouraged the diplomats from insisting on deeper involvement in the
Chinese civil war, now such concern encouraged a more assertive policy in
Asia. The secretary of state, to be sure, remained a key dissenter regarding
Taiwan, but he was increasingly surrounded by advisers who counseled
toughness, and Acheson himself had already accepted a degree of American
intervention in Indochina.

The prospects for containing Communism on the Asian mainland were
poor, and this fact suggests the inadequacy of the policy of "letting the dust
settle" in China. Although it remains uncertain that a constructive relationship was feasible between the United States and China, there can be no
doubt that continued American aid to and recognition of the National government eliminated the possibility. Given American policy, Communist
China had little choice but to move closer to the Soviet Union and seek to
undermine Western influence on its borders. In response, the United States
became progressively less sensitive to the rising tide of change in Asia and to
the prospects for exploiting divisions within the Communist camp. By the
spring of 1950, therefore, the Truman administration flirted with an involvement on the continent that it had painstakingly avoided in previous years,
an involvement that overestimated both the American stake in Asia and the
potential for influencing events there.

# 5 Hoping the Worst Won't Happen: Korea Policy on the Eve of War

Trends in administration policies in East Asia and throughout the world in the spring of 1950 help to explain the determined American response to the North Korean attack. What seems less understandable is why policymakers in Washington did not take greater pains to deter a major military venture by the Communist regime. In his speech of 12 January 1950, Acheson left South Korea out of the American defense perimeter in the Pacific. A move against it, he declared, would provide grounds for invoking "the commitments of the entire civilized world under the Charter of the United Nations," which "has not proved a weak reed to lean on by any people who are determined to protect their independence against outside aggression." But he gave no assurance of American material support to bolster an indigenous effort to resist invasion.[1] Less than four months after the National Press Club speech, Senator Connally asserted that, "whether we want it or not," South Korea might have to be abandoned to the Communists. Russia, he surmised, could "overrun Korea just like she would probably over-run Formosa when she gets ready to do it."[2] As Alexander L. George and Richard Smoke have observed, such statements often spark strong disclaimers, but Acheson responded merely by recounting American efforts to establish and maintain an independent republic below the thirty-eighth parallel.[3]

This response is particularly notable because intelligence reports in May indicated a buildup of North Korean tank forces and the movement to positions along the thirty-eighth parallel of recently returned Korean units of the Chinese Communist army.[4] At about the same time, Alexander Sachs, a noted economist and—during World War II—a consultant to the Office of Strategic Services, made a presentation to the State Department that included a prediction of an impending North Korean attack. Paul Nitze, the director of the Policy Planning Staff and probably the closest man in the entire department to the secretary of state, was especially impressed with Sachs's analysis.[5] Yet the administration did not act. An understanding of these events requires a closer look at decisions that had been made during 1949 regarding both Korea and American defense policy.

## The Decision for Withdrawal

In the year and a half prior to the outbreak of war, the most important United States action in Korea was the removal of its troops from that territory. On 23 March 1949, the president, on the advice of the National Security Council, determined that by 30 June the approximately 7,500 American soldiers remaining in South Korea should depart.[6] The withdrawal proceeded on schedule.

The State Department formally approved the March decision, but many in the agency remained ambivalent about it. In December 1948, Max Bishop and Walton Butterworth, the respective heads of the Division of Northeast Asian Affairs and the Office of Far Eastern Affairs, had proposed a National Security Council review of the Korea policy established during the previous April.[7] On 17 January 1949, the State Department officially requested such action.[8] Although Bishop emphasized South Korea's strategic importance vis-à-vis Japan, most diplomats viewed it as of largely political significance to the United States.[9]

Acheson did not oppose troop withdrawal. Reports from the field regarding the Rhee government's ability to handle unrest were less alarmist than during the previous fall.[10] In March 1948, "a very high Air Force officer" had assured George Kennan that American air power on Okinawa could control military operations on the peninsula.[11] Moreover, in December 1948, the United Nations General Assembly had passed a resolution calling for the withdrawal of foreign forces. The Russians had announced the departure of their troops and, therefore, the continued presence of American soldiers represented a political liability.[12] The secretary of state was preoccupied with Europe and hence concerned with avoiding overinvolvement on the Asian mainland. The continued presence of American troops in South Korea, in addition to serving as a deterrent to a military offensive by North Korea, might deeply involve the United States in a war on the peninsula, something to which Acheson had no desire to commit himself in advance.[13]

As had been the case since September 1948, the Joint Chiefs took the lead in pressing for withdrawal. In January 1949, they asked MacArthur for his views. The Far Eastern commander replied that South Korean forces could not repulse a large-scale invasion from the North, nor could they be strengthened adequately to achieve such a capacity—especially because Communist forces from Manchuria might participate in an attack. In addition, in the event of a serious threat to South Korea, the United States would be forced, for strategic and military reasons, to abandon "any pretense of active military support."[14] This analysis reflected MacArthur's growing concern for the security of Japan. The Communist advance in China, he believed, had freed Russia's military might in Asia, which increased the chance of a Soviet move against the American-occupied islands. Clearly, he hoped that soldiers removed from Korea would be used to bolster Japan.[15]

The Joint Chiefs quickly agreed with MacArthur's judgment against stationing troops in Korea.[16] Despite their interest in the security of Japan, however, they were more immediately concerned with strengthening reserve forces at home in preparation for a possible emergency in Europe. The blockade of Berlin by the Russians continued until May and, unlike Mac-Arthur, planners in Washington remained glued to a Europe-first strategy. Military leaders also preoccupied themselves with preparations for a general—as opposed to a limited—war.[17] In the event of a major armed conflict with the Soviet Union, the reasoning went, Korea was neither easily defensible nor necessary to an American offensive in Northeast Asia. Thus it was of little strategic value. Whatever offensive advantage the Russians might obtain by occupying it could be neutralized by American air power in Japan.[18]

Yet the Joint Chiefs were not simply blind to the need for preparations to respond to smaller military ventures by Communist forces. Military attitudes were in large measure an outgrowth of financial pressures on the Defense Department and the intense competition for funds among the armed services that arose therefrom. Presidential and congressional decisions on defense spending for fiscal 1950 brought interservice rivalries to a peak. During the fall of 1948, Secretary of Defense Forrestal, a proponent of balanced forces as a means of responding to emergencies short of total war, had attempted to persuade Truman to renounce the $15 billion ceiling that had been placed on the military budget earlier in the year.[19] The Joint Chiefs originally had requested $30 billion for fiscal 1950, but eventually whittled this figure down to $23.6 billion. Forrestal then reduced the sum to $16.9 billion. Deeply concerned about a possible federal budget deficit and aware of the political risks of asking for new taxes, however, the president stood fast on his initial guidelines.[20]

Henceforth, strategic planning became a scramble among the armed services for the largest possible share of the arbitrary limit.[21] The air force was the most aggressive of the services. Led by its dynamic civilian secretary, Stuart Symington, this new branch had already begun an offensive on Capitol Hill against Forrestal's balanced-force concept. In the face of administration plans for an increase in the army's size, Symington argued that the only conceivable enemy of the United States was Russia; that its ground forces could not be matched; and that, therefore, American security must be maintained through a strong air force. Most legislators agreed. Thus, in defense appropriations for fiscal years 1949 and 1950, Congress added funds to administration requests for the air force, but reduced those for the army.[22] The president could not overrule the cuts in the army budget, but he could and did refuse to spend the increased appropriations for the air force.[23] One result was that, as American troops withdrew from Korea, the operational capability of American air forces in East Asia also declined precipitously.[24]

To a degree, the army had itself to blame for its poor showing in Congress. Although the soldiers held their own in deliberations within the administration, their statements on Capitol Hill confirmed the air force's arguments. Army Chief of Staff Omar Bradley concentrated in his testimony on the need to prepare for World War III. In such an event, he believed, the foremost need would be a capacity to launch a "strong retaliatory blow against the Soviet

Union aimed at . . . crippling the enemy's industry, national prestige, and morale."[25] Occupation duties distracted the army from larger strategic issues, and its greater determination than the other branches to make the unification of the armed forces a success discouraged its leaders from engaging in open debate before congressional committees.[26] The army also had longstanding institutional ties with the air force, which had been broken only recently. Unlike the tradition of army-navy rivalry, therefore, a degree of identification remained among army officials with the development of air power.

The most important consideration, however, was that the arbitrary limit imposed by the White House on defense spending made impossible the maintenance of a military establishment capable of responding effectively to all contingencies. If the United States was not to spend enough on its armed forces to be prepared for both total and limited war, it made sense to give higher priority to warding off a strategic defeat—a successful Soviet attack on the American homeland and secondarily on Western Europe or Japan— rather than a tactical setback, like the forceful communization of South Korea. The United States, after all, stood a better chance of recovering from the latter development than from the former.[27]

## Jitters on the Eve of Withdrawal

In June 1949, despite its failure to articulate an alternative to preparations largely for total war, the army was uneasy about the impending American withdrawal from Korea. On the twentieth of that month, Bradley presented a study to the Joint Chiefs outlining American options in the event of a North Korean attack on South Korea. In such an event, the study conceded, the commitment of American troops would be militarily "unsound," but might be necessary because of "political considerations."[28]

The new concern of the army had two sources. First, its officials had recently testified before the House Foreign Affairs Committee that South Korea was better armed than North Korea and had a good chance of holding its own in a one-on-one military engagement with its hostile neighbor.[29] This judgment was partially an outgrowth of the purpose for which the army officials testified. The National Security Council had already rendered its decision to withdraw American troops, yet the administration wanted to finance South Korea's economic development. Major General Charles L. Bolté and his assistant, Brigadier General Thomas B. Timberman, appeared before the House Foreign Affairs Committee to defend both actions. Representatives Judd, Vorys, Lodge, and Helen Gahagan Douglas (Democrat-California) all expressed doubts as to the wisdom of total troop withdrawal, and hesitated to support economic aid to an area that appeared destined to fall into the Communist orbit.[30]

In defending administration policy, therefore, army representatives deliberately overestimated South Korea's strength in comparison to North Korea,[31] a ploy that could not help but make them uneasy. As American soldiers departed from the peninsula, to be sure, they left behind arms and ammunition whose replacement cost was $110 million and which brought South Korea's firepower to perhaps a par with that of North Korea. The South Korean army also appeared to be somewhat larger than its northern counterpart.[32] Size and equipment, however, were only two criteria for comparing military strength.

North Korean units were far better trained and led than their counterparts in the south, a fact made clear by clashes in late May 1949 on the Ongjin peninsula, an area in western Korea along the thirty-eighth parallel. Despite a numerical advantage of four to one, South Korean field commanders requested reinforcements. Contrary to the long-standing advice of Brigadier General William L. Roberts, head of the American military advisory group, to avoid diverting troops to relatively insignificant sectors, the republic's top military officers complied with panicky calls from the scene. The numerical superiority of defending forces did not prevent the northerners from penetrating three miles into South Korea, or from removing civilians and supplies from alien territory.[33] The persistence of unrest in the south added to the republic's military weakness. Although the Rhee regime had recently improved its position in relation to internal disruptive forces, a large percentage of South Korea's armed strength continued to be engaged in suppressing guerrilla bands below the thirty-eighth parallel.[34]

Although some analysts still regarded North and South Korean armed forces as "fairly evenly balanced," intelligence reports of May and June indicated that the North Korean army was rapidly expanding in both personnel and military equipment. The Chinese Communist armies in Manchuria, which reportedly included at least sixty thousand Korean nationals, might provide battle-hardened soldiers, and the Soviet Union, which in March had concluded an arms pact with North Korea, might supply substantial quantities of war matériel.[35] Even if a balance of military forces did exist, it might only be temporary, and thus army officials knew that their optimistic testimony before the House Foreign Affairs Committee might make them vulnerable to future criticism. The comments of several of the Representatives reflected a measure of support within Congress for an American troop presence in South Korea, thus further encouraging the army to reopen the question of American policy on the peninsula.

The army's encounter with Judd and company came on the heels of renewed overtures to the military by the State Department. During May 1949, violence below the thirty-eighth parallel had increased significantly, as had Rhee's belligerence toward the north. The Office of Far Eastern Affairs feared that civil war might follow the American troop withdrawal. Bishop and Niles W. Bond, the assistant chief of the Division of Northeast Asian Affairs, believed that the Joint Chiefs should be approached so as to make plans for such a contingency.[36] In sum, pressures in Washington from both inside and outside the administration suggested to top army officers that the Korean situation warranted a new look.

The air force and navy had little cause to share the army's concern because they had never had much to do with the Korean problem. Committing troops to the peninsula would merely give the army justification for requesting funds that might otherwise be allocated to the other services. Louis Johnson's takeover of the Defense Department in March had led to the most economy-conscious operation of the military establishment in the postwar era. In such an atmosphere, a chief of staff was unlikely to accept the reopening of an issue that might lead to a cut in his branch's share of a shoestring budget.[37] Moreover, the air force, imbued with the giddy self-confidence of a new agency, believed its planes in Japan and Okinawa could respond effectively to any contingency in Korea.[38]

Although the State Department's Office of Far Eastern Affairs remained dubious about American withdrawal, there was no effort to bring the issue before the National Security Council. In May, Acheson almost made such a move, but he backed off when Ambassador Muccio declined to propose the action.[39] Irritation with pressures from the Rhee government played a role here. South Korean officials, as Muccio put it, "moved heaven and earth to have withdrawal deferred."[40] Such efforts included public assertions of the South Korean army's weakness. In exchange for giving his blessing to the departure of American troops, Rhee demanded one of three things: the formation of a Pacific pact similar to NATO, an agreement between the United States and South Korea for mutual defense against "aggressor nations," or a public pledge from Washington to defend South Korea.[41] The Korean leader's concern was understandable, especially in view of the United States refusal to intervene in China to save Chiang. The State Department, however, regarded such concrete commitments as inappropriate. In such circumstances, Butterworth and his subordinates felt that public announcements of South Korea's vulnerability weakened the indigenous population's "confidence and will to survive" and encouraged adventurism in North Korea.[42] The diplomats resented South Korean pressure tactics, which reminded them of Chiang's constant efforts to get the United States to bail him out of trouble.

Yet, like it or not, they fully recognized that the American commitment to the Republic of Korea was far greater than that to Nationalist China. The National Security Council policy paper of March 1949 had concluded that "U.S. disengagement" from Korea would lead to "Communist control" of the entire peninsula and "would be interpreted as a betrayal by the U.S. of its friends and allies in the Far East." A victory by "Soviet dominated forces" would also "constitute a severe blow to the prestige and influence" of the United Nations. Thus, despite the State Department's failure to persistently oppose the final withdrawal of army forces from Korea, it did move more aggressively in other areas both to strengthen South Korea and convey a sense of America's stake in that nation's defense. The American military advisory group was established on a permanent and expanded basis. Arms aid also continued, and now for an army of 65,000 instead of 50,000 men.[43] The Bureau of the Budget had originally smothered a proposal for more than $17 million for Korea in the military assistance bill of 1949. Countermoves from the Office of Far Eastern Affairs, however, led the president to support the program, albeit at the reduced level of $10,970,000.[44] In early June, the State Department presented to Congress an economic assistance bill providing the Republic of Korea with $150 million for fiscal year 1950. In his accompanying message, Truman, in a move that contrasted sharply with his approach to China, likened the program to that for Western Europe.[45] During the ensuing weeks, he and Acheson exerted considerable pressure on Congress to act expeditiously on the measure.[46]

Finally, the State Department prepared a resolution for the United Nations General Assembly that would prolong the international organization's involvement in Korea. On 21 September, in a speech before "the town meeting of the world," Acheson asserted that a United Nations commission was needed in Korea to "observe and report on any details which might lead to military conflict . . . , to use the influence of the United Nations to avert the potential threat of internal strife . . . , and to explore further the possibility of unification."[47] To the secretary of state, the presence of international observers would discourage each side from launching major military operations against the other. The United States proceeded to sponsor a resolution, along with Nationalist China and Australia, that provided for a new commission. The resolution passed easily.[48] If the commission failed to prevent war on the peninsula, it at least played a pivotal role in placing the primary responsibility for the initiation of hostilities on North Korea.

## The Failure of Deterrence

Despite State Department efforts to protect the American commitment to South Korea, the question arises as to what more might have been done. The most obvious possibilities were to bolster American forces in Japan and order MacArthur to take an active interest in the Korean situation. Interestingly enough, the Truman administration followed courses directly opposite to these. Not only was American air power in Japan being reduced, but the troops leaving Korea were going to Hawaii and the continental United States, rather than being reassigned to Japan.[49] Washington also lessened MacArthur's responsibilities on the peninsula. Previously, he had exercised operational control over United States forces there; now he was merely to provide logistic support for the military advisory group to the coastline of Korea and the means for an emergency evacuation of American personnel.[50]

There is no evidence that State Department officials pressed the Joint Chiefs to bolster American forces in Japan as a counter to the withdrawal from Korea. If they did, however, military leaders surely pointed to declining American capabilities. In the face of this trend, the resulting preoccupation with planning for total war, and the Joint Chiefs' view regarding the commitment of American forces to Korea, the army probably saw its primary need as keeping its men in the best possible condition for combat. Upon the commencement of any hostilities with Russia, of course, the air force was to provide a breathing spell during which American manpower and industrial resources could mobilize. The greatest role of the army would be in the later stages of the conflict.[51] Even so, its leaders hoped to maintain toeholds in Europe, probably in the Pyrenees, and in the Middle East.[52] If such a stand was to be made, the bulk of American ground forces would already have to be concentrated and in a high state of readiness. The stationing of large numbers of soldiers in occupation commands in East Asia—where war plans called for a "strategic defensive" based on the offshore islands, including Taiwan—would be costly and would undermine the primary army goals.[53]

The air force also had its sights pointed eastward. Because the Soviet industrial heartland was in Eastern Europe, Western Europe and the Middle East were the logical staging areas for most of America's strategic bombing forces. Because budgetary limitations were reducing capabilities in strategic and tactical areas, air power in Japan stood to be cut before that in Europe. Under the White House spending guidelines, therefore, the State Department could make no better case for reinforcing Japan than for maintaining forces in Korea.

If the State Department merits criticism in this respect, it is for failing either to accommodate its Korean policy to the administration's attitude toward defense expenditures, or to attack that attitude at an earlier date. The study that led to NSC 68 began in the fall of 1949, but the defense budget for fiscal year 1951 approved by the White House in December was for merely $13 billion. At the same time, adjustments occurred in programs for fiscal year 1950: personnel strength of the armed forces was to be reduced by 30 June 1950 to 1.46 million, a drop-off of nearly 150,000 men from the end of the previous fiscal year. The army and navy were to sustain the cuts. The State Department did not even participate in these decisions.[54]

The diplomats also had little to do with minimizing MacArthur's role in Korea. Although the Joint Chiefs had the final word in making such assignments, the Far Eastern commander himself exerted considerable pressure. Based on his experience in exercising operational control over the Joint Military Advisory Group to the Republic of the Philippines, he was not inclined to assume a similar relationship with the advisers in Korea, unless given the authority to specify their objectives. The Joint Chiefs understandably desired to keep this power for themselves, so they simply reduced MacArthur's tasks in Korea.[55]

In his later account of Pyongyang-Moscow relations prior to North Korea's attack, former Soviet leader Nikita Khrushchev implies that, had MacArthur visited Seoul or shown an active interest in South Korean security following the American withdrawal, the outbreak of war might have been averted. In late 1949, Khrushchev recalls, Premier Kim Il-sung of North Korea on a visit to Moscow pressed for a military offensive against the south. Early in 1950, Kim returned to the Soviet capital with specific plans. Stalin hesitated, fearing the American response. But, when his advisers and Mao Tse-tung—then in Moscow negotiating an alliance with the Soviet Union—assured him that the United States was unlikely to intervene, he gave the go-ahead.[56] Because rapid American military support for South Korea required the use of occupation forces from Japan, visits by MacArthur or other top officials in Tokyo to Seoul, the thirty-eighth parallel, and such potential sites for troop landings as Inchon and Pusan might have served as warning signals to the Kremlin.

In fairness to the State Department, some efforts were made to show an American interest in South Korea. The navy was persuaded to have an American cruiser and two destroyers visit Inchon in the fall of 1949.[57] When, on 19 January 1950, the House of Representatives narrowly defeated an aid bill for the Republic of Korea, Acheson took immediate steps to reverse the setback. In a public letter to the president, he declared that the masses of Asia looked to American action in Korea "as a measure of the seriousness of our concern with the freedom and welfare of peoples maintaining their independence in the face of great obstacles."[58] Administration efforts soon led to Congress's passage of a similar assistance measure. At the same time, on a well-publicized tour of Asia, Ambassador-at-Large Philip Jessup visited South Korea.[59] Six months later, John Foster Dulles made a similar stop. In speaking to the republic's National Assembly, he asserted: "You are not alone; you will never be alone, as long as you continue to play worthily your part in the great design of human freedom."[60]

Still, these actions did not fall into a consistent pattern that conveyed a deep American commitment. The House's initial rejection of the aid bill for South Korea displayed a division within the federal government, which was rooted largely in pessimism among some legislators regarding South Korea's prospects after the Communist victory in China and in partisanship over Taiwan policy.[61] The incident illustrated the difficulty at home of sustaining a firm Korea policy while cutting American losses in China. Jessup's stop in South Korea coincided with Acheson's National Press Club speech, which excluded that area from America's defense perimeter in the Pacific. Dulles's words were vague, and they came six weeks after the administration's feeble response to Senator Connally's statement regarding Korea's probable fall to

Communism. Moreover, while Dulles was in Seoul, Secretary of Defense Johnson and General Bradley were in Tokyo, but, like other top American military officials who had crossed the Pacific in the last twelve months, they did not set foot in Korea.

To some extent, MacArthur's relationship to Washington officialdom, as well as the status of relations between American diplomatic and military personnel in the nation's capital, explain the State Department's failure to use the Far Eastern commander or the Joint Chiefs as instruments of deterrence in Korea. By 1949, MacArthur had long exercised considerable independence in his operations in Japan. His solid and sometimes brilliant record of military achievement, his seniority over all active military men in the United States, his domineering but frequently charming demeanor, and his distance, both physical and mental, from events at home—all discouraged his supposed masters in the Pentagon from pushing him hard in directions he did not want to go. State Department officials also approached him with caution. In the face of his general lack of interest in Korea, the administration hesitated to force on him a more active role there.[62]

The withdrawal from Korea also occurred at a low point in relations between the Defense and State departments. Extremely touchy about his prerogatives as secretary of defense, and suspicious of most career military men, Johnson had imposed severe restrictions upon communications between the Pentagon and the State Department.[63] Under such circumstances, and given the well-known inclination of the Joint Chiefs to write off South Korea, diplomatic personnel shrank from pressing military leaders to take a more active and visible role regarding the situation there.

The preoccupation of Acheson with Europe, and of leading State Department Asian specialists with Japan, China, and Indochina, discouraged junior officials such as Max Bishop and Niles Bond from stressing the Korean problem to their superiors. After the spring and summer of 1949, when basic decisions were made and executed, it became difficult to draw top-level men to a relatively peripheral question. It had received some such attention in the reevaluation of early 1949, but, once that process was finished, it was not likely to be started all over again. In such circumstances, efforts at deterring a North Korean attack were bound to be less than diligent.

The attitudes of most American officials, both in the field and in Washington, toward the South Koreans also compromised deterrence. Throughout 1949 and early 1950, dissatisfaction continued regarding the performance of the Rhee government. The executive and legislative branches engaged in intense bickering, land reforms passed by the National Assembly were slow to be carried out, and Rhee was more inclined to handle criticism through strong-armed methods rather than compromise. In the summer of 1949, United Nations observers were especially annoyed by the arrest of several members of the legislature for alleged subversive activities.[64]

Although keenly aware of Rhee's shortcomings, Ambassador Muccio defended the South Korean president against his harshest critics. In a dispatch to Washington on 12 September, Muccio observed that:

> The Government of the Republic of Korea . . . is hardly more than thirty miles . . . from where its soldiers and police are frequently engaged in armed conflict with an aggressive enemy. In various places in South Korea, numerous bands of communist guerrillas . . . raid, murder and plunder the nearby countryside. Daily there are armed attacks on isolated police boxes, villages, or railway stations. Daily communication centers are sabotaged, wires are out, generators are destroyed, rails are torn-up. Almost daily someone is murdered by communist terrorist gangs, acting under directions from North Korea. Within the past three months there have been at least four fairly large battles fought along the thirty-eighth parallel. . . . The Pyongyang radio fills the air with demands for the liquidation of every member of the Government . . . and with appeals to the army and the police to turn their weapons on their leaders on behalf of the communist order. At Yosu, last October . . . , one regiment did so. . . . Government leaders do not forget that what was possible once might occur again. . . . Consequently it has been difficult for me privately to advise the Korean President against certain extreme actions which his Government has taken. . . . In the state of public fear, it is difficult to insist to the president that his advisers may be misinformed or that his decisions are unsound.

Muccio chided those who advocated the abandonment of the South Koreans "because they have imperfectly grasped those practices of democratic government which have taken so many centuries to develop in the Occidental world."[65]

Yet both the American ambassador and officials in Washington understood that the sources of widespread popular discontent went deeper than the subversive efforts of North Korea. When Jessup spoke to the National Assembly in January 1950, he urged his audience to recognize that strength was "not simply a matter of arms and force [but] of economic growth and social health and vigorous institutions, public and private."[66] The comment reflected the widespread American belief that, like the Nationalist Chinese earlier, the South Koreans should spend less time pressuring the United States for aid and more time carrying out American advice.

An even more pointed American statement appeared in April 1950, this time in the form of a State Department note to the government in Seoul. On 31 March, shortly after Jessup issued his report on conditions in Korea, Rhee had announced that legislative elections previously scheduled for May would be put off until November. The State Department took the opportunity to express American discontent, both with the decision to postpone elections and the failure to curb an ominous inflationary spiral. In a note of 7 April, the State Department warned that, unless satisfactory action was taken in both cases, the United States would "reexamine" its assistance program.[67]

To a degree, such statements achieved their purpose. Elections took place on 30 May, and efforts to control inflation intensified.[68] Nevertheless, Moscow and Pyongyang may have read open expressions of dissatisfaction with South Korea's performance as further evidence that, in the end, the United States would abandon Rhee to the same fate as Chiang Kai-shek.

Suspicions of the South Koreans also influenced the American response to intelligence reports relating to North Korean intentions. A South Korean spy network was the primary source of information on activities north of the thirty-eighth parallel, and American officials doubted the honesty and forthrightness of their Korean counterparts.[69] Rhee, they knew, wanted to unite the peninsula under his rule, by force if necessary. During the summer of 1949, his forces launched numerous raids into North Korea. The American embassy in Seoul was so fearful of a major South Korean military offensive that it permitted the distribution of American ammunition only in quantities that restricted operations to a few days at a time.[70] When South Korean officials warned of an impending attack from the north, Muccio and Roberts often wondered if they were simply being manipulated into requesting more arms from Washington, aid that would be used for a march north.

Past events and current perceptions bolstered American suspicions of reports that North Korea was about to launch a large-scale attack. Predictions of this sort had been made since October 1946, when General Hodge actually accepted evidence of an impending invasion. As James Schnabel, a member of the G-2 operation of the Far Eastern Command, later observed, "[by] late 1949, talk of a North Korean invasion was almost routine in intelligence circles."[71] Aware of past false alarms, analysts tended to be skeptical. At the end of the year, Major General Charles A. Willoughby, chief of MacArthur's intelligence arm, cited several reports that North Korea would move in the coming March or April, but he viewed such a prospect as "unlikely."[72] In February and March 1950, he passed on to Washington reports that an attack would occur in March or June, but again he expressed doubts. North Korea had not exhausted its chances of capturing the south, he said, "through guerrillas and psychological warfare." Thus a conventional military attack was premature. Moreover, the Far Eastern Command viewed Moscow as being more interested in Communist efforts in Southeast Asia, far away from American troops in Japan. Unless such activities received a setback, Tokyo concluded, the Korean situation probably would be kept in the background.[73]

In May and June, Seoul, Washington, and Tokyo received numerous reports of a general strengthening of North Korean forces. On 19 June, the Central Intelligence Agency reported that

Trained and equipped units of the Communist 'People's Army' are being deployed southward in the area of the thirty-eighth Parallel. 'People's Army' and Border Constabulary units here equal or surpass the strength of southern Korean army units similarly deployed. Tanks and heavy artillery have also been moved close to the Parallel in recent months.

Yet an ensuing analysis implied that the "coordinated campaign involving political pressure within southern Korea, subversion, propaganda, intimidation, economic pressure, and military actions by infiltration of guerrilla forces" would, for the present, take precedence over any plans for a major invasion.[74]

When North Korea renewed a propaganda offensive early in June, Willoughby concluded that the Russians believed the time ripe for an "attempt to subjugate the South Korean Government by political means, especially since the guerrilla campaign in South Korea recently has met with serious reverses."[75] Even Muccio, the most perceptive American official on the scene, did not view an attack as imminent.[76]

Schnabel notes that American officials considered North Korean activities along the thirty-eighth parallel to represent a long-standing Communist practice of rotating the locations of their best-equipped units.[77] Reports that, during March and April 1950, residents just north of the thirty-eighth parallel had been forced to evacuate their homes led Willoughby to speculate on the "[n]eed for additional troop billets, a general tightening of security measures, and armed clashes along the border." He also remarked that the people had been resettled on collective farms, which might be part of the effort to collectivize agriculture.[78]

Despite his failure to anticipate the attack of 25 June, Ambassador Muccio recognized South Korea's weakness. Since the fall of 1949, he had been pressing Washington for more military assistance. In October he wrote that the military aid program for fiscal year 1950—submitted by the Army Advisory Group—was based on requirements for a ground force of 65,000 men. Yet the South Korean army had recently been expanded to 100,000 men, which was not excessive in the face of the growth of North Korean forces. Thus Muccio pressed for increased military aid to South Korea.[79]

His pleas culminated in May 1950, when he visited Washington. As before, he proposed a doubling of funds for South Korea under the Mutual Defense Assistance Program. Monies were needed to provide tactical air power, fittings for naval vessels, and equipment for at least 65,000 troops.[80] Muccio even took his case to the National Security Council, where military officials told him they were not interested in expanding aid to South Korea unless his department found it necessary for political reasons.[81] He received encouragement from the State Department, especially on the possibility of halting the cannibalization of obsolete planes in the Far Eastern Command that might be used in Korea. On his return trip to Seoul, he stopped in Tokyo in an attempt to firm up a decision on the matter. He thought he had MacArthur's approval for the transfer of the aircraft to South Korea, but, upon returning to the peninsula, he received word to the contrary.[82] In early June, frustrated by his efforts within the executive branch, Muccio submitted a report to Congress stating that

> the undeniable material superiority of the North Korean forces would provide North Korea with a margin of victory in the event of a fullscale invasion of the Republic. Such superiority is particularly evident in the matter of heavy infantry support weapons, tanks, and combat aircraft with which the USSR has supplied and continues to supply its Korean puppet. It has been aggravated also by the recent Communist success in China which have increased considerably the military potential of the North, particularly by releasing undetermined numbers of Korean troops from the Chinese Communist armies for service in Korea. The threat to the Republic will continue as long as there exists in the North an aggressive Communist regime desiring the conquest and domination of the South.[83]

This evaluation conflicted with several other recent reports to the legislative branch. Senators Smith, Knowland, and Theodore Green (Democrat-Rhode Island) all had visited the peninsula between the fall of 1949 and the following spring and had left with favorable impressions of South Korea's capabilities.[84] American officials in Korea, concerned about Congress's hesitation to continue assistance in the face of the apparent U.S. retreat from the Asian mainland, emphasized the achievements of the aid programs, and did not give the lawmakers a realistic appraisal of local conditions.

Testimony by William C. Foster, a deputy administrator of the economic mission to South Korea, also decreased the impact of Muccio's warning to Congress. On 13 June 1950, Foster told the Senate Appropriations Committee that South Korea was "prepared to meet any challenge by North Korean forces." This estimate, he stated, was based on "official sources," probably General Roberts and other military officials in Korea.[85]

The exact views of the head of the Army Advisory Group remain somewhat unclear. In August 1949, he reported to Washington that North Korea did not have the capacity to conquer the south.[86] Two months later, on a visit to Tokyo, he expressed confidence in South Korea's defensive capabilities.[87] From this point onward, his reports became ambiguous, even at times contradictory. In November and December, Roberts requested equipment, including fighter planes, for a South Korean air force to counter the recent acquisition by North Korea of Soviet aircraft. He also asked for three-inch guns for Coast Guard vessels, signal and engineer equipment, 105 mm. howitzers, machine guns, and mortars.[88] In his semiannual report of January 1950, Roberts observed that there was a "growing air threat from North

Korea" and that the condition of the Coast Guard was "of growing concern." The military assistance program of $10 million for fiscal year 1950 could "do no more than maintain the limited equipment now on hand," he claimed, and this equipment was itself inadequate for the South Korean army. In their present condition, Roberts concluded, the republic's forces could maintain internal security, but could "offer only limited resistance to an invasion from the north." In another section of the report, however, Roberts outlined a plan for defense against a North Korean attack; if the South Koreans followed it, he asserted, they could "contain and repel" the offensive "if no Chinese Communist troops are committed."[89] Presumably, this judgment assumed the proper equipping of South Korean forces. In March, Roberts wrote to General Bolté of the Army's Plans and Operations Division that "If South Korea were attacked today by the inferior ground forces of North Korea plus their Air Corps, I feel that South Korea would take a bloody nose. Again, then, knowing these people somewhat, I feel that they would follow the apparent winner and South Korea would be gobbled up to be added to the rest of Red Asia."[90] But, in April, Roberts told newsmen that raids along the thirty-eighth parallel had decreased considerably in recent months, and that it was as safe in Korea as in the United States. A month later, he told reporters covering the National Assembly elections of 30 May that no buildup of North Korean forces was in progress along the thirty-eighth parallel.[91]

By the time war broke out, Roberts had retired from his post and was on his way back to the United States. When questioned by the press regarding the North Korean offensive, he expressed confidence in South Korea's capabilities. According to the *New York Times*, he said that a "full-scale attack . . . was just what was needed to complete the training of the South Korean Army." Although concerned about the enemy's air power, he considered North Korea's use of tanks only a "slight" advantage because Korea's terrain was unsuitable for such weapons.[92] A few days before the North Korean attack, Colonel W. H. Sterling Wright, acting head of the military advisory group, told William R. Mathews of the *Arizona Star* that South Korea could contain any offensive from across the thirty-eighth parallel.[93] Yet the semiannual report of the American advisers, written in mid-June, concluded that "Korea is threatened with the same disaster that befell China." The South Korean army was so poorly supplied that it could not sustain defensive operations for more than fifteen days.[94]

Military advisers were genuinely concerned about the supply situation in South Korea and North Korea's air power, but felt compelled to exude confidence in statements that might become public. They believed that the high morale of South Korean troops was a major ingredient in their strength and may have feared that pessimistic comments would do more harm than good.

The military advisers may have been less aggressive than Muccio in pressing Washington for more aid because they were aware that the Joint Chiefs had little interest in Korea. In contrast, the State Department took the American stake in it more seriously. A comparison of the status of Muccio and Roberts within their own services reflected this difference. The top American diplomat in Korea became a career minister, the highest rank within the diplomatic service, at age 47; the leading American military man on the peninsula was about to retire at a rank several steps below that of full general.[95] Muccio was more confident than Roberts not only of his department's concern about Korea, but about his own standing within the department. He also had greater respect than Roberts for South Korean leaders and for Koreans in general.

Why did Muccio—and in some measure his military colleagues—accept the reports of Korean agents on North Korean military strength while rejecting those predicting an invasion? The answer is probably threefold. First, it is far easier to establish an enemy's physical strength than its intentions. North Korean orders to attack were such a carefully guarded secret that, according to United States estimates, two divisional chiefs of staff in the People's Army received no definite word of the operation until around 18 June.[96] Second, when—in April and May 1950—the largest buildup of North Korea's forces occurred, several warnings of an impending attack had already proven false and this undermined the credibility of new ones. Third, although by the spring of 1950 the Rhee regime had succeeded in greatly weakening the leftist guerrilla movement in the south, American intelligence regarded subversive activities as an ongoing threat to the republic that the North Koreans would give a longer trial before risking an overt military move.[97]

The question remains as to why the Truman administration failed to respond in a more positive fashion to the warnings from Seoul. Although $10.2 million had been allotted to South Korea in the Mutual Defense Assistance Act passed on 6 October 1949, by the following June only a few hundred dollars worth of signal equipment had reached the peninsula.[98] Washington took no final action on proposals for supplemental aid.

Procedural problems caused some of the delays in the implementation of the legislation of October 1949. Congress did not pass an appropriation to activate the authorization earlier in the month until 28 October. Three months then passed before bilateral agreements were concluded with South Korea on the program's execution. Survey teams working under the administrator of the Mutual Defense Assistance Program took two more months in conferring with Korean officials.[99]

Additional delays occurred because of the general state of the American defense establishment. As with past programs, the limited availability of many items and the need to service much of the matériel that was on hand necessitated the establishment of priorities. Deliveries to NATO countries, plus Greece, Turkey, and Iran naturally took precedence over those to Korea.

As a result, much of the equipment and ammunition desired by South Korea needed to come from commercial suppliers under new procurement contracts.[100] Under such circumstances, the Joint Chiefs were understandably cool toward more sizable outlays for South Korea. The local balance of forces was disadvantageous to America's friends in areas of greater strategic significance than Korea. Until requirements were on the way to being met in crucial places, it was unwise to think about expanding aid to a peripheral country such as South Korea.

The State Department, on the other hand, believed that American credibility was at stake on the peninsula, and thus was more concerned about the security of the young nation. Some officials knew that a North Korean attack, though not imminent, was a distinct possibility. They initially supported Muccio's May 1950 request for obsolete planes in the Far Eastern Command and other military equipment. The former project was probably held up because it ran afoul of military efforts to divert the planes to Taiwan. MacArthur already had advised against the creation of a South Korean air force; he argued that it was unnecessary for maintaining internal order, would increase the chances of war on the peninsula, and would bolster Communist claims that the United States was fostering an arms race there.[101] In May, his attitude, as well as that of the Joint Chiefs, was reinforced by renewed pressures from the Nationalists for aid to strengthen their air force.[102]

Under State Department pressure, the Defense Department expressed a willingness to permit supplemental aid to the South Korean army prior to any revision of American policy.[103] Yet increased assistance necessitated availability studies of the needed matériels and then the adjustment of priorities for shipment to various countries. On 19 May, Dean Rusk turned the matter over to the Foreign Military Assistance Coordinating Committee for final approval. Five weeks later, when North Korean forces moved aross the thirty-eighth parallel, that committee still had not rendered a decision.[104]

In the spring of 1950, Acheson was more fearful of a Communist action in Berlin, Greece, Turkey, or Iran, or in Indochina, where an armed conflict was already in progress and where the revolutionary tide could easily flow into adjacent areas. His desire to carry out a military aid program to bolster the French effort there overshadowed the Korean question. Rusk considered the Taiwan issue to be preeminent. Furthermore, the estimates of Roberts were less alarmist than Muccio's. (The semiannual report of mid-June arrived in Washington too late to have any impact.) MacArthur, in Tokyo, appeared unworried. When Secretary of Defense Johnson and General Bradley visited him only days before the outbreak of war, his staff—which depended largely on American army officials in Korea for their information—estimated that the republic could "maintain itself, unless the Soviets openly support North Korea in an armed invasion."[105] Thus Muccio stood alone on the American side in the intensity of his warnings, and even he did not view a North

Korean attack as imminent. Under such circumstances, it is easily understood why the State Department did not respond to his pleas with a greater sense of urgency.

## Korea on the Eve of War

Ultimately, American efforts to bolster South Korea were just successful enough to push the regime in Pyongyang over the brink from subversive activities to open military attack. Unlike the problems in China, those below the thirty-eighth parallel were small enough in scope to be influenced by minimal American aid. In addition, South Korea was so clearly dependent for its survival on the United States that Rhee, however difficult, was more susceptible than Chiang to American pressure. Contrary to the situation in Indochina, the United States found in Rhee a leader with both genuine nationalist credentials and substantial political skill. That skill, to be sure, had proven inadequate to unify right-wing forces behind his leadership. The 30 May elections for seats in the National Assembly represented a setback to Rhee's efforts to consolidate his regime. Factionalism among the anti-Communists remained a nagging constraint on the young nation's development. But this political turmoil was not accompanied by a strengthened guerrilla movement in the countryside. The spring of 1950, in fact, was a period of relative calm in the republic's ongoing and increasingly successful struggle against armed subversion from within.[106]

By that time, a variety of circumstances—both inside and outside Korea—had converged to make an explosion on the peninsula likely. To outsiders, the United States, though determined to maintain its position in Japan, appeared to lack the resolve to protect South Korea. To the Kremlin, therefore, a North Korean march southward would extend Russia's buffer zone in the east and conceivably make America's task in Japan more difficult. Conversely, to deny Kim Il-sung the opportunity to achieve the Korean aspiration of national unity—especially in the face of Mao's support for the venture—might undermine Stalin's influence in Pyongyang and even lower the Soviet Union's status among Asian Communists.

To Kim, conditions in Korea in mid-1950 probably offered the best opportunity he was likely to have to consolidate his power over the entire country. Guerrilla activities had been widespread in the south for well over three years, but they showed no immediate prospect for success in toppling the republic. Economic conditions below the thirty-eighth parallel had improved somewhat over the past year, which reduced one source of unrest.[107] The balance of military forces favored the north, yet Rhee had recently created twenty-one combat police battalions and expanded greatly his air force personnel. Equipment for these new units was not readily available, to be sure, but the government in Pyongyang may have feared it would arrive in the near future. When it did, the northern advantage might disappear, and Rhee might even carry out his oft-repeated threat to unify the peninsula forcefully.[108]

In sum, although the Truman administration had succeeded temporarily in its effort to build a viable state below the thirty-eighth parallel, its failure over the previous two and a half years to coordinate military strength and foreign policy objectives or to convey to the Communists the depth of America's commitment to South Korea, together with military conditions on the peninsula and the successful revolution in China, invited a conflict that would influence United States policy in East Asia for decades.

# PART IV
## Containment, Liberation, and Confrontation: American Policy in the Early Months of the Korean War

The United States failed to employ an effective strategy of deterrence in Korea, but, when Communist forces moved south of the thirty-eighth parallel on 25 June 1950, Washington officials barely hesitated before taking extensive military action. When South Korean forces proved unable to resist the offensive, American troops were rushed to the peninsula. This move represented a reversal of policy only in the narrow sense that it placed American soldiers back into an area from which they had previously been withdrawn. In fact, in view of State Department thinking on Korea going back at least four years, large-scale military intervention was the logical and—in retrospect—the predictable response to North Korean action. The diplomats perceived a major threat to American credibility abroad, among allies and enemies alike. President Truman agreed, and military leaders acceded with barely a whimper.

Other responses to the North Korean attack were also predictable. The stepped-up aid to the French in Indochina and to the Philippines merely built upon past decisions and policies. The announcement that the Seventh Fleet was being imposed between Taiwan and the mainland to prevent an invasion going either to or from the island represented a reversal of policy. It was a reversal, however, consistent in the new circumstances with Truman administration statements of the previous January, and predictable in the context of an increasingly alarmist climate in Washington.

To say the American response was logical and predictable, nevertheless, is not to deny that the outbreak of war in Korea was a pivotal event in the development of United States policy in Asia. Surely it was. It made possible the rapid implementation of NSC 68 and solidified NATO as a concrete military structure. It also provided a great boost to the idea of German rearmament. Without war in Korea, Taiwan probably would have fallen to the Communists within months, which would remove a major source of friction between Peking and Washington. The Communist regime might well have gained admission to the United Nations. Such an event would have increased American contacts with the Mao government and eliminated another barrier to fruitful relations between the two sides.

Still, the outbreak of war in Korea did not eradicate the long-term possibility of worthwhile interaction between the United States and mainland China. Only the massive Chinese counteroffensive in Korea in late November did that. Only then did American policy regarding Taiwan, the admission of Peking into the United Nations, and recognition of that regime become set for the foreseeable future. And China's intervention occurred only after American troops crossed the thirty-eighth parallel. A chance to avoid a major Sino-American confrontation may even have remained right up until 24 November, when General MacArthur launched his "home-by-Christmas" offensive. Had the United States halted its armies at the narrow neck of the peninsula—or even slightly north of that point—a bitter and extended conflict might not have materialized.

Why in early October did the United States move north of the thirty-eighth parallel? Why, in the face of Chinese intervention three weeks later, did the Truman administration fail to halt its troops short of the Yalu? The answers are complex, but they point clearly to many of the earlier forces that had shaped American policy. First among these forces was an ongoing concern for American credibility abroad, especially in the Communist world. The mere containment of the North Korean attack, it was argued in the State Department, would encourage future aggression, both on the peninsula and elsewhere. Moscow would perceive that the worst possible outcome of Communist aggression was the eventual reestablishment of the status quo ante. Thus, aggression would have few liabilities and numerous potential advantages. If United Nations forces united Korea, however, Stalin and his henchmen would realize that aggression could have serious drawbacks. The first direct Communist attack across an established boundary since World War II, therefore, might be the last.

Yet the American move into North Korea also rested on the assumption that neither the Soviet Union nor Communist China would intervene directly in the conflict. If Russia or China were to become involved, Washington believed, they would move before United Nations forces reached the thirty-eighth parallel. When neither did, the way seemed clear. Whereas the estimate of Soviet intentions turned out to be correct, that regarding China was wrong. It was so in large part because many American leaders underestimated Communist Chinese strength. From 1947 to 1949, State Department analysts had questioned the capacity of the Communists to unite and rule China. Now American officials doubted Peking's willingness and/or ability to intervene abroad in the face of severe economic and political problems at home.

In November 1950, concerns about American credibility and perceptions of Communist Chinese strength again influenced Washington policy-makers. Hesitation after the initial clashes with Chinese soldiers, it was believed, might convey to Peking a sense of American weakness and foster aggressiveness in the enemy. Given Peking's internal problems and limited military capabilities, on the other hand, a firm American policy might carry the day. Yet in the United States there was considerable uneasiness with this reasoning. Ultimately it prevailed, but only after considerable anguish.

In the circumstances of doubt existing in Washington during the first three weeks of November, personalities and institutions played a key role. General MacArthur in Tokyo became a central figure in decision making. From 9 November onward, he took a hard line on the question of a continued United Nations advance in Korea. His prestige in the United States, both with government officials and the people at large, had never been higher. His apparent certainty that aggressiveness would produce victory carried decisive weight among confused and uncertain leaders at home. Recently appointed Secretary of Defense George Marshall also had great influence. His support of the Joint Chiefs in advocating a bold policy weakened whatever inclination existed in the State Department to alter MacArthur's orders. Finally, the legacy of several years of conflict over American Asian policy between the diplomats and military leaders probably firmed up the Pentagon in its determination to support the field commander. In the fall of 1950, therefore, a variety of forces coalesced to produce a confrontation that would have tragic consequences for at least a generation afterward.

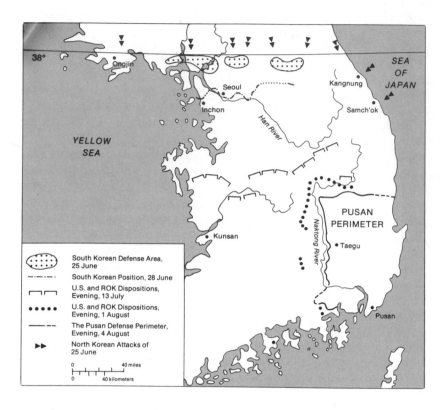

MAP 2. The War in Korea, 25 June–4 August 1950

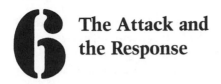

# The Attack and the Response

## The Crisis Week: The Three Stages of Intervention

At four o'clock on Sunday morning, 25 June, North Korean armed forces launched major attacks at seven points along the thirty-eighth parallel and amphibious landings in two areas on the eastern coast of South Korea.[1] The offensive took the south by surprise. Many South Korean troops stationed along the thirty-eighth parallel were away on weekend passes. Because General Roberts had left the peninsula en route to the United States and a new assignment, the American military advisory group was without a permanent commander. Its acting chief, Colonel W. H. Sterling Wright, was in Tokyo.[2]

Policymakers in the United States were also caught off guard. The attack occurred at about three o'clock Saturday afternoon, Washington time. President Truman was in his home town of Independence, Missouri, and Secretary Acheson was at his farm in Maryland. The first official word of fighting in Korea reached the State Department at 9:26 P.M. Ambassador Muccio reported that the North Korean attack appeared to be "an all-out offensive against the Republic of Korea."[3] By midnight all top administration officials, except Paul Nitze, who was salmon fishing in Nova Scotia, and George Kennan, who lacked a telephone at his Pennsylvania farm, had received the news. The seven days between the North Korean attack and the commitment on 30 June of American combat troops to the peninsula have received scrutiny in several published works and therefore warrant only brief review in this volume.[4]

American action occurred in three stages. In the first, the United States took the Korean issue to the Security Council of the United Nations. The decision to do this was made on 24 June, only hours after Washington officialdom received word of the attack. It was perhaps the only move in the crisis period that had been planned in advance.[5]

When the Security Council convened in emergency session on the following afternoon, the United States presented a resolution calling on North Korea to cease hostilities and withdraw its forces to the thirty-eighth parallel. The United Nations Commission on Korea was to observe such a retreat and inform the Security Council of the implementation of the resolution. Members of the Security Council were "to render every assistance to the United Nations" in executing these measures and "to refrain from giving assistance to North Korean authorities."[6] The Security Council passed the proposals—by a 9-0 margin (Yugoslavia abstained)—with only minor adjustments in wording.[7] The action was made possible by the absence of the Soviet Union, which had been boycotting the body since mid-January to protest the continued seating of Nationalist rather than Communist China. American leaders regarded the resolution as providing adequate authority for the use of non-Korean forces to reestablish the thirty-eighth parallel as a boundary.[8]

In Tokyo, MacArthur already had decided to meet South Korean requests for ten fighter planes and for some arms and ammunition readily available to the Far Eastern Command. He informed Washington of this move on Sunday morning (EDT).[9]

Later that day, the State Department notified Ambassador Muccio that American military advisers were to stay with South Korean units for as long as possible.[10] This move reflected, at an early point in the crisis, a sense of a deep United States commitment on the peninsula. Less than three years earlier, on the China issue, American diplomats in Washington had resisted proposals to send military officials to advise Nationalist combat units for fear that this action would begin an irreversible pattern of involvement in the civil war there. Yet a similar move occurred regarding Korea without the president's knowledge. And there is no evidence that anyone brought up the matter at the high-level conference that followed.

The second stage of decision concerned the commitment of theater air and naval forces to action in South Korea and in the Taiwan strait. It commenced on Sunday evening when the president brought together his leading advisers for a meeting at Blair House.[11] At his request, Acheson took the lead in making proposals. He advocated four specific moves: the formal approval of MacArthur's action to supply the South Koreans with arms and ammunition from the Far Eastern Command, the protection by American air forces in Japan of Kimpo airport outside Seoul during the evacuation of United States dependents, the movement of the Seventh Fleet from the Philippines to the straits of Taiwan to prevent any attack from the mainland of the offshore islands or vice versa, and the increase of American aid to Indochina. Acheson also suggested consideration of additional assistance for South Korea in support of the resolution already adopted by the Security Council.[12]

After military leaders and other State Department officials had spoken, Truman outlined his decisions. MacArthur was to continue his efforts to supply the South Koreans. He was to send a survey group to the peninsula and provide air cover for the evacuation of American women and children. The Seventh Fleet was to proceed northward from the Philippines toward Japan, and fleet units from California were to debark for Hawaii. The air force should prepare—but not execute—plans to destroy Soviet air bases in East Asia. The State and Defense departments should study places where further Soviet moves might occur. The State Department was to draft a statement outlining all actions taken by the United States, to be presented to Congress by the president on Tuesday.[13]

The next major decisions were made on the following night at another top-level meeting at Blair House. In the twenty-four hours between the two conferences, the situation in Korea became clearer in two respects. First, North Korea obviously had no intention of obeying the Security Council resolution calling for a cessation of hostilities and the reestablishment of the thirty-eighth parallel boundary. Second, South Korea certainly needed the assistance of American forces to repulse the attack. Rhee's forces could not hold Seoul and were in some danger of "imminent collapse."[14] If further deterioration was to be averted, the United States must act.

Acheson recommended that American air and naval forces in the western Pacific support the South Koreans with extensive action below the thirty-eighth parallel, that the Seventh Fleet prevent a Chinese Communist attack on Taiwan and vice versa, and that American military forces in the Philippines—as well as other aid to that country—be increased. Lastly, he proposed stepped-up assistance to Indochina, including a sizable American military mission. The president immediately approved all these points, as well as a suggestion that he issue a statement on the following day outlining American moves.[15] The secretary of state offered a State Department draft that Truman agreed to study during the night.[16]

John Hickerson, assistant secretary of state for United Nations affairs, read a draft resolution that was to be presented to the Security Council on the following afternoon. The resolution called on members of the United Nations to render such assistance to the Republic of Korea as was necessary to repulse the attack. The president approved this measure and stated he wanted as many nations involved in the enterprise as possible. After Dean Rusk noted the possibility of a Soviet veto, Truman accepted Louis Johnson's assertion that it made necessary an announcement of American action to assist South Korea before the Security Council deliberated on the proposal.[17]

The participants also addressed the question of dealing with Congress. Earlier in the day, Truman had approached Senator Connally on the legality of committing American forces in Korea without the prior approval of Congress. Rather than risk an extensive debate by asking for authorization from Capitol Hill, the Texan encouraged the president to act on his own.[18] As a believer in a strong executive, the president surely agreed with Connally.[19] Thus, discussion at the second Blair House meeting centered on determining which members of the House and Senate would be invited to a White House briefing on the following day. A list of fourteen lawmakers was finally agreed upon.[20]

Nearly three days were to pass before the Truman administration made further decisions on Korea. The period from the end of the second Blair

House meeting late Monday evening to the convening of the National Security Council at five o'clock Thursday afternoon was one of implementation. During this time, MacArthur made the only decision of consequence involving American military action, when, on Thursday morning (Korean time) and without the knowledge of Washington, he ordered planes in his command to bomb airfields north of the thirty-eighth parallel.[21]

On Tuesday, 27 June (EDT) Truman met with congressional leaders to review American actions and released a statement to the press outlining them. The president's guests from Capitol Hill were unanimous in their support of administration policy.[22] This approval was best expressed by two Republican senators who commented to the press upon leaving the meeting. Styles Bridges declared, "I think it is damned good action." H. Alexander Smith stated that he was "very pleased."[23]

They soon had much company. Shortly after the White House meeting, Truman released his statement summarizing American action. It evoked support and relief throughout the nation. Governor Thomas E. Dewey of New York wired the president that his course "was necessary to the security of our country and the free world."[24] Senator William F. Knowland, like Bridges and Smith a prominent critic of administration Asian policy, praised Truman's moves and called on all Americans to back them. Several other Republicans, as well as Democrats, made similar remarks on the Senate floor.[25] After House majority leader John W. McCormack (Democrat-Massachusetts) read the president's announcement in the lower chamber, those present—with the exception of Vito Marcantonio, the American Labor Party Representative from New York—stood up and applauded. The House then voted 315-4 to extend the Selective Service Act for one year. In New York, the stock market recovered from a sharp drop in prices on the previous day.[26] The prevailing feeling of Monday, characterized by reporter Richard L. Strout as "apathetic fatalism" grounded in the belief that the administration was "impotent to act in the sudden crisis," disappeared.[27]

Several Republicans, however, did question the president's authority to commit American forces abroad without explicit congressional sanction. Senator Robert A. Taft presented this view most forcefully in a speech on Wednesday afternoon on the floor of the upper house. Yet he stated he would support a resolution approving the use of American forces already sent to Korea.[28]

Friendly nations abroad also responded favorably. Leading officials in Great Britain, France, and Italy announced their support of the president's actions.[29] On 28 June, the Labor government in London announced it was putting British naval forces in Northeast Asia at the disposal of the United States.[30] Earlier reports from the Netherlands, Australia, Canada, Pakistan, Turkey, Belgium, Japan, and India indicated widespread support in those nations for a strong American stance.[31]

This attitude also manifested itself in the United Nations. At 3:00 P.M. on

27 June, the Security Council met for the second time since the North Korean attack. Soviet Ambassador Jacob A. Malik did not attend. American Ambassador Warren Austin presented a resolution calling on members of the United Nations to "furnish such assistance to the Republic of Korea as may be necessary to repel the armed attack and to restore international peace and security in the area."[32] Just before midnight, the Security Council passed the American proposal. Great Britain, France, Nationalist China, Cuba, Equador, Norway, and the United States voted in the affirmative. Egypt and India, whose representatives had not yet received instructions from home, abstained. Only Yugoslavia opposed the measure.[33]

The response of Moscow and Peking naturally contrasted sharply with that in the West. Like North Korea, the two leading Communist powers claimed that South Korea had initiated hostilities with military moves north of the thirty-eighth parallel.[34] In a front page editorial on 28 June, *Pravda*, the Soviet Communist party newspaper, characterized American action of the previous day as "direct aggression against the Korean People's Democratic Republic and the Chinese People's Republic."[35] A day later, *Jen Min Jih Pao*, the official party paper in Peking, printed a statement by Foreign Minister Chou En-lai asserting that the United States had ordered Syngman Rhee to attack his northern neighbor as a "pretext" for American "aggression" against Taiwan, Korea, Indochina, and the Philippines. Following Chou's declaration was a polemic by party chairman Mao Tse-tung that ended with a call to the people of China and the world to "arise" and "[d]efeat every provocation of American imperialism!"[36]

Despite the Sino-Soviet verbal barrage against American action, there was no concrete evidence that Moscow or Peking intended to enter directly into the Korean fighting. At noon on 29 June, the State Department received the Soviet reply to an American note on Korea. The Russian communique reiterated the official Soviet position that hostilities "were provoked by" South Korea. The Soviet Union, it continued, regarded foreign interference "in the internal affairs of Korea" as unwarranted. Finally, the Kremlin justified its absence from the Security Council on the ground that the refusal of the body to seat Communist China as a permanent member made legally binding decisions impossible.[37] The State Department regarded this response as additional evidence of the Kremlin's desire to avoid direct involvement in Korea.[38] Combined with the more heated statements emanating from Peking, the Soviet note led the president to conclude that "the Soviets are going to let the Chinese do the fighting for them," but even then probably only indirectly through the return to the peninsula of Korean nationals who had fought for the Communists in Manchuria.[39]

Despite the apparent decision of Russia and China to avoid direct intervention, and the use of American air and naval power in the area, South Korean forces continued to retreat. Late on Wednesday morning (Korean time), North Korean troops marched into Seoul while the defending army moved southward across the Han River. Prior to the completion of the withdrawal, a panicky South Korean officer ordered the destruction of bridges over the river. As a result, his troops were cut off from many of their transport vehicles, supplies, and heavy weapons.[40] Major General John H. Church, who had been sent to the peninsula by MacArthur to survey the military situation, reported to Tokyo that only American troops could reestablish the thirty-eighth parallel.[41] When the National Security Council met in Washington on Wednesday afternoon (EDT), however, information was too indefinite to warrant an immediate decision to deploy American army units.[42]

By late Thursday morning, 29 June, this was no longer the case. At 11:55 A.M., after the receipt of reports that South Korea had a precarious hold on the south bank of the Han River, Johnson called the president and requested another top-level meeting.[43] Truman immediately arranged for a conference at the White House for 5:00 P.M. Thus began the final stage of decision in the Korean crisis, the stage in which American troops finally were committed to combat on the peninsula.

Before leading administration officials assembled, the Joint Chiefs prepared recommendations and gained State Department approval for them. The military leaders, still unaware that MacArthur had already done so, proposed to extend American air and naval operations into North Korea. They also advocated sending American ground forces to secure the air, naval, and communications facilities at the port of Pusan, well south of the scene of combat.[44] At this point, the Joint Chiefs did not envision the early use of American troops in combat zones. U.S. soldiers in the Pusan area were merely to protect the military facilities of that city and assist in the supply of South Korean forces at the front.[45]

Military leaders in Washington were hesitant to send large numbers of combat troops to Korea. They feared that, in the event of conflict with Russia, such a move would make impossible the effective execution of emergency war plans. These plans, although relegating East Asia to a status of secondary importance, called for the defense of Japan, Okinawa, and the Philippines. Major General Charles L. Bolté, an Army assistant chief of staff, pointed out that the replacement of army units sent to Korea from Japan with soldiers from "the small strategic reserve" in the United States would compromise America's "war readiness in other areas."[46] Army officials also feared the basic unpreparedness of their troops for large-scale combat.[47] Former elements of the Chinese Communist armies were known to be taking part in the North Korean offensive. While these soldiers had been fighting in a civil war in Manchuria, their American counterparts in Japan had become accustomed to standing on street corners in Tokyo whistling at girls. General Thomas S. Timberman, an assistant to Bolté, later observed that many of North Korea's invaders could crawl on their bellies farther than American men in Japan could walk on their feet.[48]

Truman responded enthusiastically to reports of India's support for the Security Council resolution of 27 June, and of offers from Australia, New Zealand, Canada, and the Netherlands of planes and naval facilities for use in the Korean enterprise.[49] After the meeting, Acheson returned to the White House with a message from Chiang Kai-shek that thirty-three thousand Nationalist troops were available for action on the peninsula if they could be transported and supplied by the United States.[50] Ever desirous of emphasizing the collective nature of efforts to repulse North Korea, the president liked the idea. The secretary of state, however, urged caution. As a result, Truman postponed a decision on the question until he could discuss it with all his top advisers.[51]

Such a discussion was not long in coming. The immediate impetus for a White House conference that commenced at 9:30 A.M. Friday, 30 June, was MacArthur's recommendation, received in Washington six and a half hours earlier after a personal visit to the peninsula, for the commitment of American troops to the center of the fighting in Korea. A regimental combat team should be sent at once, he stated, and a future buildup of two divisions might be necessary. The Far Eastern commander's rationale for the proposal was twofold. First, South Korean units held onto the south bank of the Han River only precariously. If this line broke, the Communists might overrun the entire peninsula. Second, even if the Han River line was held, South Korean forces lacked the capacity for a counteroffensive. Thus if the status quo ante was to be reestablished, American troops were essential.[52] (Actually, by the time MacArthur's message reached the Pentagon, North Korean forces had crossed the Han and were pushing southward toward Suwon.)[53] Upon receipt of MacArthur's recommendation, the officer on duty at the Defense Department contacted General Collins. The army chief of staff went immediately to the Pentagon and, by 3:40 A.M. was engaged in a teleconference with the Far Eastern commander. Dean Rusk, representing the State Department, also participated. Collins immediately authorized the dispatch of a regimental combat team to the Pusan area, but he thought the president would want to consult with his advisers before approving the introduction of American troops into the battle area. MacArthur, however, pressed for greater latitude, declaring that "a clear-cut decision without delay is imperative."[54] Collins then called Secretary of the Army Frank Pace and requested that he phone the president while the teleconference was in progress. Truman was reached at Blair House at 4:57 A.M. and gave the go-ahead on the commitment of a regimental combat team to forward positions in Korea. He refused to authorize a buildup of two American divisions until another top-level conference could be held.[55]

After receiving a briefing at 7:00 A.M. from Colonel Henry Ahalt of the Defense Department staff, the president arranged for such a conference.[56] By 9:30 that morning, all his leading foreign policy advisers had arrived for a meeting in the White House Cabinet Room. In addition to MacArthur's rec-

ommendation for a buildup of two American divisions in Korea, the participants discussed Chiang's offer of the previous day. Truman still favored acceptance of the generalissimo's proposal for the use of thirty-three thousand
of his soldiers in Korea. When all others present demurred, however, the
commander in chief retreated. The military doubted the usefulness of the
troops, and thought American transport planes could be better employed in
handling U.S. forces and supplies. The diplomats feared that direct involvement of the Nationalists in Korea might encourage the Chinese Communists to initiate military action of their own. No one, on the other hand, objected to sending two American divisions to the peninsula, or to Admiral
Forrest Sherman's proposal for a naval blockade of North Korea.[57] With
these moves, the United States was committed, in fact as well as in theory,
to the defense of South Korea. Of the issues faced in the preceding days, only
that of the legislature's role in the intervention remained to be resolved. It
was not until 3 July that this matter was discussed in detail by Truman and
his top advisers.

At 11:00 A.M. on 30 June, however, the president did meet with fifteen
congressional leaders in the White House Cabinet Room. He gave a short
summary of recent American actions, excluding only the decision to commit United States army units directly to combat areas. Instead, he stated
that the current plan was only to send American soldiers to Pusan to keep
communications and supply lines open, a lie designed to avoid leaks that
would reveal to the enemy American troop movements.[58] A White House
press release, issued while the meeting was in progress, mentioned the
American naval blockade of North Korea and air operations north of the
thirty-eighth parallel, but stated only that MacArthur had "been authorized
to use certain supporting ground units."[59]

At this meeting, Senator Wherry argued forcefully that Congress should
have been consulted before the commitment of American ground troops in
Korea. The president assured the Nebraskan that the legislative branch
would be told if "any large scale actions were to take place." This response
reflected the prevailing assumption at the time that American military operations in Korea would be very limited in both scope and duration.[60] Truman
also emphasized that his moves to date had been emergency ones taken under his authority as commander in chief.[61] Apparently, Senator Smith suggested a congressional resolution approving the administration's acts.[62]
When Wherry persisted in his criticism, Congressman Dewey Short expressed the view, which he claimed reflected the opinion of nearly everyone
on Capitol Hill, that Congress was in debt to the president for the high
quality of his leadership in the crisis.[63]

When, on 3 July, Truman met with his subordinates at Blair House to discuss relations with Congress, top military and foreign policy officials were
accompanied by Secretaries John Snyder and Charles Brannan of the Treasury and Agriculture departments, respectively, Postmaster General Jesse

Donaldson, Senate Majority Leader Scott Lucas, and recently appointed presidential assistant Averell Harriman. At the meeting of 30 June with leaders from Capitol Hill, the president had asked his secretary of state to prepare a recommendation on the question of presenting a resolution to Congress. On 3 July, Acheson suggested a presidential report to Congress on American action in Korea and a joint resolution, initiated from within the Congress, approving that course. The second idea was rejected rather quickly, largely because it might stir debate and confusion regarding the president's powers as commander in chief, but the first sparked considerable discussion. The majority feared that a report to Congress would lead to a debate that, in turn, would undermine the prevailing consensus at home on the Korean intervention and embarrass the United States abroad. Most people on Capitol Hill were content without a report, it was argued, and the few who were not were irreconcilable. Truman decided not to call back congressmen from their 4 July recess; rather he would consult with their leaders when they returned on 10 July.[64] When, on 19 July, he sent a special message to Congress, it was aimed primarily at gaining legislative approval for a rapid expansion of American military forces, rather than at maintaining general support for specific action in Korea.[65]

## The Korean Intervention: An Interpretation

The Truman administration's response to the North Korean attack across the thirty-eighth parallel raises a host of questions for the historian, few of which can be answered simply. First, why did Washington choose to intervene militarily in Korea? The use of air and naval forces is fairly easy to explain because that action cost little in terms of America's ability to execute its general war plans in the event Communist nations attacked in more critical areas. The movement of most of the Seventh Fleet from the Philippines to the Yellow Sea, in fact, put that unit in a better position to defend Japan, the most critical territory to American security in the entire western Pacific. Air and naval action, in sum, involved low-risk operations that were clearly appropriate in the face of America's relationship to the Republic of Korea.

In contrast, the commitment of American ground forces did disrupt the Pentagon's war plans. Three basic conditions made the action conceivable, the last two of which simply had not been anticipated in advance. First was America's atomic and industrial advantage over Russia. This superiority enabled the United States to take conventional action at a strategically peripheral point without making itself vulnerable to an overwhelming setback in a more important area.[66] Second was the absence of Soviet military actions in other places, or of evidence of preparations for such moves. By 29 June, it seemed likely that the North Korean attack was an isolated operation. Third was the apparent decision of Moscow and Peking not to commit their own troops to the peninsula. Such an intervention would have prevented the United States from maintaining a beachhead on the peninsula.[67]

If these three conditions made American ground action conceivable, they did not necessarily make it desirable. What did this was the State Department's strong belief—to which President Truman subscribed—that the United States would lose something of major consequence if it did not repulse the attack. The North Korean move led American leaders to fear a repeat of the 1930s, when the "democratic" powers in the West had permitted Japan, Italy, and Germany to get away with aggression. Successful aggression by one nation had encouraged it by others, and, in the end, a world war had resulted. Now, in 1950, America's submission to aggression would encourage similar Communist moves elsewhere.[68] Furthermore, if the United States failed to show determination at this time, friendly nations in Europe and worldwide would question its reliability. Collective security in the West would suffer a severe blow.[69]

Why was the North Korean attack labeled "aggression"? Why didn't American leaders perceive the outbreak of fighting on the peninsula as simply a civil conflict between contending political factions? Truman and his advisers did not do so because they regarded the thirty-eighth parallel as an established international boundary, one that had been set temporarily in 1945 to delineate Soviet and American occupation zones, but which later had gained permanence and legitimacy—unless altered by mutual consent. The first step in this process was the failure of Moscow and Washington to agree on procedures for unification; the second was the creation of a United Nations–sponsored government below the line. Given the central roles of Russia and the United States in Korea since 1945, the North Korean attack became, indirectly, an act of the Soviet Union, one that could compromise America's credibility worldwide.[70]

The timing of the Korean crisis also merits discussion. The North Korean attack came when the Truman administration's Asian policy was under intense attack from the Republican opposition, and when an off-year election campaign was on the horizon. It also came less than a year after the Soviet Union's explosion of an atomic device and the Communist conquest of China, and while the Rhee regime had the guerrilla problem under at least temporary control. Surely these factors helped tip the scales toward American intervention. Yet, with the possible exception of the situation within South Korea, these were secondary not primary considerations. The perception of a substantial American stake in Korea long antedated the disturbing events of the summer and fall of 1949 and the major GOP offensive against American "timidity" in Asia. Had it been radically different from what it was, the domestic political climate might have prevented large-scale American involvement. As it was, it merely reinforced Truman's and Acheson's strong inclination to commit American troops.[71]

International developments during the past eleven months had certainly alarmed American leaders and given special significance to the North Korean attack. Those developments encouraged Washington to view the offensive as reflecting a new willingness on the part of Moscow to use force in achieving its objectives. Thus American action beyond Korea—in Taiwan, Indochina, and even Western Europe—appeared more necessary than it might have been before 1949. Again, however, international events between August 1949 and June 1950 did not create the belief that the United States had a commitment to South Korea.

On the other hand, the apparent durability of the republic against its internal enemies served to both accentuate that commitment and make effective American action seem plausible. June 1950 saw Rhee in a typically precarious position vis-à-vis his opponents in the National Assembly, but Rhee and the republic were by no means synonymous in the minds of American decision makers. And South Korean forces had recently made great strides in combatting guerrillas within their midst. Had the North Korean offensive been supported by massive uprisings below the thirty-eighth parallel, Washington might well have made different judgments regarding the necessity for and possible effectiveness of strong American countermeasures. In a word, at no time since the withdrawal of American troops in 1949 did conditions within South Korea encourage a firm U.S. response to a North Korean invasion as much as did those of June 1950.

Considering the position of the Joint Chiefs on Korea since September 1947, their support for American ground action on the peninsula may seem surprising. David Detzer offers at least a partial explanation for the apparent reversal when he observes that "the reality of an assault on South Korea was different than the theory."[72] In the crisis situation, as never before, all eyes centered on Korea. For the first time in three years, budgetary constraints were nonexistent. It soon became clear to all in attendance at top-level meetings that the president was inclined toward whatever intervention was necessary to save South Korea, and that he looked first to his secretary of state for advice. It also was clear that Acheson agreed with Truman. Thus, although the Joint Chiefs expressed reservations about committing ground troops in the first days of the crisis, when South Korea proved incapable of defending itself and MacArthur assured Washington that American soldiers from Japan could save the day without compromising the island nation's defense, military men did not hesitate. They immediately pressed for the commitment of troops.[73] Had their deliberations taken place in a vacuum, the Joint Chiefs might well have made different decisions. Given the views of both their commander in chief and their field commander, however, they grasped eagerly at the opportunity for decisive action, one they surely hoped would direct greater attention at home to the need for coordinating means and ends in American foreign policy.

Yet, in the army, the crisis conditions merely brought to the surface feelings that had laid dormant for three years. Recall the army studies of early 1947 concluding that the United States had much at stake in Korea.[74] Recall Chief of Staff Eisenhower's comment in the same period that the United States would lose more by withdrawing from the peninsula than it would spend in maintaining its position there.[75] Recall even the army analysis of June 1949 hinting that, if North Korea crossed the thirty-eighth parallel, armed intervention might be necessary for political reasons.[76] It is not surprising, therefore, that—within three days of the North Korean attack—the army produced a paper which, while noting the dangers of American military involvement in Korea, offered an expansive list of advantages in "successful" United States action there. Such action, it was asserted, would:

1 Create universal respect for United States determination to support the United Nations Charter principles with physical measures.
2 Enhance the prestige of United States leadership.
3 Make a profoundly favorable impression on the Japanese.
4 Bolster the West German government's orientation toward the West.
5 Probably firm up the British attitude against Communist China.
6 Lift interest and effort to obtain more concrete action under NATO.
7 Bolster French morale on its Indochina program.[77]

MacArthur's advocacy of committing ground troops is more perplexing. The Far Eastern commander had never resisted the withdrawal of American soldiers from Korea; in fact, he had pressed for it. Although this stance probably was in part an outgrowth of the limited resources available to his command, he had a well-deserved reputation for letting Washington know when, in his mind, American military strength in the Pacific was inadequate. During 1949 and 1950, he agitated against reductions in United States air and ground forces in Japan and for military assistance to Taiwan, but he uttered not a word about South Korea's weakness. Then, more than two days after the outbreak of war on the peninsula, he told John Foster Dulles in Tokyo that anyone who advocated an American challenge to Communist military power on the Asian mainland "ought to have his head examined."[78]

MacArthur's eventual advocacy of sending American troops to Korea is explicable through an analysis of his personality and perception of the world about him. The general was now seventy years old, but he maintained a strong sense of personal destiny, one in which God, country, and self sometimes became closely intermingled. As a would-be poet of the American fleet in the Pacific noted in 1944, one day the Lord was even likely to "hear a deep voice say, 'Move over God its Mac.'"[79] MacArthur was a rabid "Asia-firster" who, nevertheless, had soft-pedaled his views immediately after World War II. In part, this was because he was preoccupied with reigning over Japan; in part, it was because he was interested in a run for the presidency in 1948 and probably did not want to bind himself too rigidly to a position that would stir controversy and narrow his political base.[80]

In 1949, however, critics of American policy became louder and more numerous, and their echo undoubtedly reached the Dai Ichi Building in Tokyo. MacArthur became more aggressive in espousing a forward policy in Asia. Whereas in February he told Secretary of the Army Kenneth Royall that he was "not in a position to discuss the internal situation of China or to advise in detail on a policy for China," seven months later he told a group of visiting congressmen that only three things were needed to turn the tide there against the Communists: "a ringing declaration that the United States will support any and every one . . . opposed to Communism," the placing of some five hundred fighter planes and a limited number of volunteer airmen "in the hands of some 'war horse' similar to General Chennault," and the allocation of surplus ships to the Nationalist navy sufficient to blockade and destroy the coastal cities of the mainland.[81] He did not dwell on this position, but— when visited by dignitaries from back home in the ensuing months—he pushed vigorously for aid to Taiwan.

Korea did not enter into his campaign for three reasons. First, there was no major constituency in the United States pressing for expanded aid to that country. Second, he genuinely believed that it was both less easily defended and less important to American security than Taiwan. Third, he did not perceive a major threat to the Republic of Korea from forces in North Korea. He was either unaware of, or disagreed with, Muccio's reports. In the fall of 1949, he had probably heard General Roberts brag about South Korean strength, and, at the time of the attack, may have been misled by the estimates of Roberts's temporary successor, Colonel Sterling Wright. In the first two days of hostilities, MacArthur showed great confidence in South Korea's ability to defend itself with minimal outside aid.[82]

Yet even after MacArthur had traveled to Korea and realized that only American troops could halt the North Korean advance, he delayed for over eighteen hours before recommending to Washington their dispatch to the peninsula.[83] This hesitation suggests that he continued to have reservations about such a move. His ultimate decision to advocate the commitment rested in the new circumstances created by the crisis. By 30 June (Tokyo time) it was evident, somewhat to MacArthur's surprise, that his superiors at home would be receptive to a call for action. It was also clear that the situation provided an opportunity to direct new attention toward Asia in the United States. Here MacArthur's perception of the national interest coincided with his own. American involvement in an Asian war would give him the chance to act out his destiny, first on the battlefield, then perhaps in the White House. "I am ready to serve at any time in any capacity, anywhere," he declared to a reporter on 25 June.[84] Direct American intervention would not only enhance his reputation, but it would also help protect him from future revelations that, in 1949, he had advised against the retention of United States troops in Korea and later had failed to anticipate the North Korean attack. Finally, by 30 June, it seemed likely to him, as well as to the

Joint Chiefs, that the crisis was a local one, that American soldiers sent to the peninsula would face largely Korean rather than Chinese and/or Soviet forces. To him, therefore, ground operations would be quite limited in both size and duration. They would not compromise American action elsewhere because the need for such action was limited. By the end of June, he had already conceived of an American counteroffensive on the peninsula via an amphibious landing at Inchon. The projected date for the maneuver was 22 July.[85] As in the Philippines on the eve of World War II, MacArthur grossly underestimated the strength of enemy forces vis-à-vis his own.

## The Korean Intervention: An Evaluation

Despite MacArthur's initial underestimation of North Korea's strength, the fact remains that, in less than three months, the United States and South Korea did halt and throw back the enemy advance. This must be kept in mind in any evaluation of the Korean intervention. The Korean War as it is known today—a three-year conflict taking more than thirty thousand American lives and involving the United States in bitter fighting with the Communist Chinese—occurred because the Truman administration attempted to unify the peninsula with American troops. Had United States ground forces halted at the thirty-eighth parallel in early October 1950, full-scale American participation in hostilities probably would have ended then and there. Thus any cost-benefit analysis of the American intervention in Korea must accept the fact that it could have been far cheaper for the United States than the Korean War actually was.

It also must be noted that analogies between the American intervention in Korea in 1950 and Vietnam in the 1960s are inexact. In the North Korean attack, a conventional army moved across a demarcation line established by Soviet and American occupation forces in 1945 and solidified by actions of both powers in the following years. North Vietnam's movement into South Vietnam prior to 1965 differed in both method and scale. Whereas in 1947 and 1948, the Soviet Union was the main impediment to the peaceful unification of Korea, after 1955 the United States played that role in Vietnam. In 1950, American action in Korea had the enthusiastic backing of governments in Western Europe. In the early 1960s, on the other hand, the European allies of the United States were less intent on strong action to contain Communism in Vietnam. In 1950, American commitments to defend key areas of the non-Communist world were largely untested. Although Washington's obligation to South Korea was never explicit, it was very real in the eyes of friendly nations that had supported recent United States policy in the United Nations. In the early 1960s, the legitimacy of America's commitments to Western Europe and Japan were more firmly established and the depth of United States responsibility to South Vietnam was not so clear. Despite the obvious shortcomings of the Rhee regime, its domestic strength was substantially greater and its origins better grounded in nationalist sentiments than the American-sponsored governments of South Vietnam in later years. Although American intervention in Vietnam as well as in Korea initially enjoyed considerable public support, the venture of 1950 was accompanied by far less official deception than that more than a decade later.

Circumstances in Korea in 1950 also differed fundamentally from those in China three years before. The American commitment to South Korea was more direct than that to Nationalist China. Whereas the immediate threat to the Rhee government was from a regime created and armed by the Russians, that challenging Chiang Kai-shek had stronger indigenous roots and had never depended on the Soviet Union for its war-making power. The United States stood a far better chance of successful intervention in 1950 in South Korea than it had in 1947 in China. Rhee's rule was imperfect, but the Republic of Korea had shown a greater capacity than Nationalist China to put to good use American economic and military aid.

In the final analysis, American military intervention in South Korea was advisable because the United States had a commitment—no less important because it was unstated—to defend that area against unprovoked attack;[86] because the Republic of Korea, if secured from invasion, showed definite signs of being a going concern; and because the United States had the conventional capability for rapid and effective action. This is not to suggest that the refusal of the United States to take military action in Korea would have led to the collapse of the non-Communist world in the face of Russian and Chinese hordes. Far from it. There is much reason to believe, in fact, that Korea was a special case, one in which no Soviet troops were needed to defeat the enemy and in which the United States had failed to convey a willingness to use force; that administration fears of a series of Communist moves along the Soviet periphery were, in an immediate sense, unfounded. It is not even certain that Korea under Communist domination would have been a close ally of Russia. Surely, Kim Il-sung's need for Kremlin support would have declined once his enemies in the south were eliminated. Yet the crisis on the peninsula occurred at a time of great insecurity in Western Europe, while NATO was in early infancy and did not even extend to southern Europe and the eastern Mediterranean, and when the American connection to Japan was not well defined. In such circumstances, the limited use of force in Korea could bolster confidence in American leadership in crucial areas and solidify relationships that would help stabilize international politics in an era of intense rivalry between the superpowers.

But American intervention in Korea was justified only as a short-term, low-cost operation, and thus the process of intervention deserves careful scrutiny. The central question here is whether or not the Truman administration acted in a manner most conducive to the early and least costly achievement of its purposes. In a narrow sense, the basic American objective following the outbreak of war was to reestablish the thirty-eighth parallel as a border between North and South Korea. In larger terms, American leaders sought to avoid widening the combat beyond the peninsula, while strengthening the forces for international stability and the containment of Soviet influence.

To probe the Russian position, and to convey to the Kremlin that the United States sought to avoid a confrontation with the Soviet Union, Acheson asked Moscow to disclaim "responsibility for this unprovoked and irresponsible act" and to press North Korea to withdraw its forces to the thirty-eighth parallel.[87] The White House erred perhaps when, late on 27 June, it authorized release to the public of this information. As historian Gaddis Smith has noted, this move "denied the Soviet government a chance to save face," thereby reducing what little chance existed that Moscow would induce Pyongyang to terminate the offensive.[88] The Soviet reply on 29 June blamed hostilities on South Korea and indirectly the United States, condemned outside intervention in the affairs of the peninsula, and declared illegal the Security Council resolutions of 25 and 27 June.[89]

The American note avoided any direct charge of Soviet complicity in the attack, but its publication and its tone reflected two assumptions: that private talks with the Russians were unlikely to be productive, and that the North Korean attack was part of a larger Soviet strategy to weaken the West. American leaders were probably correct in believing that North Korea had acted only with Soviet consent.[90] Yet, despite their recognition of the possibility that Stalin had simply miscalculated the American response, they gave too little weight to the prospect that, after a show of resolve from the United States, he would seek to end the Korean enterprise, even if this meant giving up an ally's temporary military advantage. Acheson was perhaps too rigid in his view that successful negotiations could occur only when the United States had established local situations of military strength.

On the military front, the immediate use of American air power against North Korean forces might have been advantageous. Such action, especially if combined with efforts to secure Kimpo airport, might have countered the edge held by North Korea over the defending army and prevented the rout of South Korean units. The rapid commitment of American planes would have been a signal to Pyongyang and Moscow that the United States would not stand aside and permit a Communist conquest of the peninsula. Had an American military move occurred within twenty-four hours of the attack, North Korea might have retreated without too great a loss of face.

But there were serious drawbacks to instantaneous American military action. It would have involved the United States deeply in a situation for which the Truman administration had done limited advance planning and at a time when South Korea's needs remained uncertain. It also would have preceded the formation of a coalition of non-Communist states favorable to its position. Had rapid American military intervention been immediately decisive, the question might have arisen as to whether or not the United States had overreacted to another minor fracas along the thirty-eighth parallel. Had initial American operations failed to halt the North Korean advance, the impact of obtaining United Nations support later on might have been reduced. The Security Council resolution of 25 June, of course, largely eliminated this problem.

The risks entailed in presenting the Korean crisis to the United Nations were slight in comparison to the potential advantages. Past involvement of the international body in the affairs of the peninsula made the American move in the Security Council a logical first step in responding to the outbreak of war. If a Soviet veto prevented the Security Council from passing American resolutions, the issue could have been referred to the General Assembly. If speedy action in both bodies proved impossible, which was unlikely, the United States could have attempted to contain the North Korean attack on its own.

A successful effort to obtain United Nations sanction of military measures to restore the thirty-eighth parallel offered the psychological advantage of acting in Korea in the name of collective security and in concert with other nations, including the emerging Asian power, India. In an age of revulsion in the Third World against past exploitation by the West—and of Communist efforts to profit from that revulsion—the explicit support of non-Western countries in the Korean endeavor was not to be taken lightly.

The military advantages of collective action were less impressive. The United States was the only non-Communist power with significant physical might in Northeast Asia. Material assistance from other states was likely to reach significant proportions only if the Korean venture became a lengthy one. In such an event, the difficulties of coordinating operations among contingents from several nations would remain a serious impediment to efficient multinational military efforts. On the other hand, America's assumption of the brunt of the human and material sacrifices might give it greater leeway in both tactics and strategy.

The Truman administration's presentation on 27 June of a second resolution to the Security Council probably was unnecessary. Russia's return to that body to exercise its veto power, though considered unlikely by State Department officials, remained a possibility. And the introduction of a measure calling explicitly for a resort to arms suggested that its adoption was a prerequisite to legitimate American military action. Trygve Lie, secretary-general of the United Nations, later justified Truman's order for American aid and naval support to South Korea prior to the passage of the second resolution with two arguments: first, military sanctions against North Korea were "fully within the spirit of the Council's resolution of 25 June"; and second, "diplomatic consultations" prior to the president's decision indicated "that there were seven votes—the required majority in the Council for authorizing armed assistance to the Republic of Korea."[91] These points may be well used with nearly equal weight in favor of eliminating the second resolution altogether.

This minor tactical point is overshadowed by two other aspects of the Korean intervention. The Truman administration's failure to ask for congressional approval of its course immediately following the commitment of American ground forces was a serious mistake. From a legal standpoint, the president's decision to act alone may be argued with considerable force on both sides. Surely the constitutionality of his action would have been more clear-cut had it been reinforced by a congressional resolution giving explicit sanction. Yet that is different from saying that he was obligated to gain approval from Capitol Hill.[92]

From a political perspective, however, the administration certainly should have sought legislative ratification, at least of the commitment of ground forces. Formal congressional approval of administration moves might well have lessened criticism of the intervention. Despite the original enthusiasm in Washington for Truman's tough stance in Korea, the secretary of state recognized that the administration could not count on such backing over the long haul, especially if "firm leadership . . . should involve casualties and taxes."[93] To be sure, much of the future criticism of the executive was politically motivated and would not have been blunted by Congress's passage in June or July 1950 of a resolution of support. Yet, at least one avenue of attack would have been closed.

Moreover, most negative comments at the time of the commitment of American soldiers were restricted to procedural rather than substantive matters. Taft and Wherry argued not that the United States should concede South Korea to the Communists, but rather that Congress should play an active and formal role in any military intervention. Perhaps such partisans would have assailed Truman for sending American troops into battle prior to gaining congressional authorization. This argument, however, seemed so narrow and contentious at the time that it would have been received with derision. Republicans who had recently attacked the Democrats for their timidity in Asia were not in a strong position to question the necessarily swift and decisive action of the president. Given the general public and political approval for the course adopted, some isolated criticism probably would have served to solidify rather than undermine support for the administration.

Truman might have minimized any surrender of presidential authority by avoiding any suggestion in a resolution that congressional approval of his action was legally mandatory. Instead of sending a draft resolution to Congress directly from the executive branch, he also might have had Democratic leaders on Capitol Hill present a measure on their own.[94]

The last day of June was the best time to seek congressional approval. A move then would have followed immediately the commitment of ground forces in Korea and maximized its impact. Senators and Representatives, anxious to return home for rest and to tend to political duties related to the November elections, would have been in a receptive mood for quick action. For effect and in the interests of rapid passage, therefore, 30 June was the opportune moment for the presentation of a resolution.

This fact emphasized the need for deliberation on domestic political matters contemporaneously with those on possible actions abroad. To Truman, consideration of political maneuvers at the beginning of the Korean crisis may have seemed overly cynical, or even unpatriotic. When, at the first Blair House meeting, Under Secretary of State Webb raised the domestic political issue, the president responded curtly, "We're not going to talk about politics. I'll handle the political affairs."[95] In his determination to act in the national interest, he may have forgotten temporarily that America's well-being does not invariably conflict with the administration's partisan advantage.

Two of MacArthur's acts during the crisis—his commencing of arms shipments to South Korea on 25 June and his order to bomb targets north of the thirty-eighth parallel on 29 June—are disturbing in view of subsequent developments. Both moves occurred without Washington's consent. The first MacArthur reported to the Pentagon almost immediately. The arms assistance was approved at the first Blair House meeting. The second move was not reported to his superiors, but almost twenty-four hours later the president did order the bombing of military targets in North Korea.[96] Truman and Acheson, nevertheless, already showed irritation with the Far Eastern commander for his failure to keep them abreast of events in Korea. The president instructed Secretary of Defense Johnson to order MacArthur "to submit complete daily reports."[97]

MacArthur, of course, possessed a reputation for independence going back at least as far as World War II. The minimal constraints imposed on him as head of the American occupation of Japan had fostered his sense of autonomy. The information available to Washington in late June was too thin to warrant major disciplinary action, especially in the emergency situation. Yet the general's past record and present conduct should have produced greater wariness on the part of top officials in the United States than in fact it did.

MacArthur deserves some credit in the crisis, however, for his trip to Korea and his brief appearance at the front on 29 June. To some, the trip tempted fate rather too much, but it certainly bolstered morale among both South Koreans and Americans on the scene. Ambassador Muccio's conduct in the days after the attack also played a significant role in instilling hope and determination in the Rhee government. His actions at the end of June and in early July were a key to the maintenance of indigenous resistance to the North Korean advance. This resistance, in turn, was essential to the eventual establishment of a stable front around Pusan.[98]

## American Moves outside Korea:
## An Explanation and Evaluation

Whereas the pluses outweigh—if not outnumber—the minuses in the Truman administration's actions regarding Korea, the reverse is certainly the case with regard to moves elsewhere. Only on the matter of increased aid to the Philippines—where American commitments were substantial—did the United States act wisely. Stepped-up assistance to the French and the Bao Dai regime in Indochina merely involved the United States more deeply in a cause that was bound to fail. Unilateral intervention on the side of colonialism in one area at a time when the United States proceeded in the name of collective security and self-determination in another compromised the gains to be obtained in the latter endeavor. Finally, intensified American involvement at several points along the periphery of China could not help but push Peking into greater dependence on Moscow.

Similar objections apply to the imposition of the Seventh Fleet in the straits of Taiwan. As a result of budgetary constraints, American naval power in the western Pacific was seriously understrength. Given the navy's tasks in Korea, few ships or planes were left to protect Chiang Kai-shek. Until late July, little was done around Taiwan except reconnaissance flights with navy airplanes. A month after the Korean attack, a destroyer division traveled southward from the Yellow Sea through the Taiwanese straits, but on 1 August it headed north again. On 4 August, the Seventh Fleet formed a new task group, consisting of only three destroyers, to patrol the waters separating Taiwan from the mainland. Thus the announcement that the United States would prevent a Communist attack on the Nationalists' last stronghold was largely a bluff.[99]

Although Taiwan was not a colony in the same sense that Indochina was—or had been—Chiang was essentially a discredited ruler with little native support on the island. Intervention to save him was not likely to be popular with most other nations, in Asia or elsewhere. It would be especially distasteful to Communist China, whose ties with the Soviet Union the United States had been trying to undermine.

What explains the Truman administration's moves regarding Taiwan and Indochina? Since World War II, international stability had been a primary objective of American leaders. To them, North Korea's offensive represented a threat in this area, both because of its potential long-term impact on the United States as a stabilizing influence worldwide and because it might represent the beginning of a series of moves by Communist forces at other points on the Sino-Soviet periphery. As recently as 19 June, Far Eastern Command intelligence had stated its belief that Indochina was "the next objective of communism" in Asia. Although an early Communist offensive in that French territory appeared more likely than against Chiang's fortress, reports indicated that Chinese troops and ships on the mainland opposite the island had recently increased substantially.[100] In the crisis created by the North Korean attack, the danger existed of an escalation process producing circumstances in which the United States could not respond in a conventional manner in areas crucial to its interests. Decision makers in Washington then would confront the unenviable choice between accepting major defeats or of using atomic weapons, probably on the Soviet homeland. The use of American power in the strait of Taiwan, therefore, as well as the increased aid to the Philippines and Indochina, represented a signal to Peking and Moscow that the United States was prepared to respond to Communist probes in several places. By raising the specter of escalation, ending perhaps in great power confrontation, American officials actually sought to reduce the chances of that eventuality.[101]

The State Department also was concerned about the impact in Japan of simultaneous Communist victories in Taiwan and Korea.[102] Furthermore, Acheson undoubtedly was sensitive to the need for unity during the crisis, both within the administration and in the nation at large. Surely he suspected, before going to Blair House on 25 June, that Johnson, who had just returned from Tokyo and talks with General MacArthur, would press for action regarding Taiwan. Surely, Acheson guessed that the crisis would provide a boost for pro-Chiang forces in Congress. Surely such considerations reinforced his inclination to propose action to neutralize the island.

It is difficult to avoid the conclusion that the State Department could have achieved its objective of deterrence without announcing an increase in aid to Taiwan and Indochina. The president simply might have issued a general statement that attacks by Communist forces in areas other than Korea would have serious consequences. The point could have been reinforced with Taiwan through conspicuous flights by American planes along the coast opposite the island. Until late July, this was the only American military action taken there anyway.

Such a course might have left Johnson, the Joint Chiefs, and some prominent members of Congress dissatisfied. Yet Acheson had fought and won battles with the Pentagon in the past, and Truman clearly was not enthusiastic about the neutralization of Taiwan. When the secretary of state first proposed it on 25 June, the president postponed decision for twenty-four hours. Upon approving the move at the second Blair House meeting, Truman showed his uneasiness by asserting that the United States would not give the Chinese Nationalists "a nickel."[103] Had the secretary of state advocated tactics short of a temporary but explicit commitment to defend Taiwan, Truman—in all likelihood—would have been receptive.

Domestic politics may have been a more serious problem. On 27 June, however, Truman compounded the potential for later difficulties by issuing the following rationale for the neutralization of Taiwan:

The attack upon Korea makes it plain beyond all doubt that Communism has passed beyond the use of subversion to conquer independent
nations and will now use armed invasion and war. . . . In these circumstances the occupation of Formosa by Communist forces would be a
direct threat to the security of the Pacific area and to the United States
forces performing their lawful and necessary functions in that area.[104]

This reasoning bears the mark of the military rather than the diplomatic
mind. Because the secretary of state had taken the initiative on Taiwan at
the Blair House meetings, and had proposed action satisfactory to military
leaders, the secretary of defense and the Joint Chiefs had had little cause for
extensive comment. Yet their belief that the United States should prevent a
Communist conquest of the island probably rested more on a concern to
protect the southern flank of American forces engaged in Korea than on the
more subtle political and strategic calculations of the State Department.
Johnson and Bradley, therefore, probably sought to incorporate the Pentagon's thinking in the president's statement.

Whatever the origins of the statement, it certainly undermined the State
Department view that neutralization should be restricted in time to the duration of the fighting in Korea. After all, if the island was *militarily* important in a crisis elsewhere in Asia, it merited protection before and after, as
well as during, hostilities. A better public declaration would have been that
the United States was intervening in the strait of Taiwan to avoid the outbreak of fighting outside Korea and a possible cycle of escalation that could
end in great power confrontation. This reasoning made sense of a course that
was certain to provoke intense scrutiny at home. In addition, it might have
helped to prevent future misunderstandings within the executive branch as
to the precise nature of American policy.

Finally, it is far from certain that domestic pressures necessitated the Truman administration's action. A public campaign had been waged before—
and with a large measure of success—to avoid direct involvement in the
Chinese civil war. Had it been waged again, there is no telling what the outcome would have been. The Truman administration, however, probably
would have suffered no greater embarrassment on the Taiwan issue, both at
home and abroad, than it actually did as the summer of 1950 progressed.

## Inconvenient Distractions:
## The British and Indian Peace Initiatives

Much to the discomfort of the Truman administration, settlement of the Taiwan question almost immediately became linked in international maneuvers to the Korean crisis. To American diplomats, the ultimate

fate of the island was secondary to the developing situation in Korea. It was on the peninsula, after all, that Communist "aggression" had occurred. It was in response to this event that the United Nations, encouraged by the United States, had called for collective action "to restore international peace and security in the area." The United Nations had not sanctioned American intervention in the strait of Taiwan, and several non-Communist nations felt the move unwise. If the situation in Korea provided the Truman administration with an opportunity to strengthen the forces of collective security against Communist expansion, that regarding Taiwan could only embarrass the United States in foreign lands.

Great Britain and India, two major nations supporting U.S. action in Korea, soon acted contrary to American wishes. Neither country backed the American move regarding Taiwan. Great Britain feared the impact it might have on Western relations with Communist China; India disliked intervention in the internal affairs of an Asian nation.[105] In early July, British diplomats in Moscow and Washington approached the United States and the Soviet Union in an attempt to arrange a cease-fire in Korea. In the latter capital, Great Britain mentioned a possible exchange of American withdrawal from the strait of Taiwan and Communist Chinese admission into the United Nations for the establishment of the status quo ante in Korea.[106]

Acheson immediately rejected the idea. On 10 July, he wrote to the British Foreign Office and asserted that the questions of the future of Taiwan and of Chinese Communist admission to the United Nations must "be considered on their merits and not under the duress and blackmail then being employed" by the Communist world. Concessions by the United States, the secretary of state argued, "would whet Communist appetites and bring on other aggressions elsewhere." The United States, he added, sought a peaceful solution of the Taiwan issue, either through United Nations auspices or in a peace treaty between the United States and its World War II allies and Japan, the island's former colonial master.[107]

The Indian initiative was more persistent and more complicated than that of the British, though its substance and timing were somewhat similar. At the beginning of July, Indian diplomats in Peking, Washington, Moscow, and New York moved in what Acheson later characterized as "multisplendored confusion."[108] The schemes they outlined differed substantially, depending on the place of their presentation and their transmitter. The first proposal came from Sarvepalli Radhakrishnan, the Indian ambassador to the Soviet Union. He suggested that the United States support the admission of Communist China to the United Nations and that, in turn, the Security Council, with Russia and Communist China participating, support an immediate cease-fire in Korea, the retreat of North Korean forces to the thirty-eighth parallel, and United Nations mediation for the creation of a "united, independent Korea."[109] Meanwhile, in Peking, K. M. Panikkar, India's ambassador to Communist China, had proposed to the Chinese merely that the Korean problem could be solved in the Security Council with, as he later recalled, the new regime "taking her legitimate place."[110]

India informed the United States that Communist China was receptive to the plan. The Kremlin, on the other hand, rejected the proposal regarding Korea, probably because it resembled the Washington rather than the Peking version. Despite the pleas of George F. Kennan, the Truman administration made no effort to exploit a possible division between the Communist powers. Again, the prevailing opinion in official Washington was that North Korean aggression should not be rewarded with American concessions elsewhere.[111]

On 13 July, Indian Prime Minister Jawaharlal Nehru, choosing to be encouraged by the Chinese response rather than discouraged by those of the Soviet Union and the United States, sent identical letters to Stalin and Acheson. Nehru's proposal corresponded to Panikkar's earlier one in Peking.[112] In Washington, Vijaya Lakshmi Pandit, the Indian leader's sister, followed up the move with a personal call on the secretary of state. She argued that Moscow was looking for a solution to the Korean tangle. An American demand for a quid pro quo for Communist Chinese entry into the United Nations, she insisted, would be exploited by the Communists as demonstrating Washington's lack of desire for a peaceful solution in Korea. If Peking became unreasonable after taking its seat in the Security Council, she believed, it would suffer a setback at the hands of world opinion.[113] Despite this pressure—and despite a favorable reply to the Nehru note by Stalin on 15 July—Acheson, with the president's approval, stuck to his previous stand with the British.[114]

This response reflected not only the Truman administration's belief in separating the Korean problem from isssues relating to China, but its determination to chart its own course in the crisis, even in the face of pressures from outside the Communist camp.

Truman and Acheson may be criticized for their overly negative attitude. To be sure, the specific proposals put forth by London and New Delhi left much to be desired. Certainly, if the issues of Korea, Taiwan, and Chinese representation in the United Nations were to be linked, concrete movement on the first should at least have been simultaneous with that on the second and third. Even if such a procedure occurred, serious opposition was bound to arise in the domestic political arena to any deal that would enhance Communist China's position in Taiwan or the United Nations.

Still, Acheson erred in rejecting out of hand the linking of the three issues, and in discouraging Great Britain and India, especially the latter, from continuing their efforts for peace. The initial Indian proposal to the United States included the prospect of uniting Korea. However unlikely agreement was between the Communist powers and the United States on this point, the Truman administration might have picked up on this aspect of India's plan. Because the present crisis had resulted from the division of Korea, its resolution and the prevention of future trouble could reasonably be connected to political unification of the peninsula. Had American flexibility regarding Taiwan and Chinese Communist representation in the United Nations been tied to progress toward a unified Korea satisfactory to the United States, the onus for stifling India's initiative might have been partially transferred to the Communist side. Ultimately the United States could have accepted the status quo ante bellum in Korea in return for concrete assurances that such a settlement would not result in a renewed offensive from the north. Because India was a potential counterweight to Communist Chinese influence in Asia, the United States should have sought to avoid irritating New Delhi.[115]

A probe of the Communist camp also might have uncovered a crack in the Sino-Soviet front. Communist China's priorities in this case probably were directed toward Taiwan, whereas Russian eyes focused on Korea.[116] The fallacy in the secretary of state's position rested in two assumptions: first, that, to be worthwhile, negotiations had to stand a reasonable chance of leading to an end of hostilities in Korea on terms acceptable to the United States; and, second, that a retreat on Taiwan and Communist Chinese admission to the United Nations represented concessions that would encourage future aggression. The American position regarding representation of Taiwan and Peking in the international body had been altered in response to the North Korean invasion. Taiwan had been neutralized and Washington had commenced active lobbying among its allies to prevent Communist Chinese entry into the United Nations.[117] This being the case, it was perfectly logical to move back to positions held prior to 25 June simultaneously with the resolution of the Korean matter.

Kennan appears to have been the only high-ranking State Department official to urge diplomatic flexibility. He regarded Korea as an area of American weakness and thought that the peninsula was of little strategic importance to the United States. Although supporting American intervention there, he viewed the action as "negative," one that should be terminated at the earliest possible moment. Communist Chinese admission to the United Nations, he argued, could do little harm to the United States. If the withdrawal of American opposition to that move could be connected to a restoration of the thirty-eighth parallel in Korea, the Truman administration would do well to grasp the opportunity.[118]

Dulles, who now frequently participated in top-level talks on foreign policy, objected to this view. He argued that an exchange of the sort outlined by Kennan would appear to the public as an American retreat. He also suggested that a deal would undermine support for the administration's crash program for bolstering America's military capabilities.[119]

These arguments, in addition to the fear that American concessions in the face of North Korea's aggression might spark future Communist adventures, undoubtedly carried weight with Acheson. But the secretary of state also put the British and Indian initiatives into a larger context. The North Korean attack reinforced his view that the Russians would exploit cases in which they or especially their satellites had the military advantage over anti-Communist forces. Until the scales tipped in favor of the United States or its allies, it was useless to try to bargain with Moscow. The appropriate course was to move forward rapidly with a major expansion of America's physical power. Thus, beginning with a presidential message to Congress on 19 July, the administration launched a campaign that by October had resulted in passage of twice the funds previously anticipated for fiscal year 1951 for the armed services and for military assistance abroad.[120]

## Flexible Policy, Inflexible Diplomacy

In mid-August, India renewed its effort for a peaceful settlement in Korea. On the eleventh, in an informal meeting of non-Communist members of the Security Council, Sir Benegal Rau, the Indian delegate to the United Nations, proposed the creation of a committee of nonpermanent representatives on the Security Council.[121] Three days later, in the Security Council, he suggested that the group study all recommendations for an end to the fighting on the peninsula, "including proposals for the future of Korea," and submit its conclusions to the parent body "by a specified date."[122]

Rau did not immediately present a motion to the Security Council because he wanted first to receive some response from the United States and the Soviet Union. During the remainder of August, considerable maneuvering occurred behind the scenes. The Indian delegate never introduced the plan in a formal manner. Initially, Jacob Malik, the Soviet representative, who had returned to the council to assume its presidency during August, threatened to veto any proposal that made binding the resolutions of 25 and 27 June. Warren Austin, the American delegate, then expressed concern that a failure to explicitly reaffirm these measures in instructions to the committee would imply that the measures were invalid, thus giving the Russians a source of propaganda damaging to the United States.[123] This second Indian initiative, therefore, ended in failure.

Again, the United States may have missed an opportunity in the diplomatic sphere. Although its fears about a study group were not totally unfounded, implementation of the Indian proposal might have led to a significant victory for the United States. Of the six nonpermanent members of the Security Council, all but Yugoslavia had supported the resolution of 25 June—and that nation had abstained. Only Yugoslavia and Egypt did not endorse the resolution that passed two days later. Yugoslavia voted against the measure, but was later critical of the Soviet position in the Korean conflict. Because a majority of the nonpermanent members supported both resolutions, it was unlikely that a committee would submit a report that was inconsistent with them. Moreover, none of the proposed members of the group were in the Soviet camp, and, therefore, the chances were good that its report would be unsatisfactory to the Kremlin.

The Truman administration's response to the Indian initiative of August reflected once more its disinclination to grapple with the Russians in the diplomatic sphere. It also reflected a desire to avoid any move in the United Nations that might interfere with America's freedom of action in Korea. Although on 29 June Secretary Acheson stated that United States operations were "solely for the purpose of restoring the Republic of Korea to the status prior to the invasion from the North," studies were soon being made within the administration as to whether American ground forces should cross the thirty-eighth parallel.[124]

Two events sparked this activity. First, on 13 July, the Columbia Broadcasting System (CBS) reported a statement by South Korean President Syngman Rhee to the effect that North Korean aggression "had obliterated the thirty-eighth parallel and that no peace and order could be maintained in Korea as long as the division [of the peninsula] at the thirty-eighth parallel remained." In response, "an American army spokesman" allegedly asserted that United States forces had intervened merely to push the invaders north of that line and would "use force if necessary" to halt South Korean troops there.[125] Second, on 12 July, at a briefing in Tokyo of Generals J. Lawton Collins and Hoyt Vandenberg, the army and air force chiefs of staff, respectively, General MacArthur expressed confidence that the North Korean advance would be halted and a counteroffensive launched by United Nations forces. He also stated his intention to destroy North Korea's forces rather than simply drive them back across the thirty-eighth parallel.[126]

By 15 July, a debate raged within the State Department between the Policy Planning Staff, headed by Paul Nitze but still influenced by Kennan, and the Division of Northeast Asian Affairs, led by John Allison. Herbert Feis of the former branch urged that the United States government publicly disassociate itself from Rhee's statement. Otherwise, he argued, a rift with our allies might occur, the Chinese Communists and Russians might send their own troops into the fighting, and Soviet charges of American aggression in Korea might gain credibility outside the Communist world.[127]

Allison, who was already a bit miffed over his being passed over in promotions to class one in the foreign service, replied heatedly to this analysis.[128] Perpetuating the division of Korea, he exclaimed, would make "impossible" the implementation of the Security Council resolution of 27 June calling for a restoration of "peace and security in the area." If the United States accepted the status quo antebellum, it would lose the confidence of South Koreans and "leave the aggressors . . . unpunished," thereby encouraging aggression elsewhere. Finally, Allison rejected the claim that a military venture into North Korea would put off America's allies. Most of our friends, he believed, agreed that the continued division of Korea was "utterly unrealistic." A diplomatic offensive by the United States could eliminate most allied opposition to such military action. He urged that the United States avoid any public commitment to halt its troops at the thirty-eighth parallel or to accept a restoration of the status quo as of 25 June.[129]

While middle-level State Department officials debated the issue, Collins and Vandenberg returned from the western Pacific and reported on conditions in Korea to President Truman. On 17 July, the chief executive instructed the National Security Council to prepare recommendations on what the United States should do once North Korean forces had been pushed back to the thirty-eighth parallel.[130] At the same time, the Joint Strategic Survey Committee, a staff organization of the Joint Chiefs, launched a study of the matter. Thus, well before the United States forces had halted the North Korean advance, governmental machinery in Washington had commenced deliberations on what should be done once the tide of battle turned.

Despite this activity, Secretary of State Acheson was not particularly interested in the question. He cabled Ambassador Muccio that United States officials must avoid public statements commiting their country to a future course of action. To him, it was simply too early to establish policy to meet circumstances that could not be clearly foreseen.[131]

Yet, in the State Department, the matter continued to stir debate. On 24 July, in response to the Policy Planning Staff arguments, Allison advocated throwing caution to the wind:

> there is grave danger of conflict with the USSR and the Communist Chinese whatever we do from now on—but I fail to see what advantage we gain by a compromise with clear moral principles and a shirking of our duty to make clear once and for all that aggression does not pay—that he who violates the decent opinions of mankind must take the consequences and that he who takes the sword will perish by the sword. . . . That this may mean war on a global scale is true—the American people should be told and told what it will mean to them. . . . When all legal and moral right is on our side, why should we hesitate?[132]

Had the secretary of state responded to this diatribe, he would have noted that, despite America's superiority in atomic weapons, the United States was not necessarily militarily superior to the Soviet Union, at least for the short term; that, with global war an increasingly likely prospect, Korea was a poor place to commit large numbers of American troops, not only because of its limited strategic significance to the United States, but also because the peninsula's location gave the Soviets a military advantage there; and that American adventurism in Korea might create divisions within the Allied camp that would undermine collective efforts in the event war spread to Europe. In sum, Acheson stood closer to the Policy Planning Staff, which on 22 July concluded the following:

> In the unlikely event that there is a complete disintegration of North Korean forces together with a failure of the Kremlin and Communist China to take any action whatever to exert influence in North Korea, United Nations forces acting in pursuance of an additional Security Council resolution, might move into North Korea in order to assist in the establishment of a united and independent Korea.[133]

Still, Allison made his mark, to some extent because he had the support of his immediate superior, Assistant Secretary of State for the Far East Dean Rusk. The Policy Planning Staff paper of 22 July conceded that under certain conditions American ground forces might move into North Korea, a position that injected an element of flexibility into the earlier stance of Feis. Three days later, the Nitze-headed group gave further ground when it concluded that

> The necessity to maintain a realistic balance between our military strength on the one hand and commitments and risks on the other hand, together with the need for additional information which depends upon political and military developments in the near future, make it impossible to take decisions now regarding our future course of action in Korea.[134]

Thus, during July, the Policy Planning Staff moved from an initial position of total opposition to any move across the thirty-eighth parallel to one of defining narrowly the conditions under which such operations might be undertaken, and finally to a simple wait-and-see attitude. This last posture remained a good distance from that of Allison, but it left open an option that the group had previously sought to eliminate. From late July onward, there was no high level State Department official, with the exception of Kennan, who consistently took a stand against a United Nations move into North Korea.[135] And Kennan, who did not enjoy Acheson's confidence, left for the Institute for Advanced Study at the end of August.

In some respects, the Department of Defense accepted the Policy Planning Staff's position of late July. The Pentagon advocated a military effort to unify Korea, but only under two conditions: that the United States mobilized sufficient resources to both "gain its military objectives in Korea" and strengthen "its military position in areas of strategic importance"; and that the Soviet Union neither intervened in Korea nor initiated general hostilities.[136] Like the Policy Planning Staff, the military men regarded Soviet intervention in North Korea—either through the use of its own or Communist Chinese troops—as a major possibility once it became clear that United

Nations forces would not be pushed off the peninsula. Most important, both groups anticipated that such a Soviet move would occur *before* United Nations ground operations reached the thirty-eighth parallel.[137]

But the Department of Defense analysis went far beyond State Department papers in outlining the advantages of unifying Korea under a non-Communist regime. The diplomats, including Allison, viewed the advantages essentially in defensive terms: that is, Korea should be united so as to prevent a future North Korean attack across the thirty-eighth parallel, to discourage Communist aggression in the future by punishing it in the present, and to avoid both the wrath and demoralization of South Koreans, who yearned for national unity. The Policy Planning Staff also anticipated public and congressional pressure for a "final" solution in Korea.[138] Military planners, however, viewed the unification of the peninsula in a broader light. They anticipated that such a

> [p]enetration of the Soviet orbit . . . would disturb the strategic complex which the USSR is organizing between its own Far Eastern territories and the contiguous areas. Manchuria, the pivot of this complex outside the USSR, would lose its captive status, for a free and strong Korea could provide an outlet for Manchuria's resources and could also provide non-communist contact with the people there and in North China.[139]

The unification of Korea might lead the Communist Chinese to reassess their "dependent" relationship with Moscow. It would also boost the morale of anti-Communist forces throughout Asia. Thus, total victory in Korea would help to reverse "the dangerous strategic trend in the Far East" of the past twelve months.[140]

This analysis fit into the pattern of military thinking on China going back to 1947. For several years, the Joint Chiefs and the State Department had been split on China policy. For several years, the latter agency had frustrated the former in its preference for a more forward approach to the country. Now, because of the opportunity presented by war in Korea, military leaders were anxious to undo at least some of the perceived damage to American interests resulting from past State Department domination of the policy-making process.

Yet another factor inclining the Joint Chiefs toward an aggressive Korea policy was the towering presence of MacArthur as field commander of United Nations forces. In mid-July 1950, he pressed Generals Collins and Vandenberg for a policy aimed at destroying North Korea. Every American ship in the Pacific, he thought, should be engaged in a rapid buildup of supplies and troops in Asia. "To hell with the concept of business as usual," he declared to Collins and Vandenberg. "It is how you play your poor hands rather than your good ones which counts in the long run."[141]

MacArthur held an exalted position with the Joint Chiefs. He had received his first commission in the United States Army in 1903, twelve years before chairman of the Joint Chiefs Omar Bradley. He became Army chief of staff in 1930, eleven years before Bradley received his first star. On the eve of the war in 1941, he came out of retirement to become commander of United States forces in the western Pacific. During the next four years, he served brilliantly in the fight against Japan. At war's end, he took on the huge task of commander of Allied occupation forces in the defeated island nation. Most observers felt he made the transition from field commander to military statesman with ease.

There were other reasons as well for MacArthur's influence on the Joint Chiefs. First, he was the commander in the field in wartime, and military tradition dictated that his views on Korea be given the utmost consideration. Second, his personal presence was Olympian. As one retired general recently recalled, "He could charm the birds off the trees."[142] The outbreak of war in Korea insured that his audience in Tokyo would include, more often than ever before, top personages from Washington. His persuasive powers, formidable as they often were at a distance, were all the more so in person. Third, he was almost universally regarded as an expert on Asia, despite the fact that he spoke no Oriental languages and had traveled little on the mainland.

It would be a mistake, nonetheless, to view MacArthur's influence as decisive on the issue of an American military campaign in North Korea. Certain of the views presented by the Far Eastern commander to Collins and Vandenberg during their Tokyo visit of July did reappear in the Defense Department paper of the 31st discussed above. American bombing near the northern border of Korea appeared to be a possible means of preventing a major Soviet or Chinese intervention on the peninsula. Also, a rapid American buildup and counteroffensive would tend to discourage such intervention.[143] This last assertion, and the view that unification of the country under non-Communist rule would tend to draw Communist China away from Russia, may have rested, at least in part, on MacArthur's belief that "it is the pattern of Oriental psychology to respect and follow aggressive, resolute and dynamic leadership—to quickly turn on a leadership characterized by timidity or vacillation."[144] Yet, on broad issues, it is likely that MacArthur merely strengthened preexisting inclinations. He did not modify the Europe-first orientation of the Joint Chiefs, but he did play upon their long-standing discontent with American policy in Asia. In mid-summer, his influence was secondary; from late October onward, however, it would become more central.

The key points here are that, in August, the Truman administration sought to keep all options open regarding Korea and that the Indian initiative appeared to threaten that objective. As the month progressed, the United States moved increasingly toward a strategy of mobilizing American and world opinion in favor of the unification of Korea. On 10 August, in a speech before the Security Council, Ambassador Warren Austin asked, "Shall only part of the country [Korea] be assured . . . freedom?" Answering his own query, he stated:

> I think not. . . . Korea's prospects would be dark if any action of the United Nations were to condemn it to exist as 'half slave and half free' or even one-third slave and two-thirds free. The United Nations has consistently worked for a unified country, an independent Korea. The United Nations will not want to turn from that objective now.[145]

Austin followed with a similar statement a week later.[146] These statements surely had prior clearance at the policymaking level in Washington.[147]

On 27 August, in an interview with CBS commentator Eric Sevareid, Ambassador-at-Large Philip Jessup expanded on Austin's statements. "Decisions on future military steps [would] . . . be made," he stated, "to meet the circumstances as they developed." The United States would not act unilaterally, but it would support the United Nations in giving the Korean people an opportunity to "freely decide on their own form of government."[148] Four days later, in a radio broadcast, President Truman asserted that "the Koreans have a right to be free, independent, and united." The United States, "under the guidance of the United Nations," would "do [its] . . . part to help them enjoy that right."[149]

Final decisions on American objectives in Korea were to await military developments. Because United Nations troops were still holding somewhat precariously to a defensive perimeter around Pusan on the southeastern tip of the peninsula, it was too early to make definite plans for the reunification of the country. Little doubt existed within the administration, however, that the continued division of Korea was undesirable. The only issue that remained open was whether friendly forces could subdue North Korea at a cost acceptable to the United States. Prior to the American counteroffensive in mid-September, the Truman administration sought to avoid any initiative in the United Nations that might restrict its freedom to act once the military balance changed in Korea.

The evolving American attitude on Korea resulted in a shift in the Chinese Communist position regarding the peninsula. Before 20 August, statements emanating from Peking gave top priority to Taiwan rather than Korea. On that date, however, Chou En-lai sent a message to the United Nations in which he asserted that, because Korea bordered on China, its people could not "but be concerned about a solution of the Korean question."[150] The problem could be solved peacefully, he continued, and the People's Republic of China must be present when it was discussed in the Security Council. Thirteen days earlier, *Jen Min Jih Pao* had endorsed a Soviet proposal of 4 August that Communist China, North Korea, and South Korea attend United Nations deliberations regarding the peninsula on an ad hoc basis.[151]

As scholar Allen Whiting has pointed out, the Sino-Soviet posture of early

August might be interpreted as an indication that the two Communist powers were genuinely interested in a restoration of the status quo ante in Korea. Malik's return to the Security Council, despite the continued presence of the Nationalist Chinese representative on that body, constituted a significant alteration of the previous Soviet position. So did the Kremlin's apparent willingness to recognize South Korea's status as equal to that of North Korea, at least for the temporary purpose of their appearance before the international organization.[152]

But, when Austin suggested that the peninsula should be united under anti-Communist rule, the Sino-Soviet stance broadened to include a threat of an expanded conflict unless the fighting in Korea soon came to an end. Two days after Chou's message of 20 August, Malik expounded this theme in a harsh attack on American policy.[153] On 26 August, the Chinese Communist periodical *World Culture* published an article that reiterated Chou's position and included the assertion "North Korea's defense is our defense."[154]

These apparent signals, however, were missed by top administration officials in Washington. There is no evidence that, during August, the State Department viewed the Soviet position in the Security Council as anything but a continuation of its past policy of complete antagonism toward the United States and its course in Korea. In fairness to American diplomats, Malik's general comportment clouded any conciliatory or warning cues that he might have sought to convey to the United States.[155] On the other hand, with administration goals in Korea in a state of flux, and with Acheson inclined to negotiate with the Russians only from "situations of strength," American leaders were perhaps less able than they should have been to perceive shifts in the Sino-Soviet stance and their possible significance.[156]

## Taiwan in the Limelight

While the Truman administration moved in the United Nations to head off an early effort by India to define war aims in Korea, the Taiwan issue moved to center stage, both at home and abroad. In an overt sense, the question emerged because MacArthur believed that under no circumstances should the island be permitted to fall into Communist hands and because he sought to influence American policy on the matter. The Far Eastern commander's actions in relation to Taiwan, however, must be understood in the context of his military responsibilities, the political climate in the United States, and divisions within the executive branch in Washington.

On 8 July, when MacArthur became commander in chief of the United Nations Command, he already directed American armed forces in East Asia. His operational control of the Seventh Fleet had commenced late on 25 June (Washington time), when, as a result of decisions made at the first Blair

House meeting, American naval units were ordered to proceed northward from the Philippines to Japan.[157]

From a military standpoint, there were advantages in combining MacArthur's responsibilities regarding Taiwan with those in Korea. Because the Seventh Fleet had missions in both the strait of Taiwan and in Korea and because American army units in the western Pacific had missions at several points along the island chain running from Japan to the Philippines as well as in Korea, a need existed for a commander in chief on the scene to coordinate operations.

Yet there were obvious political liabilities in giving one man the titles of Commander in Chief, United Nations Command, and Commander in Chief, Far East. MacArthur now had responsibilities for executing the unpopular American policy on Taiwan, in addition to carrying out United Nations goals in Korea. This fact clouded the distinction between the action of the international organization in the crisis and that taken independently by the United States. On the surface, this may have appeared as an advantage to the United States, but in reality it could only irritate some nations that supported the Korean enterprise and encourage the Communists to emphasize in their propaganda American intervention in the Chinese civil war. Furthermore, MacArthur's strong views on Taiwan and his independent nature did not augur well for his handling of dual role in the manner desired by Washington.

On these grounds, MacArthur should have been assigned the leadership of United Nations operations, but replaced in his position as Far Eastern commander by a high-ranking military man from Washington. Yet, such a move might have created problems in other areas. MacArthur, his loyal subordinates in Tokyo, and Republican critics of administration policy in the United States might have regarded it as an unjustifiable demotion. The result might have been a reduction in the effectiveness of American operations in East Asia and an increase in partisan debate at home. Although in retrospect such risks were worthwhile, there is no evidence that administration officials gave serious consideration to any option other than the one chosen. Before long, leading State Department personnel may have wished they had.

On 31 July, MacArthur arrived in Taipei for two days of talks with Chiang Kai-shek. Upon returning to Tokyo—and several days before reporting to Washington on the trip—the Far Eastern commander released a statement in which he stressed the military nature of his discussions with the Chinese leader. MacArthur declared that plans had been completed for coordinating Nationalist and American forces in the event of an offensive against the island. He lauded the generalissimo for his "indomitable determination to resist Communist domination" and asserted that Chiang's resolve "parallels the common interests and purpose of Americans, that all people in the Pacific should be free—not slaves."[158] Chiang reciprocated with a declaration that his meetings with MacArthur had established a basis for the joint defense of Taiwan and for "Sino-American military cooperation." Now that the Nationalists could "work closely with our old comrade in arms," he proclaimed, victory was certain.[159]

The incident seriously embarrassed the Truman administration. In the United States, the MacArthur-Chiang statements resulted in a storm of press speculation. Newsmen wondered if secret agreements had been reached between the two men and if the Far Eastern commander had received clearance for his trip from Washington.[160] At the United Nations, where Jacob Malik was about to return to the Security Council, the trip was characterized, in James Reston's words, as "a triumph of mistiming."[161] MacArthur's actions added to the uneasiness in neutral and allied capitals that American China policy might lead to a broadening of the military conflict in Asia.[162] In China, *Jen Min Jih Pao* labeled the comments of MacArthur and Chiang as evidence of "American aggression and invasion of Taiwan."[163]

The State Department, which had not been told of MacArthur's planned excursion to Taiwan, and whose representatives there had been virtually ignored by the Far Eastern commander, first received a report on the trip from William Sebald, its political adviser in Tokyo.[164] Sebald, who had not accompanied MacArthur, passed on the general's private statement upon his return. Only "military problems of a technical nature" had arisen, he claimed, but he feared that the task of defending the island would be increased by the "unfriendly" attitude toward Chiang of American diplomats in Taipei.[165] From those representatives in the Taiwanese capital, the State Department heard that the Far Eastern commander planned to transfer American fighter squadrons to the Nationalist-held territory.[166]

The report of the State Department officials in Taipei was especially disturbing to Truman and Acheson because the Joint Chiefs had recently informed MacArthur of their proposal that American planes break up Chinese Communist troop concentrations on the mainland opposite Taiwan. On 4 August, therefore, Truman ordered Secretary of Defense Johnson to send a sharp message to MacArthur reminding him that only "the President as Commander-in-Chief has the authority to order or authorize preventive action against . . . the mainland."[167] To delineate the precise nature of American policy regarding Taiwan to the Far Eastern commander, Truman dispatched Averell Harriman, his trusted special assistant on foreign policy, to Tokyo.

In visiting Taiwan, MacArthur clearly did not exceed his authority. In fact, military considerations justified such a move, if not by the Far Eastern commander himself, at least by one of his leading subordinates. During July, American officials, both in the western Pacific and in Washington, worried that the Chinese Communists would attack the island at any moment.[168] Unknown at the time was the fact that the number of Chinese Communist forces on the mainland opposite Taiwan decreased following American intervention in Korea.[169] In early July, to be sure, American intelligence officials in Hong Kong were told that elements of General Chen Yi's Third Field Army were moving northward from positions adjacent to the strait of Taiwan.[170] Later in the month, however, the Nationalists reported a Communist artillery barrage against Quemoy.[171] They also claimed that preparations for the invasion of Taiwan had been increased.[172] After the unexpected North Korean move of June, the Joint Chiefs were sufficiently worried to recommend substantial arms aid to Chiang, a survey by the Tokyo command of Nationalist military requirements, and reconnaissance flights by American aircraft to determine the likelihood of military operations against Taiwan. In late July, the National Security Council approved the measures.[173]

In the face of this uncertainty regarding Chinese Communist intentions and the limited American forces available to defend Taiwan, MacArthur had good reason to want a firsthand look at the state of Chiang's defenses. His trip to the island and his statement thereafter might even be viewed as a deterrent to a possible military offensive from the mainland.

The State Department, however, should have been consulted about the journey before it occurred. The military survey approved by the National Security Council, after all, was not intended to be led by the Far Eastern commander himself.[174] When, on 29 July, he informed the Joint Chiefs of his upcoming trip, they replied that, until certain policy questions were resolved by the State and Defense departments, he might wish to send a senior officer to Taiwan rather than go himself. Thus, the Joint Chiefs recognized the political sensitivity of the matter. Yet they told MacArthur that he was free to travel to the island if he thought it necessary.[175]

That the State Department was not consulted demonstrates the poor coordination between American military and diplomatic officials in Washington while Louis Johnson headed the Defense Department. The incident also reflects a divergence on the Taiwan issue between the two departments and a disinclination on the part of the Joint Chiefs to take strong measures to control their commander in the field. MacArthur's conduct, in turn, probably was influenced by his presumption that he had at least the tacit support of military leaders at home.

Had MacArthur's trip been the last time that his actions regarding Taiwan embarrassed the Truman administration, the incident soon would have been forgotten. Probably both out of personal pique over the commotion surrounding his Taiwan trip and because he saw an opportunity to influence American policy, however, MacArthur took public issue with his political superiors in Washington.

Hints of what was to come appeared in Harriman's official review of his meetings with MacArthur and in the general's press release following his talks with the presidential envoy. Truman's special assistant reported to the White House that the Far Eastern commander understood the administration's desire to avoid long-term commitments to Chiang and to prevent the generalissimo from initiating major action against the mainland, but he had "a strange idea that we should back anybody who will fight communism." Harriman cited MacArthur's statement that "he would, as a soldier, obey any orders that he received from the President," but added that such obedience would be "without full conviction."[176]

After Harriman's departure from Tokyo, MacArthur released a statement claiming that his trip to Taiwan had been "maliciously misrepresented to the public by those who invariably in the past have propagandized a policy of defeatism and appeasement in the Pacific." "The American people," he hoped, "will not be misled by sly insinuations, brash speculations and bold misstatements so insidiously fed them . . . by persons 10,000 miles away from the actual events . . . to promote disunity and destroy faith and confidence in American purposes and institutions and American representatives at this time of great world peril."[177]

MacArthur followed up this veiled attack on the advocates of a modicum of American restraint in Asia with a more explicit and detailed dissent from American China policy. The United Nations commander recently had been invited to address the annual encampment of the Veterans of Foreign Wars (VFW), scheduled for the end of August. Although he declined to make a personal appearance, MacArthur sent a lengthy dispatch to the organization to be read in his absence. Three days before its scheduled delivery, advance copies were in the hands of the press.

The communication began with an analysis of the strategic significance of Taiwan. MacArthur reiterated, albeit in more general terms, the arguments that he had expounded in June in a top-secret memorandum presented to Bradley and Johnson.[178] He went beyond this earlier piece, however, in attempting to counter the assertion that the American defense of Taiwan would alienate the people of Asia. "Those who speak thus," he argued, "do not understand the Orient." They failed to grasp that the peoples of East Asia were drawn to vigorous and forceful leadership. "Nothing in the last five years," he exclaimed, "has so inspired the Far East as the American determination to preserve the bulwarks of our Pacific Ocean's strategic position from future encroachment."[179]

This statement demonstrated a serious misunderstanding, perhaps even an unawareness, of the intense nationalism that was such a major force in Asia, and of its frequently anti-Western character. MacArthur's exposition on the "Oriental mentality" serves to emphasize that his experience with Asia after World War II was largely restricted to Japan and that, even before 1945, his contact with the continent itself was very limited.

But the imperfect hold on reality of MacArthur did not disturb administration officials so much as the fact that he was challenging established American policy at a particularly sensitive moment. On 24 August, Chou En-lai commenced a Chinese Communist verbal barrage against the United States with a demand that the Security Council "condemn . . . and take immediate measures to bring about the complete withdrawal of all United States armed invading forces from Taiwan and from other territories belonging to China."[180]

In reply to this demand and the charge of an American invasion of Chinese lands, Truman directed Ambassador Austin to address a note to Secretary-General Trygve Lie explaining United States policy regarding Taiwan. The communique made seven points: (1) the United States had "not encroached on . . . the territory of China"; (2) Communist China had planned to attack Taiwan at a time when such action would have endangered United Nations forces in Korea; (3) American intervention in the straits of Taiwan was "an impartial neutralizing action" directed at both the Nationalists and the Communists and was not aimed at acquiring a special position for the United States; (4) the operation was "without prejudice to the political settlement of the status of the island," which should be worked out through "international action"; (5) the United States continued in its attitudes of friendship "for the Chinese people" and for "the integrity of China"; (6) Washington "would welcome United Nations consideration of the case of Formosa"; (7) nevertheless, the immediate question before the Security Council was "the complaint of aggression against the Republic of Korea." This matter merited full consideration before the Security Council moved on to other matters.[181]

The first five points largely reiterated Truman's comments on Taiwan in his 19 July message to Congress.[182] The seventh followed the American position during August in the face of Malik's efforts to place the Taiwan matter ahead of Korea on the Security Council agenda. The sixth represented a shift in American policy resulting from the charges of Communist China and pressure from Great Britain.

The Truman administration was ambivalent toward early United Nations consideration of the Taiwan question. Although the "neutralization" policy was supposedly only temporary, considerable sentiment existed within the executive branch in favor of a long-term effort to prevent Taiwan's fall to the Communists. Pressures from the China bloc in Congress continued along the same line. Despite their support for Truman's course in Korea, the Republicans were determined to make American postwar policy toward Asia a primary issue in the upcoming off-year elections. Some in the GOP emphasized past mistakes rather than current directions, but others dwelled on both.[183] The less Taiwan appeared in the headlines and the less it came up in United Nations discussions, the greater flexibility the administration could maintain on the issue.

Balancing this consideration was the fact that an investigation by the international organization would help repudiate allegations of an American invasion of the island. Nevertheless, given the scant support abroad for American intervention in the strait of Taiwan, much sentiment might emerge for the United Nations to reach beyond mere fact-finding in an effort to resolve the Taiwan problem permanently. The presentation of resolutions distasteful to the United States would be likely. These might include calls for an end to American involvement in the Chinese civil war, for a multinational trusteeship on the island, or for political integration with the mainland. Under the conditions prevailing in the summer of 1950, the first possibility was unacceptable to the United States. And earlier studies by the State Department had indicated that serious problems would accompany the second. The United States probably could block action by either the Security Council or the General Assembly. Yet this course might have serious political repercussions abroad. Until the situation in Asia became clarified, therefore, the preservation of the status quo regarding Taiwan had distinct advantages for the United States.

In August, however, Soviet and Communist Chinese attacks on the American position, in addition to pressures from Great Britain and India, forced the administration's hand.[184] In such a context, MacArthur's expression of discontent with established policy could not go unchallenged. Truman had to persuade allies, neutrals, and Communist China that his attitude toward Taiwan differed from the Far Eastern commander's and that America's course was set in the White House in Washington, not the Dai Ichi building in Tokyo. This effort was likely to stir up controversy at home, where MacArthur reigned as a hero to Republican critics of the administration's strategy in Asia.

On 26 August, at a White House meeting with the secretaries of state, defense, and treasury, the Joint Chiefs, and Harriman, the president directed that MacArthur be ordered to withdraw his message to the Veterans of Foreign Wars. Truman would send him a copy of Ambassador Austin's letter to Trygve Lie to make clear to him why his statement had to be retracted.[185]

The president also considered relieving MacArthur of his posts as Far Eastern and United Nations commander while allowing him to remain in Tokyo as the head of the occupation in Japan.[186] Truman later recalled that he rejected this move because it "would have been difficult to avoid the appearance of a demotion and I had no desire to hurt General MacArthur personally."[187] Although it is reasonable to assume that a fear of the domestic political repercussions entered into Truman's calculations, the tone of his personal note of explanation to the Far Eastern commander indicates that the president had some concern for his subordinate's morale.[188] Unfortunately, this sensitivity may have undermined MacArthur's understanding of Truman's determination to remain master of his own house.

Despite MacArthur's withdrawal of his message, it appeared in full in the 1 September issue of *U.S. News and World Report*.[189] The press's possession of the paper, in fact, had led MacArthur, upon receipt of the retraction order from Louis Johnson, to advise the secretary of defense that the move would be an embarrassing mistake for the administration. Johnson, who sympathized with the Far Eastern commander on the Taiwan issue, hedged.

When word got back to the president of Johnson's hesitation, the commander in chief stood his ground.[190] He followed up the incident with an announcement on 31 August that, after the Korean War, the Seventh Fleet would be removed from the strait of Taiwan.[191]

A day later, the president made a major television and radio address. In addition to reaffirming America's limited aims regarding Taiwan and implying that the United States, with United Nations assistance and approval, would attempt to unify Korea, he expressed the desire to avoid an expansion of the war beyond the peninsula. This statement sought to reassure America's allies and Communist China that the United States had no intention of launching an aggressive war against the leading Communist powers.[192]

Along with the MacArthur incident, three developments made this gesture necessary. On 25 August, Secretary of the Navy Francis B. Matthews publicly suggested that the United States start "a war to compel cooperation for peace."[193] Two days later, Peking claimed that American aircraft crossed the Yalu River and strafed parts of Talitsu and Antung. In the face of numerous reports of Communist Chinese troop movements northward to Manchuria, this charge, which American officials soon conceded might be true, appeared ominous.[194]

Four days after Truman delivered his speech, he decided to ask for Johnson's resignation.[195] This decision—long in the making—was precipitated by the secretary of defense's hesitation in carrying out Truman's directive regarding MacArthur's VFW letter and by rumors that Johnson was privately advocating a preventive war against Russia.[196]

Despite the Truman administration's efforts to soften the political impact of its Taiwan policy, the issue remained an irritant in America's foreign relations. On 29 August, the Security Council voted in favor of considering Communist China's charge of aggression against the United States. The United States voted for the measure, but opposed inviting representatives of the Peking regime to attend discussions on the issue.[197] A month later, however, over continued American objections, the Security Council passed a resolution inviting Peking to participate in the discussions of Taiwan beginning on 15 November.[198]

On the domestic political front, the Truman administration also ran into difficulties over Taiwan. After Communist China's shelling of Quemoy on 24 July, some voices arose in the press and Congress in favor of "unleashing" Chiang Kai-shek against the mainland.[199] More widespread protests emerged a month later when Truman demanded that MacArthur withdraw his letter to the Veterans of Foreign Wars. Senate Minority Leader Kenneth Wherry spoke for many Republicans on Capitol Hill in asserting that

> The vagueness and complete lack of direction to the Administration's policies in the Far East are intolerable at a time when our boys are fighting and dying in Korea. Only our faith in the rugged Americanism

of General MacArthur buoys our hopes in that conflict. Let us hear from General MacArthur, and woe to him who dares to say he shall not speak.[200]

The more restrained Senator H. Alexander Smith wrote to Dulles expressing his concern that a deal might be made whereby the Communists would retreat in Korea in exchange for American concessions regarding Taiwan.[201] The Hearst and McCormick newspaper chains also continued to attack what they called the Truman administration's timidity on the Taiwan issue.[202]

Contemporary State Department surveys, however, revealed widespread support for the Truman-Acheson position. A majority of writers editorializing on the MacArthur incident supported the president.[203] A September poll by the National Opinion Research Center indicated that 35 percent of the public approved United States Taiwan policy, and only eleven percent disapproved. The remainder had no opinion.[204] With public support for the Korean intervention holding firm, the Truman administration had reason to believe that Democratic candidates in the upcoming election could effectively counter the Republican offensive against its policies in Asia. This was especially true after mid-September, when the tide in Korea changed dramatically in favor of United Nations forces.[205]

Moreover, the Truman administration made some progress in obtaining congressional support for programs that the China bloc might have used as bargaining ploys. Little opposition arose to proposals from the executive branch for increases in military spending. More resistance emerged on foreign economic aid. In August, Congress reduced funds for Marshall Plan countries by $200 million. The Point Four Program received only $15 million, almost $12 million less than the White House had lobbied for.[206] Yet these cuts were not crippling. More than pressure from Asia-firsters, they reflected the widespread feeling that expanded appropriations for defense must be balanced, at least partially, by trimming elsewhere. Backing in the press, the public, and Congress for an enlarged American military role in Western Europe was substantial.[207] Thus, the pro-Chiang forces on Capitol Hill continued to carry less weight on legislation relating directly to foreign ventures than they had in late 1947 and early 1948.

## The Surge of the Communists-in-Government Issue

Nevertheless, a danger to the Truman administration's foreign policy loomed on the horizon in the form of the Communists-in-government issue. On the eve of the war in Korea, it seemed that the Democrats might emerge relatively unscathed by the furor created by Senator McCarthy's charges of widespread Communist infiltration into the State Department. In early June 1950, seven Republicans in the upper house issued a "Declaration of Conscience" criticizing the methods of their colleague from Wisconsin.[208] Three weeks later, three Republican chief executives reproved McCarthy at a GOP governors' conference.[209]

The Truman administration may have concluded from such developments, along with the overwhelmingly favorable public response to its swift action in Korea, that the Communists-in-government issue could be removed from the political landscape prior to the fall election campaign.[210] In any event, the option of a presidential appointment of a nonpartisan executive commission to study McCarthy's charges, which had been under active consideration before the North Korean attack, was temporarily set aside.[211] In mid-July, when the Tydings subcommittee submitted a report to the Senate of McCarthy's claims, the White House treated it as conclusive.

This reaction was a serious mistake. The report accused McCarthy of "conscious falsehoods" and found none of his charges to be true, but the two Republican members of the subcommittee, Henry Cabot Lodge of Massachusetts and Bourke B. Hickenlooper of Iowa, dissented from this view. The investigation, they asserted, had been biased and superficial. Senate approval of the majority opinion came only after a highly partisan debate and close vote.[212] With some justice, Republicans could now accuse the Democrats of trying to sweep the Communists-in-government issue under the rug before the fall election campaign.

The Democratic stand on the Tydings subcommittee report, therefore, eliminated any chance that the matter would be played down in the ensuing months. One early result of the GOP offensive aimed at the November election was congressional passage of an internal security bill, popularly labeled the McCarran Act after the chairman of the Senate Judiciary Committee, Pat McCarran. The measure was obnoxious to all those, including the president, concerned with the protection of civil rights. In late September, in response to Truman's veto, the House and Senate voted overwhelmingly to override. The Democratic leadership in the upper chamber, fearful of the political consequences of opposing the legislation, abandoned the White House.[213]

This event was the beginning of a pattern of extreme sensitivity among Democrats on Capitol Hill regarding the explosiveness of the Communists-in-government issue. Historian Robert Griffith has argued persuasively that, at the time, the impact of the general question—and of McCarthy in particular—was seriously overrated.[214] But reality itself frequently has less impact on human behavior than people's perception of it. However courageous Truman may have been in vetoing the McCarran bill, the response of most congressional Democrats to his move, the intensifying attacks of Republicans on the administration's attitude toward internal subversion, and the linking of this matter to American policy in East Asia could not help but emphasize to the White House the desirability of maintaining the status quo on Taiwan and of pursuing operations in Korea onward toward total victory.

## Dangerous Portents

On the eve of the United Nations counteroffensive at Inchon on 15 September, Truman administration policies regarding both Korea and China were in a state of flux. On 11 September, to be sure, the president approved NSC 81, a major position paper on Korea.[215] Yet, as in late July, decision makers thought it too early to render final judgments on crossing the thirty-eighth parallel. The key question remained: would the Soviet Union and/or Communist China intervene directly in North Korea? Would America's friends in the United Nations support major non-Communist ground operations north of the line?

On the second question, State Department officials were increasingly confident that the answer was in the affirmative.[216] They regarded this matter as particularly important because allied unity, especially if expressed in concrete form in a resolution by the United Nations, might discourage China and Russia from intervening militarily in North Korea.[217]

Yet the State Department, as well as the Joint Chiefs, continued to view Soviet action as likely, provided the Kremlin felt it "would not involve a substantial risk of global war."[218] Because Soviet movement into North Korea after American troops had entered that territory would inevitably result in a clash between the superpowers—which easily could escalate into World War III—Russia probably would act before United Nations ground forces reached the thirty-eighth parallel. Chinese intervention in North Korea was possible, though less likely, because the Soviet Union regarded that area as its own sphere of influence.

NSC 81 anticipated that MacArthur would be given authority to move ground forces beyond the thirty-eighth parallel "provided that at the time of such operations there has been no entry into North Korea by major Soviet or Chinese Communist forces, no announcement of intended entry, nor a threat to counter our operations militarily in North Korea."[219] American officials hoped North Korean forces would be so thoroughly destroyed in the south that only Republic of Korea troops would be needed for operations in the north. This eventuality would not necessarily reduce the likelihood of Russian or Chinese intervention, but it would lessen the risk that such intervention would lead to general war.[220]

The prospects for outside intervention, however, could be diminished by avoiding American ground operations near the Soviet or Chinese borders. Hence, "It should be the policy not to include any non-Korean units in any U. N. ground forces which may be used in the northeastern province [of North Korea] bordering the Soviet Union or in the area along the Manchurian border."[221] This aspect of NSC 81 represented the only significant alteration of a State Department draft of 1 September. The earlier paper had stated simply that "[i]n no circumstances should . . . [non-Korean] forces be used" in those regions.[222] Undoubtedly, military officials made the change.

In view of subsequent events, it is clear that military leaders regarded the words "It should be the policy" as less absolute than "In no circumstances." State Department planners, however, may not have grasped this fact until later. The change reflected a somewhat lesser concern on the part of military men for Soviet and Chinese sensitivity to American activity near their borders.[223]

NSC 81 made no provision for an American approach to the Soviet Union. The paper merely stated that, if the Kremlin initiated diplomatic action to end the conflict while hostilities continued below the thirty-eighth parallel, the United States "should be prepared to negotiate a settlement favorable to us." Such a settlement should "not leave the aggressor in an advantageous position that would invite a repetition of the aggression," nor should it "undermine the authority and strength of the United Nations."[224]

With the exception of Kennan, no one advocated direct American overtures to Russia.[225] In late August, the Policy Planning Staff did devise a plan for the peaceful unification of the peninsula, but it was to be advanced only in the event that the Kremlin indicated a willingness, "before the tide of battle . . . turned . . . to negotiate a settlement involving the withdrawal of the North Koreans to the thirty-eigh[th] parallel." In brief, the proposal went like this: North Korean forces would retreat to positions north of the thirty-eighth parallel, while American troops advanced to the thirty-sixth parallel and their South Korean counterparts to the thirty-eighth. Then the United Nations Commission would move into the north to supervise the demobilization and disarmament of Communist forces. The United Nations body would proceed to conduct elections to provide northern representation in the government of the Republic of Korea. Upon the request of the commission, South Korean constabulary units could enter North Korea to assist in this process.[226]

Although no one suggested that this plan serve as a framework for an initiative to Moscow, John Paton Davies, the China expert on the Policy Planning Staff, and John K. Emmerson of the Division of Northeast Asian Affairs did favor a more subtle maneuver. They wanted to inform India of the proposal under the assumption that, from New Delhi, it would "reach Peiping's ears," and eventually fall into the hands of the Kremlin. This process, they reasoned, "would irritate the Russians, promote the cleavage [presumably between Moscow and Peking], and might possibly intrigue the Chinese Communists."[227]

Rusk rejected the plan. He argued that the Korean issue was "primarily a concern for" the Security Council and United Nations members who currently supported the collective action on the peninsula. Implementation of the plan would commit the United States to a particular approach to Korea's unification prior to its clearance with other friendly nations. Such a commitment would "tend to create . . . future complications" abroad. Furthermore, it had not been established as "a Government position" within the executive branch at home as well. In any event, "the existing military situation in Korea and the position of both Moscow and Peiping" made consideration of the plan outside the Security Council premature. Rusk conceded, nevertheless, that the substance of the proposals for a settlement of the Korean problem had much merit and should "be kept on ice for possible future use."[228]

It is doubtful that Rusk rejected the Davies-Emmerson idea without first approaching Acheson.[229] Thus, the response reveals much about top-level State Department attitudes. It reflects the significance accorded the maintenance of unity within the non-Communist camp. More broadly, it suggests once again the disinclination of Acheson to deal with the leading Communist powers in anything but an adversary relationship. To him, complex maneuvers with the Russians and the Chinese were likely only to result in confusion and division in the allied camp. They were best avoided, therefore, or at least postponed until it was clear that other alternatives were less satisfactory. If Acheson thought in depth about the circumstances under which an American diplomatic initiative would be worthwhile—and there is no evidence he did—he probably felt it would be in response to an unambiguous threat by the Soviet Union and/or Communist China, following a reversal of the military balance in South Korea, that one or both nations would enter into the north if United Nations forces crossed the thirty-eighth parallel.

Uncertainty regarding Korea played a major role in the formulation of China policy. The primary issue here was the present and future status of Taiwan. The United States sought first to avoid an outbreak of hostilities in that area and then to avert a diplomatic confrontation with its European allies and India. The latter problem was the more acute, but in mid-September it appeared to be at least temporarily resolved. On the fourteenth of the month, in a meeting with the foreign ministers of Great Britain and France, Acheson proposed that the General Assembly create a United Nations commission to investigate the long-term status of Taiwan. It would submit a report and recommendations during the following year. In the meantime, the Security Council could grapple with the immediate problem of alleged American aggression against China. British and French officials expressed satisfaction with this approach.[230]

The Pentagon did not share the State Department's flexibility. It opposed "any United Nations solution for Formosa which might enhance the military position of the U.S.S.R. in the Far East."[231] Clearly, military men now desired a long-term American commitment to the island's defense. This split between the State and Defense departments produced no immediate clash, however, because the diplomats conceded that the status quo regarding Taiwan must be maintained at least until the end of hostilities in Korea.

In sum, American China policy had become enslaved to events on the peninsula. This fact serves to emphasize the fateful nature of decisions made from late June 1950 onward and the degree to which the climate of urgency in Washington distracted attention from the goal of weaning Peking from

Moscow's influence. After the shocks of late 1949 and early 1950, executive officials grasped eagerly at the opportunity for bold action. Some elements in the State Department counseled a measure of caution, and even held their own on the Taiwan issue, but, in the charged atmosphere surrounding them, their voices stood less and less chance for a sympathetic hearing. However justified the initial effort to contain the North Korean attack, the auxiliary moves, along with the general course followed during July and August, threatened to eliminate whatever chance remained for the United States to evolve a realistic policy in Asia.

So the summer of 1950 was a period of confrontation for the Truman administration. In foreign relations, the prevailing view was that a sizable increase in the physical strength of the West must temporarily overshadow sophisticated diplomacy. Simultaneous pursuit of the two endeavors seemed unwarranted or impossible. On the domestic front, administration leaders attempted to remove the internal security issue from the political scene rather than merely blunt its impact. This effort helped to destroy the temporary lull in partisan debate engendered by the conflict overseas. By September, therefore, American officials were in a weak position to respond prudently to a sudden reversal in the balance of military forces in Korea.

# 7 The Adventure

Early on 15 September (Korea time) 1950, the American X Corps of just under seventy thousand men, backed by massive air and naval bombardment, commenced landings at Inchon, some twenty miles from Seoul on the west coast of Korea. These units met little resistance. Their advance was rapid, their losses slight. Within eleven days, they had seized control of the South Korean capital and linked up with elements of the Eighth Army, which on 23 September had burst out of the Pusan perimeter. North Korean forces were now in a headlong and often disorderly retreat toward the thirty-eighth parallel. By the end of the month, United Nations ground operations approached that boundary. At the beginning of October, South Korean troops crossed into the north. A week later, their American counterparts followed. North Korea's military machine, which less than three months earlier had been close to dominating the entire peninsula, was now in rout and threatened with extinction.

## Planning a Counteroffensive: MacArthur Opts for Boldness

Despite unimpeachable evidence that plans in Washington for crossing the thirty-eighth parallel were far advanced prior to mid-September, it is difficult to deny that the outcome of the Inchon operation exerted a major influence on the decision to send United Nations forces into North Korea. In a general sense, MacArthur had conceived the assault on Inchon within days of the outbreak of war in Korea. Originally, his gross underestimation of North Korean strength had led him to believe that it could be conducted in late July. By 10 July, however, the failure of American and South Korean forces to halt the North Korean onslaught had necessitated an indefinite cancellation of the plan. When Generals Collins and Vandenberg arrived in Tokyo three days later, MacArthur told them of his broad strategy aimed at destroying North Korea's army, though he conceded that the military situation did not permit the setting of a date for a United Nations offensive.[1]

Inchon as a site for military operations presented three major drawbacks. First, the tides in the city's harbor made approaches by sizable vessels feasible only once every month, and even then for only a few hours along narrow channels. Any landing, therefore, had to be timed precisely. Moreover, the heavily fortified island of Wolmi-do, which dominated the harbor, served as a major barrier to an advance by unfriendly forces. Second, to reach the city

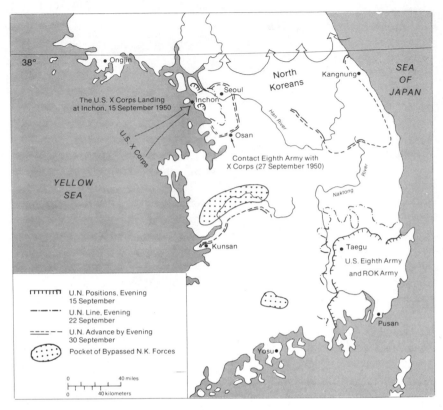

MAP 3. The Defeat of the North Korean Forces

from the beaches, marines would be forced to scale seawalls that were twelve to fourteen feet high. After overcoming this barrier, the invading force would face an enemy sheltered by many substantial buildings. Third, Inchon was so far north as to make difficult the rapid linkage of soldiers there with those on the southern tip of the peninsula. As the summer progressed and the American Eighth Army retreated to a small perimeter around Pusan, this problem took on major proportions. Uncertainty grew over the capacity of the United Nations troops to break out of this defensive position and join up with forces far to the north. If such an effort proved impossible, overwhelming North Korean strength might be concentrated against units at or near Inchon.[2]

MacArthur recognized these problems. In fact, on 23 July, when he ordered his Joint Strategic Plans and Operations Group to commence work on specific plans for an amphibious envelopment, he directed that alternate landing sites also be considered. Inchon, nonetheless, remained in the forefront of his mind. By mid-August, a detailed draft had emerged for an offensive at Inchon, targeted for 15 September. The Far Eastern commander was more convinced than ever that his original inclination was sound.³

Others had doubts. The projected leaders of the landing and assault forces, Major General Oliver P. Smith of the first Marine Division and Rear Admiral James H. Doyle, questioned MacArthur's assumptions and cited the natural obstacles of the Inchon site as well as the questionable offensive capabilities of the Eighth Army. In Washington, the Joint Chiefs had received little information regarding MacArthur's plan. Aware of his earlier miscalculations and of the limited resources immediately available to the United States, they were deeply concerned that he might undertake an operation that was beyond his means. As a result, General Collins and Admiral Sherman arrived at Tokyo on 21 August for a firsthand report.⁴

On 23 and 24 August, at high-level meetings in the Japanese capital, the pros and cons of the Inchon site were discussed thoroughly. Naval and marine officers in the Far Eastern Command led the opposition to MacArthur's plan. At a crucial point, the Far Eastern commander took the floor, and, with what General Collins later called a "brilliant exposition," left his audience "spellbound."⁵ MacArthur concluded with the declaration, "Never will the eagle of victory perch on the banner of a commander who won't take a chance!"⁶ Admiral Sherman and a few others continued to harbor doubts, but they were insufficient to thwart the plans of the top military officials on the scene. When Collins and Sherman returned to the United States, they briefed the president, the secretary of defense, and Generals Bradley and Vandenberg. On 28 August, the Joint Chiefs approved the Inchon operation. They suggested, however, that plans also be established for a landing near Kunsan, farther to the south. The military leaders also asked MacArthur to keep them informed of any new information regarding the upcoming offensive.⁷

The military tradition of granting a commander in the field much leeway in determining the means by which he accomplished desirable goals stood squarely in the path of any inclination among the Joint Chiefs to alter MacArthur's plans. The Far Eastern commander's reputation, his seniority, and his assertiveness, demonstrated most recently in his letter to the Veterans of Foreign Wars, represented further impediments.

Nevertheless, the arguments in favor of the Inchon site impressed military planners in Washington. Its proximity to Seoul and its location well north of the position of most North Korean troops represented advantages of considerable strategic significance. The capture of Seoul soon after a landing would be a major psychological blow to the enemy and would sever its main north-south supply route. On the way from Inchon to Seoul, moreover, United Nations forces could capture Kimpo airfield, which would serve as an excellent advance base for American air operations. Unlike other landing points farther south, Inchon was far enough north to provide the starting point for an envelopment that might trap the entire North Korean army below the thirty-eighth parallel. MacArthur's plan, therefore, offered the possibility of a total victory in the near future. Because the Joint Chiefs were eager for an early termination of American operations on the peninsula and because the destruction of North Korea's army would assist in this endeavor, the Inchon operation held a major advantage over the alternatives.[8]

Yet, if United Nations forces encountered serious difficulties in landing, the offensive potential of the counterattack would be compromised. The amount of enemy resistance that was likely to be confronted at Inchon was the key in determining the wisdom of the plan. MacArthur believed that the bulk of Communist strength was committed to the Pusan area and that few reserves were available to the North Koreans in the vicinity of Inchon. Furthermore, he argued, the natural barriers to landing at Inchon would prevent the North Koreans from anticipating a move there. The element of surprise would benefit American units.[9]

The intelligence briefing given Sherman and Collins in Tokyo was shaky on the matter of enemy strength around Inchon.[10] This and other considerations gave the Joint Chiefs second thoughts about the operation, even after they had communicated their general approval to MacArthur. In early September, the North Koreans launched another major offensive against the Pusan perimeter. This move was an ugly reminder of the precarious hold maintained by United Nations forces in Korea. To military leaders in Washington, it also served to emphasize that nearly all the reserves of the American Eighth Army had been committed to combat and that no reinforcements could be sent to the Far Eastern Command from the United States for several months. In short, if the counterattack failed, United Nations forces might be pushed off the peninsula.[11]

MacArthur's failure to submit his final plans for the upcoming offensive heightened this fear. On 5 September, the Joint Chiefs wired Tokyo requesting information on any modification in tactics. The Far Eastern commander assured Washington that no changes were in the offing and that by 11 September he would dispatch by officer-courier a detailed outline of the operation.[12]

Still dissatisfied, the Joint Chiefs asked for reevaluation of the projected landing in view of the Eighth Army's difficulties on the Pusan perimeter. MacArthur's reply exuded optimism. "There is no slightest possibility," he declared, "of our forces being ejected from the Pusan beachhead." The rapid linking of the Eighth Army with United Nations forces to the northwest, though desirable, was not essential to the success of the counterattack. The move at Inchon, MacArthur concluded, was the only means of avoiding a costly war of attrition in which the Communists, who had a greater capacity for reinforcement, would hold a decided advantage.[13]

This response ended the formal inquiries from Washington. For the purposes of future analysis, however, the most important point is that doubts regarding the wisdom of the maneuver had long existed in top military circles in Washington, and continued to exist—at least privately—right up to its execution. When the counteroffensive succeeded brilliantly, the Joint Chiefs became less inclined than ever before to question MacArthur's judgment.

## Inchon and the International Climate

Although this fact was to become critical from mid-October onward, the Inchon landing exerted an immediate influence on international politics. With the alteration of the balance of forces on the peninsula, the Soviet Union sent out strong signals that it was interested in negotiations on Korea. In New York, Russian diplomats pursued what was for them a conciliatory course. On 21 September, Soviet Foreign Minister Andrei Vishinsky delivered a comparatively sober speech to the opening session of the General Assembly. Rather than centering on United States Taiwan policy and Communist China's admission to the United Nations—as his subordinates had done during August—he expressed concern regarding the war in Korea, relations among the five permanent members of the Security Council, and the trend toward rearmament in Western Europe.[14] The speech seemed to be more than the usual Soviet propaganda tirade. James Reston observed that Soviet diplomats had abandoned their "stone faces" in private to become "elaborately jovial." The Soviet delegates to the United Nations not only attended a reception for Acheson at the Waldorf-Astoria, they also actually "appeared to be enjoying themselves." They talked openly about the necessity of ending the Korean War.[15]

At the beginning of October, more explicit signals appeared. On 29 September, Great Britain and seven other nations had introduced a resolution, partially drafted by the United States, to the General Assembly. The resolution included four recommendations, the most significant of which called for "appropriate steps" to "insure conditions of stability throughout Korea" and for United Nations-supervised elections over the entire peninsula to establish "a unified, independent, and democratic government" for the country.[16]

Russia responded to Britain's presentation with a resolution of its own. In several respects, this countermeasure was unsatisfactory to the United States. It did, however, call for United Nations-supervised elections throughout the peninsula, which was a major alteration of the Kremlin's position since 1947. And Vishinsky expressed a desire to negotiate on the resolutions through a subcommittee of the First Committee.[17]

Vishinsky also approved private talks on Korea between a low-level Soviet diplomat and the Norwegian representatives to the United Nations. In these discussions, the Russian mentioned the possibility of disarming the North Koreans and permitting a United Nations commission to conduct elections.[18] When, on 7 October, American troops entered the north, however, the Soviets broke off the contact.[19]

Although the United States did not reject talks out of hand, American leaders feared that negotiations would place them under irresistible pressure from allies and neutrals to halt at least temporarily United Nations ground operations at the thirty-eighth parallel.[20] The success at Inchon had given friendly forces tremendous momentum. An opportunity appeared to be at hand for total military victory at little cost in time and resources. To halt United Nations troops in the midst of their rapid march north would hurt morale, especially within South Korea's contingents, and give North Korean soldiers, some thirty thousand of which had eluded entrapment in the South, time to regroup. Thus, although Washington did not openly reject diplomacy, it did shy away from procedures that might have compromised its military advantage on the peninsula. Had the American counteroffensive been less dramatic in its impact and had the United Nations advance been slower and with greater sacrifice, the Truman administration might well have regarded negotiations as more attractive.

## Inchon and American Perceptions

Yet the Inchon landing influenced American policy only because leaders in Washington held certain beliefs. These included the convictions that any show of hesitation or uncertainty by the United States would produce increased intransigence in Moscow and Peking; that negotiations with Communists were not generally productive, and were often harmful; and that, for the present, the Soviet Union and Communist China wished to avoid a direct military confrontation with the United States. The first two beliefs, of course, are closely related and have been a major preoccupation of this book. On Korea, the first may be traced back at least to late 1946, the second to September 1947. The third also had a history going back well before 1950, yet it deserves further elaboration in the specific context of Korea after the Inchon counteroffensive.

The view that Moscow and Peking wanted to avert hostilities with the United States led, in turn, to the conclusion that, if either of the top Communist powers were going to intervene directly in North Korea, they would do so well before United Nations forces reached the thirty-eighth parallel. This conclusion rested on two assumptions, namely that if major Chinese or Russian units moved into North Korea, American troops would not enter that territory; and that Moscow and Peking recognized this fact. Thus, when no foreign soldiers entered North Korea immediately following the Inchon landing—and the Soviets assumed a relatively conciliatory posture in New York—the way seemed clear for a United Nations military offensive to unify the peninsula.

The fallacies in this thinking are clear. First, Washington overestimated Moscow's ability to read American intentions. Because the Kremlin was uncertain as to how the United States would react to Soviet intervention in North Korea, such intervention involved major risks. Then, Washington misread the failure of Russia or China to send troops into Korea as a confession of helplessness to influence events on the peninsula. On the one hand, top American officials failed to grasp Russia's cautiousness regarding its own role in Korea; on the other hand, they miscalculated Russia's ability and willingness to play the Chinese card at a later date.

Perceptions of Peking's intentions were influenced by reports from China indicating that the Mao regime would avoid direct involvement. Information flowing into Washington, to be sure, was often contradictory. On 5 September, and again a week later, James R. Wilkinson, the American consul general at Hong Kong, reported to Washington that Chinese sources on the mainland indicated that the government planned to send forces into North Korea if American troops entered that area.[21] On 23 September, the American embassy at Taipei transmitted a report from the Nationalist Chinese defense minister, which was "partially confirmed by [an] outside source," that Communist China would send 250,000 troops into Korea.[22] Earlier intelligence reports from both London and Tokyo had disclosed that since July large numbers of soldiers had been moving from southern and central China into Manchuria.[23] Yet, on 20 September, Loy Henderson, the American ambassador to India, relayed to Washington the assessment of K. M. Panikkar, his Indian counterpart in Peking. Pannikar stated that the Chinese Communists had

> shown no undue interest [in Korea] beyond expression[s] of sympathy.
> Even that has been notably slackened during the last two weeks. In
> such circumstances direct participation of China in Korean fighting
> seems beyond [the] range of possibility unless of course a world war
> starts as a result of UN forces passing beyond the thirty-eighth parallel
> and [the] Soviet Union deciding directly to intervene.[24]

Additional evidence supporting this conclusion included the failure of the Chinese to take "even elementary precaution against air raids of their cities," which, given the recent experience of North Korean cities, were likely to accompany a Sino-American clash. Also, aside from "the strengthening of defenses in Manchuria," there were no apparent military preparations in progress in China. In the following days, Wilkinson presented information that reinforced Panikkar's view. Three reports from the mainland indicated that, because of the Peking regime's desire for entry into the United Nations and its preoccupation with internal reconstruction, it would provide only limited and indirect support to North Korea.[25]

It is easy to see why the reports from Panikkar were more persuasive than those from Taipei. The National government, Washington surmised, hoped to further alienate the United States from the Communist government on the mainland by presenting evidence of that regime's aggressive intent. The Indian ambassador and his government also appeared likely to overstate the prospects of Communist Chinese intervention, albeit for a different reason. The Indians generally sought to restrain the United States from action that might result in an expanded conflict. Hence, when Panikkar concluded that Peking would not send forces across the Yalu, State Department officials took special notice.

Panikkar's analysis also gained special credence because it fit prevailing State Department attitudes regarding Communist China. Acheson's condescension toward that nation appeared most baldly on 10 September in an interview with CBS commentator Eric Severaid:

> Now, I give the people of Peiping credit for being intelligent enough to see what is happening to them. Why they should want to further their own dismemberment and destruction by getting at cross purposes with all the free nations of the world who are inherently their friends and have always been friends of the Chinese as against this imperialism coming down from the Soviet Union I cannot see. And since there is nothing in it for them, I don't see why they should yield to what is undoubtedly pressures from the Communist movement to get into the Korean row.[26]

In substance, this remark had at least a kernel of truth. Russian influence in Manchuria was considerable, and, in all likelihood, the Sino-Soviet relationship was less than smooth. One intelligence report of late August indicated that the Chinese were irritated by the Soviet attempt to direct their activities and embroil them in the Korean conflict.[27] Surely, the Peking regime was not anxious to confront the United States at a time when its tasks at home—both political and economic—were so burdensome.

Yet Acheson's suggestion that "free nations" were the friends of the Chinese, and that, deep down, the Communists knew this, was arrogant and naive. It revealed a basic insensitivity to the depth of Communist resentment toward the United States for its past and present support of the Nationalist Chinese. It reflected a failure to grasp the deep-seated fear and apprehension in Peking regarding American intentions in Asia. Finally, it demonstrated an underestimation of Communist determination—even in the face of severe domestic problems—to prevent the forces of a hostile great power from marching to China's border.

Despite these misperceptions, reports from China from the end of September onward produced considerable unease in Washington. On 27 September, the British reported that Panikkar had altered his views somewhat; now he believed China "had decided on a more aggressive policy" and would intervene indirectly in Korea on an expanded scale.[28] Two days later, Alan Kirk, the American ambassador in Moscow, reported word from the Dutch foreign office that its chargé in Peking believed the Communists were actively considering military intervention if American troops crossed the thirty-eighth parallel.[29] At the beginning of October, the American embassy in the Netherlands repeated this warning from the Dutch diplomat in China.[30] From Hong Kong, Wilkinson sent a partial text of a 30 September speech by Chou En-lai stating that "the Chinese people absolutely will not tolerate foreign aggression nor will they supinely tolerate seeing their neighbors being savagely invaded by imperialists."[31] Finally, on 3 October, the State Department received word of Panikkar's midnight meeting with Chou in which the latter stated that China would intervene in Korea if the United States sent its troops into the north.[32]

Livingston Merchant, Rusk's top assistant, asserted at a meeting in Under Secretary of State James Webb's office that the report should be treated "with extreme seriousness" and not be discounted as a bluff.[33] U. Alexis Johnson, deputy director of the Division of Northeast Asian Affairs, suggested to Rusk that consideration be given to using only South Korean troops "for the subjugation of North Korea."[34] O. Edmund Clubb made somewhat similar proposals.[35]

Yet these counsels of caution were rejected. To flinch when the Chinese threatened or remonstrated was, to Acheson, most distasteful to contemplate. "Hesitation and timidity," he argued on 4 October would create "greater risk [than a] firm and courageous" stand.[36] As with many other decisions by the United States in Asia over the previous four years, that regarding an offensive in North Korea had become linked to concern for American credibility abroad.

By early October, moreover, the momentum for sending American troops across the thirty-eighth parallel was nearly irresistible. On 27 September, Washington had sent orders to MacArthur authorizing an American campaign in the north.[37] Two days later, eight friendly nations had presented a resolution to the General Assembly approving such action. In the midst of a heated congressional election campaign, a substantial majority of both editorial writers and those questioned in a national poll favored a military effort to unify Korea.[38] Short of clear evidence that Soviet or Chinese troops had crossed into North Korea, or a direct threat of Soviet entry, there was no stopping the northward march of United Nations forces.[39]

## The Diplomatic Option: An Evaluation

The prospects for productive negotiations on Korea remain uncertain. Perhaps Russia sought merely to undermine American resolve, or to enhance its own image as a force for peace in the world. Nevertheless, there was much in the situation of the early fall of 1950 to produce disquiet in the Kremlin. The United States was more determined than ever to move toward a peace treaty with Japan. Congress and the president finally appeared willing to accept a level of military spending commensurate with American objectives abroad. West German rearmament appeared to be on the horizon. The balance of forces in Korea had shifted greatly to the disadvantage of the Communists. Direct Soviet intervention could reverse this development, at least temporarily, but it might also bring about the unleashing of American military-industrial power against the Soviet homeland. Large-scale Chinese Communist intervention in Korea could probably turn the tide on the peninsula, but such action was unpalatable to Peking, which had serious domestic problems to contend with. And China's assumption of the major burdens in Korea might eventually weaken Soviet influence over the Communist movement in Asia and elsewhere.[40] Finally, if, as Soviet premier Nikita Khrushchev later suggested, the Kremlin did not anticipate the sharp American response to the North Korean attack in June, it may be that in the fall Soviet leaders were uncertain what Washington's response would be to Chinese intervention in Korea. They may even have feared direct American retaliation against Russia.[41]

Ultimately, these considerations may not have been sufficient to make Moscow and Peking accept a settlement in Korea satisfactory to the Truman administration. A secretary of state intent on keeping his options open, however, should have made an effort to find out if this was the case. Simultaneous overtures to the Russians and the Chinese might even have revealed divisions within the Communist camp.

Domestic politics offered no major deterrent to talks because the American people traditionally approved negotiations even when they stood little chance of success.[42] Fifty-two percent of the Americans questioned in a national poll completed in mid-October believed that a meeting between Truman and Stalin to seek an end to their countries' differences was a "good idea." Only 35 percent viewed it as a "poor idea."[43]

This public response said nothing about the political risk of halting American troops at the thirty-eighth parallel for a time while discussions took place. Certainly such a course would have stimulated serious dissent in Congress and the press. Nevertheless, had the United States moved toward negotiations well before October, their conclusion—or at least a sense of their prospects—might have been attained before American troops were ready to enter North Korea. And public dissent might have been reduced had the Truman administration, from mid-August onward, publicly delineated the dangers of a military campaign in the north rather than emphasizing the need for political unity in Korea. In any event, military operations on the northern half of the peninsula—especially if they involved no American ground forces—did not necessarily preclude East-West diplomatic activity regarding Korea's future.

But Acheson was more intent on negotiations to solidify the Western alliance against Communist expansion than with talks on Korea. As Adam Ulam has observed, the secretary of state, ever suspicious of Soviet motives and none too sensitive to subtle signals emanating from Moscow—where officials sought to convey a desire to bargain while obscuring Russian weakness—perceived neither the strength of the American position in the fall of 1950 nor the limits to which that position could be enhanced.[44] As a result of this failure, the United States embarked on a dangerous course in Korea before exploring prospects for an advantageous settlement without a successful American military venture in North Korea.

That venture was particularly ill-advised in view of allied and neutral opinion. Although the British continued to support American policy, Peking's threat of intervention made them extremely uneasy.[45] In the General Assembly, India maneuvered furiously to reconcile the eight-power and Soviet resolutions on Korea. Sir Benegal Rau, head of the Indian delegation, proposed the creation of a special subcommittee to seek a compromise. This move coincided with an effort by Secretary-General Trygve Lie to negotiate an agreement on a unified Korea. He hoped that Pyongyang would disband its forces and allow a United Nations commission into North Korea to conduct an election, which, in turn, would serve as a basis for the unification of the peninsula. If North Korea rejected this plan, Lie was willing to support a United Nations effort to consolidate the territory militarily as a prelude to political unification.[46]

Ambassador Austin objected to the Indian proposal on the ground that it would delay action on the British resolution, thereby "permitting the aggressor to prolong his activities."[47] In an attempt to meet Austin's objections, Rau agreed that the projected subcommittee would have to submit any proposals before 6 October.[48] The Soviet Union reacted favorably to India's initiative.[49] As in July and August, however, Indian efforts failed. On 4 October, the First Committee defeated India's plan by a vote of 32-24 with three abstentions.[50]

Although the eight-power resolution eventually passed the General Assembly by a 47-5 margin, the support for the Indian maneuver in the First Committee suggests widespread unease with American Korea policy. India's opposition to an immediate American move across the thirty-eighth parallel was especially important because of that nation's stature in Asia and because New Delhi's relations with Peking were under increasing strain over the latter's pressure on Tibet.[51] The fall of 1950, therefore, was an especially opportune time for the United States to build a more constructive relationship with India.

At the very least, Washington should have halted American troops at the thirty-eighth parallel and pursued negotiations in New York. Even permitting South Korean soldiers to move into the north presented certain problems. In all likelihood, they could not have destroyed enemy forces or pacified the territory. Thus, a South Korean campaign raised the specter of indecisive fighting on the peninsula over an interminable period. Yet had the United States halted South Korean units at the thirty-eighth parallel in October 1950, considerable resentment would have arisen, both within the Rhee government and throughout the general populace. American soldiers, in fact, might have found themselves forcefully restraining their South Korean counterparts. However imperfect these choices may have been, they were far less dangerous in their implications than a possible Sino-American clash in Korea. That would raise questions in Western Europe regarding the prudence of the United States and weaken relations with India. Most importantly, it would produce a major drain on American resources in an area of secondary strategic importance, and, for the short term at least, solidify Peking's allegiance to Moscow.

It was silly to argue that a failure to punish the Communist world for the North Korean attack would encourage future aggression. Certainly, the American response to the June crisis, both locally and worldwide, was such as to discourage future Communist adventurism in Korea or elsewhere and to bolster confidence in the West in American leadership. In sum, by October the United States had profited much internationally from its action in Korea. Now, in trying to gain a little more, it was about to incur a serious deficit.

## Crossing the Thirty-eighth Parallel: The Personal Dimension

Before moving on to the fateful military campaign in North Korea, a few words are in order on the role of personalities. Would the outcome in early October have been different had someone other than Rusk been the officer in charge of American policy toward East Asia, or had someone other than Allison been director of the Division of Northeast Asian Affairs? It is clear that these two men were among the least likely to support a cautious policy regarding military activities in North Korea. It is clear that Merchant and Clubb, just below Rusk, and Johnson, just below Allison, were more deeply disturbed by the risks entailed in an American advance beyond the thirty-eighth parallel.

What if, in the spring of 1950, W. Walton Butterworth had been retained as assistant secretary of state for the Far East? He was a Princeton graduate of the same class as Kennan. Like Kennan—who was a good friend—he was a career foreign service officer. Unlike Rusk, Butterworth was independently wealthy, a man who had no financial need to keep his job. Although a team player, he was a tough, forceful personality in the intricate game of bureaucratic politics. More than Rusk, he was a coolheaded realist, suspicious of narrow moral and legal arguments. His broad views on China were moderate. Whereas Rusk had begun his career in government in the military during World War II and had maintained close contacts with army officials afterward, Butterworth had no background in the armed services and generally held military men in contempt. Although he could often see both sides of an issue, he rarely had difficulty making up his mind which was correct. On the other hand, decisiveness was never one of Rusk's outstanding qualities. Finally, Clubb had served under Butterworth in China during 1946 and 1947, and the latter had great esteem for his subordinate's knowledge of and judgment in matters Chinese.[52]

Would Butterworth have given greater weight than did Rusk to Clubb's analysis of early October—as well as to Johnson's and Merchant's apprehensions? Would he have pushed them vigorously with Acheson? Perhaps so, but to what degree? It would have taken a strong man indeed to resist forcefully the momentous pressures that existed in early October, and Butterworth was not totally immune to domestic politics. Surely, his position would have been strengthened had Johnson been in Allison's place. Then, the two men who bore the greatest responsibility for reporting to Acheson on Korea might have been of one mind; and the secretary of state was not one who readily ignored strong advice from below. Yet, given his attitudes toward China and the likelihood that, if the Truman administration halted the American advance at the thirty-eighth parallel, a politically risky confrontation with the victorious MacArthur would ensue, it remains doubtful that the evidence available in early October could have been brought to bear upon Acheson forcefully enough to change his mind. The most that can be said is that a Butterworth-Johnson combination in the State Department from the summer onward might have led to somewhat different circumstances in early October, and thus to a different policy outcome.

It can be said with greater assurance that, in late September, personalities had a substantial impact on the framing of a new directive for MacArthur. It has already been shown that planners in Washington anticipated that no American troops would be used in the provinces bordering on Russia and China, but that the State Department was less flexible on the issue than the Defense Department.[53] The orders sent to MacArthur on 27 September stated the following: "Under no circumstances . . . will your forces cross the Manchurian or U.S.S.R. borders of Korea, and, as a matter of policy, no non-Korean ground forces will be used in the northeast provinces bordering the Soviet Union or in the area along the Manchurian border."[54] The distinction made between action in Manchuria or Russia and action in Korea's border provinces implied that the prohibition against the second was less firm than that against the first. Military men understood that a difference existed between a mandatory order and a statement as a matter of policy, though the precise nature of that difference was uncertain.[55] In any event, State Department officials spotted the discrepancy in the Joint Chiefs' draft of the new instructions and took up the matter with the Pentagon.[56]

At this point, a recent change in personnel at the top of the Defense Department became significant. On 21 September, General Marshall became secretary of defense, replacing the recently fired Louis Johnson, whose relations with the State Department had been at best frigid, at worst explosive. In contrast, Marshall had outstanding relations with the diplomats. During the first six months of Marshall's stewardship of the State Department, Acheson had been his top assistant. The secretary of state was a great admirer of the general, as were the president and virtually all top State Department officials. With Johnson at the helm in the Pentagon, Acheson had encountered no peer in influence at the White House on foreign policy matters. With Marshall's accession, he on occasion did. Although Acheson did not hesitate to initiate and perpetuate disagreements with a Johnson-led Defense Department, when Marshall took over the secretary of state became less combative. So did his subordinates.

As Paul Nitze later recalled, had Johnson responded to the State Department inquiry regarding MacArthur's new orders, the diplomats probably would have resisted pressure to retain an element of flexibility on American troop involvement in the extreme northern provinces of Korea. When Marshall did so, however, they simply suppressed their doubts.[57] Certainly timing was important here because the issue arose during the peak of optimism in Washington following the Inchon counteroffensive and at a moment when Acheson was in New York, preoccupied with talks on the NATO alliance and with proceedings at the United Nations. It appears, nonetheless, that Marshall's presence in Washington, which three years earlier had been crucial in America's avoidance of a deepening clash with the Communists in China, now served to increase significantly the prospects of such confrontation in Korea. But this fact would become apparent only in the weeks after President Truman's 15 October meeting with MacArthur at Wake Island.

## Optimism Reigns: The March North Begins

During the two weeks following the crossing of the thirty-eighth parallel by American troops, the Truman administration presented a confident face to the public. In its early stages, the advance into North Korea met with little resistance. Beneath the surface, however, three matters caused serious concern to top Washington officials.

First was the possibility of Communist Chinese intervention. Although threats of such action from Peking did not prevent American ground operations in North Korea, they did result in the sending of further orders to the Far Eastern Command. On 9 October, in an expansion of the orders of 27 September, the Joint Chiefs told MacArthur that "in the event of an open or covert employment anywhere in Korea of major Chinese Communist units, without prior announcement, you should continue the action as long as, in your judgment, action by forces now under your control offers a reasonable chance of success." The Far Eastern commander was to "obtain authorization from Washington prior to taking any military action against objectives in Chinese territory."[58]

Between 8 and 14 October, Communist China repeated its warnings in domestic newspapers, and intelligence reports indicated that Chinese troops were massing in Manchuria in areas near the Yalu River. Still, an army analysis concluded that they were unlikely to cross into Korea on a major scale. Without Soviet air and naval support, Chinese intervention might not be as decisive as at an earlier date, and Soviet aid would increase Russian influence in Manchuria. Moreover, an attack on American forces might lead to countermeasures that could threaten the existence of Mao's regime.[59] The intelligence branch of the Far Eastern Command held similar views, and asserted that Peking and Moscow probably had ruled out "further expensive investment in support of a lost cause."[60] Thus, fears in Washington were not adequate to alter the American course in Korea.

A second matter of concern was that of setting up a government in areas of North Korea as they were occupied by United Nations forces. The ultimate problems were those of transferring authority from military to civilian rule and of creating a government for all of Korea. If United Nations policy prior to the outbreak of the Korean War was to be implemented, the Republic of Korea, headed by Syngman Rhee, would logically extend its authority over the entire country. Northern Korea would be represented in the national government through the election of one hundred people to the National Assembly.

Yet this policy had serious liabilities. Inside Korea, Rhee was sure to try to boost conservative elements into a position of domination in the legislature. Success in that effort would cause trouble in territories previously governed by the People's Republic because the conservatives would certainly attempt to reverse some of the reforms instituted by the Communists. In Asia and elsewhere, Communists could be counted on to make use of an application of past United Nations policy to cast doubt on the legitimacy of the international, and especially the United States, military effort. Any victory by Rhee would hinder an American effort to counter the Communist portrayal of the

United States as a reactionary power, as well as irritate India and America's allies.

On the other hand, Rhee and his political supporters would surely oppose any attempt by the United Nations and the United States to alter the course provided for in the General Assembly resolution of November 1947. That the United Nations was aware of its dilemma is suggested by the General Assembly's failure to define its policy regarding national elections and the permanent status of the Republic of Korea. A decision as to who was to exercise temporary authority in territories of North Korea occupied by United Nations forces, however, could not be postponed. On 12 October, the United Nations Interim Committee of the General Assembly voted that the Unified Command, under General MacArthur, would temporarily be responsible for civil administration in North Korea. The Republic of Korea was to exercise authority only in the south.[61] Rhee objected loudly to this arrangement, but the United States stood behind the decision.[62] Thus, the worries of the administration in pursuing its policy of unifying Korea did not end with the threat of Chinese intervention.

A final matter of concern regarding the Korean question was that of American air activity around the Soviet and Manchurian borders. Although the directive of 27 September forbade American air operations over Russia, on 9 October (American time) two U.S. planes, apparently by mistake, attacked a Soviet air base sixty-two miles from the Korean border. The base was located only eighteen miles from the important Russian port of Vladivostok. On 10 October, the Soviet Union issued a strong public protest.[63] Nine days later, the State Department acknowledged the attack and offered to pay for any damage to Soviet property.[64]

The incident may have provided some impetus for the president's trip to the western Pacific to talk to MacArthur. Yet domestic politics were the primary motive for Truman's pilgrimage to Wake Island. Surely, it was not intended as a major policymaking event. Acheson was not informed in advance of Truman's decision to go, and the secretary neither attended nor desired to do so.[65] As former presidential aide Charles Murphy has recalled, the trip was the idea of the White House staff, which viewed it as good public relations for the Democratic party on election eve.[66]

The details of the meeting are not significant here. What is important is that MacArthur left it with a greater sense of freedom than when he arrived. In his talks with the president, Harriman, Rusk, General Bradley, and others, the Far Eastern commander exuded confidence on Korea.[67] He asserted it was unlikely that the Communist Chinese would intervene, and that, if they did, United Nations forces would easily prevail. The latter claim was especially crucial because later on it would add to Washington's deliberations the question of Peking's capabilities rather than merely its intentions. In a private meeting, MacArthur even apologized to the commander in chief for the VFW letter.[68] When, more than a decade later, Truman recalled that

MacArthur "kissed my ass" at the meeting, he erred only in a literal sense.[69] Acheson described the mood of the presidential party upon its return to the United States as "full of optimism and confidence in the General."[70] And MacArthur returned to Tokyo equally assured of his own authority to do as he pleased in Korea. On 17 October, he ordered United Nations soldiers to move fifty to a hundred miles into provinces bordering on Manchuria and the Soviet Union. A week later, he removed all restrictions on the use of non-Korean troops near the peninsula's northern boundary.[71]

Apparently the Joint Chiefs did not take notice of the first move. After the second, however, in a wire to MacArthur, they stated that though he "undoubtedly had sound reasons for issuing these instructions they would like to be informed of them."[72] The Far Eastern commander replied that "military necessity" dictated his move. South Korean forces, he asserted, were inadequate to hold North Korea's border regions. He had legal justification for his action, he continued, because the Joint Chiefs had stated that their directive of 27 September was not final. Moreover, the restrictions on non-Korean troops had been stated as a matter of policy rather than a mandatory order. A communique from Marshall two days later had loosened even that restraint by stating, "We want you to feel unhampered tactically and strategically to proceed north of the thirty-eighth parallel." MacArthur concluded by saying that the "entire subject was covered in my conference at Wake Island."[73]

The Joint Chiefs, as General Collins later observed, "at least tacitly accepted MacArthur's defense of his order by making no move to countermand it."[74] On 26 October, however, President Truman stated publicly that it was his understanding that only Korean troops would approach the Yalu.[75] Mac-Arthur was kind enough to clarify the matter for the commander in chief— and for the American people—with a declaration that the United Nations' mission was simply "to clear Korea."[76]

The Wake Island conference was not totally responsible for MacArthur's moves. The wording of the instructions sent him on 27 September was at least partially to blame. Yet the minutes of MacArthur's meeting with Truman, Bradley, Rusk, and other leading administration officials indicate that the "proconsul of the East" implied at one point that non-Korean troops would be permitted into the extreme northern provinces of the peninsula. When questioned on the feasibility of using Indian soldiers for occupation duties along the Soviet and Chinese borders, he stated the following: "It would be indefensible from a military point of view. I am going to put South Korean troops up there. They will be the buffer. The other troops will be pulled back south of a line from twenty miles north of Pyongyang to Hamhung."[77] Assuming that the wording of the minutes is precise, Mac-Arthur's statement that non-Korean troops would be "pulled back" to the narrow neck indicated that he initially intended to use them north of that line. No one questioned him on the matter. The point may have passed over the heads of the Washington officials present. It is likely, however, that Mac-

Arthur regarded this episode as additional justification for moving American troops into the border provinces.

MacArthur's action was significant for three reasons. First, the orders of 17 and 24 October committed non-Korean forces to a continuing offensive beyond the most convenient point for defensive operations between the thirty-eighth parallel and the Yalu. Henceforth, supply lines became seriously overextended, thereby rendering American troops increasingly vulnerable to counterattack. Second, the continuing northward march of American troops could not help but increase anxieties in Peking, and increase the likelihood of a clash between Chinese and American forces. Third, the action insured that the first contact between United Nations ground troops and the Chinese, if it occurred, would take place after American soldiers had advanced beyond the narrow neck. It would be more difficult to defuse an impending crisis, therefore, because to hold at that line would now involve a *retreat* of American forces rather than merely *the halting of* an advance. Given the prevailing state of mind in Washington regarding the dangers of showing timidity in the face of Communist pressure, neither prospect was attractive, but the first was far less so than the second. Thus, the move by American forces beyond the narrow neck increased the chances of both a major Sino-American confrontation and a military setback for the United States.

The role of MacArthur in this matter is an issue that historians will never resolve with certainty. Surely, most other military men in his place would have requested permission from Washington before sending American troops beyond the narrow neck.[78] Surely, in such circumstances the Joint Chiefs would have sought the views of the State Department. It is less certain, however, what decision would have been reached. The Joint Chiefs had long feared a stalemate in Korea. Their worries remained, even after the United Nations counteroffensive of mid-September. With time, enemy soldiers who escaped across the thirty-eighth parallel, combined with the organized but not fully trained North Korean units that had been held back from the June offensive, could become a substantial force. It was important, therefore, to destroy the entire North Korean army quickly. The South Koreans alone could not accomplish this task.

The position of the Defense Department during September indicates that, if a need arose, it would favor American ground activity north of the narrow neck. Intelligence reports and Chou's warning in early October did increase unease within the military regarding the likelihood of Chinese intervention. Yet MacArthur's statement at Wake Island that there was little chance of a Chinese move into North Korea and that, if such a move did occur, United Nations forces would still emerge victorious was reassuring. It must be kept in mind that the Far Eastern commander's influence in Washington was at a peak after Inchon, not only because the landing there had been such a success, but because he had stuck to his plan in the face of serious doubts among the Joint Chiefs. As historian David Rees has noted, that triumph was one of "imagination and intuition," rather than "logic and science."[79] For this very reason, military leaders later hesitated to question Mac-Arthur's plans, facts to the contrary notwithstanding.[80] Before 25 October, there was far too little evidence of Chinese intervention to have led the Joint Chiefs to oppose his actions, even had he requested permission from Washington beforehand.

It is also unlikely that the State Department would have opposed his order of 17 October. The diplomats, after all, were not immune to MacArthur's influence, nor were most of them inclined toward caution. They may at least have hedged a week later, however, at granting him total freedom for ground operations within North Korea, and, had State Department doubts led to significant delay in approving MacArthur's orders, that order might never have been issued. This is so because on 25 October South Korean forces made their initial contact with Chinese soldiers. Had this incident occurred and been confirmed in Washington prior to MacArthur's announcement that all Korea was open to American troops, it would have been easier politically, both at home and abroad, for the Truman administration to halt them well short of the Manchurian border. Such a move could then have been explained as being grounded in previous orders rather than in direct Chinese pressure. From late October onward, therefore, it is possible—even probable—that MacArthur exerted a major influence on the actions (or inactions) of Washington. His role was important both because he had tremendous personal prestige after Inchon and because he took liberties with his instructions that most others would have avoided. Still, his influence was greatly enhanced by prevailing attitudes in Washington regarding China.

## Courting Disaster

On 25 October, at Onjong, less than forty miles south of the Manchurian border in northwestern Korea, the republic's First Division met stiff resistance from Chinese soldiers. Many of these "volunteers"—as Peking labelled them—were killed in battle and some were captured. In the following days, South Korean and American troops—in both the eastern and western sectors—made extensive contact with Chinese units.[81]

In Tokyo, strong anxieties emerged. On 28 October, a Far Eastern Command intelligence summary estimated that 316,000 "regular Chinese ground forces," in addition to 274,000 security troops, were in Manchuria. All of the regulars, the report continued, "could be employed in the Korean War . . . [and] the bulk of [them] . . . are now in positions along the Yalu River at numerous crossing sites."[82] These figures conflicted sharply with those cited by MacArthur at Wake Island.[83] Yet G-2 chief, General Charles A. Willoughby, argued that "the auspicious time for intervention has long

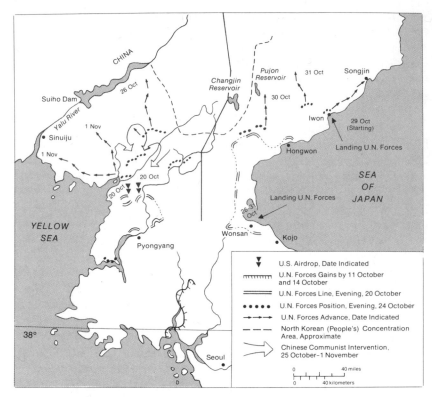

MAP 4. U.N. Forces Advance to the Yalu, 11 October–1 November 1950

since passed; it is difficult to believe that such a move, if planned, would have been postponed to a time when remnant North Korean forces have been reduced to a low point of effectiveness."[84]

In Washington, General Bradley also expressed considerable puzzlement. Peking's actions were "halfway between" the possibilities of large-scale and marginal involvement in Korea that the Joint Chiefs had previously envisaged.[85] General Collins viewed the reported crossings of the Yalu as an effort to save face after the public declarations by Chou En-lai of support for North Korea. Collins conceded, however, that, despite China's lack of air power and limited strength in artillery, its forces could seriously threaten United States troops.[86] In early November, therefore, the Joint Chiefs set aside plans for cutting back reinforcements to Korea.[87]

In the State Department, Clubb argued that the intervention could "not be conceived as other than direct." It was "unlikely," moreover, that the involvement was so limited as to present a danger that the Chinese would be "promptly bloodied and thrown out by [a] force that they themselves have consistently characterized as 'a paper tiger.'" Chinese action probably had been coordinated with the Soviet Union, he observed, and might well be the first step in a broadening of the conflict to areas beyond Korea.[88] On 3 November, Edward Barrett, the assistant secretary of state for public affairs, insisted that Chinese Communist propaganda alone suggested a massive intervention in Korea.[89] Even Wilkinson in Hong Kong, who throughout October had belittled the chances of large-scale Chinese involvement on the peninsula, was worried.[90] Yet no one proposed a halt to the United Nations advance. Despite Clubb's fears, he hoped that "a sound drubbing could be administered to Communist Chinese forces."

It was not until 7 November that Washington officialdom gave serious consideration to altering MacArthur's mission. On the previous day, in response to a denial of his request for permission to bomb the Yalu bridges, he had wired the Joint Chiefs that "Men and material in large force are pouring across all bridges over the Yalu from Manchuria. This movement not only jeopardizes but threatens the ultimate destruction of the forces under my command."[91] In response to this estimate, President Truman gave MacArthur the authority to bomb the Korean side of the bridges. Simultaneously, Clubb and Davies drew up detailed presentations on American options.[92] Both agreed that Communist China might "be on the rampage."[93] Both feared that a show of weakness would reinforce Chinese aggressiveness. Clubb noted that "Communists frequently adopt a threatening posture with the cold-blooded purpose of so frightening their enemies that the latter will surrender without a fight."[94] Both men advocated a combination of moderation and firmness. Davies wanted mobilization at home, negotiations with the Chinese, and abstention from any air attacks on Manchuria. Clubb emphasized the need to build up friendly forces in Korea with contingents from nations other than the United States and South Korea. He regarded the maintenance of a collective front in Korea as all-important. Although he did not explicitly propose an end to any United Nations military advance, he did state, "This should be a period of some slowing up of military operations to permit political estimates and discussions with our allies, to the end that, in our haste to win a battle, we shall not lose the war."[95] He was not optimistic regarding the possibilities for fruitful negotiations with the Communist powers, but he believed that talks should be pursued anyway, both with China and Russia.[96] He even suggested that the United States might dangle before Soviet eyes the prospect of discussions on Germany.

On 8 November, the Central Intelligence Agency (CIA) presented the strongest case to date in favor of halting the United Nations advance in North Korea. (Actually, United Nations forces had temporarily stopped their forward movement, both because of Chinese resistance and logistical problems.) In a paper subscribed to by the intelligence branches of the State Department and the armed services, the CIA concluded that combined Chinese and North Korean forces in Korea had the capacity to force their enemy to withdraw to "defensive positions farther south." Furthermore, China could probably make available 350,000 troops "for sustained ground operations in Korea . . . within thirty to sixty days."[97] If the military situation in North Korea was stabilized, however, the Chinese might "well consider that, with advantageous terrain and the onset of winter, their forces now in Korea are sufficient to accomplish their immediate purposes."[98] The policy proposal implicit in this analysis was that United Nations forces should seek to establish a defensive position in North Korea.

On the same day, the Joint Chiefs informed MacArthur that the National Security Council would meet on 9 November to discuss a possible alteration of his mission. At the same time, they prepared an option paper for presentation at that meeting. The paper outlined three alternatives: (1) a withdrawal of United Nations forces; (2) the establishment of a defensive line at the present locations of United Nations troops; and (3) a forward movement of those troops. The first was "totally unacceptable" from the standpoint of America's worldwide prestige. The second "might be a temporary expedient pending clarification of the military and political problems raised by Chinese intervention." The third might "require some augmentation of military strength in Korea even if the Chinese Communist scale of effort is not materially increased." The military leaders concluded that the State Department should seek a political settlement to the Korea situation, but that MacArthur's mission should not, for the present, be changed.[99]

These recommendations served as the basis for the National Security Council meeting of 9 November. All those present seemed to favor negotiations with China. Acheson introduced the possibility of establishing a ten-mile demilitarized zone on both sides of the Yalu. This idea originated with the thought that the Chinese simply wanted a *cordon sanitaire* on their border. Apparently, the secretary of state met no opposition. It was agreed that the United States should seek diplomatic contacts with Peking.

Yet no one proposed a halt—even temporarily—to offensive operations in North Korea so as to avoid initiating large-scale Sino-American hostilities. Why? Here the evidence is less than conclusive. Clearly, there remained some hope that a quick military victory could be attained in Korea. No one could be certain on this point until United Nations forces moved northward and engaged the enemy. The greater the delay in doing this, the more troops and supplies the Chinese could move across the Yalu.[100] As long as a favorable military decision remained a prospect, therefore, none of MacArthur's superiors were prepared to alter his plans for an end-the-war offensive.

Personalities as well as common attitudes toward China were decisive at this point. Only hours before the National Security Council meeting, some purple prose had arrived in Washington in MacArthur's name. "It would be fatal," he declared, "to weaken the fundamental and basic policy of the United Nations to destroy all resisting armed forces in Korea and bring that country into a united and free nation." Now that he could use his air power throughout Korea, he asserted, he could "deny reinforcements coming across the Yalu in sufficient strength to prevent the destruction of those forces . . . arrayed against me in Korea." He projected an offensive "on or about November 15" for the purpose of "driving to the border and securing all of North Korea." Any lesser move would "completely destroy the morale of my forces." It also would "condemn us to an indefinite retention of our military forces along difficult defense lines in North Korea and unquestionably arouse such resentment among the South Koreans that their forces would collapse or might even turn against us." The idea that the Chinese in Korea might restrain themselves from moving southward if left unmolested, he claimed, was "wishful thinking at the very worst."[101] MacArthur concluded by drawing an analogy between the current British desire to give the Chinese a small strip of North Korea and their appeasement of Nazi Germany twelve years earlier. "To give up any portion of North Korea to the aggression of the Chinese Communists," he warned, "would be the greatest defeat of the free world in modern times." He recommended "with all the earnestness that I possess that there be no weakening at this crucial moment and that we press on to complete victory which I believe can be achieved if our determination and indomitable will do not desert us."[102]

MacArthur was not entirely alone in his views. Acheson and the Joint Chiefs had many of the same fears. Certainly, they feared that a hint of timidity would further embolden China. Surely, they sought to avoid an interminable commitment of American troops to Korea.

The balance of military forces on the peninsula, however, was far more unsettling to them than to MacArthur. Intelligence reports already suggested that the Chinese buildup south of the Yalu might be too much for United Nations units to overcome—and Bradley viewed the bombing of the Yalu bridges as unlikely to stop the flow of Chinese soldiers into North Korea.[103] Moreover, Washington officials were deeply concerned about the impact of a Sino-American confrontation on the European theater. Great Britain and France both worried that expanded American commitments in Asia would compromise commitments to NATO. MacArthur cared little about allied sentiments, or about American interests outside Asia. Nor was he apprehensive about a Sino-American clash in Korea.

Had a general with less self-assurance and less prestige been in Tokyo at the time—in a word, had MacArthur not been the Far Eastern commander—Washington probably would at least have postponed a United Nations advance. In contrast to circumstances five weeks earlier, by the second week of November leaders in Washington had sufficient evidence of large-scale Chinese involvement in Korea to accept a cautious course. Yet, in the face of MacArthur's assurances, they could not overcome their own strong distaste for and fear of Communist China and face up to reality. In the crisis, MacArthur simply brought out the worst in them rather than the best.

In fairness to MacArthur, he undoubtedly assumed that massive Chinese intervention in Korea would force Truman to order direct American action against the mainland.[104] Events later showed that this was not the case, but, prior to December, Washington officials had not reached a decision on the matter, much less communicated it to their field commander.

On the other hand, had MacArthur been informed of a decision that under no circumstances would the United States retaliate directly against mainland China, it is uncertain that he would have altered his course in Korea. As a man prone to overestimate the strength of his own forces and one who also possessed great confidence in his ability to grasp the "Oriental mentality," such news from his superiors back home might not have altered his determination to resume the military offensive. Surely, he would have protested strongly any timidity in dealing with Peking. Worse still, the protest might have been public. Had he been ordered to halt short of the Yalu, it is even likely that he would have launched a public debate—and no one in the administration welcomed that. On 7 November, after all, the Democrats had suffered substantial losses to the Republicans in an off-year election. Especially prominent in the GOP campaign that fall were attacks on the alleged weakness of Truman's policy in Asia. Acheson was often singled out for criticism by opposition politicians. After election day, some Democrats even blamed the secretary of state personally for the setback.[105] Under such circumstances, not even a man with Acheson's backbone could relish an open confrontation with "the sorcerer of Inchon."[106]

## Taiwan Policy Hardens

As a situation in Korea became more and more uncertain, the Truman administration grew increasingly unwilling to take risks on the Taiwan issue. In late September 1950, the General Assembly set 15 November as the date to take up the question. In the intervening period, Great Britain drafted a resolution on Taiwan for presentation to the international body. It called for a United Nations commission to study the matter and make recommendations.[107] State Department officials were uneasy with the draft right from the start, for it implied that the commission should follow closely the Cairo declaration of 1943, which projected the return of the territory to China. With Dulles taking the lead and Acheson approving, American diplomats set to work on revising the British draft so as to leave open the possibility of a recommendation for Taiwan's autonomy.[108] While the conflict in Korea continued, the United States was determined to prevent Communist conquest of the island, but, even after the Korean issue was resolved, Washington was prepared to lobby intensively to keep it separated from the mainland—or at least neutralized militarily.

In early November, as preparations for dealing with the Taiwan question in the General Assembly neared completion, the State Department moved ever closer to opposition to any United Nations involvement that might increase pressure on the United States to abandon the island to Communism. Chinese intervention in Korea was undoubtedly a factor here. With the termination of hostilities on the peninsula less and less a certainty, the diplomats were inclined to favor postponement of General Assembly deliberations on Taiwan. In fact, on 15 November, Dulles proposed this approach to the First Committee, which approved it almost unanimously.[109] Discussions on the issue in the General Assembly or its subunits did not resume until 1951. On 28 November, the Security Council commenced debate on the matter, with a Communist Chinese official participating. By this time, however, the Chinese counteroffensive in Korea had begun and the American position on Taiwan had, for all practical purposes, solidified for a generation. Even the "neutralization" of the island became insufficient because the United States turned to collaboration with the Nationalists in using Taiwan as a base for attacks on the mainland.

It remains uncertain whether or not the unification of Korea under United Nations auspices in late 1950 would have resulted in a flexible American policy regarding Taiwan. Opposition to empowering a United Nations commission to make recommendations on the island's fate—or to follow any proposals contrary to perceived American interests—went deeper in many circles than immediate anxieties about the situation in Korea. The Joint Chiefs now pressed for a long-term policy of keeping Taiwan out of enemy hands. Rusk and Dulles, like many people in Congress and the public, had been sympathetic to such a course even before the outbreak of war in Korea. To be sure, the president's and the secretary of state's distaste for Chiang and their sensitivity to the political drawbacks at the international level of continuing support for the Nationalists were more keen than most other nonspecialists on China. Yet, since January, their hostility toward Peking had mounted, and after the congressional elections of November the Truman administration was in a more precarious position at home than at any time since 1948. Still, the GOP remained the minority party in both houses, and total victory in Korea offered the prospect of rejuvenating the presidency of a man who had recovered from setbacks in the past.

## The Final Plunge

Certainly, in those tense November days in Washington, the men charged with determining American policy could not detach themselves from the domestic climate. Yet fear of a public debate with MacArthur was merely one of several considerations that influenced the decision makers. It carried weight because of the uncertainty in all circles regarding

Chinese capabilities and intentions—and because in these circumstances such factors as concern for American credibility, military tradition, and personalities came into play.

In the two weeks after the National Security Council met on 9 November, the State Department moved on several fronts with regard to Korea. First, Acheson sought to establish contact with Peking with the aim of probing Chinese Communist intentions and possibly negotiating on Korea. Initially, he made overtures through Sweden, which had relations with the Mao regime.[110] That approach led nowhere, but on 16 November the State Department received a report from New Delhi that the Communist Chinese delegation assigned to discuss the Taiwan issue before the Security Council had been granted extensive authority to talk about Korea, both inside and outside the United Nations. Panikkar was the source, however, and he was not even fully trusted by the Indians. Moreover, the Indian ambassador in Peking stated that the delegation was scheduled to arrive in New York on 19 November; it did not actually do so until five days later, the same day MacArthur launched his "end-the-war offensive."[111]

On 20 November, nevertheless, a Polish delegate to the United Nations leaked alleged Chinese peace proposals to the press. They included a withdrawal of Chinese troops from Korea in return for the creation of a North Korean-controlled buffer zone below the Yalu, and withdrawal of American recognition of and aid to Nationalist China.[112] These terms, however, were far from acceptable to the United States and sparked no new diplomatic moves in Washington.

The second front for American maneuver was the public arena. There, Washington sought to reassure Peking that the United States had no aggressive designs on China. On 15 November, Acheson and Rusk spoke to this effect before a National Conference on Foreign Policy, held at the State Department.[113] At a press conference on the following day, President Truman stated that the United States "never at any time entertained any intention to carry hostilities into China."[114]

In truth, the United States was actively considering sending its planes into Manchuria in pursuit of their Chinese counterparts, which were attacking United Nations forces in North Korea. Only the strong objections of America's European allies prevented Washington from going ahead with this action.[115]

This fact reveals the framework for American moves on the third front, the United Nations. The State Department regarded unity in the non-Communist camp as crucial. The mustering of allied support for the American position would strengthen the United States politically—and perhaps militarily—in the event the conflict broadened. Hopefully, it also would discourage the Chinese from large-scale involvement in Korea. On 10 November, the United States and five other nations presented a resolution to the Security Council calling on China "to refrain from assisting or encouraging the North Korean authorities" and to withdraw its troops from the penin-sula. At the same time, the United States requested that the United Nations commission on Korea "assist in the settlement of any problems" of concern to China and the Soviet Union in areas along the Korean border.[116]

The United States backed away from an initial inclination to bring the resolution to an early vote—which surely would have sparked a Soviet veto. From 13 November onward, the State Department became increasingly pre-occupied with the idea of establishing a buffer zone along the Yalu River. This preoccupation grew out of pressures from Great Britain and France as well as a continuing concern about Chinese intentions and capabilities.[117] After 7 November, Chinese troops had broken off contact with United Na-tions forces, but American diplomats remained deeply concerned. Peking did not appear anxious to negotiate, and reports from the mainland through Brussels and the Hague provided little reassurance that the Chinese would melt away in the face of a United Nations offensive.[118] In the meantime, American units in North Korea remained precariously split, the Eighth Army in the west more than fifty miles north of Pyongyang and the X Corps widely dispersed far to the east. General Willoughby of Far Eastern intel-ligence expressed particular concern about a Chinese buildup on the north-ern and western rims of X Corps positions.[119]

On 17 November, John Paton Davies of the Policy Planning Staff finally proposed a halt to United Nations offensive operations. "The bulk of the evi-dence," he argued, pointed "to the probability that the Kremlin and Peiping are committed at least to holding the northern fringe of Korea—and, that, against our present force they have the military capability of doing so." In such circumstances, the United States was unlikely "to outdo the enemy short of pressing phase by phase to the ultimate action: initiating atomic warfare." The most attractive option, he concluded, was to declare the termi-nation of major military operations and seek the establishment of a demili-tarized zone south of the Yalu. This course would force Peking and Moscow "to bear the onus for initiating clearly aggressive action" and, therefore, would "probably give them pause."[120]

How widespread such thinking was in the State Department remains un-certain. If officials other than Davies expounded similar views, documents that prove it have yet to surface. On the other hand, General Bolté in the Pentagon had information that "certain elements" in the diplomatic agency were pressing for a halt to offensive operations by United Nations forces. A good chance existed, he thought, that the view would be put forth at an up-coming State-Defense meeting.[121]

The meeting took place on 21 November, but no one from the State De-partment made such a proposal. Discussion centered on possible methods of reassuring the Chinese of America's limited aims, while at the same time giving MacArthur freedom of action within North Korea. The proceedings were a pathetic display of powerful men desperately seeking to avert disaster without provoking the wrath of a subordinate six thousand miles away.[122] The best they could come up with was a plan for United Nations forces to move back from the Yalu after enemy resistance ceased, with South Korean troops holding the high land dominating the approaches to the river and other units falling back in reserve. On 24 November, the Joint Chiefs relayed this proposal to MacArthur as a mere suggestion.[123] Predictably, the Far Eastern commander demurred.[124] He had won the battle in Washington hands down, though, now, on the battlefield, he would not be so lucky.

Communications between the State and Defense departments were exceedingly good at this time, and it is reasonable to assume that Acheson at least sensed the Pentagon's views on Korea. Certainly, military leaders had strong doubts about Chinese power and designs, but MacArthur's expressions of confidence from 9 November onward deterred them from halting the United Nations advance.[125] Bolté, who was the last major military figure from Washington to visit Japan and Korea, had been impressed by MacArthur's confidence and determination. In a private meeting in Tokyo between the two men, the Far Eastern commander had exclaimed, "Bolté, we've got 'em!"[126] Upon his return to Washington, Bolté took the lead in opposing any meddling with MacArthur's directives. United Nations forces, he believed, could under "circumstances now prevailing" hold any position in North Korea. The chances for localizing the conflict would improve if Communist forces were driven from the peninsula. A show of strength by the United Nations would deter further aggression; weakness would have the opposite effect. "History," he concluded, "has proved that negotiating with Communists is as fruitless as it is repulsive." He urged the Joint Chiefs to oppose any suggestion by the secretary of state to alter MacArthur's orders.[127]

With a Johnson-led defense establishment, Acheson might have chosen confrontation. With a Marshall-led defense establishment, he preferred conciliation. Surely the secretary of state harbored many of the same feelings toward the Chinese as did Bolté, but, without the ingredients of a willful field commander, prestigious leadership in the Pentagon, and a volatile political climate nationwide, Acheson's choices in November 1950 might well have been different. Had they been so, the president probably would have taken his advice and Marshall would have conceded gracefully. Yet, in the prevailing circumstances of doubt and fear, a strong, often arrogant, man chose to follow rather than to lead, and he would regret it for the rest of his life.

# Conclusion

It is impossible to determine with any assurance if, by mid-November 1950, a Sino-American confrontation could have been averted. Since 1946, Chinese Communist hostility toward the United States had grown steadily. Revolutionary ideology contributed to this trend, but, at several points in the half of a decade after World War II, Mao and his cohorts demonstrated more flexibility in their attitude toward the United States than American decision makers showed toward them. Washington's persistent support of the National government would have provoked antagonism among Chiang's opponents no matter what their world view. With United Nations forces positioned vulnerably in North Korea in the fall of 1950, it is entirely possible that Peking would have launched a major offensive even had Truman halted MacArthur's advance.

Yet much can be said for the argument that, short of the American march toward the Yalu that commenced on 24 November, the Chinese would have avoided a major clash with the United States. As Davies pointed out, responding defensively to an approach of unfriendly forces to one's borders was quite a different enterprise politically than frontally attacking stationary units many miles from the international boundary. Furthermore, Mao's hold at home was not totally secure. Hostilities with the United States in Korea were likely to spark American-supported attacks on the mainland from Taiwan. Certainly, a confrontation on the peninsula would retard internal economic reconstruction and growth. American leaders, therefore, had much reason for believing that Mao was not anxious to engage the United States in Korea. At the very least, it can be said that had United Nations forces halted after the initial contacts with Chinese troops, the United States would have been in a far stronger position, both militarily and politically, to counter Peking's moves. Ironically, Washington chose a course that offered minimal prospects for "negotiations from strength."

Events in the fall of 1950 abound with ironies. General Marshall, a leading architect of America's Europe-first and Pacific island-hopping strategy during World War II and the pivotal figure in 1947 in preventing the United States from making an irreversible commitment in China, returned to the government just in time to play a major part in a policy that resulted in Sino-American confrontation. The military man, who as secretary of state had stymied the Joint Chiefs on the China issue, did not do so as secretary of defense, when his institutional authority over them was more direct than before.

Whereas the failure of the Truman administration to protect adequately its commitment to South Korea played a central part in the commencement

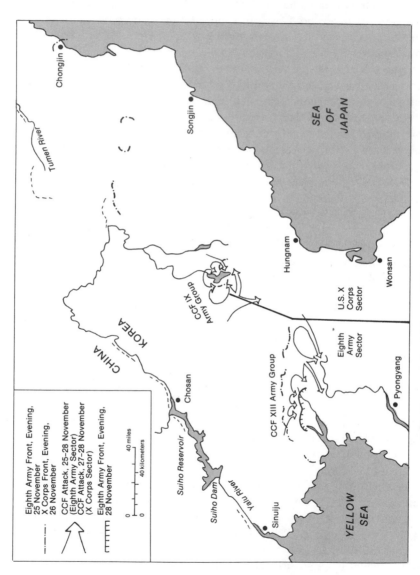

MAP 5. The Communist Chinese Offensive, 25–28 November 1950

of hostilities in June 1950, the overexertion of American power on the peninsula five months later led to an expansion of the conflict. General MacArthur, who during 1948 and 1949 had influenced materially the decision to withdraw American soldiers from South Korea, later took a critical hand both in sending American troops back and in setting them on a course that would greatly increase the need for their presence there indefinitely.

Despite Dean Acheson's improved relationship with the Pentagon after Louis Johnson's dismissal, his effectiveness in dealing with the Korean War may actually have decreased. After speaking eloquently in January 1950 against a course that would draw Peking's attention away from its natural divergence of interest with Moscow, ten months later Acheson permitted a campaign in North Korea that, temporarily at least, did just that.

Between mid-1947 and September 1950, the containment strategy dominated American foreign policy. When the concept was not applied, it was because the Truman administration decided that limited American capabilities made inadvisable an all-out protection of unessential American interests. In September 1950, however, the United States adopted a policy of liberation in Korea and soon paid dearly for this exception to its generally defensive conduct. In the face of a massive Chinese counteroffensive, American leaders rapidly adjusted their goals. To Acheson, containment—that is, a settlement along the thirty-eighth parallel—now carried "moral force." The problem had become how to achieve even that outcome. The United States was back in the position it had faced in July and August, only a new, more formidable enemy had entered the field, and America's friends tended "to criticize us rather than the Chinese Communists." If the war expanded into China and eventually erupted into general hostilities with Russia, the secretary of state feared that "soon . . . we would fight without allies on our side."[1] Yet to withdraw from Korea or to make concessions regarding Taiwan and China's seat in the United Nations would convey weakness and undermine American leadership in Western Europe and Japan. Although the worst fears in Washington did not come to bear, America's experiment with liberation had momentous costs—in American lives and treasure, in American politics, and in American foreign policy.

Perhaps the supreme irony is that the Chinese Communist intervention in Korea served in the long run to undermine the Sino-Soviet alliance.[2] China's assumption of burdens on the peninsula that Russia was unwilling to risk bolstered Peking's prestige worldwide and ultimately encouraged Mao to reject Moscow's leadership of international Communism.

On the other hand, the Sino-American clash hardened Washington's attitudes toward the Mao regime and prevented an early exploitation of the rift between Peking and Moscow. In part, the miscalculation of China's intentions in September and early October 1950 was rooted in the belief that Sino-Soviet interests diverged in Northeast Asia, that Chinese intervention in Korea would serve Russian but not Chinese interests. When China did enter the fighting, therefore, American leaders naturally assumed that Peking viewed its interests and those of Moscow as one. China's rulers, according to Acheson, were "better pupils [of the Kremlin] even than the Eastern European satellites."[3] In the climate engendered by the bitter fighting in Korea, few officials were to challenge that conclusion for more than a decade.

Yet an explanation of the Sino-American confrontation must center not on ironies but on persistent trends in American thought, interacting with international events. Although perceptions of Communist China hardened noticeably after November 1950, throughout the period of this study American leaders viewed Communism in China as disadvantageous to the United States. In 1947, Marshall had struggled gallantly against expanded involvement in China largely because he doubted America's ability to influence the outcome of the civil war there.[4] Distaste for the Chinese Communists, which increased steadily from the spring of 1950 onward in the face of their harsh treatment of U.S. diplomats, the growing Communist threat in Indochina, the conclusion of a Sino-Soviet alliance, and the bombastic rhetoric emanating from Peking had much to do after June 1950 with the disinclination of MacArthur, the Joint Chiefs, and the State Department to negotiate on the Korean issue. Despite its consistent recognition of the possibility of a Sino-Soviet split, the Truman administration never acted positively to exploit a conflict of interest between the two powers. In the months prior to the outbreak of war in Korea, in fact, American policy in Asia increasingly emphasized the containment of Communist influence rather than the redirecting of Mao's attention to Soviet penetration in the north.

Throughout the 1947–50 period, an underestimation of Communist strength influenced American policy. Initially, it encouraged the State Department to oppose a broadened commitment to Chiang Kai-shek. In late 1948 and 1949, it discouraged the United States from approaching Mao for fear that such a move would make more manageable his task of uniting and ruling China. In the fall of 1950, perceptions of Mao's weakness at home fostered beliefs in Washington that China would avoid deep involvement in Korea.

Ethnocentrism produced this misperception. American officials, including the China experts, regarded the Middle Kingdom as a backward nation—politically, economically, militarily—to which the United States had frequently lent a helping hand in the past and which would continue to need American assistance in the future. When the Communists showed a lack of appreciation for past efforts by the United States on behalf of China or questioned its motives, diplomats sought explanations in the realm of ideology rather than in external stimuli like American behavior. Introspection was notably absent from American thought. When Communist China counterattacked in Korea, therefore, Acheson, rather than viewing the action as a response to a threatening U.S. move toward the Manchurian border, labeled it aggression against the United Nations. To British Foreign Minister Clement Atlee, he declared, "For fifty years we have tried to be friends with the Chinese. They have now attacked us with their armies and have denounced us violently. They have done great harm to the work of fifty years."[5]

Even so, such haughtiness was combined with genuine fear. Especially prominent in American thinking between 1947 and 1950 was a belief that the United States must build credibility abroad. This view discouraged the Truman administration from expanding American commitments to Nationalist China, but it also helped prevent a total abandonment of the Chiang regime and led to enlarged obligations in Korea at a time when American military strength was in decline. In June 1950, a need to uphold an American commitment made intervention in Korea appear necessary. Three months later, as in September 1947, limited American military strength in the area did not prevent decision makers in Washington from taking on larger tasks on the peninsula. Under prevailing conditions in Korea, American leaders favored a military campaign in the north as a deterrent to future "aggression." Then, in November, they refused to halt the campaign in the face of Chinese intervention, in part because they feared the consequences of any show of weakness. In a word, the strongest nation in the world evinced a keen sensitivity to others' perceptions of its power. To American policy elites, the central issue was not one of potential but of actual power. In the late 1930s, the United States had possessed the potential to influence events in Europe and Asia, but it had lacked the will. To avoid another world conflict, it was now imperative that America demonstrate—both to itself and to others—its will to shape events abroad.

The sense of insecurity grew substantially as a result of events from August 1949 onward. First, the Soviet Union exploded an atomic device well ahead of schedule, then the Communists rapidly consolidated their power in China. In early 1950, they joined the Soviets in a military alliance and in recognizing the Ho Chi Minh regime in Vietnam. The spring brought reports of the stationing of Soviet planes in China. The United States had done much over the past three years to contain Communism, but it seemed not to have been enough. American leaders anticipated that the next four years would be ones of increasing peril, as the Soviet Union expanded its atomic arsenal as well as its long-range bomber force and the revolutionary tide in the underdeveloped world gained momentum. The North Korean attack in June, therefore, took place during a period of heightening urgency in Washington. Although that fact was not crucial in the initial American intervention on the peninsula, it was a key to American moves elsewhere and in the march north of the thirty-eighth parallel in the fall.[6]

Yet misjudgments about Communist Chinese capabilities and concern for American credibility alone did not always shape United States policy. Domestic politics sometimes provided a nagging constraint on decision makers. In 1947, it contributed to a major shift among military officials regarding America's presence in Korea. Congressional cuts in defense spending and later slashes in income taxes contributed to the decision to withdraw American troops from the peninsula. This move, in turn, encouraged North Korean adventurism. In 1948, concern for the well-being in Congress of the European Recovery Program led the Truman administration to send to Capitol Hill a sizable proposal of aid for Nationalist China. In early 1949, pressure from the legislative branch at a time when the White House sought approval for the North Atlantic Treaty and military aid for Western Europe discouraged the president from abandoning Chiang. In the summer and fall of 1950, public opinion and Republican attacks on alleged Democratic timidity in Asia encouraged those in power to follow an overly aggressive course in Korea. They perceived a need for a concrete victory abroad to reduce both partisan recriminations and general talk of preventive war against the Soviet Union, and the unification of Korea appeared to meet that need perfectly.[7]

Personalities and institutions also played a role at critical moments. The Joint Chiefs and the State Department had serious disagreements over both China and Korea policy throughout the period. Between September 1947 and June 1950, such differences compromised efforts by the diplomats to protect American commitments to South Korea. During the same period, pressures on China from military leaders compounded the State Department's problems in limiting American involvement in the civil war. During the fall of 1950, despite the close working relationship between the State and Defense departments, the memory of old defeats regarding China policy probably added to the determination of military leaders to support MacArthur. In late 1950, as in 1947, the Joint Chiefs were wrong about China; now they demanded the opportunity to prove it.

Marshall, who in 1947 had denied them this opportunity, now supported their position. By 1950, he was a tired and ill man, who could not even put in a full workday. He had been brought back into the Truman administration to make peace between the State and Defense departments, and between the military and civilian elements in the latter agency. Officials from the president on down continued to look to him for leadership, but, perhaps in part because he feared that an early end to the war would halt American rearmament as much as he feared a conflict with China, he upheld MacArthur.[8]

The Far Eastern commander's prestige, of course, peaked after Inchon. So did his self-assurance. The man who only five months before had declared that anyone who challenged Communist power on the Asian mainland "ought to have his head examined" now advocated just such a course. As his capacity to influence American policy grew, therefore, so too did his misunderstanding of events. In Korea, he seriously miscalculated Chinese strength and intentions; in Washington, he misread the ultimate reaction to a Chinese counteroffensive on the peninsula.

On the latter point, however, it is essential to go back in time several months—or even years. From the very beginning of the Korean War, Washington had been tolerant of MacArthur's independence. At most, he had been given a slap on the wrist—and then only in the case of the VFW letter regarding Taiwan. Even before June 1950, the Truman administration had been lax in pressing its will upon him. He had ruled Japan virtually as an independent monarch. In 1949 and early 1950, the State Department had failed to insist that he take a more active role in Korea. At the same time, Washington had failed to reprimand him for his lobbying among visiting dignitaries from Congress for a more assertive China policy. Thus, by the fall of 1950, he had considerable experience in charting his own course. He had much reason to believe that a firm hand with his superiors back home would produce the desired results.

To a substantial degree MacArthur was correct, in part because Washington shared his views, albeit in less extreme form. In varying degrees, State and Defense department officials had always underestimated Communist Chinese capabilities. Washington had constantly feared that any show of hesitation in the international arena would embolden America's enemies. When, on 9 November, in a communique to the Joint Chiefs, MacArthur invoked the "Munich analogy," he was hardly breaking new ground. His presence in Tokyo simply magnified such factors in the Truman administration's deliberations. The Far Eastern commander played a pivotal role not because he was the "village idiot," but because he was not. Individuals can influence history, to be sure, but only in the degree to which they represent the best or the worst in those around them.

Perhaps the most tragic aspect of the road to confrontation with China in late 1950 is that, had any one of several factors been absent on the American side, it probably would have been averted. Had the field commander been less willful and less intimidating to his superiors than MacArthur, had Truman and his colleagues—especially Acheson—been less beleaguered on the political front at home, had Johnson been at the helm of the Defense Department instead of Marshall, had American intelligence known before 24 November that some 200,000 Chinese troops were in Korea—had any of these pieces of the puzzle been altered, the history of the Korean War might look very different.

Yet the biggest piece of all was the mixture of arrogance and insecurity about the world that existed in the minds of U.S. leaders. They were arrogant at times in overestimating their nation's ability to shape events in Korea; they were insecure in exaggerating America's need to hold firm in certain situations both there and in China. A strong sense of self-righteousness magnified these aspects of their thought. Thus, they often lacked sensitivity to the legitimate interests of others and failed to assess America's needs realistically in relation to its capabilities. Rarely does a nation have the capacity and the will combined to achieve all that it would like in the international arena. Powerful as it was, the United States in 1950 was no exception. The essential point missed by American decision makers was that America was not—nor did it need to be—a major military power on the continent of Asia. Regrettably, the Sino-American conflict in Korea was not only rooted in ignorance of this fact, but it also taught certain lessons that encouraged Washington to ignore it in the future.

# Notes

## Abbreviations Used in Notes

CR     U.S. Congress, *Congressional Record*.

CWP    U.S. Department of State, *United States Relations with China with Special Reference to the Period 1944–1949*, 1949.

DA     Dean Acheson Papers, Harry S. Truman Library, Independence, Mo.

DSB    U.S. Department of State, *Department of State Bulletin*.

DSOD   U.S. Department of State, Office of Public Opinion Studies, "Daily Summaries of Opinion Development," Record Group 59, National Archives, Washington, D.C.

FEC    Far Eastern Command.

FR     U.S. Department of State, *Foreign Relations of the United States*, 1955–77.

GE     George Elsey Papers, Harry S. Truman Library, Independence, Mo.

HAS    H. Alexander Smith Papers, Princeton University Libraries, Princeton, N.J.

HST    Harry S. Truman Papers, Harry S. Truman Library, Independence, Mo.

IS     Far Eastern Command, *Intelligence Summaries*, Record Group 260, Federal Records Center, Suitland, Md.

JFD    John Foster Dulles Papers, Princeton University Libraries, Princeton, N.J.

MSFE   U.S. Congress, Senate, Armed Services and Foreign Relations Committees, *Military Situation in the Far East*, 82d Cong., 1st sess., 1951.

NSC    National Security Council.

NYT    *New York Times*.

PS     "Princeton Seminars," available in Xerox form in the Dean G. Acheson Papers, Harry S. Truman Library, Independence, Mo.

RG     Record Group (National Archives and Federal Records Center).

TS     Top Secret (now declassified).

USVR   U.S. Congress, House, Armed Services Committee, *United States–Vietnam Relations, 1945–1967*, vol. 8, 1971.

## Introduction

1. *MSFE*, p. 3295.

2. *PS*, 13 February 1954.

3. On the Communist issue in American politics, see Alan D. Harper, *The Politics of Loyalty*, and Robert Griffith, *The Politics of Fear*.

4. Cabell Phillips, *The Truman Presidency*, pp. 402–24; Alonzo L. Hamby, *Beyond the New Deal*, pp. 460–66.

5. *CWP*, p. xvi.

6. Gaddis Smith, *Dean Acheson*, pp. 125–26.

7. U.S. Department of State, *American Foreign Policy, 1950–1955*, pp. 2311–17.

8. *DSB*, 23 (18 September 1950):463.

9. John Lewis Gaddis, "Was the Truman Doctrine a Real Turning Point?" p. 397.

10. *MSFE*, p. 659. See also Acheson's presentation to the National Security Council of 28 November 1950, in Harry S. Truman, *Memoirs*, 2:341.

11. *MSFE*, p. 703.

12. *USVR*, 8:488.

13. The list includes the crisis over Iran in 1946, the British withdrawal from

Greece and the proclamation of the Truman Doctrine in 1947, the Communist victory in China and the Soviet explosion of an atomic device in 1949, and the formulation of NSC 68 and the outbreak of war in Korea in 1950.

14. The "neutralization" of Taiwan on 27 June 1950 was initially intended to last only for the duration of the fighting in Korea.

15. David Halberstam, *The Best and the Brightest*, p. 298.

16. See President Johnson's speech at the Johns Hopkins University in April 1965. *DSB*, 52 (26 April 1965): 606–10.

17. Frank M. Robinson and Earl Kemp, eds., *Report of the U.S. Senate Hearings— The Truth about Vietnam*, pp. 25, 35.

18. Tang Tsou, *America's Failure in China*; Soon Sung Cho, *Korea in World Politics*.

19. Jonathan Schell, *Time of Illusion*, pp. 337–87.

20. Smith, *Acheson*, p. 423.


## Chapter 1

1. John Leighton Stuart, *Fifty Years in China*, p. 177.

2. *CWP*, p. 311.

3. Ibid., pp. 116–17.

4. See George F. Kennan's observations on this point in U.S. Congress, Senate, Foreign Relations Committee, *State Department Employee Loyalty Investigation*, pp. 2120–21. See also Vladimir Dedijer, *Tito*, p. 322, and Milovan Djilas, *Conversations with Stalin*, p. 182. Chinese Communist behavior became somewhat bolder in the fall of 1945 as a result of gains made, with some illicit Soviet help, in Manchuria. This trend changed in late November, however, when the Soviets turned again toward a pro-Nationalist position. See James Byron Reardon-Anderson, "The Foreign Policy of Self-Reliance," chapter 8.

5. The presence of Soviet forces in Manchuria not only made Chiang more dependent on American aid, but it perhaps made him less inclined to pursue an all-out military effort against the Communists.

6. Paul A. Varg, *The Closing of the Door*, p. 218.

7. Michael Schaller, *The U.S. Crusade in China*, p. 97. This volume is certain to become a standard work on Sino-American relations during World War II.

8. U.S. Congress, Senate, Committee on the Judiciary, *Morgenthau Diary, China*, 2:1486–88, 1678–83.

9. Varg, *Closing of the Door*, pp. 187–88.

10. For an analysis of the political implications of the negotiations by Mao Tse-tung, see his *Selected Works of Mao Tse-tung*, 4:47–51.

11. On the Marshall mission, see Varg, *Closing of the Door*, chapters 10–12.

12. Schaller, *U.S. Crusade in China*, p. 182; Warren Cohen, "The Development of Chinese Communist Attitudes toward the United States."

13. John S. Service, *The Amerasia Papers*, pp. 681–85.

14. See Schaller, *U.S. Crusade in China*, chapter 9.

15. On Hurley, see Russell Buhite, *Patrick J. Hurley and American Foreign Policy*.

16. Schaller, *U.S. Crusade in China*, pp. 204–6.

17. *CWP*, pp. 312–13. For letters of protest from Chinese Communist military commanders to American officials in Manchuria and North China, see Box 1, John F. Melby Papers.

18. See John F. Melby's report "Chungking Press Reaction over Ambassador Hurley's Resignation," Box 1, Melby Papers. See also Reardon-Anderson, "The Foreign Policy of Self-Reliance," pp. 319–24.

19. On the relationship between Marshall and Stilwell, see Barbara W. Tuchman's *Stilwell and the American Experience in China*.

20. *CWP*, pp. 312, 969–70; "United States Military Aid to Foreign Governments in Post-War Period as Authorized by Congress," 13 October 1947, Box 40, Series 47.3, RG 51.

21. James E. Webb to George Y. Harvey, 21 October 1947, Box 40, Series 47.3, RG 51.

22. *CWP*, pp. 226, 180–81, 311–14.

23. Tang Tsou, *America's Failure in China*, pp. 327–31. See also Reardon-Anderson, "The Foreign Policy of Self-Reliance," pp. 268–69, 279–80, 345.

24. O. Edmund Clubb, *China and Russia*, p. 357. See also Reardon-Anderson, "The Foreign Policy of Self-Reliance," p. 353.

25. See W. Walton Butterworth's analysis of 31 October 1946, in *FR, 1946*, 10:455–57. At the time, Butterworth was the minister-counselor at the American embassy in Nanking.

26. Stuart to Byrnes, 2, 21 December 1946, ibid., 10:580–81, 651–52; Minutes of Meeting between General Marshall and Dr. Wei Taoming, 9 December 1946, ibid., 10:602–5.

27. Notes on Meeting Between General Marshall and Generalissimo Chiang Kai-shek, 1 December 1946, ibid., 10:577.

28. Tsou, *America's Failure in China*, p. 122.

29. Because he was the ambassador, Stuart had constant contact with American foreign service men who were less sentimental than their boss. Stuart's public and official expressions of opinion, therefore, were more moderate than Judd's. As a Republican politician in Washington, Judd had different associations and less reason to restrain himself in supporting the generalissimo. Still, Stuart's sentimentalism regarding China frequently influenced his judgment. John F. Melby, *The Mandate of Heaven*, pp. 80–89; Philip C. Sprouse, Oral History. On Judd, see Floyd Russel Goodno, "Walter H. Judd."

30. W. A. Swanberg, *Luce and His Empire*.

31. Joseph C. Keeley's *The China Lobby Man* is a sympathetic portrait of Kohlberg and his activities.

32. For Marshall's fear of this, see *FR, 1946*, 10:690.

33. E. J. Kahn, Jr., *The China Hands*, pp. 185–86.

34. For the backgrounds of the China experts, see ibid. and U.S. Department of State, *Biographic Register, 1950*. On Vincent, see Gary May, *China Scapegoat*.

35. *FR, 1946*, 10:680. Jim Peck's "America and the Chinese Revolution: An Interpretation" is an excellent historiographical essay dealing with the interaction of the United States and Chinese culture. See Ernest R. May and James C. Thomson, eds., *American–East Asian Relations*, pp. 319–55. For a perceptive analysis of the revulsion of American reporters and scholars in China toward Chiang's government, see Kenneth E. Shewmaker, *Americans and the Chinese Communists*, pp. 320–46. Although Shewmaker deals with people whose purposes and perspectives were different from American diplomats, much of his analysis could be applied to this latter group.

36. Chiang Kai-shek, *China's Destiny and Chinese Economic Theory*, pp. 157–82.

37. John King Fairbank, *The United States and China*, 2d ed., p. 192.

38. Ibid., pp. 221–22.

39. Marshall to President Truman, 28 December 1946, *FR, 1946*, 10:661–65; John Robinson Beal, *Marshall in China*.

40. Colonel Marshall S. Carter to Marshall, 23 November 1946, *FR, 1946*, 10:559.

41. See Akira Iriye, *Across the Pacific*, chapters 7 and 8, and Warren Cohen, *America's Response to China*, p. 148.

42. On the independence movements, see Robert A. Scalapino and Chong-sik Lee, *Communism in Korea*.

43. For a discussion of State Department perceptions of the provisional government in mid-1945, see William George Morris, "The Korean Trusteeship, 1941–1947," p. 36.

44. On the influence of past events on American thinking, see John Lewis Gaddis, *The United States and the Origins of the Cold War*, chapter 1.

45. Morris, "Korean Trusteeship," chapters 1–3.

46. Speech of 15 November 1942, quoted in Soon Sung Cho, *Korea in World Politics*, p. 17.

47. American Draft of the Communiqué, n.d., *FR: Conferences at Cairo and Tehran 1943*, pp. 399–404, 869; Robert E. Sherwood, *Roosevelt and Hopkins*, p. 777. Truman, *Memoirs*, 2:316.

48. Minutes of Roosevelt-Stalin Meeting, 8 February 1945, *FR: The Conferences at Malta and Yalta 1945*, p. 770.

49. Ibid., pp. 358–59; *FR, 1944*, 5:1226, 1240–41.

50. James I. Matray, "An End to Indifference" and "The Reluctant Crusade," pp. 94–102.

51. In addition to concessions in Manchuria, the Yalta agreement gave to Russia the southern half of Sakhalin and the adjacent islands.

52. Gaddis, *U.S. and the Origins of the Cold War*, p. 13.

53. This is a theme of William L. Neumann's *After Victory*.

54. For a detailed account of the State Department and the Korean issue during World War II, see Morris, "Korean Trusteeship," chapters 1–3.

55. Briefing Book Paper: Inter-Allied Consultation Regarding Korea, n.d., *FR: Diplomatic Papers, Conferences at Malta and Yalta 1945*, p. 361; Briefing Book Paper: Interim Administration for Korea and Possible Soviet Attitudes, June 29, 1945, *FR: The Conference of Berlin (The Potsdam Conference), 1945*, 1:313.

56. Matray, "The Reluctant Crusade," pp. 94–102 and Mark Paul, "Diplomacy Delayed."

57. Provision was made, however, for the eventual participation of Great Britain and China. Morris, "Korean Trusteeship," pp. 119–20.

58. *FR, 1945*, 6:1309.

59. Soon Sung Cho, *Korea in World Politics*, pp. 54–55.

60. The best sources on Korean communism are Dae-sook Suh, *The Korean Communist Movement*, and Scalapino and Lee, *Communism in Korea*.

61. Roy E. Appleman interview with author. Appleman was an American officer in the occupation.

62. In January 1946, a subordinate described him as follows: "His way was the direct way. He hated mystery, subterfuge and insinuation. The Russians tried his soul by their constant secretiveness and by refusing to talk things over with him. They became, 'Those suspicious Russian bastards!'" See A. Keep, "The Old Man," in USAFIK (U.S. Armed Forces in Korea), XXIV Corps, G-2, Historical Section, RG 332.

63. Morris, "Korean Trusteeship," p. 123; Gregory Henderson, *Korea*, p. 123. Neither man perceived, for instance, the fragmentation of the Korean Communist movement outlined so impressively in Suh, *Korean Communist Movement*, and Scalapino and Lee, *Communism in Korea*.

64. U.S. Department of State, *Biographic Register, 1948*, p. 121; Morris, "Korean Trusteeship," p. 119.

65. Cho, *Korea in World Politics*, pp. 69–70. Bruce Cumings's "American Policy in the Korean Liberation," in *Without Parallel*, ed. by Frank Baldwin, pp. 39–108, is a critical analysis of Hodge and the American occupation. Cumings, Suh in *Korean Communist Movement*, and Scalapino and Lee in *Communism in Korea* all agree that the People's Republic was not initially Communist-dominated.

66. For pleas from South Korea for an initiative from Washington, see *FR, 1945*, 6:1059–60, 1070–72.

67. William R. Langdon to Dean Acheson, 11 November 1945, ibid., pp. 1130–33.

68. Harry S. Truman, *Memoirs*, 2:319; Cho, *Korea in World Politics*, pp. 103–5; *FR, 1945*, 6:597–643.

69. The text of the agreement on Korea is in U.S. Department of State, *Moscow Meeting of Foreign Ministers*, pp. 14–16.

70. George F. Kennan, *Memoirs, 1925–1950*, pp. 287–88.

71. Hodge had been instructed by Washington not to try to explain or justify the trusteeship agreement. Morris, "Korean Trusteeship," p. 157.

72. Cho, *Korea in World Politics*, p. 108. Hodge complained that the State Department had failed to take his advice and keep him informed of Washington policy. Hodge to Joint Chiefs, 2 February 1946, RG 218.

73. FEC, "History of United States Army Forces in Korea," 2:88–92.

74. Ibid., pp. 116–17.

75. General Headquarters, XXIV Corps, "G-2 Summary," 6–16 September 1945, XXIV Corps, G-2, Historical Section, RG 332.

76. *FR, 1946*, 8:625–26.

77. Hodge to Byrnes, 8 May 1946, ibid., 8:665–66.

78. Proposed Message to General of the Army Douglas MacArthur Drafted in the Department of State, ibid., 8:645.

79. Langdon to Marshall, 8, 24 May 1946, ibid., 8:669–70, 686–89. FEC, "U.S. Army Forces in Korea," contains much information on American efforts to form a centrist coalition.

80. FEC, "U.S. Army Forces in Korea," 2:118–20.

81. Hodge to MacArthur, 8 October 1946, XXIV Corps, G-2, Historical Section, RG 332.

82. General Headquarters, XXIV Corps, "G-2 Summary, Period 1 December 1946 to 8 December 1946," XXIV Corps, G-2, Historical Section, RG 332.

83. FEC, "U.S. Army Forces in Korea," 3:30–32.

84. U.S. Department of the Army, Supreme Commander, Allied Powers, Japan, *Summation of U.S. Military Government Activities in Korea*, 13, 15, and 18 (October and December 1946 and March 1947).

85. Koon Woo Nam, *The North Korean Communist Leadership*, pp. 36–41.

86. Hodge to M. P. Goodfellow, 7 July 1946, Box 1, M. Preston Goodfellow Papers.

87. Central Intelligence Group, "The Situation in Korea," 3 January 1947, p. 10, RG 260.

88. For examples of State Department concern for America's image abroad, see *DSB*, 14 (6 January 1946):7–10, and (24 February 1946):294–97.

89. Robert Jervis, *Perception and Misperception in International Politics*, p. 284.

90. *FR, 1946*, 8:697.

91. Ibid., 8:708.

92. Ibid., 8:706.

93. Ibid., 8:713.

**Chapter 2**

1. *CWP*, p. 695.

2. Ibid., p. 219.

3. On Marshall and Stilwell, see Barbara Tuchman, *Stilwell and the American Experience in China*. On the evolution of Marshall's views between late 1945 and early 1947, see Gary May, *China Scapegoat*, chapter 5. On Marshall's first experience in China, see Forrest Pogue, *George C. Marshall*, 1:227–46.

4. George Elsey interview with the author. On 25 February, Truman wrote the following to Aubrey Williams, publisher of the *Southern Farmer*: "General Marshall is better acquainted with the situation [in China] than anybody in the U.S. . . . I believe his judgment is to be trusted on the best approach to working that delicate situation out." Box 173, President's Secretary's Files, *HST*.

5. In his memoirs, Truman describes Marshall as "one of the most astute and profound men I have ever known." Harry S. Truman, *Memoirs*, 2:112. For other adulatory comments by Marshall's colleagues, see the George Elsey, Frank Pace, and Philip Sprouse Oral Histories.

6. Charles E. Bohlen, *Witness to History*, p. 259.

7. Sprouse to Vincent, undated but clearly in early February 1947, *FR, 1947*, 7:786–89.

8. Vincent to Marshall, 7 February 1947, ibid., 7:791.

9. Stuart to Marshall, 6, 17 January 1947, ibid., 7:6–12, 18.

10. *CWP*, pp. 232–33, 710–19.

11. Stuart to Acheson, 28 March 1947, *FR, 1947*, 7:73–80.

12. Ringwalt to Vincent, 4 April 1947, ibid., 7:813–14.

13. Carter to Vincent, 15 April 1947, ibid., 7:819–20.

14. Forrestal to Acheson, 16 April 1947, ibid., 7:959.

15. *CWP*, p. 970.

16. Ringwalt to Vincent, 5 May 1947, *FR, 1947*, 7:831–33.

17. *CWP*, p. 356.

18. Ibid., pp. 944–45, 968. Marshall had approved the general provisions of this order on 20 February. It was not carried out until June largely because of problems between the War and Navy departments regarding the precise nature of the Naval Advisory Group (i.e., its relation to the Army Advisory Group). Marshall's failure to push for the order's implementation suggests that his support for it was more a result of pressures within the administration than a belief in the program's usefulness.

19. See, for instance, Joint Chiefs of Staff memorandum, 22 October 1945, *FR, 1945*, 7:590–98.

20. Norstad to Patterson, 7 February 1947, 091 China, RG 319.

21. Lyman P. Van Slyke, ed., *The Chinese Communist Movement*.

22. Norstad to Patterson, 7 February 1947, 091 China, RG 319.

23. Patterson to Marshall, 11 February 1947, 091 China, RG 319. For Alsop's efforts to promote his views, see Alsop to Patterson, 8 November 1947, Box 18, Patterson Papers; Alsop to George Kennan, 18 February 1948, Box 3, Alsop Papers; and Alsop to Albert C. Wedemeyer, 28 January 1947, Box 2, ibid. In the first letter cited above, Alsop apologized for losing his temper in a recent conversation between the two on China. Although Patterson agreed with Alsop on American policy toward China, the secretary of war was an avid admirer of Marshall. For Lucas's views, see Lucas to Stuart, 28 June 1947, *FR, 1947*, 7:860–63. Earlier in the year, Brigadier General Thomas Timberman had been sent by the army to China to put an end to the direct involvement of American "advisers" under Lucas in air missions against the Communists. Timberman interview with the author.

24. Forrestal to Marshall, 30 January 1947, *FR, 1947*, 7:943–44.

25. Walter Millis, ed., *The Forrestal Diaries*, p. 175.

26. Ibid.

27. Ibid., p. 177.

28. Minutes of Meeting of the Secretaries of State, War, and Navy, 12 February 1947, *FR, 1947*, 7:795–97.

29. See note 18 above.

30. Minutes of Conference concerning China, 20 February 1947, *FR, 1947*, 7:946–50.

31. Ibid.

32. Patterson to Marshall, 26 February 1947, *FR, 1947*, 7:799–803.

33. Forrestal to Marshall, 27 February 1947, ibid., 7:804.

34. Marshall to Vincent, 27 February 1947, ibid., 7:803–4.

35. For Marshall's replies to Patterson and Forrestal, see ibid., 7:805–9.

36. Marshall to Vincent, 27 February 1947, ibid., 7:803–4.

37. Vincent to Marshall, 3 February 1947, ibid., 7:1297.

38. Ibid., pp. 1082–83.

39. Vincent to Marshall, 4 March 1947, ibid., 7:1085.

40. Vincent to Marshall, 14 March 1947, ibid., 7:1088–89.

41. Vincent to Willard Thorp, 18 March 1947, ibid., 7:1092; Vincent to Marshall, 27 March 1947, ibid., 7:1093–94.

42. James Alan Fetzer, "Congress and China, 1941–1950," pp. 79–80, 100–101. On Judd, see Floyd Russel Goodno, "Walter H. Judd."

43. Justus D. Doenecke, *Not to the Swift*, p. 46.

44. William M. Leary, Jr., "Portrait of a Cold Warrior."

45. Chennault to Vandenberg, 17 January 1947, Vandenberg to Chennault, 28 January 1947, Box 2, Vandenberg Papers.

46. James Alan Fetzer, "Senator Vandenberg and the American Commitment to China." Vandenberg's speech in Cleveland of 11 January 1947, urging a reorientation of China policy, may have been seen by the administration as a warning of things to

come. On this speech and Vandenberg's concern about China, see Arthur S. Vandenberg, Jr., *The Private Papers of Senator Vandenberg*, p. 522.

47. Fetzer, "Congress and China," p. 103.

48. Vincent to Acheson, 3 February 1947, *FR, 1947,* 7:1296.

49. Vincent to Marshall, 28 February 1947, ibid., p. 1083.

50. Ross Y. Koen, *The China Lobby in American Politics*, pp. 163–64.

51. Bridges to Vandenberg, 7 April 1947, File 27, Folder 174, Bridges Papers; Bridges to Vandenberg, 24 March 1947, Vandenberg to Bridges, 25 March 1947, Box 2, Vandenberg Papers; May, *China Scapegoat*, pp. 160–67.

52. Fetzer, "Congress and China," p. 121.

53. U.S. Congress, House, Foreign Affairs Committee, *Assistance to Greece and Turkey*, pp. 16–18, 47–49.

54. Memorandum by the Joint Chiefs of Staff to the State-War-Navy Coordinating Committee, 9 June 1947, *FR, 1947,* 7:838–48; U.S. Joint Chiefs of Staff (Schnabel), *The History of the Joint Chiefs of Staff*, 1:437–38, 447.

55. This paper of 10 May 1947 did "not represent the final views of the Joint Chiefs" because revisions were "being considered." Ibid., 7:849n. Subsequent studies, however, left China below nations of the Near East and Western Europe on the list of priorities for arms.

56. Vincent to Marshall, 20 June 1947, ibid., 7:849.

57. In his *The Truman Administration and China, 1945–1949* (p. 35), Ernest R. May neglects the Vincent memorandum discussed above when arguing against the size factor as a major deterrent to large-scale American intervention.

58. Minutes of Meeting of the Secretaries of State, War, and Navy, 26 June 1947, *FR, 1947,* 7:850–51. See also Millis, *Forrestal Diaries*, pp. 285–88.

59. Marshall S. Carter to Marshall, 9 July 1947, 091 China, RG 319.

60. Fetzer, "Congress and China," pp. 125–26; Albert C. Wedemeyer, *Wedemeyer Reports*, p. 383.

61. Marshall to Lovett, 2 July 1947, *FR, 1947,* 7:635–36.

62. Wedemeyer to Marshall, 2 July 1947, ibid., 7:637; Admiral William Leahy, "Notes on China," 12 July 1947, William Leahy Papers. At the time, Leahy was military chief of staff in the White House.

63. Wedemeyer, *Wedemeyer Reports*, p. 62; General Charles L. Bolté interview with the author. Bolté was a longtime associate of both men.

64. Memorandum of Conversation, by the Secretary of State, 8 May 1947, *FR, 1947,* 7:1115; *CWP*, pp. 364–65; Millis, *Forrestal Diaries*, p. 285.

65. John F. Melby to "Maggie," 5 November 1947, Box 6, John F. Melby Papers.

66. Wedemeyer to Marshall, 29 July 1947, *FR, 1947,* 7:682–84.

67. Stuart to Marshall, 24 August 1947, ibid., 7:759–61; Melby to Butterworth, 25 August 1947, Box 1, Melby Papers.

68. Melby to Butterworth, 25 August 1947, Box 1, Melby Papers.

69. Stuart to Marshall, 4 October 1947, *FR, 1947,* 7:307–8.

70. Stuart to Marshall, 4 September 1947, ibid., 7:284–85.

71. John F. Melby, *The Mandate of Heaven*, pp. 80–89.

72. Memorandum Prepared in the Embassy in China for the Minister-Counselor of Embassy, 5 July 1947, *FR, 1947,* 7:222–28. See also Memorandum by the First Secretary of the Embassy in China, 31 July 1947, ibid., 7:693–95; and Memorandum by the Second Secretary of the Embassy in China, n.d., ibid., 7:678–82. The second secretary was Melby, whose approving description of Butterworth's earlier attitude is quoted above. It is fair to assume that the first memorandum cited above reflected the views of Butterworth.

73. Notes of Cooke for the Wedemeyer Mission, 25 July 1947, Central Security-Classified Records of the Offices of the Secretary of the Navy/Chief of Naval Operations.

74. Sprouse to Wedemeyer, 23 August 1947, *FR, 1947,* 7:741–59.

75. Wedemeyer to Randall Gould, 23 August 1947, Box 1, Randall Gould Papers.

76. The Wedemeyer report on China is printed in *CWP*, pp. 764–67.

77. Sprouse Oral History.

78. *CWP*, p. 767.
79. Ibid., p. 260.
80. Wedemeyer, *Wedemeyer Reports*, p. 383.
81. Rusk to Butterworth, 13 October 1947, *FR, 1947*, 7:320–24.
82. Ivan D. Yeaton, "Memoirs," pp. 129–30, Box 1, Ivan D. Yeaton Papers.
83. Norstad to Eisenhower, 16 November 1946, 092 (TS), RG 319.
84. Memorandum for the Record, 13 June 1946, 092 (TS), ibid.
85. Wedemeyer to Members of the Mission, 7 September 1947, *FR, 1947*, 7:769–70.
86. Sprouse Oral History.
87. *CWP*, pp. 262–64, 269.
88. Ibid., p. 270.
89. Ibid., pp. 810–13; Butterworth to Marshall, 15 October 1947, *FR, 1947*, 7:895–96; Lovett to Stuart, 24 October 1947, ibid., 7:901.
90. Minutes of the Meeting of the Committee of Two, 3 November 1947, ibid., 7:909.
91. U.S. Congress, Senate, Foreign Relations Committee, *Interim Aid for Europe*, pp. 2–10, 43.
92. *CWP*, p. 367.
93. Ibid., pp. 325–26.
94. Stuart to Marshall, 11 October 1947, *FR, 1947*, 7:892.
95. Butterworth to Marshall, 11 November 1947, ibid., 7:917–18.
96. *NYT*, 10 November 1947, p. 1.
97. On 14 October, Vandenberg wrote that he was unsympathetic to a European aid program unless aid also was granted to China. Vandenberg to C. Reid Webber, 14 October 1947, Box 3, Arthur H. Vandenberg Papers.
98. William C. Bullitt, "Report on China."
99. *DSOD*, 9, 10 October 1947.
100. Kennan to Marshall, 4 November 1947, Policy Planning Staff Files, RG 59.
101. *CR*, 93 (12 November 1947): 10704.
102. U.S. Congress, House, Appropriations Committee, *Third Supplemental Appropriations Bill for 1948*, pp. 227–28, 245–48.
103. For an account of Vandenberg's role, see Fetzer, "Senator Vandenberg and the American Commitment to China," pp. 291–92.
104. For testimony before the Senate Appropriations Committee, see U.S. Congress, Senate, Appropriations Committee, *Third Supplemental Appropriations Bill for 1948*. Allen's statement is quoted in W. A. Swanberg, *Luce and His Empire*, pp. 252–53. Another account of domestic political pressures on the Truman administration in late 1947 is in Koen, *The China Lobby*, pp. 88–91.
105. Vandenberg told this to State Department officials in late 1947. Butterworth interview with the author.
106. On the support of most in the China bloc for aid to Europe, see Fetzer, "Congress and China," pp. 87–92.
107. *NYT*, 27 November 1947, p. 26.
108. *Time* 50 (1 December 1947): 16.
109. See, for example, Warren Cohen, *America's Response to China*, pp. 195–96, and William Stueck, "Domestic Politics, Far Eastern Strategy, and the Early Months of the Korean War," pp. 11–12.
110. *PS*, 22 July 1953.
111. U.S. Department of State, Office of Public Opinion Studies, "Monthly Survey of American Opinion on International Affairs," October, November, and December 1947, RG 59.
112. Ibid., March 1947.
113. Later in this chapter, it is pointed out that polls of March and April 1948 indicated that a plurality of Americans favored military aid to Chiang. This pattern emerged, however, only after a concerted effort by the China bloc in Congress and the press as well as the Communist coup in Czechoslovakia. Had the Truman ad-

ministration made a concerted effort to reveal the risks of increased military assistance to the Nationalists, this trend probably could have been avoided.

114. For a contrary view, see May, *Truman Administration and China*, p. 35.

115. Richard Barnet, *Intervention and Revolution*, pp. 124–26.

116. See chapter 3 below.

117. *PS*, 22 July 1953.

118. Nimitz to the Secretary of the Joint Chiefs of Staff, 9 June 1947, Navy Plans Division Files.

119. Actually, because reforms of a scope envisioned by the State Department would have threatened Chiang's control of the National government, it seems doubtful that the generalissimo would have met American desires under any circumstances.

120. "Index Numbers of Wholesale Prices in Principal Cities," *China Economist*, 14 February 1949, in Box 98, Arthur N. Young Papers.

121. Ward to Marshall, 9 January 1948, *FR, 1948*, 7:26–27.

122. Clubb to Marshall, 11 February 1948, ibid., 7:90.

123. For more details on the development of the China aid program, see William Stueck, "American Policy Toward China and Korea, 1947–1950," pp. 153–57.

124. *NYT*, 8 February 1948, Section IV, p. 3; Vandenberg to William Knowland, 11 December 1948, Box 3, Vandenberg Papers.

125. Marshall to the President and the Cabinet, 5 March 1948, Box 154, President's Secretary's Files, *HST*.

126. *NYT*, 14 March 1948, Section IV, p. 1.

127. Ibid.

128. Fetzer, "Senator Vandenberg and the American Commitment to China," p. 293.

129. U.S. Congress, Senate, Foreign Relations Committee, *Foreign Relief Assistance Act of 1948*, pp. 422–23, 437, 443–44, 446–47.

130. For Vandenberg's tactics of gentle persuasion within his committee, see ibid., pp. 447, 453, 457, 468, 475. For the committee's report, see U.S. Congress, Senate, Foreign Relations Committee, *Senate Report 1026: Aid to China*.

131. For the conference committee bill, see U.S. Congress, *Conference Report 1655: Foreign Assistance Act of 1948*.

132. *DSOD*, 16 February 1948.

133. These articles are available in Box 4, Milton E. Miles Papers.

134. U.S. Congress, House of Representatives, Foreign Affairs Committee, *United States Foreign Policy for a Postwar Recovery Program*; *DSOD*, 11 March 1948.

135. U.S. Department of State, Office of Public Opinion Studies, "Fortnightly Survey of American Opinion on International Affairs," March, April, May 1948, RG 59.

136. U.S. Department of State, Office of Public Opinion Studies, "Monthly Survey of American Opinion on International Affairs," April 1948, RG 59.

137. Memorandum by Rear Admiral Sidney W. Souers, 26 March 1948, *FR, 1948*, 8:45–50.

138. On Budget Bureau concern with wastage in aid to China, see Bureau of the Budget Staff Recommendation, n.d., Series 47.1, Box 61, RG 51, and a Budget Bureau memorandum of 16 February 1948, initialed "HA" and addressed to K. L. Murphy, in Box 10, James E. Webb Papers.

139. Lovett to Marshall, 2 April 1948, *FR, 1948*, 8:51.

140. *CR*, 94 (2 April 1948):4060–61.

141. Marshall to Bridges, 1 July 1948, *FR, 1948*, 8:75.

142. Lovett to Stuart, 6 April 1948, ibid., 8:75–76; Marshall to Bridges, 1 July 1948, ibid., 8:105.

143. Ibid., 8:105–6; *CWP*, pp. 946–47.

144. Marshall to Bridges, 1 July 1948, *FR, 1948*, 8:106.

145. Ibid., 8:107.

146. Bridges to Marshall, 28 June 1948, ibid., 8:102–3.

147. Bridges and Taber to Truman, 1 July 1948, ibid., 8:107.

148. Memorandum of Conversation by Marshall, 11 June 1948, ibid., 8:90–99. The hearing must have been in executive session because no published record exists. For evidence that Wedemeyer pushed in Senate hearings for American supervision of Chiang's use of the grants, see Wedemeyer to Senator Hugh Butler, 14 June 1948, 091 China, RG 319.

149. Memorandum of Conversation by Lovett, 9 July 1948, *FR, 1948*, 8:109–11.

150. Truman to Marshall, 28 July 1948, ibid., 8:124–25. For negotiations on arms aid between the State Department and the Chinese embassy in Washington, see "Diary," 13 July 1948, Box 217, and "Notes of Conversation," 9 April, 23 June, 15 July, and 20 September 1948, Box 124, Wellington Koo Papers. Koo was the Chinese ambassador to the United States.

151. Sprouse to Butterworth, 16 July 1948, *FR, 1948*, 8:114.

152. Marshall to Royall, 9 August 1948, ibid., 8:135–36.

153. *NYT*, 23 June 1948, p. 6.

154. *NYT*, 26 June 1948, p. 1; 1 October 1948, pp. 1, 16–17; 16 October 1948, p. 7; 28 October 1948, p. 24.

155. Republican disunity on China comes through clearly in U.S. Congress, Senate, Foreign Relations Committee, *Foreign Relief Assistance Act of 1948.*

156. On 11 December 1948, Vandenberg, in explaining why the Republicans did not make more of the China issue in the presidential campaign, wrote that it "would only have precipitated and underscored a discussion of Chiang's weaknesses and would have nullified any remnant of his prestige." Vandenberg, *Private Papers of Senator Vandenberg*, p. 527.

157. H. G. Sparrow to Wedemeyer, n.d. (obviously in August 1948), and handwritten note by Wedemeyer to his staff, dated 16 August 1948, 091 China (TS), RG 319.

158. Wedemeyer to General Omar N. Bradley (army chief of staff), 9 October 1948, Wedemeyer to Forrestal, 9 October 1948, 091 China (TS), RG 319.

159. *NYT*, 30 October 1948, p. 5.

160. *NYT*, 1 November 1948, p. 2.

161. *DSOD*, 18 November 1948.

162. Ibid., 15 November 1948.

163. Ibid., 17 November 1948.

164. Ibid., 18 November 1948.

165. Memorandum for the Record by Lieutenant Colonel M. F. Gilchrist, Jr., 15 November 1948, 091 China (TS), RG 319.

166. Clubb to Marshall (with attachment), 11 June 1948, Box 7016, RG 59.

167. Commander, U.S. Naval Forces, Western Pacific, "Chronological Record of Events—NavWesPac 9 April 1948 to 28 August 1949," Naval Archives, Washington Navy Yard. See also Badger to Admiral Louis Denfield (chief of naval operations), 16 July 1948, Box 1, Oscar C. Badger Papers.

168. Lewis Clark to Butterworth, 27 August 1948, *FR, 1948*, 8:140.

169. Clark to Butterworth, 7 September 1948, ibid., 8:165–67.

170. Clark to Butterworth, 27 August 1948, ibid., 8:139. Because Tsingtao, in north China, was the location of the largest American naval facility in China, Badger also had an obvious interest in the area.

171. Clark to Butterworth, 7 September 1948, Badger to Denfield, 24 August 1948, ibid., 8:165, 169–70.

172. Joint Chiefs of Staff to Forrestal, 9 September 1948, ibid., 8:167–69.

173. Stueck, "American Policy Toward China and Korea," pp. 167–69.

174. By mid-November, some eight hundred tons of small arms and ammunition had arrived in China from MacArthur's Pacific command. Wedemeyer to Royall, 1 November 1948, 091 China (TS), RG 319; *CWP*, p. 953.

175. Lovett to Forrestal, 15 October 1948, Forrestal to Lovett, 3 November 1948, *FR, 1948*, 8:178–79, 189–91.

176. Stuart to Marshall, 17 May 1948, ibid., 7:237–38; Robert Allen Griffin to Senator William Knowland, 18 August 1948, Box 3, Vandenberg Papers. Griffin was the deputy director of the ECA mission in China.

177. H. Bradford Westerfield, *Foreign Policy and Party Politics*, p. 267.

178. In early 1948, Taft spoke out on the issue only in general terms, but was critical of administration policy. *NYT*, 13 February 1948, p. 3.

179. Although a member of the Foreign Relations Committee, Smith did not devote much attention to the China question until November 1948. See his diary for 1948 in *HAS*. Knowland's interest in China began only slightly earlier and was related to letters he received from his friend Allen Griffin. Griffin to Knowland, 18 August, 30 September 1948, Box 3, Vandenberg Papers.

180. Dean Acheson, *Present at the Creation*, p. 95.

181. *CWP*, p. 358.

182. *MSFE*, pp. 2762–63.

183. On the process of transferring surplus items to China, see Royall to Marshall, 24 February 1948, Wedemeyer to Eisenhower, 18 February 1948, and Ringwalt to Butterworth, 18 March 1948, *FR, 1948*, 8 : 18–22, 33–34. On Chinese stalling in placing orders, see Wedemeyer to Royall, 1 November 1948, 091 China (TS), RG 319.

184. *MSFE*, pp. 2762–63.

185. Tang Tsou, *America's Failure in China*, p. 483.

186. Badger to Stuart, 9 May 1948, Denfield to Badger, 1 November 1948, Wedemeyer to Barr, 25 October 1948, Badger to Denfield, 9 November 1948, Box 1, Badger Papers. See also Clark to Butterworth, 7 September 1948, Stuart to Marshall, 11 July 1948, Badger to Denfield, 3 May 1948, Acheson to Forrestal, 28 May 1948, Forrestal to Acheson, 17 June 1948, *FR, 1948*, 8 : 165–67, 266–67, 310–11, 316–17, 319–20.

187. Wedemeyer to Royall, 1 November 1948, 091 China (TS), RG 319.

188. Clubb to Stuart, 3 January 1948, *FR, 1948*, 7 : 5–8.

189. Stuart to Marshall, 9 February 1948, ibid., 7 : 86–87.

190. *NYT*, 1 February 1948, Section IV, p. 3; *DSOD*, 28 January, 4 February 1948.

191. For Bridges's attack on the administration, see *NYT*, 22 January 1948, p. 2.

192. Stuart to Marshall, 31 January 1948, *FR, 1948*, 8 : 9.

193. Stuart to Marshall, 14 May 1948, ibid., 7 : 231.

194. Stuart to Marshall, 29 April 1948, ibid., 7 : 212. For the report of a perceptive private observer, see Ernest Price to Wayne Morse, 11 July 1948, Ernest B. Price Papers. Price had been a foreign service officer in China from 1914 to 1929. In 1948, he was an executive of the Standard Vacuum Oil Company in Shanghai.

195. Stuart to Marshall, 14 July 1948, *FR, 1948*, 7 : 357–59.

196. Butterworth to John Cabot, 28 May 1948, Box 904, RG 59.

197. Marshall to Stuart, 16 July 1948, *FR, 1948*, 7 : 363.

198. Although Li purported to be anti-Communist, he recognized the need to work with the Communists in a coalition, at least temporarily. See James E. McKenna to Stuart, 21 May 1948, ibid., 7 : 248–51.

199. Stuart to Marshall, 6 November 1948, ibid., 8 : 645.

200. Lapham to Hoffman, 26 October 1948, ibid., 8 : 655.

201. Clubb to Marshall, 24 November 1948, Cleveland to Lapham, 2 December 1948, ibid., 8 : 152–53, 660.

202. Butterworth to Lovett, 8 November 1948, Cleveland to Lapham, 2 December 1948, ibid., 8 : 646–47, 659.

203. Stuart to Marshall, 4 December 1948, ibid., 8 : 662–63.

204. Memorandum by Butterworth, 30 December 1948, ibid., 8 : 667–68.

205. Harlan Cleveland to Lapham, 2 December 1948, ibid., 8 : 660–61.

206. Stuart to Marshall, 6 December 1948, Stuart to Marshall, 21 November 1948, ibid., 7 : 631–32, 593–94; Sprouse Oral History. For recent scholarly debate in this matter, see Nakajima Mineo, "The Sino-Soviet Confrontation in Historical Perspective," and Okabe Tatsumi, "The Cold War and China," in Yonosuke Nagai and Akira Iriye, eds., *The Origins of the Cold War in Asia*, and Michael H. Hunt, "Mao Tsetung and the Issue of Accommodation with the United States, 1948–1950," and Steven M. Goldstein, "Chinese Communist Policy toward the United States: Opportunities and Constraints, 1944–1950," in Dorothy Borg and Waldo Heinrichs, eds., *Uncertain Years*.

207. Stuart to Marshall, 26 October 1948, Clark to Butterworth, 8 November 1948, *FR, 1948*, 7:519–20, 553–55.

208. Chapter 4 below discusses the divisions that existed within Communist ranks regarding contacts with the United States and America's need for economic intercourse with China. Some Communists were, indeed, interested in American economic aid, but that is another thing altogether from suggesting that such assistance was crucial to Communist prospects or that, to obtain it, the Communists were willing to submit to American desires on major issues without a previous American move away from the Nationalists.

209. James Byron Reardon-Anderson, "The Foreign Policy of Self-Reliance," p. 419.

210. The Lapham proposal was not envisioned as a direct overture to the Communists but as a possible means of maintaining contact with groups of various sympathies, and of demonstrating that the United States could rise above the intense partisanship of the times in the interests of the Chinese people. This said, however, it remains true that, because the initiative was a first step away from total support for the nationalists, it might have served as an important signal to the Communists.

211. Stuart to Acheson, 5 February 1949, *FR, 1949*, 8:110.

212. Stuart to Marshall, 20 October 1948, *FR, 1948*, 7:520.

213. Memorandum by the Policy Planning Staff, 7 September 1948, ibid., 8:152–53.

214. John Paton Davies to Melby, 1 March 1948, Box 6, Melby Papers.

## Chapter 3

1. Minutes of meeting of Secretaries of State, War, and Navy, 29 January 1947, 337 SANACC, RG 319.

2. Hodge to M. Preston Goodfellow, 28 January 1947, M. Preston Goodfellow Papers.

3. Ibid.; XXIV Corps, G-2, Historical Section, "G-2 Summary, Period January 19 to January 26, 1947," RG 332.

4. Gregory Henderson, *Korea*, pp. 137, 419.

5. Walter Millis, ed., *The Forrestal Diaries*, p. 265.

6. Minutes of War Council Meetings, 17 October 1946, 15 January 1947, Box 23, Robert P. Patterson Papers; U.S. Congress, Senate, Appropriations Committee, *Military Establishment Appropriations Bill for 1948*, p. 3.

7. Patterson to Alexander P. deSeversky, 8 February 1947, Box 27, Patterson Papers.

8. Headquarters, United States Armed Forces in Korea, Office of the Assistant Chief of Staff, G-2, "Dr. Rhee's Lobby in America and Its Recent Activities," Box 7129, RG 59; Memorandum of Conversation, by John Z. Williams, 20 January 1947, Box 3827, ibid.

9. Eisenhower to MacArthur, 9 February 1947, 091 Korea (TS), RG 319.

10. Norstad to Patterson, 4 January 1947, ibid.

11. Chamberlin to Norstad, 11 February 1947, ibid.

12. See Patterson's diary of the trip in Box 27, Patterson Papers.

13. To compare the views of the civilian chiefs with those of the military, see the papers cited in notes 10 and 11 above and Howard C. Peterson to Patterson, 1 March 1947, 092, RG 319. On the general agreement regarding an immediate course of action, see Memorandum for the Record, by Brigadier General G. A. Lincoln, 4 March 1947, ibid.

14. Vincent to Marshall, 27 January 1947, *FR, 1947*, 6:601–3.

15. Ibid.

16. Edwin Martin to Arthur Bunce, 5 February 1947, Box C-213, RG 59.

17. J. Weldon Jones, James Penfield, and A. V. Arnold to Marshall, 25 February 1947, Box 7129, ibid.

18. The War Department representative on the committee was a soldier, Major General A. V. Arnold, not a civilian.

19. Draft Report of Special Interdepartmental Committee on Korea, 25 February 1947, *FR, 1947*, 6:613.

20. Vincent and Joseph C. Grew to the Secretary of State, 28 February 1947, ibid., 6:618–19. The Budget Bureau representative on the interdepartmental Committee was J. Weldon Jones, the assistant director in charge of the Fiscal Division.

21. Peterson to Patterson, 1 March 1947, 092, RG 319.

22. Dean Acheson, *Present at the Creation*, pp. 217–19.

23. Dean Acheson, *Sketches from Life of Men I have Known*, pp. 151–52.

24. Summary of Conclusions of Staff Meeting in the State Department, 8 April 1947, and Edwin M. Martin to Wood, 31 March 1947, Box C-213, RG 59; Vincent to Acheson, 8 April 1947, Vincent to Hilldring, 27 March 1947, and Hilldring to Vincent, 25 March 1947, Box 3827, ibid.

25. *FR, 1947*, 6:626–28.

26. See, for instance, *CR*, 93 (10 April 1947):3297.

27. *CR*, 93 (16 April 1947):3482.

28. *CR*, 93 (25 April 1947):3774.

29. War Council Meeting Minutes, 7 July 1947, Box 23, Patterson Papers.

30. *FR, 1947*, 6:690n.

31. *DSB*, 16 (20 April 1947):716.

32. U.S. Department of State, *Korea's Independence*, pp. 35–37.

33. For Hodge's letter, see ibid., pp. 28–32.

34. U.S. Department of the Army, Supreme Commander, Allied Powers, Japan, *Summation of U.S. Military Government Activities in Korea*, 21 (June 1947):16–26.

35. Jacobs to Marshall, 26 June 1947, *FR, 1947*, 6:679.

36. Jacobs to Marshall, 28 June 1947, ibid., 6:681.

37. Jacobs to Marshall, 20 June 1947, Box 3827, RG 59. Rhee constantly attempted to discredit Hodge's moves by suggesting they were contrary to American policy.

38. For the development of Rhee's views as 1947 progressed, see Oliver to Hilldring, 28 February 1947, Vincent to Hilldring, 27 January 1947, ibid.; and Hodge to Marshall, 7 July 1947, *FR, 1947*, 6:691–93. Such a solution to the Korean problem became more attractive to American policymakers as the chance for agreement with the Soviet Union grew more remote. Rhee was inclined to interpret publicly American policy in a manner that would enhance his own position. Unless his views were rebutted explicitly in private talks with American officials in Washington, he tended to take liberties with statements made during such conversations.

39. Major General Albert E. Brown, "Development of a Political Program," 20 February 1947, Box 3827, RG 59.

40. Jacobs to Marshall, 28 June 1947, *FR, 1947*, 6:680–82.

41. For precise figures, see Soon Sung Cho, *Korea in World Politics*, pp. 148–49. Detailed records of Joint Commission proceedings are available in XXIV Corps, G-2, Historical Section, RG 332.

42. Jacobs to Marshall, 25 July 1947, Hodge to Marshall, 12 August 1947, *FR, 1947*, 6:731–33, 751–52.

43. Jacobs to Marshall, 26 August 1947, ibid., 6:769–71.

44. Lovett to the American embassy in the Soviet Union, 26 August 1947, ibid., 6:771–74. The Lovett letter was dated according to Washington time. The date in Korea was 27 August.

45. Molotov to Marshall, 3 September 1947, ibid., 6:779–81.

46. For detailed studies of the United Nations and the Korean question, see Leon Gordenker, *The United Nations and the Peaceful Unification of Korea*, Leland Goodrich, *Korea*, and Cho, *Korea in World Politics*, pp. 161–83.

47. Hodge to Marshall, 3 July 1947, Jacobs to Marshall, 21 July 1947, *FR, 1947*, 6:686–87, 710–11.

48. MacArthur to Marshall, 2 July 1947, ibid., 6:683.

49. Jacobs to Marshall, 25 July 1947, ibid., 6:733.

50. Jacobs to Marshall, 21 July 1947, ibid., 6:710–11.

51. *CR*, 93 (25 July 1947):10234.

52. No consensus existed on the likelihood of an increased Soviet willingness to make concessions. Walton Butterworth regarded the chances as slight that the United Nations would succeed in unifying Korea. Dean Rusk, director of the Office of Special Political Affairs, was more optimistic, as was also Philip Jessup, an American representative to the United Nations. Butterworth, Rusk, and Jessup interviews with the author.

53. *FR, 1947*, 6:738.

54. Ibid., 6:817–18.

55. "Strategic Importance of Korea," Annex to Appendix B, 16 September 1947, 092, RG 319. The State Department plan referred to was that outlined in Lovett's letter to Molotov of 26 August.

56. Wedemeyer to Truman, 19 September 1947, Box 173, President's Secretary's Files, *HST*.

57. Butterworth to Lovett, 1 October 1947, *FR, 1947*, 6:820–21.

58. Smith to Marshall, 28 August 1947, ibid., 6:775–76.

59. Lovett to Austin, 18 September 1947, ibid., 6:794–96.

60. "Report to the President on China-Korea," Appendix E to Part III, September 1947, ibid., 6:798–803.

61. Niles Bond interview with the author. On Jacobs's background, see U.S. Department of State, *Biographic Register, 1948*, p. 268.

62. Jacobs to Marshall, 19 September 1947, *FR, 1947*, 6:803–7.

63. For estimates of North Korean armed strength, see Hodge to the Joint Chiefs, 30 August 1947, Box 130, RG 218; Central Intelligence Group, "Korea," 15 August 1947, Part III, p. 1, RG 260.

64. Jacobs to Marshall, 26 September 1947, *FR, 1947*, 6:816.

65. Goodrich, *Korea*, p. 41; Cho, *Korea in World Politics*, pp. 182–83.

66. Jacobs to Marshall, 19 September 1947, *FR, 1947*, 6:803–7; "Transcript of General Hodge Verbal Summary to General Wedemeyer on 27 August 1947," XXIV Corps, G-2, Historical Section, RG 332.

67. General Headquarters, XXIV Corps, "G-2 Summary, Period October 5 to October 12, 1948," RG 332.

68. Oliver to Hilldring, 24 July 1947, Box 3827, RG 59; Memorandum of conversation between Charles E. Saltzman, James K. Penfield, B. C. Limb, and Oliver, 23 September 1947, Box 3838, ibid.

69. State Department officials concluded at the end of September that "nothing should be done which make it impossible for the Soviets to agree with the U.S. on a solution to the Korean problem." See Butterworth to Lovett, 1 October 1947, *FR, 1947*, 6:820.

70. Austin to Lie, 17 October 1947, ibid., 6:832–35.

71. United Nations General Assembly, *Official Records*, Session 2, Comms. 1–2 (1947), p. 606.

72. Robert E. Riggs, *Politics in the United Nations*.

73. Dusan J. Djonovich, ed., *United Nations Resolutions*, Series 1, Vol. 1, pp. 207–9.

74. United Nations General Assembly, *Official Records*, Session 2, Comms. 1–2 (1947), pp. 281–82.

75. Ibid., pp. 260–61.

76. In October, the interim legislative assembly voted to send Rhee as a delegate to the United Nations. Jacobs to Marshall, 23 October 1947, Box C-214, RG 59.

77. After the Soviet proposal for simultaneous withdrawal on 26 September, Rhee abruptly reversed his earlier position favoring such action.

78. Jacobs to Marshall, 21 July 1947, *FR, 1947*, 6:71.

79. Dae-sook Suh, *The Korean Communist Movement*; Robert A. Scalapino and Chong-Sik Lee, *Communism in Korea*, 1; chapters 1–5.

80. Scalapino and Lee, *Communism in Korea*, 1:315; Robert R. Simmons, *The Strained Alliance*, chapter 2.

81. By early November, Rhee had reversed his view on the simultaneous withdrawal of foreign troops once again. Hodge to the Department of the Army, 3 November 1947, *FR, 1947*, 6:852. In withdrawing, the United States could have emphasized the desire of most Koreans for an end to the occupation. Protests from Rhee might have been countered by pointing to his erratic position on the issue.

82. Washington had anticipated a Soviet proposal for joint withdrawal since the spring.

83. On American concerns regarding Japan, see Max Bishop to Penfield, 14 August 1947, Lovett to Marshall, 26 August 1947, and Hugh Borton to Butterworth, 9 October 1947, *FR, 1947*, 6:492–94, 505, 537–43.

84. The Russians did, of course, march into western Poland and Finland in 1939 and 1940, but only after an agreement with Germany, the one nation in a position to resist the move.

85. Marshall to Langdon, 6 January 1948, *FR, 1948*, 6:1083.

86. Gordenker, *United Nations*, pp. 56, 60–63.

87. Jacobs to Marshall, 5 February 1948, *FR, 1948*, 6:1093.

88. See a confidential report (undated but obviously in early 1948) by John Foster Dulles, an American delegate, in Box 1, Supplement of 1971, *JFD*.

89. Gordenker, *United Nations*, pp. 72–74.

90. Truman to Mackenzie King, 5 January 1948, Memorandum of Conversation by Lovett, 3 January 1948, *FR, 1948*, 6:1081–83, 1079.

91. Jacobs to Marshall, 5 February 1948, Lewis W. Douglas (ambassador to Great Britain) to Marshall, 20 February 1948, ibid., 6:1093–94, 1121.

92. Gordenker, *United Nations*, pp. 58–59.

93. Jacobs to Marshall, 3 February 1948, Jacobs to Marshall, 12 February 1948, *FR, 1948*, 6:1105–9.

94. U.S. Department of the Army, Supreme Commander, Allied Forces, Japan, *South Korean Interim Government Activities*, 30 (March 1948):153.

95. Ibid., pp. 153–54.

96. Gordenker, *United Nations*, pp. 77–85; Langdon to Marshall, 12 March 1948, *FR, 1948*, 6:1154–55.

97. *FR, 1948*, 6:1153.

98. Hodge to Marshall, 8 April 1948, Box 7125, RG 59.

99. Jacobs to Marshall, 14 April 1948, *FR, 1948*, 6:1178–79.

100. Ibid., 6:1178n.

101. The election date was moved back twenty-four hours because on 9 May an eclipse of the sun was to occur. Hodge felt superstitious Koreans might regard the day as one of "ill-omen." *NYT*, 4 April 1948, p. 11.

102. Jacobs to Marshall, 28 April 1948, *FR, 1948*, 6:1184.

103. Jacobs to Marshall, 22 April 1948, ibid., 6:1180.

104. U.S. Department of the Army, Supreme Commander, Allied Powers, Japan, *South Korean Interim Government Activities*, 32 (May 1948):147.

105. Jacobs to Marshall, 23 February 1948, *FR, 1948*, 6:1090.

106. *NYT*, 9 May 1948, pp. 1, 32; 10 May 1948, pp. 1, 3.

107. Jacobs to Marshall, 12 May 1948, Box 7125, RG 59; U.S. Department of the Army, Supreme Commander, Allied Powers, Japan, *South Korean Interim Government Activities*, 32 (May 1948):182.

108. Ibid., pp. 137–42.

109. The question of the openness of the elections can be debated endlessly. Three months prior to the election, Jacobs wrote a perceptive analysis of Rhee's position. This analysis suggests the difficulty of judging, in traditional terms, the "will" of the Korean people. Rhee was, Jacobs asserted, "the outstanding leader in a confused, ill-informed society lacking in leadership—no doubt a bad, self-seeking and unwise leader, but nevertheless a dominating, shrewd, positive, feared character. His large following has nothing to do with love or veneration for the man. . . . It is . . . the

result of a wide belief that Rhee is the source of all present and future political power in South Korea, the supreme protector of vested interests and the existing order of things, and that he is the man on whom to stake all one's fortunes. Although treatment of him by the United States and events at times should have created doubts on this score, his unfailing success, through a variety of circumstances in stealing every important and historical public show in South Korea confirms and reconfirms this belief." Jacobs to Marshall, 9 February 1948, Box 7125, RG 59.

110. Butterworth to Marshall, 4 March 1948, *FR, 1948*, 6:1137–39.

111. T. N. Depuy to MacArthur, 16 October 1947, 091 Korea (TS), RG 319.

112. Brigadier General S. L. Scott to the Plans and Operations Division, 16 October 1947, ibid.

113. Scott to the Plans and Operations Division, 21 November 1947, ibid.

114. Lieutenant Colonel J. W. Mann (for MacArthur) to George A. Lincoln, 5 December 1947, Hall to the Plans and Operations Division, 5 January 1948, MacArthur to the Plans and Operations Division, 6 February 1948, ibid.

115. Report by the National Security Council on the Position of the United States with Respect to Korea, 2 April 1948, *FR, 1948*, 6:1168–69. The National Security Council came into being in September 1947 under the terms of the National Security Act. The council was the supreme coordinating agency in the area of foreign policy.

116. Central Intelligence Agency, "The Current Situation in Korea," 18 March 1948, RG 260.

117. Report by the National Security Council on the Position of the United States With Respect to Korea, 2 April 1948, *FR, 1948*, 6:1164–69.

118. Ibid., 6:1169.

119. Lovett to Draper, 19 May 1948, *FR, 1948*, 6:1200–01.

120. Millis, *Forrestal Diaries*, pp. 401, 418, 436–38.

121. For figures on American economic aid to South Korea after World War II, see U.S. Congress, House, Foreign Affairs Committee, *Korean Aid*, pp. 37, 57, and 105.

122. Jacobs to Marshall, 12 February 1948, Box 7125, RG 59.

123. Cf. Jacobs to Marshall, 26 May 1948, *FR, 1948*, 6:1207–10 to Jacobs to Marshall, 19 September 1947, *FR, 1947*, 6:803–7.

124. Muccio was a foreign service officer of the class of career minister. Between 1926 and 1935, he served in China. This was his last experience in Asia prior to 1948. U.S. Department of State, *Biographic Register, 1950*, p. 3641.

125. Jacobs to Marshall, 13 May 1948, *FR, 1948*, 6:1196.

126. Gordenker, *United Nations*, pp. 108–13.

127. United Nations General Assembly, *Official Records*, Session 3, Part 2, Supplement 9 (A/575/Add 3), 1948, p. 3; Hodge to Marshall, 28 June 1948, *FR, 1948*, 6:1229–30.

128. Jacobs to Marshall, 11 July 1948, *FR, 1948*, 6:1238; Scalapino and Lee, *Communism in Korea*, 1:372–73.

129. Ibid.

130. Ibid., pp. 306–7, 310.

131. Ibid., pp. 307–8; Muccio to Marshall, 4 November 1948, Box 7126, RG 59.

132. Muccio to Marshall, 4 November 1948, Box 7126, RG 59.

133. Muccio to Marshall, 12 November 1948, *FR, 1948*, 6:1326.

134. Joungwon A. Kim, *Divided Korea*, pp. 115–23.

135. Muccio to Marshall, 12 November 1948, *FR, 1948*, 6:1326.

136. Muccio to Marshall, 18 November 1948, ibid., 6:1331.

137. Dusan J. Djonovich, ed., *United Nations Resolutions*, Series 1, 2:89–90.

138. Foy D. Kohler (chargé in the Soviet Union) to Marshall, 19 September 1948, *FR, 1948*, 6:1306.

139. Bishop to Butterworth, 17 December 1948, ibid., pp. 1337–40. Allison became deputy director of the Office of Far Eastern Affairs.

140. Niles Bond interview with the author.

141. On the State Department's increasing concern with Japan during 1948, see George F. Kennan, *Memoirs, 1925–1950*, pp. 392–418.

142. Bishop to Butterworth, 17 December 1948, *FR, 1948*, 6:1338.

143. Dean Acheson, *Present*, p. 249.

144. Butterworth to Lovett, 17 December 1948, quoted in *FR, 1948*, 6:1343n.

145. Marshall to Lovett, 16 November 1948, ibid., 6:1328.

146. Marshall to Hoffman, 17 September 1948, Hoffman to Marshall, 1 October 1948, ibid., 6:1303–5, 1312–13.

147. Muccio to Bond, 22 November 1948, Box 7130, RG 59.

148. It is impossible to determine the precise number of Koreans in the Chinese Communist armies. One hundred thousand is a reasonable estimate. Simmons, *The Strained Alliance*, p. 118.

149. On Truman's belief in balanced budgets and congressional pressures for tax reduction, see Herbert Stein, *The Fiscal Revolution in America*, pp. 206–8, and Susan Hartmann, *Truman and the 80th Congress*, pp. 74–79, 134–36. Truman vetoed tax cuts in 1947 and 1948, but in April of the latter year was overridden by Congress.

For a revealing statement regarding the expansion of the armed forces, see "Statement by the President to the Secretary of Defense, the Secretaries of the Three Departments, and the Three Chiefs of Staff," 13 May 1948, Box 8, James E. Webb Papers. For a retrospective and spirited defense of administration policy regarding defense spending, see James Webb to Paul Y. Hammond, 3 April 1957, Box 51, ibid. For a contemporary appraisal by Webb's top assistant, see "Statement by Frank Pace before the Committee on National Military Establishment, October 7, 1948," Box 14, Frank Pace Papers. The President's Council of Economic Advisers held views similar to Webb and Pace. See Edwin G. Nourse, "What Effect Will Armament Spending Have on the Business Outlook?" pp. 40–46.

Millis, *Forrestal Diaries* is an excellent source on both Forrestal's battles with the White House over defense spending and with the Joint Chiefs over unification of the armed services. Useful secondary works include Edward A. Kolodjiez, *The Uncommon Defense and Congress*, pp. 89–97; Warner Schilling, ed., *Strategy, Politics, and Defense Budgets*, pp. 1–266; and Paul Y. Hammond, "Super Carriers and B-36 Bombers: Appropriations, Strategy, Politics," in Harold Stein, ed., *American Civil-Military Relations*, pp. 471–90.

150. Muccio to Marshall, 17 January 1949, Box 7127, RG 59.

151. Biddle to Wedemeyer, 5 March 1948, 091 Korea (TS), RG 319.

152. Nikita Khrushchev, *Khrushchev Remembers*, p. 368.

## Chapter 4

1. Dean Acheson, *Morning and Noon*, p. 165; Dean Acheson, *Present at the Creation*, p. 104.

2. Acheson, *Present*, pp. 136–37.

3. Ibid., p. 250.

4. Ibid., pp. 89–115.

5. "Diary," 6 January 1949, *HAS*; *NYT*, 26 January 1949, p. 1; H. Bradford Westerfield, *Foreign Policy and Party Politics*, pp. 326–27; David N. Farnsworth, *The Senate Committee on Foreign Relations*, p. 26.

6. Westerfield, *Foreign Policy and Party Politics*, p. 327.

7. Arthur H. Vandenberg, Jr., *The Private Papers of Senator Vandenberg*, p. 469.

8. *PS*, 15 July 1953.

9. Westerfield, *Foreign Policy and Party Politics*, p. 328. Although the Senate confirmed Acheson overwhelmingly, Republican Senator H. Alexander Smith, an avid supporter of interparty cooperation on foreign policy, commented privately, "It is unfortunate that there is a feeling of distrust with regard to him." "Diary," 19 January 1949, *HAS*.

10. Dean Acheson, *Sketches from Life of Men I Have Known*, p. 133.

11. Acheson, *Present*, p. 101.

12. Acheson, *Sketches*, pp. 133–34.

13. James Reston, "Secretary Acheson: A First-Year Audit," p. 37.

14. *PS*, 22 July 1953; Acheson, *Present*, p. 306.

15. Griffin to Knowland, 18 August, 30 September 1948, Knowland to Vandenberg, 2 September, 19 October 1948, Box 3, Arthur H. Vandenberg Papers. See also Knowland to Griffin, 8 September, 19 November 1948, Box 1, Robert Allen Griffin Papers.

16. *PS*, 22 July 1953.

17. Smith to Acheson, 31 January 1949, Box 98, *HAS*.

18. See Smith's "Diary" from January through June 1948 in *HAS*. Smith devoted considerable time to a displaced persons bill and the Taft-Hartley Act.

19. Ibid., 2, 7 December 1948.

20. Ibid., 6, 21 December 1948.

21. William M. Leary, Jr., "Smith of New Jersey," pp. 5, 12, 24–25, 75.

22. Ibid., pp. 132–33.

23. *CR*, 95 (1949):1950–51.

24. Ibid., pp. 1530, 1532–33.

25. *NYT*, 11 March 1949, p. 13.

26. U.S. Congress, Senate, Foreign Relations Committee, *Economic Assistance to China and Korea*, p. 3.

27. Acheson, *Present*, p. 105; McCarran to Smith, 26 February 1949, Box 98, *HAS*.

28. *FR, 1949*, 9:482–83.

29. Vandenberg noted in his diary merely that Barkley expressed agreement with his view. Vandenberg, Jr., *Private Papers*, pp. 530–31. On 7 February, however, Marshall S. Carter, special assistant to the secretary of state, wrote that those present from Congress were unanimous in their agreement with Vandenberg. *FR, 1949*, 9:485–86.

30. Memorandum of Conversation with the President, by Acheson, 7 February 1949, *FR, 1949*, 9:486.

31. Smith to Acheson, 31 January 1949, Box 98, *HAS*.

32. Ibid.

33. Stone to Webb, 27 January 1949, Box 3499, RG 59.

34. Patterson to Smith, 21 February 1949, Box 98, *HAS*.

35. Butterworth to Acheson, 18 February 1949, Box 3499, RG 59.

36. Joint Chiefs to Forrestal, 24 November 1948, *FR, 1949*, 9:261–62.

37. Joint Chiefs to Forrestal, 10 February 1949, ibid., 9:284–86.

38. Report by the National Security Council on the Current Position of the United States with Respect to Formosa, 3 February 1949, Acheson to Sidney Souers, 18 February 1949, ibid., 9:281–82, 288–89.

39. Acheson to Merchant, 2 March 1949, Merchant to Acheson, 6 March 1949, ibid., 9:293–94, 297.

40. Statement by Acheson at the Thirty-fifth Meeting of the National Security Council on the Formosan Problem, 1 March 1949, ibid., 9:294–96.

41. Memorandum Prepared in the Office of Far Eastern Affairs, 14 January 1949, Stuart to Acheson, 23 March 1949, Butterworth to Acheson, 15 April 1949, Cabot to Acheson, 28 April 1949, ibid., 9:599–601, 633, 635, 639–40.

42. Memorandum Prepared in the Office of Far Eastern Affairs, Acheson to Merchant, 2 March 1949, ibid., 9:599–601, 293; Westerfield, *Foreign Policy and Party Politics*, pp. 345–50; Tang Tsou, *America's Failure in China*, pp. 500–501; James Alan Fetzer, "Congress and China," pp. 183–86. Butterworth noted, however, that the State Department was supporting continuation of the China aid program "in large measure" to keep up assistance to Taiwan. Acheson to Stuart, 24 March 1949, *FR, 1949*, 9:304.

43. Draft Report by the National Security Council on United States Policy regarding Trade with China, 28 February 1949, Souers to the National Security Council, 3 March 1949, *FR, 1949*, 9:826–34.

44. Clubb to Acheson, 15 March 1949, Stuart to Acheson, 18 March 1949, Memorandum of Conversation, by Sprouse, 6 January 1949, ibid., 9:913–15, 917–18, 5–6.
45. Acheson to Clubb, 3 February 1949, ibid., 9:11.
46. Stuart to Acheson, 29 April 1949, ibid., 9:13.
47. Acheson to Certain Diplomatic and Consular Officers, 6 May 1949, ibid., 9:17.
48. Acheson to Stuart, 13 May 1949, ibid., 9:21–23.
49. Stuart to Acheson, 14 May, 8 June 1949, ibid., 8:745–46, 754.
50. Clubb to Acheson, 1 June 1949, ibid., 8:357–60.
51. Webb to Clubb, 14 June 1949, ibid., 8:384–85.
52. Memorandum of Conversation with the President, by Webb, 16 June 1949, ibid., 8:388.
53. Clubb to Acheson, 24, 27 June 1949, ibid., 8:397–99.
54. Stuart to Acheson, 30 June 1949, Davies to Kennan, 30 June 1949, ibid., 8:766–67, 768–69; U.S. Congress, Senate, Foreign Relations Committee, *The United States and Communist China in 1949 and 1950*, p. 10.
55. Acheson to Stuart, 1 July 1949, *FR, 1949*, 8:769.
56. Memorandum of Conversation, by Webb, 16 June 1949, ibid., 8:388.
57. *FR, 1949*, 9:17, 23, 43; Stuart to Acheson, 30 June 1949, ibid., 8:767. In his dispatch to Stuart rejecting the overture, Acheson stated that the "[p]rincipal reasons for [a] negative decision are those contained" in the ambassador's telegram of 30 June, which outlined pros and cons without taking a strong stand on either side. See Acheson to Stuart, 1 July 1949, ibid., 8:769.
58. John Cabot Oral History; John Melby to Livingston Merchant, 14 January 1949, Melby to Frederic Schultheis, 14 January 1949, Box 6, John F. Melby Papers.
59. Stuart to Acheson, 30 June 1949, *FR, 1949*, 8:767.
60. *CR*, 95 (1949):8294.
61. Ibid., p. 8406. In mid-June, after the Nationalists announced their intention to move government headquarters from Canton to Chungking, Acheson decided to send a first secretary to the latter city rather than simply give the American consul there responsibility for maintaining contact with the declining regime. The secretary of state labeled "U.S. public opinion" as one reason for the decision. Acheson to Stuart, 30 June 1949, *FR, 1949*, 8:704.
62. Rusk interview with the author.
63. Gaddis Smith, "Mr. Acheson Answers Some Questions," p. 2.
64. See Davies's reports in *CWP*, pp. 564–75, especially that of 7 November 1944 (p. 573).
65. Memorandum by Davies, "American Policy in Asia," 19 February 1944, quoted in Michael Schaller, *The U.S. Crusade in China*, p. 157.
66. Memorandum by Davies, 24 August 1949, *FR, 1949*, 9:536–40.
67. Ibid., 9:536n.
68. Clubb to Acheson, 11 July 1950, ibid., 8:779.
69. Mao Tse-tung, *On People's Democratic Dictatorship*.
70. Cabot to Acheson, 31 May 1949, Box 895, RG 59.
71. Quoted in Clubb to Acheson, 20 June 1949, ibid.
72. Stuart to Acheson, 15 June 1949, ibid.
73. Nancy Bernkopf Tucker, "An Unlikely Peace."
74. Warren W. Tozer, "Last Bridge to China."
75. Cabot to Acheson, 7 July 1949, *FR, 1949*, 9:1262.
76. On the British attitude toward recognition, see the British Embassy to the Department of State, 19 March 1949, ibid., 9:11–12; on the French position, see David Bruce to Acheson, 20 May 1949, ibid., 9:26–27.
77. Cabot to Acheson, 7 July 1949, ibid., 9:1263.
78. Stuart to Acheson, 14 July 1950, ibid., 8:784–85.
79. Stuart to Acheson, 20 July 1949, ibid., 8:448. Tillman Durdin's articles in the *New York Times* of 17 and 18 September 1949 (p. 5 and Section I, p. 26, respectively) discuss evidence of divisions in the Communist camp. State Department officials regarded Durdin as one of the most astute American journalists reporting on the China scene.

80. Stuart to Acheson, 23 June 1949, Ward to Acheson, 11 December 1949, *FR, 1949*, 8:971, 1048.

81. Clark to Acheson, 23 June 1949, ibid., 8:1103–4.

82. J. Wesley Jones (counselor of embassy in Nanking) to Acheson, 7 August 1949, ibid., 8:1126.

83. Withholding overt military aid from Taiwan and continuing trade with Communist-held areas in China were negative policies aimed at giving the Communists no clear reason for devoting their primary attention to American hostility, which was far different from seeking actively to disrupt Sino-Soviet relations. In May, Yugoslavia informed the British that it would close its frontier with Greece and cease aid to the Greek Communists. This move followed initial American inaction on Yugoslav requests for economic assistance, and U.S. diplomats may have concluded that similar firmness with the Chinese Communists also would produce concessions.

84. Seymour Topping, *Journey between Two Chinas*, pp. 89–90.

85. Claire Lee Chennault, *Way of a Fighter*, pp. xvii–xx.

86. On Goodwin's activities, see Chen Chih-mai to Wellington Koo, 31 January 1949, Box 180, Koo Papers. On Chennault, see Arthur to Chennault, 2 February, 7 April 1949, Reel 12, Claire Lee Chennault Papers; and F. H. Russell (director, Office of Public Affairs) to Bohlen, 27 January 1949, Box 3499, RG 59.

87. *CR*, 95 (1949):5480–84; Reel 12, Chennault Papers.

88. Claire Lee Chennault, "Hold 'Em! Harass 'Em! Hamstring 'Em!—The Chennault Plan," pp. 25–28.

89. *NYT*, 4 May 1949, pp. 1, 20.

90. Smith to H. Kenaston Twitchell, 15 August 1949, Box 98, *HAS*. On 24 June, Chennault wrote Hearst suggesting that David P. Sentner be sent to China to report for the Hearst papers. Reel 12, Chennault Papers. The letter followed publication on 20 June of a Sentner interview with Colonel David Li, a member of the Chinese Purchasing Mission in Washington, in which Li disputed the administration view that Nationalist armies lacked the will to fight. Sentner did make the trip.

91. Smith to Knowland, 7 June 1949, Box 98, *HAS*.

92. Claire Lee Chennault, "Last Call for China."

93. Senator John McClellan to Chennault, 29 July 1949, Reel 12, Chennault Papers.

94. Chennault's correspondence with Congressmen is in Reel 12, ibid.

95. *CR*, 95 (1949):6306.

96. Senator Fulbright, who was later to become the great sage on American involvement in Vietnam in the 1960s, suggested that monies requested by the administration for economic recovery and development in South Korea be committed instead to the Chennault plan. Fulbright received little support for his idea in the Senate Foreign Relations Committee. Fulbright to Chennault, 29 July 1949, Reel 12, Chennault Papers.

97. Webb to Butterworth, 10 May 1949, Butterworth to Webb, 10 May 1949, Memorandum of Conversation, by Webb, 11 May 1949, Webb to Stuart, 25 May 1949, Stuart to Acheson, 30 May 1949, Clark to Acheson, 6 June 1949, *FR, 1949*, 9:517, 519–27.

98. Arthur to Chennault, 2 February, 7 April 1949, Reel 10, Chennault Papers; Smith to Twitchell, 15 July, 15 August 1949, Box 98, *HAS*.

99. Vandenberg, Jr., *Private Papers*, p. 534.

100. *CR*, 95 (1949):8292–98.

101. Smith to Twitchell, 15 July, 15 August 1949, Box 98, *HAS*.

102. *CR*, 95 (1949):D655.

103. U.S. Congress, House, Foreign Affairs Committee, *Military Assistance Act of 1949*.

104. *NYT*, 16 August 1949, p. 1.

105. Westerfield, *Foreign Policy and Party Politics*, p. 357.

106. Fetzer, "Congress and China," p. 200.

107. *CR*, 95 (1949):12636–40, 12757.

108. *NYT,* 12 September 1949, p. 1.
109. Fetzer, "Congress and China," pp. 204–6.
110. Sprouse to Allison, 28 January 1949, Box 3499, RG 59.
111. U.S. Congress, Senate, Foreign Relations and Armed Services Committees, *Military Assistance Program,* pp. 37–38.
112. U.S. Congress, Senate, Foreign Relations Committee, *Nomination of Philip C. Jessup,* p. 603.
113. *USVR,* 8:152–265.
114. Smith to Jessup, 13 December 1949, Acheson to Smith, 30 June 1949, Smith to Twitchell, 15 July 1949, Smith to Acheson, 31 January 1949, Box 98, *HAS.*
115. For the background on the publishing of this book, see *FR, 1949,* 9:1365–1409.
116. Acheson, *Present,* p. 302. In a public opinion poll taken shortly after the *White Paper*'s appearance, only 36 percent of those questioned had heard anything about the work. Of that group, 53 percent disapproved of past American China policy and only 26 percent approved. Arthur N. Feraru, "Public Opinion Polls on China," p. 131.
117. Feraru, "Public Opinion Polls on China," p. 131.
118. Acheson, *Present,* p. 303.
119. Butterworth and Jessup interviews with the author.
120. U.S. Congress, Senate, Judiciary Committee, *Institute of Pacific Relations,* pp. 1551–1682.
121. U.S. Congress, Senate, Foreign Relations Committee, *Reviews of the World Situation,* pp. 94–95.
122. Clubb to Acheson, 2 October 1949, *FR, 1949,* 9:93–94.
123. Clubb to Acheson, 8 October 1949, ibid., 9:112–14.
124. Clubb to Acheson, 11 October 1949, ibid., 9:121.
125. Kirk to Acheson, 7 October 1949, ibid., 9:106–8.
126. Webb to Clubb, 6 October 1949, ibid., 9:103.
127. Webb to Pete Jarman (ambassador to Australia), 21 September 1949, William Sebald (acting political adviser in Japan) to Acheson, 7 October 1949, Memorandum of Conversation, by Sprouse, 1 November 1949, Julius C. Holmes (chargé in the United Kingdom) to Acheson, 16 December 1949, ibid., 9:91, 105, 149–51, 224.
128. Memorandum of Conversation, by Acheson, 12 October 1949, ibid., 9:124–25.
129. Tsou, *America's Failure in China,* p. 518.
130. H. Schuyler Foster, Jr. (assistant chief in charge of Special Activities Branch), to Francis M. Fisher (Policy Information Office, Office of Far Eastern Affairs) and Sprouse, 7 July 1949, Box 3499, RG 59; Feraru, "Public Opinion Polls on China," p. 131.
131. Press Clipping, *New York World-Telegram,* 29 November 1949, Box 98, *HAS.*
132. Tom Connally Papers, Box 222; *NYT,* 30 December 1949, p. 1.
133. *NYT,* 8 January 1950, Section IV, p. 3.
134. Memorandum of Conversation, by Merchant, 23 November 1949, *FR, 1949,* 9:198.
135. *NYT,* 15 January 1950, p. 1.
136. Acheson, *Present,* p. 344; Memorandum of Conversation, by Acheson, 13 September 1949, Memorandum of Conversation, by Acheson, 17 September 1949, Memorandum of Conversation, by Sprouse, 14 November 1949, *FR, 1949,* 9:81–85, 90, 190–91.
In U.S. Congress, Senate, Foreign Relations Committee, *U.S. and Communist China in 1949 and 1950* (pp. 17–18), it is suggested that in March 1950 the American position on recognition softened, that proper treatment of American diplomats in China became the only prerequisite. This view is based on a strained reading of speeches by Acheson and Loy Henderson, the American ambassador to India. See *DSB,* 22 (27 March 1950):469 and (10 April 1950):565–66.
137. *FR, 1950,* 6:313n.
138. Acheson to Clubb, 22 March 1950, ibid., 6:322.

139. Clubb to Acheson, 11 April 1950, ibid., 6:329.

140. Memorandum of Conversation, by Sprouse, 14 November 1949, Memorandum of Conversation, by Acheson, 12 October 1949, *FR, 1949*, 9:190–91, 124–25.

141. Memorandum of Conversation with the President, by Acheson, 17 November 1949, Box 64, *DA*.

142. Memorandum of Conversation, by Butterworth, 9 September 1949, Memorandum of Conversation, by Acheson, 13 September 1949, *FR, 1949*, 9:78, 83.

143. Acheson to Certain Diplomatic and Consular Officers, 16 December 1949, ibid., 9:222–23.

144. George M. Abbot (consul general at Saigon) to Acheson, 19 December 1949, Edwin F. Stanton (ambassador to Thailand) to Acheson, 20 December 1949, Myron M. Cowen (ambassador in the Philippines) to Acheson, 20 December 1949, Henry B. Day (chargé in Burma) to Acheson, 27 December 1949; ibid., 9:227–28, 231–35, 246. On State Department concern on this point, see also Memorandum of Conversation, by Jessup, 10 November 1949, *FR, 1949*, 2:206.

145. U.S. Department of State, Office of Public Opinion Studies, "Fortnightly Survey of American Opinion on International Affairs," October 1949, p. 4, RG 59.

146. U.S. Department of State, Office of Public Opinion Studies, "Fortnightly Survey of American Opinion on International Affairs," November 1949, p. 3, ibid.

147. U.S. Department of State, Office of Public Opinion Studies, "Opinion and Activities of American Private Organizations and Groups," 26 September, 24, 31 October, 21 November, 12 December 1949, ibid.

148. U.S. Department of State, Office of Public Opinion Studies, "Opinion and Activities of American Private Organizations and Groups," 17, 24 October, 5, 12 December 1949, ibid.

149. No direct evidence exists to support this hypothesis, but Kao's leanings toward Moscow and his inclinations toward independence from Peking seem certain. Harrison E. Salisbury, *War between Russia and China*, pp. 95–97; O. Edmund Clubb, *China and Russia*, pp. 405–7; Adam B. Ulam, *The Rivals*, pp. 167–70; Robert R. Simmons, *The Strained Alliance*, pp. 57–59. For Ward's account of the incident, see the *New York Times*, 13 December 1949, p. 16.

150. Clubb to Acheson, 30 October, 2, 9 November 1949, *FR, 1949*, 8:993–95, 997–98, 1014. Gubichev was arrested in March in the Judith Coplon espionage case. He went to trial in New York in mid-October, was convicted by a jury in March 1950, and was sentenced to fifteen years in prison. Under State Department pressure, however, the judge suspended the sentence and Gubichev was immediately deported. See ibid., 5:776–805.

151. Again, the Soviets claimed the officials had diplomatic immunity. The case was resolved on 23 November after the company agreed to register under the Foreign Agents Registration Act of 1938, pleaded nolo contendere to the charges against it, and was assessed a ten thousand dollar fine. Ibid., 5:754–74.

152. Clubb to Acheson, 13 January 1950, *FR, 1950*, 6:286n.

153. Clubb, *China and Russia*, pp. 381–83.

154. C. L. Sulzberger, *A Long Row of Candles*, p. 492; Acheson to Bruce, 25 January, 11 February 1950, *FR, 1950*, 6:294–95, 308–10.

155. Clubb to Acheson, 27 September 1949, Box 3499, RG 59.

156. On 19 January 1950, the House of Representatives defeated, by a vote of 193–191, a bill for aid to South Korea. The action came after the Truman administration had announced its intention to grant no more military aid to Chiang's government on Taiwan. *NYT*, 20 January 1950, p. 1. Had Acheson refused to ask for an extension of the deadline for the commitment of funds to the Nationalists through the China Aid Act, there certainly would have been considerable outrage on Capitol Hill. But it is doubtful that this response would have led directly to the defeat of any administration foreign policy legislation. The secretary of state later conceded in his memoirs that House rejection of the Korean aid bill could have been avoided through a more intense lobbying effort by the executive. Acheson, *Present*, p. 358.

157. John Gittings, *The World and China*, pp. 178–79; Webb to Truman, 10 January 1950, *FR, 1950*, 6:270–71.

158. McConaughy to Acheson, 21 December 1949, *FR, 1949*, 8:639–41.
159. McConaughy to Acheson, 16 December 1949, ibid., 8:632–36.
160. If anything, President Truman was more hard-nosed in his sentiments than his State Department advisers. In November, he had to be talked out of instituting a blockade of coal traffic along the China coast from Shanghai northward as a means of gaining Ward's release. Memorandum of Meeting with the President, by Webb, 14 November 1949, and Acheson to Truman, 21 November 1949, *FR, 1949*, 8:1015–16.
161. *MSFE*, p. 2577.
162. Acheson to Souers, 4 August 1949, *FR, 1949*, 9:369–71.
163. Joint Chiefs of Staff to the Secretary of Defense, 9 August 1949, 091 Formosa (TS), RG 319.
164. Chennault to Johnson, 2 October 1949, Reel 12, Chennault Papers; Johnson to the Joint Chiefs, 13 September 1949, 091 China (TS), RG 319.
165. JCS 1721/37, 28 September 1949, 091 China (TS), ibid.
166. JCS 1721/38, 20 October 1949, 091 China (TS), ibid.
167. In August 1949, General Omar N. Bradley became the first chairman of the Joint Chiefs and was replaced as army chief of staff by General J. Lawton Collins. Admiral Louis E. Denfield served as chief of naval operations until October, when he was fired for objecting publicly to established defense policies. Admiral Forrest P. Sherman replaced him. The air force chief of staff was General Hoyt S. Vandenberg. Throughout the fall of 1949, the Joint Chiefs took a more cautious position on China policy than many of their subordinates.
168. J. P. Daley to C. V. R. Schuyler, 12 October 1949, 091 China (TS), RG 319.
169. Bolté to Collins, 10 November 1949, 091 China (TS), ibid.
170. Gray to Gruenther, 14 November 1949, 091 Formosa (TS), ibid.
171. Vandenberg to the Joint Chiefs, 8 November 1949, 091 Formosa (TS), ibid.
172. Schuyler to Bolté, 30 November 1949, 091 Formosa (TS), ibid.
173. Schuyler to Bolté, 22 December 1949, 091 Formosa (TS), ibid.
174. Gruenther to the Joint Chiefs, 22 December 1949, 091 Formosa (TS), ibid. By this time, events in China had undermined the desire to send substantial aid to anti-Communist forces on the mainland.
175. Joint Chiefs to Johnson, 23 December 1949, *FR, 1949*, 9:460–61.
176. Leary, "Smith of New Jersey," pp. 140–46.
177. *CR*, 96 (1950):150.
178. Ibid., pp. 156–60.
179. *NYT*, 2 December 1949, p. 15. Vandenberg leaned toward similar arguments, though he never publicized the fact. Vandenberg to John Foster Dulles, 14 December 1949, Box 9, Supplement II 1971, Part II, *JFD*.
180. *NYT*, 28, 29 November 1949, pp. 4, 15.
181. Bolté to Collins, 1 December 1949, 091 Formosa (TS), RG 319.
182. Bolté to Gilchrist, 23 November 1949, ibid.; Collins to the Joint Chiefs, 6 December 1949, ibid.
183. J. Lawton Collins, *War in Peacetime*, pp. 73–74.
184. Bolté to Gruenther, 22 November 1949, 091 Formosa (TS), RG 319.
185. Ibid.
186. *NYT*, 2 December 1949, p. 15.
187. On 29 May 1949, MacArthur forwarded his views on the strategic importance of Taiwan to the Joint Chiefs. See Memorandum on Formosa, by MacArthur, 14 June 1950, *FR, 1950*, 7:161–65.
188. Ibid.
189. Voorhees to Johnson, 14 December 1949, 091 Formosa (TS), RG 319.
190. Memorandum of Conversation, by Acheson, 29 December 1949, *FR, 1949*, 9:463–67; JCS paper of 23 December 1949, 091 Formosa (TS), RG 319.
191. *MSFE*, p. 2578.
192. Johnson's personality is discussed in a wide variety of sources. My account is based on interviews with Marx Leva (an assistant to Johnson for legislative affairs), General Charles Bolté, and Paul Nitze (director of the State Department Policy Planning Staff under Acheson), and on Acheson, *Present*, pp. 373–74.

193. *NYT*, 30 December 1949, p. 1.

194. *NYT*, 31 December 1949, p. 1.

195. Ibid.

196. *NYT*, 3 January 1950, p. 1.

197. *NYT*, 4 January 1950, p. 1.

198. Ibid., p. 14; *MSFE*, p. 1697.

199. *NYT*, 5 January 1950, p. 1.

200. Ibid.

201. Ibid.

202. *DSB*, 22 (16 January 1950): 79. Actually, $9 million also remained available from the $125 million grant in the China Aid Act of 1948.

203. Ibid., p. 80; Gaddis Smith, *Dean Acheson*, p. 131; Acheson, *Present*, pp. 350–53; *PS*, 15 July 1953.

204. *PS*, 15 July 1953; U.S. Congress, Senate, Foreign Relations Committee, *Reviews of the World Situation*, p. 150.

205. Butterworth to Rusk, 9 June 1949, *FR, 1949*, 9: 346.

206. Memorandum by Kennan, 6 July 1949, ibid., 9: 356–59.

207. Acheson to Donald D. Edgar, 30 March 1949, Acheson to Rusk, 9 June 1949, Draft Memorandum Prepared in Policy Planning Staff, 23 June 1949, Memorandum of Conversation, by Fulton Freeman, 9 September 1949, ibid., 9: 305, 346–50, 359–60, 388–90.

208. U.S. Congress, Senate, Foreign Relations Committee, *Reviews of the World Situation*, pp. 146–49.

209. *DSB*, 22 (22 January 1950): 114–15.

210. Smith, *Acheson*, p. 136.

211. *NYT*, 15 January 1950, Section IV, p. 7.

212. Joseph Barber, ed., *American Policy toward China: A Report on the Views of Leading Citizens in Twenty-three Cities*, p. 14.

213. Feraru, "Public Opinion Polls on China," p. 131.

214. Smith, *Acheson*, pp. 56–57; Acheson, *Present*, pp. 250–52.

215. Acheson, *Present*, pp. 359–61; *PS*, 10 October 1953.

216. The precise content of parts of the speech remains somewhat in doubt. See Robert Griffith, *The Politics of Fear*, pp. 48–51, and Smith, *Acheson*, p. 166.

217. Griffith, *Politics of Fear*, pp. 73–74.

218. Ibid., p. 69.

219. Ibid., pp. 77, 81.

220. See above, p. 43.

221. Griffith, *Politics of Fear*, pp. 95–96.

222. Acheson, *Present*, p. 337.

223. Westerfield, *Foreign Policy and Party Politics*, p. 371.

224. On the process of reconciliation, see Truman to Dulles, 4 April 1950, Box 50, *JFD*; and Vandenberg to Acheson, 31 March 1950, and Acheson Memorandum of Telephone Conversation with Dulles, 5 April 1950, Box 65, *DA*.

225. Acheson, *Present*, pp. 431–32.

226. *NYT*, 2 April 1950, Section IV, p. 3.

227. Acheson to Truman, 5 April 1950, Box 65, *DA*.

228. *NYT*, 16 April 1950, p. 1; Kenneth Heckler, "Bipartisan Foreign Policy," n.d., Personal Correspondence File, *GE*.

229. Acheson, *Present*, pp. 431–32.

230. Acheson to Austin, 22 March 1950, Acheson to Diplomatic Missions and Consular Offices, 23 March 1950, *FR, 1950*, 2: 243–44.

231. U.S. Congress, Senate, Foreign Relations Committee, *Economic Assistance to China and Korea*, pp. 193–94. Acheson requested that the money be made available for "the general area of China." In May 1950, Congress passed legislation making some of the funds so available. The Truman administration put the money to immediate use in Indochina. *USVR*, 8: 327.

232. Acheson to Johnson, 1 June 1950, *FR, 1950*, 6: 351–52.

233. Matthews to Johnson, 14 June 1950, Classified Correspondence of Secretary of the Navy Matthews, RG 80.

234. Paul Nitze interview with the author.

235. Elmo Roper, *You and Your Leaders*, p. 175.

236. For instance, a House foreign aid authorization bill passed on 1 April by a vote of 287–86. Although sixty-nine of the negative votes were by Republicans, seventy-eight of the minority representatives voted in favor of the bill. Critics of the administration dominated the headlines, but most commentators felt Truman would continue to succeed in holding together a majority coalition in favor of his policies. Administration programs might be cut, it was conceded, but not crippled. *NYT*, 2 April 1950, Section IV, p. 3.

237. *DSB*, 22 (23 January 1950):116.

238. Quoted from *Pravda*, 24 January 1950, by George F. Kennan in *Memoirs, 1950–1963*, p. 42.

239. Gittings, *The World and China*, pp. 173–74.

240. Quoted in Kennan, *Memoirs, 1950–1963*, pp. 43–44.

241. Acheson, *Present*, pp. 428–35.

242. Leftist groups, of course, agitated for a total American withdrawal. In early 1950, however, intelligence reports from the Far Eastern Command indicated that the dominant sentiment was by no means opposed to a continued American presence. Reports are available in RG 260.

243. David L. K. Bruce to Acheson, Charles W. Yost to George W. Perkins, 31 January 1950, *FR, 1950*, 6:704–5, 710–11. See also Noel Clinton Eggleston, "The Roots of Commitment," pp. 99–100.

244. *USVR*, 8:276–79.

245. Report to the National Security Council by the Department of State, 27 February 1950, *FR, 1950*, 6:744–47.

246. *USVR*, 8:286.

247. *NYT*, 9 May 1950, p. 1.

248. Smith, "Mr. Acheson Answers Some Questions," p. 30.

249. Acheson to Bruce, 29 March 1950, Gullion to Acheson, 8 April 1950, Bruce to Acheson, 3 February 1950, *FR, 1950*, 6:768–71, 773–76, 719–20.

250. Johnson to Acheson, 18 April 1950, ibid., 6:781.

251. Merchant to Butterworth, 7 March 1950, ibid., 6:750. See also *USVR*, 8:248, 253–58, 283, 309; and Eggleston, "The Roots of Commitment," p. 102.

252. NSC 68 is published in *FR, 1950*, 1:235–92.

253. *DSB*, 22 (23 February 1950):272–74.

254. U.S. Congress, *Reviews of the World Situation*, p. 266.

255. See, for example, Ogburn to Butterworth, 21 March 1950, *FR, 1950*, 6:766–67.

256. Butterworth to Merchant, 17 February 1950, ibid., pp. 738–39; *USVR*, 8:280–81.

257. U.S. Congress, Senate, Foreign Relations Committee, *Reviews of the World Situation*, p. 306.

258. Report of H. Kenaston Twitchell and Basil R. Entwistle, n.d., but clearly in early May 1950, Box 142, Part II, *JFD*.

259. *NYT*, 5 February 1950, p. 9; 22 April 1950, p. 6.

260. Dean Rusk interview with the author.

261. Dulles memorandum, 18 May 1950, Box 47, *JFD*.

262. Rusk to Acheson, 30 May 1950, *FR, 1950*, 6:349–50. For an insightful portrait of Rusk, see David Halberstam, *The Best and the Brightest*, pp. 308–23.

263. Problem Paper Prepared by a Working Group in the Department of State, 1 February 1950, *FR, 1950*, 6:712.

264. Clubb to Acheson, 9 April 1950, ibid., 6:327–28.

265. Remarks of McConaughy in the State Department, 2 June 1950, ibid., 6:354–56.

266. Rusk to Acheson, 26 April 1950, *FR, 1950*, 6:334–35.

267. Johnson to Acheson, 14 April 1950, ibid., 6:784.

268. Rusk to Acheson, 26 April 1950, ibid., 6:335; FEC, *IS*, 6 May 1950, RG 260; Central Intelligence Agency, "Reports of Current Soviet Military Activity in China," 21 April 1950, Box 255, President's Secretary's Files, *HST*.

269. Johnson to Acheson, 6 May 1950, *FR, 1950*, 6:339.

270. Burns to Rusk, 29 May 1950, ibid., 6:346–47.

271. For suggestive, but hardly definitive, materials on covert operations, see William M. Leary, Jr., "Aircraft and Anti-Communists," pp. 654–69. See also John D. Marks and Victor Marchetti, *The CIA and the Cult of Intelligence*, pp. 137–38. On guerrilla activities in China, see FEC, *IS*, 19 May 1950, RG 260.

272. Fisher Howe to W. Park Armstrong, 31 May 1950, Rusk to Acheson, 30 May 1950, *FR, 1950*, 6:347–51.

273. Rear Admiral A. C. Davis to General Bradley, 10 June 1950, 381 Formosa, RG 218.

274. *NYT*, 10 June 1950, pp. 1, 20; Wellington Koo, "Notes of Conversation: Assistant Secretary of Defense Paul Griffith," 7 June 1950, Box 180, Koo Papers.

275. Wellington Koo, "Notes of Conversation: John Foster Dulles," 12 June 1950, Box 180, Koo Papers.

276. Dean Rusk to the author, 12 September 1978.

277. Central Intelligence Agency, "The Current Western European Attitude toward the North Atlantic Treaty," 27 April 1950, Box 257, President's Secretary's Files, *HST*.

**Chapter 5**

1. *DSB*, 22 (23 January 1959):116.

2. *U.S. News and World Report*, 28 (May 1950):4.

3. Alexander L. George and Richard Smoke, *Deterrence in American Foreign Policy*, p. 161; *FR, 1950*, 7:67n.

4. FEC, *IS*, 10, 14 May 1950, RG 260.

5. Paul Nitze interview with the author.

6. *FR, 1949*, 7:969n. For the National Security Council paper, see ibid., 7:967–78.

7. See above, pp. 000–000.

8. U.S. Department of State, "Policy Statement: Korea," 31 January 1949, 711.95/1-3149, RG 59.

9. Ibid. See also Bishop to Butterworth, 24 May 1949, Box C-946, RG 59.

10. Muccio to Acheson, 27 January 1949, *FR, 1949*, 7:947.

11. George F. Kennan, *Memoirs, 1925–1950*, p. 511.

12. See Acheson's testimony in *MSFE*, p. 2010.

13. U.S. Department of State, "Policy Statement: Korea," 31 January 1949, 711.95/1-3149, RG 59.

14. MacArthur to the Department of the Army, 19 January 1949, 092 (TS), RG 319.

15. MacArthur to the Department of the Army, 4 December 1948, 092 (TS), ibid.

16. MacArthur to the Department of the Army, 19 January 1949, 092 (TS), ibid.

17. See, for instance, George and Smoke, *Deterrence in American Foreign Policy*, pp. 145–46.

18. See above, p. 86.

19. Edward A. Kolodziej, *The Uncommon Defense and Congress*, p. 76.

20. Ibid., pp. 91–92.

21. Ibid., p. 91.

22. Ibid., pp. 80–81, 83, 85, 106.

23. Ibid., p. 104.

24. FEC, "Requirements, Means Available, and Procedures Evolved to Accompany CINCFE Missions," 333 Pacific (TS), RG 319.

25. U.S. Congress, House, Armed Services Committee, *Military Establishment Appropriations Bill for 1950*, 4:567.

26. Kolodziej, *Uncommon Defense*, p. 94.

27. Warner Schilling, ed., *Strategy, Politics, and Defense Budgets*, p. 288.

28. Maddocks to Bradley, 23 June 1949, 091 Korea (TS), RG 319; *FR, 1949*, 7:1055; James I. Matray, "The Reluctant Crusade," pp. 463–67.

29. U.S. Congress, House, Foreign Affairs Committee, *Korean Aid*, pp. 120, 137, 163.

30. Ibid., pp. 120, 162, 177, 186.

31. Bolté and Timberman interviews with the author. For a top-secret evaluation of South Korean strength vis-à-vis North Korea that supports the interpretation presented herein, see U.S. Department of the Army, Intelligence Division, *Intelligence Review*, 157 (June 1949):42–46, RG 260.

32. South Korea was estimated to have an army of seventy-two thousand troops, seventeen thousand more than the estimated size of that of North Korea. FEC, *IS*, 15 May, 12 June 1949, RG 260.

33. FEC, *IS*, 9 June 1949, ibid. See also U.S. Department of the Army (Sawyer), *Military Advisers in Korea*, p. 69.

34. U.S. Department of the Army, *Military Advisers*, p. 67.

35. Muccio to Acheson, 11 June 1949, *FR, 1949*, 7:1042; FEC, *IS*, 12, 15 May, 4, 7 June 1949, RG 260; Roberts to Department of the Army, 23 April, 13 May, 11, 18 June 1949, Box C-946, RG 59.

36. Bishop to Butterworth, 24 May 1949, Box C-946, RG 59. The similarity of Bradley's arguments to the Joint Chiefs of 20 June and those of Bishop in the memorandum just cited suggests that the State Department approached the army.

37. In interviews with the author, both Bolté and Timberman emphasized the impact of Johnson's leadership on the atmosphere within the armed services. For the response of the other Joint Chiefs to Bradley's overture on Korea, see memorandum for the army chief of staff, 23 June, 1949, *FR, 1949*, 7:1056–57.

38. Kennan, *Memoirs, 1925–1950*, p. 511.

39. Acheson to Muccio, 9 May 1949, Muccio to Acheson, 11 May 1949, *FR, 1949*, 7:1014, 1018–19.

40. Muccio to Butterworth, 27 August 1949, Box C-946, RG 59.

41. Drumright to Acheson, 13 June 1949, Box 7127, ibid.

42. Memorandum of Conversation, by Butterworth, 2 June 1949, Box C-946, ibid.

43. *FR, 1949*, 7:969–78.

44. "Chronological Summary of United States Military Assistance to the Republic of Korea," n.d., in the possession of John Ohly. In October 1949, Ohly became deputy director of the Military Assistance Program.

45. *DSB*, 20 (19 June 1949):783.

46. Acheson memoranda of conversations, 5, 7, 14 July, 3 August 1949, Box 64, *DA*.

47. *DSB*, 19 (3 October 1949):207.

48. *FR, 1949*, 7:1090–92.

49. FEC, "Requirements, Means Available, and Procedures Evolved to Accompany CINCFE Missions," 333 Pacific (TS), RG 319.

50. U.S. Department of the Army, *Military Advisers*, pp. 46–47.

51. Kolodziej, *Uncommon Defense*, p. 94.

52. See "War Plan Fleetwood," 29 November 1948, 337 (TS), RG 319.

53. On J. Lawton Collins's pride in the readiness of army units and the role played in their continuing fitness by the recent reduction of army occupation duties, see Kolodziej, *Uncommon Defense*, p. 114.

54. Ibid., p. 112.

55. U.S. Department of the Army, *Military Advisers*, p. 46.

56. Nikita Khrushchev, *Khrushchev Remembers*, pp. 367–68. For a detailed analysis of Russia's role in the North Korean attack, see William Stueck, "The Soviet Union and the Origins of the Korean War."

57. *FR, 1949*, 7:1093n.

58. *NYT*, 22 January 1950, Section I, p. 4.

59. *NYT*, 13 January 1950, p. 3.

60. "Statement Before the Korean National Assembly," 19 June 1950, Box 104, Part I, *JFD*.

61. Charles M. Dobbs, "American Foreign Policy, the Cold War, and Korea," p. 237.

62. In an interview with the author, Dean Rusk indicated that the State Department had encouraged MacArthur to take a more active interest in areas of East Asia other than Japan, but frequently to no avail.

63. Paul Nitze interview with the author.

64. Drumright to Acheson, 8 August 1949, Box 7128, RG 59.

65. Muccio to Bond, 12 September 1949, Box 7128, ibid.

66. *NYT*, 13 January 1950, p. 3.

67. *DSB*, 22 (17 April 1950):602.

68. Memorandum by W. G. Hackler, 27 April 1950, *FR, 1950*, 7:48–49. In June, however, the inflationary situation remained "dangerous." See Central Intelligence Agency, "Current Capabilities of the Northern Korean Regime," 19 June 1950, p. 13, RG 260.

69. Democratic People's Republic of Korea, *Facts Tell*.

70. John Muccio interview with the author.

71. U.S. Department of the Army, (Schnabel), *The United States Army in the Korean War*, 3:62–63.

72. FEC, *IS*, 30 December 1949, RG 260.

73. FEC, *IS*, 25 March 1950, ibid.; *MSFE*, pp. 1991–92.

74. U.S. Central Intelligence Agency, "Current Capabilities of the North Korean Regime," 19 June 1950, pp. 11, 13, RG 260.

75. FEC, *IS*, 19 June 1950, ibid.

76. U.S. Department of the Army, *United States Army in the Korean War*, 3:63; *DSB* 22 (26 June 1950):1049.

77. U.S. Department of the Army, *United States Army in the Korean War*, 3:64–65.

78. FEC, *IS*, 24 June 1950, RG 260.

79. Muccio to Ohly, 11 October 1949, in the possession of John Ohly.

80. Minutes of Meeting between Muccio and Ohly, sometime in May 1950, in the possession of John Ohly.

81. Muccio interview with the author; *FR, 1950*, 7:78–81.

82. Muccio interview with the author.

83. *DSB*, 22 (26 June 1950):1049.

84. On Knowland's impressions, see U.S. Congress, Senate, Foreign Relations Committee, *Reviews of the World Situation*, p. 191. On Green's, see Tom Connally, *My Name Is Tom Connally*, p. 345. On Smith's, see his report of 1 December 1949, Box 98, *HAS*.

85. Collins, *War in Peacetime*, p. 42.

86. Roberts to Bolté, 19 August 1949, 091 Korea, RG 319.

87. William Sebald, *With MacArthur in Japan*, p. 182.

88. U.S. Department of the Army, *Military Advisers*, pp. 94–95, 102–3; Muccio to Acheson, 8 November 1949, *FR, 1949*, 7:1094.

89. Military Advisory Group, Korea, "Report on the Situation in Korea for the Period Ending December 31, 1949," 091 Korea (TS), RG 319.

90. Roberts to Bolté, 8 March 1950, ibid.

91. O. H. P. King, *Tail of the Paper Tiger*, pp. 330–31.

92. *NYT*, 26 June 1950, p. 3.

93. William R. Mathews, "Diary: Korea with the John Foster Dulles Mission, June 14 to June 29, 1950," pp. 7–14, William R. Mathews Papers (Dulles File).

94. U.S. Department of the Army, *Military Advisers*, p. 104.

95. Muccio rose to the rank of career minister in 1947.

96. U.S. Department of State, *North Korea: A Case Study in the Techniques of Takeover*, p. 113.

97. On South Korea's success in suppressing guerrillas, see John Merrill, "Internal Warfare in Korea, 1948–1950."

98. U.S. Department of the Army, *Military Advisers*, p. 103.

99. U.S. Congress, House, Foreign Affairs Committee, *Background Information on Korea*, p. 103.

100. Ibid., p. 34; Ohly to Rusk, 11 March 1950, in the possession of John Ohly.

101. Robert Futrell, *The United States Air Force in Korea*, p. 5.

102. On Admiral Sherman's interest in the planes, see Charles Cooke to Forrest Sherman, 14 April 1950, and Sherman to Cooke, 3 May 1950, Box 8, Charles Cooke Papers. On Nationalist pressure in Washington, see Wellington Koo, "Notes of Conversation: Paul Griffith," 3 June 1950, Box 180, Wellington Koo Papers.

103. Memorandum of Conversation, by Niles Bond, 10 May 1950, *FR, 1950*, 7:81.

104. Ibid., p. 83n.

105. General Headquarters, Supreme Commander for the Allied Powers and Far Eastern Command, "General Orientation for the Secretary of Defense and the Chairman of the Joint Chiefs of Staff," 18 June 1950, Selected Records Relating to the Korean War, Box 15, *HST*.

106. Merrill, "Internal Warfare in Korea."

107. Ibid.

108. Robert Simmons, *The Strained Alliance*, pp. 113–16.

## Chapter 6

1. For evidence that North Korea initiated hostilities, see United Nations General Assembly, *Official Records*, 5th Session, Supplement 16, p. 4; Nikita Khrushchev, *Khrushchev Remembers*, pp. 367–70; FEC, "Documentary Evidence of North Korean Aggression," Douglas A. MacArthur Papers. For a debate on the matter, see Karunker Gupta, "How Did the Korean War Begin?" and rebuttals by Chongsik Lee, W. E. Skillend, and Robert Simmons in *China Quarterly*, 14 (April–June 1973):354–68.

2. U.S. Department of the Army (Sawyer), *Military Advisers in Korea*, pp. 114–22.

3. U.S. Department of State, *United States Policy in the Korean Crisis*, p. 1.

4. Glenn D. Paige, *The Korean Decision*; David Detzer, *Thunder of the Captains*; Dean Acheson, *Present at the Creation*, pp. 402–13; Harry S. Truman, *Memoirs*, 2:333–44; J. Lawton Collins, *War in Peacetime*, pp. 1–24.

5. U.S. Congress, Senate, Foreign Relations Committee, *Reviews of the World Situation, 1949–1950*, p. 191; U.S. Congress, Senate, Appropriations Committee, *Appropriations for the Departments of State, Justice, Commerce, and the Judiciary for the Fiscal Year Ending June 30, 1952*, p. 1086.

6. U.S. Department of State, *United States Policy in the Korean Crisis*, p. 15.

7. *NYT*, 26 June 1950, p. 6.

8. Paige, *Korean Decision*, p. 121.

9. Message from General MacArthur, 25 June 1950, Box 71, *GE*.

10. U.S. Department of the Army, *Military Advisers*, p. 123; Paige, *Korean Decision*, p. 123; U.S. Department of State, *United States Policy in the Korean Crisis*, pp. 1–2.

11. Blair House was the temporary residence of the first family while the White House was being repaired.

12. Memorandum of Conversation on the Korean Situation, by Jessup, 25 June 1950, *FR, 1950*, 7:157–58.

13. Ibid., 7:160–61.

14. "Secretary Acheson's Briefing Book: Blair House Meetings," 26 June 1950, Box 71, *GE*.

15. Memorandum of Conversation on the Korean Situation, by Jessup, 26 June 1950, *FR, 1950*, 7:178–80.

16. Ibid., 7:180.

17. Ibid., 7:181, 183.

18. Tom Connally, *My Name Is Tom Connally*, p. 346.

19. Paige, *Korean Decision*, p. 149.

20. Memorandum of Conversation on the Korean Situation, by Jessup, 26 June 1950, *FR, 1950,* 7:182.

21. U.S. Department of the Army (Appleman), *The United States Army in the Korean War,* 1:33.

22. Memorandum of Conversation, by Jessup, 27 June 1950, *FR, 1950,* 7:200–202.

23. *NYT,* 28 June 1950, p. 4.

24. Ibid.

25. *CR,* 96 (27 June 1950):9228–33.

26. *NYT,* 28 June 1950, p. 1.

27. *Christian Science Monitor,* 29 June 1950, p. 4, quoted in Paige, *Korean Decision,* p. 160. For continued expressions of approval on 28 June of the president's actions, see Paige, *Korean Decision,* pp. 212–13, and *DSOD,* 28 June 1950, Box 5, RG 59.

28. *CR,* 96 (28 June 1950):9319–27. Other senators opposing the president on this point included James P. Kem (Republican-Missouri), Arthur V. Watkins (Republican-Utah), and John W. Bricker (Republican-Ohio).

29. Paige, *Korean Decision,* pp. 200–201.

30. *NYT,* 29 June 1950, p. 13.

31. Selden Chapin (Netherlands) to Acheson, Austin (United Nations) to Acheson, 26 June 1950, Loy Henderson (India) to Acheson, Murphy (Belgium) to Acheson, 27 June 1950, Memorandum of Meeting in the Office of Under Secretary of State Webb, 28 June 1950, *FR, 1950,* 7:185, 188–93, 205–8, 213; FEC, *IS,* 28 June 1950, RG 260.

32. *NYT,* 28 June 1950, p. 6.

33. On 30 June, the Egyptian representative announced he would have abstained even had he received instructions because his government viewed the crisis as merely a new development in the East-West conflict. The Indian representative, however, declared that he would have voted for the resolution had his instructions arrived.

34. Allen S. Whiting, *China Crosses the Yalu,* p. 54; Paige, *Korean Decision,* pp. 214–15.

35. *Pravda,* 28 June 1950, p. 1, quoted in Paige, *Korean Decision,* pp. 215–16.

36. *Jen Min Jih Pao,* 29 June 1950, p. 1, quoted in Paige, *Korean Decision,* pp. 210–11.

37. U.S. Department of State, *United States Policy in the Korean Crisis,* p. 64.

38. Acheson, *Present,* p. 412; Paige, *Korean Decision,* p. 248; Minutes of Meeting in the Cabinet Room of the White House, 29 June 1950, p. 5, Box 71, *GE.*

39. Minutes of Meeting in the Cabinet Room of the White House, 29 June 1950, p. 5, Box 71, *GE;* Beverly Smith, "The White House Story: Why We Went to War in Korea," p. 88.

40. U.S. Department of the Army, *United States Army in the Korean War,* 1:21–36; *NYT,* 29 June 1950, p. 1.

41. Paige, *Korean Decision,* p. 224.

42. Truman, *Memoirs,* 2:340–41.

43. Smith, "White House Story," p. 86.

44. Ibid.

45. Ibid.

46. Bolté to Pace, 28 June 1950, 091 Korea (TS), RG 319.

47. U.S. Department of the Army (Schnabel), *United States Army in the Korean War,* 3:79.

48. Timberman interview with the author.

49. Minutes of Meeting in the Cabinet Room of the White House, 29 June 1950, pp. 2–3, 6, Box 71, *GE.*

50. Merchant to Acheson, 29 June 1950, *FR, 1950,* 7:239–40.

51. Truman, *Memoirs,* 2:342; Acheson, *Present,* p. 412.

52. The document is quoted almost verbatim in U.S. Department of the Army, *United States Army in the Korean War,* 3:77–78.

53. *NYT,* 30 June 1950, p. 3.

54. Teleconference with MacArthur, 30 June 1950, pp. 1–2, Box 71, *GE*.

55. Ibid., p. 2; Truman, *Memoirs*, 2:342–43; Smith, "White House Story," p. 88.

56. President's Call to Pace and Call from Louis Johnson, 30 June 1950, Box 71, *GE*.

57. Acheson, *Present*, pp. 412–13; Truman, *Memoirs*, 2:343.

58. Minutes of Meeting in the White House Cabinet Room, 30 June 1950, pp. 1–3, Box 71, *GE*; Paige, *Korean Decision*, p. 269.

59. U.S. Department of State, *United States Policy in the Korean Crisis*, p. 24.

60. Minutes of Meeting in the White House Cabinet Room, 30 June 1950, pp. 6–9, Box 71, *GE*.

61. Ibid.

62. Acheson, *Present*, p. 413.

63. Minutes of Meeting in the White House Cabinet Room, 30 June 1950, pp. 9–10, Box 71, *GE*.

64. Ibid.

65. Gaddis Smith, *Dean Acheson*, pp. 196–97.

66. In other words, if Russia moved into Western Europe or attacked Japan, the United States could respond with an atomic offensive against Russia. If this did not immediately end the aggression, American industrial and manpower resources could be mobilized for an eventual counteroffensive that would devastate Soviet forces.

67. On 13 January 1950, Acheson, testifying before a closed session of the Senate Foreign Relations Committee, said that he did "not believe we would undertake to resist [a North Korean invasion] . . . by force." Scholar Lewis McCarroll Purifoy has argued that this statement indicates that the "Truman administration never had any intention of fighting in Korea." Actually, Acheson's statement was less than categorical, and it suggested that he had not thought much about the matter rather than that he had made a carefully calculated decision. For instance, he assumed that "South Korea could now take care of any trouble that was started by North Korea," but could not handle "any invasion which was either started by the Chinese Communists or powerfully supported by them or by the Soviet Union." What Acheson meant by "powerfully supported" is open to varied interpretations, but it does not appear that he anticipated two conditions that existed at the end of June, namely the obvious inability of the South Koreans to repel a North Korean attack, together with the apparent intention of Peking and Moscow to avoid sending in their own forces. See U.S. Congress, Senate, Foreign Relations Committee, *Reviews of the World Situation*, p. 191, and Lewis McCarroll Purifoy, *Harry Truman's China Policy*, p. 195n.

68. In *"Lessons of the Past"* (pp. 81–83), Ernest R. May develops this point at some length.

69. Rusk, Jessup, and Raymond Thurston interviews with the author. At the time, Thurston was a counselor at the American embassy in Moscow.

70. The indigenous aspects of the crisis were further clouded by the fact that the North Korean attack was not accompanied by major uprisings in the south against established authorities.

71. For contrary arguments, see Stephen Pelz, "When the Kitchen Gets Hot, Pass the Buck," and Purifoy, *Truman's China Policy*, chapter 8. Neither account offers direct evidence that domestic politics played a central role in the Korean intervention.

72. Detzer, *Thunder*, p. 93.

73. In an interview with the author, Collins emphasized MacArthur's assessment as a key to the attitude of the Joint Chiefs.

74. See above, p. 78.

75. See above, p. 75.

76. See above, p. 156.

77. Bolté to Pace, 28 June 1950, 091 Korea (TS), RG 218.

78. Memorandum of Conversation, by Dulles, 1 July 1950, Box 47, *JFD*.

79. See "Doug's Communique," written by an unidentified officer aboard Admiral William Halsey's flagship in the Pacific, in Box 138, President's Secretary's Files, *HST*.

80. David Schonberger's "The General and the Presidency," is suggestive on this point.

81. MacArthur's Briefing of the Huber Subcommittee, 5 September 1949, 091 Formosa (TS), RG 319.

82. William Sebald, *With MacArthur in Japan*, pp. 182–84; William R. Mathews, "Diary: Korea with the John Foster Dulles Mission, June 14 to June 29, 1950," pp. 5–29, William R. Mathews Papers (Dulles File).

83. Marguerite Higgins, *War in Korea*, pp. 33–34; U.S. Department of the Army, *United States Army in the Korean War*, 1:44.

84. Mathews, "Diary," p. 32; Joyce and Gabriel Kolko, *The Limits of Power*, p. 579.

85. U.S. Department of the Army, *United States Army in the Korean War*, 3:139–40.

86. Here "unprovoked" is used in a narrow rather than a broad sense. Certainly much of the Rhee regime's behavior toward the north—the threats of military action and the border raids—were provocative, but so too was much of North Korea's behavior toward the south. South Korean action was not provocative, however, to the degree that it immediately and directly put in jeopardy North Korea's existence.

87. *DSB*, 23 (3 July 1950):5.

88. Smith, *Acheson*, p. 190.

89. *DSB*, 23 (10 July 1950):48.

90. William Stueck, "The Soviet Union and the Origins of the Korean War."

91. Trygve Lie, *In the Cause of Peace*, pp. 331–32.

92. For a popular, but superficial, recent account on this issue, see Arthur M. Schlesinger, Jr., *The Imperial Presidency*, p. 137. He argues that Truman's power to use ground forces in Korea without congressional consent "was far from conclusive."

93. Acheson, *Present*, p. 411.

94. Schlesinger suggests that Truman might have followed President Woodrow Wilson's course in 1914 after the dispatch of American troops to Vera Cruz, Mexico. Wilson, in a resolution he sent to Congress approving the action, said he did "not wish to act in a matter of so grave consequence except in close conference with both Senate and House." He also claimed he could pursue the course already taken without congressional sanction and without exceeding his powers as president. Schlesinger, *Imperial Presidency*, pp. 98, 138. Such an assertion by Truman in 1950, however, would have invited controversy.

95. Paige, *Korean Decision*, p. 141.

96. U.S. Department of the Army, *United States Army in the Korean War*, 3:77n.

97. Minutes of Meeting in the Cabinet Room, 29 June 1950, p. 6, Box 71, *GE*.

98. On the human element in South Korea's continuing resistance to the North Korean advance, see Harold Joyce Noble, *Embassy at War*.

99. U.S. Department of the Navy (Field, Jr.), *History of U.S. Naval Operations: Korea*, pp. 67, 128; U.S. Seventh Fleet, "Korean Conflict, Summary Chronological Report of Operations During the Opening Days of the United Nations Effort to Support the Republic of South Korea Invaded by North Korea and the Chinese Communist Forces," Naval Archives, Washington Navy Yard.

100. FEC, *IS*, 19 June 1950, RG 260; ibid., 23 June 1950; *MSFE*, p. 2621.

101. This thinking was tied to the feeling that the Kremlin had initiated or approved the North Korean attack because it miscalculated the American response. It was hoped the reinforcement of anti-Communist forces in other areas would prevent further miscalculations. John Foster Dulles's argument in May that the United States needed to "take a dramatic and strong stand" regarding Taiwan to demonstrate to enemies of the United States that it was willing to risk war probably took on great significance to State Department officials in the face of the North Korean

attack. Dulles Memorandum on Formosa, 18 May 1950, Box 47, *JFD*. See also above, p. 000. For a suggestive statement by Acheson on the roots of American intervention in the Taiwan straits, see Acheson to Bevin, 10 July 1950, *FR, 1950*, 7:350.

102. George F. Kennan, *Memoirs, 1925–1950*, p. 513.

103. Memorandum of Conversation, by Jessup, 26 June 1950, *FR, 1950*, 7:180.

104. U.S. Department of State, *United States Policy in the Korean Crisis*, p. 18.

105. Acheson, *Present*, p. 148; Shiv Dayal, *India's Role in the Korean Question*, pp. 76–77; Ross N. Berkes and Mohinder S. Bedi, *The Diplomacy of India*, pp. 108–9; J. C. Kundra, *Indian Foreign Policy, 1947–1954*, p. 130.

106. Bevin to Franks, 7 July 1950, *FR, 1950*, 7:329–30; Acheson, *Present*, p. 418.

107. Acheson, *Present*, p. 418; Acheson to Franks, 10 July 1950, *FR, 1950*, 7:347–51.

108. Acheson, *Present*, p. 419.

109. Kirk to Acheson, 10 July 1950, *FR, 1950*, 7:340.

110. K. M. Panikkar, *In Two Chinas*, p. 103.

111. Kennan, *Memoirs, 1925–1950*, pp. 518–19; Acheson, *Present*, p. 419.

112. McGhee to Acheson, 13 July 1950, Henderson to Acheson, 13 July 1950, *FR, 1950*, 7:372–73, 376–77.

113. Acheson, *Present*, pp. 419–20.

114. Ibid., p. 420; *DSB*, 23 (31 July 1950):170–71.

115. For evidence that the American response did irritate Nehru, see Acheson, *Present*, p. 420.

116. From the moment Truman announced American intervention in the straits of Taiwan, Peking emphasized that move over the Korean matter. The action regarding Taiwan was labeled "armed aggression against the territory of China in total violation of the United Nations charter." *People's China*, 16 July 1950, p. 4, quoted in Whiting, *China Crosses the Yalu*, p. 58.

117. Bacon to Freeman, 29 June 1950, Acheson to Austin, 3 July 1950, *FR, 1950*, 2:246–47.

118. Kennan, *Memoirs, 1925–1950*, pp. 518–20.

119. Ibid., pp. 520–23. On 4 May 1950, President Truman stated at a news conference that the defense budget would be reduced in the next fiscal year. *NYT*, 5 May 1950, p. 1.

120. Acheson, *Present*, p. 421.

121. Memorandum of Conversation, by James N. Hyde, 11 August 1950, *FR, 1950*, 7:555–56.

122. United Nations Security Council, *Official Records*, Fifth Year, 487th meeting, 14 August 1950, p. 9.

123. *NYT*, 15 August 1950, p. 1; 16 August 1950, pp. 1, 5; 19 August 1950, p. 3; 20 August 1950, pp. 1, 20; 21 August 1950, pp. 1, 5; 22 August 1950, p. 1; 24 August 1950, p. 5.

124. *DSB*, 23 (10 July 1950):46.

125. John Allison to Rusk, 13 July 1950, *FR, 1950*, 7:373.

126. Summation of Remarks by General MacArthur, 13 July 1950, 333 Pacific, RG 319.

127. The memorandum is summarized by John Allison in his memorandum to Rusk of 15 July, *FR, 1950*, 7:393.

128. Raymond Thurston interview with the author. Allison had been a class two officer since May 1947. Unlike O. Edmund Clubb, however, in May 1950 he was not promoted. See U.S. Department of State, *Biographic Register, 1950*. On Allison's career, see John M. Allison, *Ambassador from the Prairie*.

129. Allison to Rusk, 15 July 1950, *FR, 1950*, 7:393–95.

130. Memorandum by James S. Loy, Jr., to the National Security Council, 17 July 1950, ibid., 7:410.

131. Acheson, *Present*, p. 451.

132. Allison to Nitze, 24 July 1950, *FR, 1950*, 7:460–61.

133. Draft Memorandum by the Policy Planning Staff, 22 July 1950, ibid., 7:452.

134. Draft Memorandum by the Policy Planning Staff, 25 July 1950, ibid., 7:472.

135. For the most detailed expression of Kennan's views on the matter of crossing the thirty-eighth parallel, see Kennan to Acheson, 21 August 1950, ibid., 7:623–28.

136. Draft Memorandum Prepared in the Department of Defense, 31 July 1950, ibid., 7:503–4.

137. Draft Memorandum Prepared by the Policy Planning Staff, 25 July 1950, Draft Memorandum Prepared in the Department of Defense, 31 July 1950, ibid., 7:471, 506–7.

138. Draft Memorandum Prepared by the Policy Planning Staff, 25 July 1950, ibid., 7:471–72. This consideration may have made the Policy Planning Staff less aggressive than it otherwise might have been in the intradepartmental rift.

139. Draft Memorandum Prepared in the Department of Defense, 31 July 1950, ibid., 7:506.

140. Ibid., 7:508.

141. Collins, *War in Peacetime*, p. 82.

142. General Thomas Timberman interview with the author.

143. Collins, *War in Peacetime*, pp. 82–83; Draft Memorandum Prepared in the Department of Defense, 31 July 1950, *FR, 1950*, 7:503.

144. *MSFE*, pp. 3479–80.

145. *DSB*, 23 (28 August 1950):330–31.

146. *NYT*, 18 August 1950, p. 1.

147. Acheson, *Present*, p. 454.

148. *DSB*, 23 (9 September 1950):375.

149. *DSB*, 23 (11 September 1950):407.

150. Quoted in Whiting, *China Crosses the Yalu*, p. 79.

151. United Nations Security Council, *Official Records*, 483d meeting, 4 August 1950; *Jen Min Jih Pao*, 7 August 1950, cited in Whiting, *China Crosses the Yalu*, p. 74.

152. Whiting, *China Crosses the Yalu*, pp. 74–75.

153. United Nations Security Council, *Official Records*, 489th meeting, 22 August 1950.

154. *World Culture*, 26 August 1950, quoted in Whiting, *China Crosses the Yalu*, pp. 84–85.

155. Whiting, *China Crosses the Yalu*, p. 75.

156. O. Edmund Clubb, then at the head of the China desk, did write three memoranda between July and October 1950 warning his superiors of a possible Chinese Communist entry into the Korean War. See O. Edmund Clubb, *The Witness and I*, pp. 88–89, and E. J. Kahn, Jr., *The China Hands*, p. 226.

157. Memorandum of Conversation, by Jessup, 26 June 1950, *FR, 1950*, 7:181.

158. *NYT*, 1 August 1950, p. 4.

159. *NYT*, 2 August 1950, p. 6.

160. U.S. Department of the Army, *United States Army in the Korean War*, 3:368–69; Truman, *Memoirs*, 2:354.

161. *NYT*, 11 August 1950, p. 11.

162. See, for instance, Minutes of Meeting in Paris with British and French Diplomats, 3 August 1950, *FR, 1950*, 6:409–10.

163. *Jen Min Jih Pao*, 5 August 1950, quoted in Whiting, *China Crosses the Yalu*, p. 82.

164. Acheson, *Present*, p. 422.

165. Courtney Whitney, *MacArthur*, pp. 373–74; Sebald to Acheson, 3 August 1950, *FR, 1950*, 6:415.

166. Strong to Acheson, 3 August 1950, *FR, 1950*, 6:410–12.

167. Joint Chiefs of Staff to MacArthur, 4 August 1950, 381 Formosa, RG 218.

168. Strong to Acheson, 14 July 1950, Kennan to Acheson, 17 July 1950, Joint Chiefs to Johnson, 28 July 1950, *FR, 1950*, 6:379–81, 395.

169. On Chinese Communist troop movements in July, see Whiting, *China Crosses the Yalu*, pp. 64–65.

170. FEC, *IS*, 5 July 1950, RG 260.

171. *NYT*, 23 July 1950, p. 12.

172. *NYT*, 20 July 1950, Section IV, p. 4; 2 August 1950, p. 6.

173. Truman, *Memoirs*, 2:397.

174. The survey group, in fact, followed MacArthur to the island, arriving on 5 August. See Karl Lott Rankin, *China Assignment*, pp. 50–51. In July, Rankin was appointed American minister and chargé d'affaires in Taipei. Although John Leighton Stuart technically remained the U.S. ambassador to China, he had not been in his post since the previous August. Before Rankin's appointment, Robert Strong, the first secretary of the embassy, was the top State Department official stationed on Taiwan.

175. Joint Chiefs to MacArthur, 29 July 1950, 381 Formosa, RG 218.

176. Extracts from Harriman Memorandum of Conversation with MacArthur, 6, 8 August, 1950, *FR, 1950*, 6:427–30.

177. Whitney, *MacArthur*, p. 375; *Time*, 56 (21 August 1950):9.

178. Memorandum on Formosa, by MacArthur, 14 June 1950, *FR, 1950*, 7:161–65.

179. *MSFE*, p. 3475.

180. *DSB*, 23 (4 September 1950):396. The "other territories" referred to here probably were the Pescadores Islands and other offshore islands still held by Chiang. Whiting, *China Crosses the Yalu*, p. 85.

181. *MSFE*, p. 3475.

182. *MSFE*, p. 3467.

183. *NYT*, 7 August 1950, p. 1; *NYT*, 14 August 1950, p. 5; Robert Taft to Bernard W. DeVander, 11 August 1950, Box 822, Robert A. Taft Papers. On Republican use of the Taiwan issue during the summer of 1950, see Ronald J. Caridi, *The Korean War and American Politics*, pp. 58–64.

184. On British concern over American policy regarding Taiwan, see *NYT*, 12 August 1950, p. 3, and 18 August 1950, p. 10.

185. Memorandum for Record of Events on 26 August 1950, *FR, 1950*, 6:453–54.

186. *MSFE*, pp. 2587, 3665; Truman, *Memoirs*, 2:405.

187. Truman, *Memoirs*, 2:405.

188. The note is printed in *MSFE*, p. 3480.

189. *U.S. News and World Report* 29 (1 September 1950):32–34.

190. Annex to Memorandum for Record of Events on 26 August 1950, *FR, 1950*, 6:455–60.

191. *NYT*, 1 September 1950, p. 4.

192. *NYT*, 2 September 1950, p. 4.

193. *Time* 56 (4 September 1950):12.

194. For a report of Chinese Communist troop movements to Manchuria, see FEC, *IS*, 26 August 1950, RG 260.

195. Notes Dictated by Charles Ross to George Elsey, 12 September 1950, Box 72, *GE*; Memorandum of Conversation with the President, by Elsey, 16 September 1950, Box 72, *GE*.

196. Hanson Baldwin, the *New York Times* writer on military affairs, wrote on 1 September that Matthews's speech had been approved by Johnson as "a trial balloon." The secretary of defense, Baldwin claimed, "has been selling the same doctrine of preventive war in private conversations around Washington." *NYT*, 1 September 1950, p. 22.

197. *NYT*, 30 August 1950, p. 5.

198. *NYT*, 30 September 1950, p. 5.

199. Caridi, *The Korean War and American Politics*, p. 59.

200. *CR* 96 (28 August 1950):13575.

201. Smith to Dulles, 6 September 1950, Box 142, *JFD*.

202. U.S. Department of State, Office of Public Affairs, "Monthly Survey of American Opinion," August 1950, Box 60, *GE*.

203. Ibid.

204. Ibid., October 1950.

205. On the general confidence within the administration, see Alonzo L. Hamby, *Beyond the New Deal*, p. 420.

206. *NYT*, 25 August 1950, p. 1.

207. U.S. Department of State, Office of Public Affairs, "Monthly Survey of American Opinion," August, October 1950, Box 60, *GE*.

208. *NYT*, 2 June 1950, p. 1.

209. H. Bradford Westerfield, *Foreign Policy and Party Politics*, p. 380.

210. Ibid., pp. 380–81.

211. Alan D. Harper, *The Politics of Loyalty*, pp. 135–40; Robert Griffith, *The Politics of Fear*, pp. 109–14.

212. *NYT*, 18 July 1950, p. 1; 21 July 1950, pp. 1, 8.

213. Harper, *Politics of Loyalty*, pp. 154–62.

214. Griffith, *Politics of Fear*, pp. 122–31.

215. *FR, 1950*, 7:712–21.

216. United States Delegation Minutes: SFM Pre 4, Draft Paper Prepared for Preliminary Tripartite Conversations of September Foreign Ministers Meeting, 31 August 1950, ibid., 7:667–69, 679–83.

217. Draft Position Paper for Meeting of Foreign Ministers in September, ibid., 7:656.

218. Draft Memorandum Prepared in the Department of State, 31 August 1950, ibid., 7:672.

219. Report by the National Security Council to the President, 9 September 1950, ibid., 7:716.

220. Ibid., 7:714.

221. Ibid., 7:714–15.

222. Draft Report by the National Security Council on United States Courses of Action with Respect to Korea, 1 September 1950, *FR, 1950*, 7:687–88.

223. This point is further demonstrated in the State-Defense conflict between mid-August and mid-September over the bombing of Rashin. See Acheson to Truman, 11 September 1950, ibid., 7:721–22. For evidence of a distaste among military leaders as far back as July for the prospect of halting American forces at the narrow neck, see Draft Memorandum Prepared in the Department of Defense, 31 July 1950, ibid., 7:503.

224. Report by the National Security Council to the President, 9 September 1950, ibid., 7:714.

225. For Kennan's view, see Kennan to Acheson, 21 August 1950, ibid., 7:627.

226. Draft Memorandum Prepared by the Policy Planning Staff, 21 August 1950, ibid., 7:615–16.

227. Emmerson to Rusk, 22 August 1950, ibid., 7:616n.

228. Memorandum of Conversation, by Emmons, 8 September 1950, ibid., 7:709.

229. This judgment is based on two foundations: first, the style of the Rusk memorandum ("It is believed . . ." "It is suggested . . .") indicates that the views of others were being taken into account; second, Rusk was a cautious man. He undoubtedly knew of the close relationship between Acheson and Nitze and of Nitze's high regard for Davies. Thus, Rusk probably would have regarded independent action on his part in this case as endangering his own position with the secretary of state. This view of the personalities involved is based on interviews with Nitze, Philip Jessup, Niles Bond, and Rusk.

230. United States Delegation Minutes of 4th Meeting of Foreign Ministers of France, the United Kingdom, and the United States, 14 September 1950, *FR, 1950*, 6:500–501.

231. Joint Chiefs to Johnson, 8 September 1950, ibid., 6:491.

## Chapter 7

1. D. D. Dickson to Bolté, 17 July 1950, 091 Korea, RG 319; Summation of Remarks of MacArthur, 13 July 1950, ibid.

2. U.S. Department of the Army (Schnabel), *United States Army in the Korean War*, 3:145–47. See also J. Lawton Collins, *War in Peacetime*, pp. 118–20.

3. U.S. Department of the Army, *United States Army in the Korean War*, 3:146.

4. For background information on this trip, see ibid., pp. 148–49; Collins, *War in Peacetime*, pp. 108, 116, 121; *MSFE*, pp. 1295, 2618.

5. Collins, *War in Peacetime*, p. 126.

6. Major General Thomas S. Timberman interview with the author.

7. Joint Chiefs to MacArthur, 28 August 1950, 383.21 Korea, RG 218.

8. Collins, *War in Peacetime*, p. 120. On the depletion of army reserve forces in the United States in the summer of 1950, see ibid., pp. 80–81, and U.S. Department of the Army, *United States Army in the Korean War*, 3:89–90, 104–5, 118–20, 123.

9. Collins, *War in Peacetime*, p. 125.

10. Ibid., p. 126.

11. Ibid., pp. 127–28; U.S. Department of the Army, *United States Army in the Korean War*, 3:152–53.

12. U.S. Department of the Army, *United States Army in the Korean War*, 3:152–53.

13. MacArthur to the Joint Chiefs, 8 September 1950, 383.21 Korea, RG 218.

14. *NYT*, 21 September 1950, pp. 6–7.

15. *NYT*, 22 September 1950, pp. 1, 8.

16. Austin to Acheson, 29 September 1950, *FR, 1950*, 7:826–28.

17. United Nations General Assembly, *Official Records*, 5th Session, 352nd Meeting (4 October 1950), pp. 48–49, 55–56.

18. John C. Ross to Rusk, 5, 6, 7 October 1950, *FR, 1950*, 7:878–80, 897, 907–10.

19. Ross to Rusk, 10 October 1950, ibid., 7:922.

20. Minutes of the Sixth Meeting of the U.S. Delegation to the United Nations General Assembly, 25 September 1950, ibid., pp. 769–72; Minutes of the Ninth Meeting of the U.S. Delegation to the United Nations General Assembly, 28 September 1950, ibid., 7:801, 803–4.

21. *FR, 1950*, 7:698, 724–25.

22. Ibid., 7:765n.

23. Ibid., 7:563; FEC, *IS*, 26 August 1950, RG 260.

24. *FR, 1950*, 7:742.

25. Ibid., 7:765, 768.

26. *DSB*, 23:(18 September 1950):460–64.

27. FEC, *IS*, 26 August 1950, RG 260.

28. Memorandum of Conversation, by Merchant, 27 September 1950, *FR, 1950*, 7:794.

29. Kirk to Acheson, 29 September 1950, ibid., 7:821–22.

30. Chapin to Acheson, 3 October 1950, ibid., 7:858.

31. Wilkinson to Acheson, 2 October 1950, ibid., 7:852.

32. Merchant to Rusk, 3 October 1950, ibid., 7:848.

33. Ibid.

34. Johnson to Rusk, 3 October 1950, *FR, 1950*, 7:849.

35. Clubb to Merchant, 4 October 1950, ibid., 7:864–66.

36. Memorandum of Conversation, by Allison, 4 October 1950, ibid., 7:868–69.

37. Webb to the United States Mission at the United Nations, 26 September 1950, ibid., 7:781–82, 793n.

38. U.S. Department of State, Office of Public Opinion Studies, "Fortnightly Survey of American Opinion on International Affairs," September, October 1950, RG 59.

39. It might be argued that a direct threat in public of Chinese Communist intervention would have led to a halt of American forces. This is doubtful, unless the threat came well before October. By then, the momentum, combined with the antagonism toward and contempt for Communist China among American officials, were such as to require more concrete evidence of Peking's intentions. A threat from Moscow, however, probably would have been taken more seriously, first because Russia was militarily stronger than China, and second because a Soviet-American confrontation in Korea was likely to escalate into a similar collision in Europe.

40. For an analysis of possible Soviet calculations in September, see Adam Ulam, *Expansion and Coexistence*, pp. 508–11 and 527–31. Ulam argues that the Soviet resolution of 2 October was not aimed toward achieving a settlement in Korea because it called for an immediate withdrawal of foreign forces from the peninsula. Such a proposal, he observes, was obviously unacceptable to the United States. This is correct, but the Russians did show a willingness to negotiate on the differences between their resolution and that of Great Britain and to permit nationwide supervision of elections by representatives of the United Nations.

41. Nikita Khrushchev, *Khrushchev Remembers*, pp. 367–70.

42. For instance, in February 1950 a national survey was taken on the question of whether or not to create a hydrogen bomb. Seventy-seven percent of those polled responded in the affirmative, and only 17 percent answered in the negative. But 48 percent believed the United States should try again to work out an agreement with Russia to control the atomic bomb before an attempt was made to make a hydrogen bomb. Forty-five percent disagreed. Only 11 percent thought negotiations with the Russians would be successful. Seventy percent thought they would be unsuccessful. U.S. Department of State, Office of Public Opinion Studies, "Fortnightly Survey of American Opinion on International Affairs," February 1950, RG 59.

43. Ibid., October 1950.

44. Ulam, *Expansion and Coexistence*, p. 510.

45. Holmes to Acheson, 4 October 1950, *FR, 1950*, 7:867; Memorandum of Conversation, by Allison, 4 October 1950, ibid., 7:868–69; Memorandum of Conversation, by Rusk, 6 October 1950, ibid., 7:893–94; Lord Tedder to Bradley, 5 October 1950, 383.21 Korea, RG 218.

46. Trygve Lie, *In the Cause of Peace*, pp. 344–45.

47. Austin's arguments are printed in United Nations, General Assembly, *Official Records*, First Committee, 350th meeting (3 October 1950), p. 55.

48. Ibid.

49. Ibid., pp. 55–56.

50. *NYT*, 5 October 1950, p. 1.

51. For documents on Indian and American exchanges regarding the Tibetan matter, see *FR, 1950*, 6:531–32, 545–51, 583–84. On 7 October, Communist China invaded Tibet.

52. This comparison of Rusk and Butterworth is based primarily on interviews with Rusk, Butterworth, Clubb, Niles Bond, and General Timberman, but also on Clubb, *The Witness and I*, pp. 87–88, and George F. Kennan, *Memoirs, 1925–1950*, p. 152.

53. See above, pp. 219–20.

54. *FR, 1950*, 7:781.

55. Generals Matthew Ridgway and J. Lawton Collins interviews with the author.

56. Nitze interview with the author.

57. Ibid.

58. Joint Chiefs to MacArthur, 9 October 1950, *FR, 1950*, 7:915.

59. U.S. Department of the Army, *United States Army in the Korean War*, 3:201.

60. FEC, *IS*, 14 October 1950, RG 260.

61. *NYT*, 13 October 1950, p. 1.

62. *NYT*, 22 October 1950, p. 1. See also U.S. Department of the Army, *United States Army in the Korean War*, 3:219–21.

63. *NYT*, 11 October 1950, p. 1.

64. *NYT*, 20 October 1950, p. 1.

65. Dean Acheson, *Present at the Creation*, p. 456.

66. Oral History, Charles Murphy. See also John Edward Wiltz, "Truman and MacArthur," p. 174.

67. Substance of Statements Made at Wake Island Conference on 15 October 1950, *FR, 1950*, 7:948–60.

68. Truman, *Memoirs*, 2:416.

69. Merle Miller, *Plain Speaking*, p. 313.

70. Acheson, *Present*, p. 457.

71. Collins, *War in Peacetime*, p. 177; U.S. Department of the Army, *United States Army in the Korean War*, 3:218.

72. U.S. Department of the Army, *United States Army in the Korean War*, 3:218.

73. Marshall to MacArthur, 29 September 1950, *FR, 1950*, 7:826.

74. Collins, *War in Peacetime*, p. 180.

75. *NYT*, 25 October 1950, p. 1.

76. *NYT*, 28 October 1950, p. 1.

77. Substance of Statements Made at Wake Island Conference on 15 October 1950, *FR, 1950*, 7:959.

78. Generals Collins and Ridgway interviews with the author.

79. David Rees, *Korea*, p. 96.

80. Collins, *War in Peacetime*, p. 141.

81. U.S. Department of the Army (Appleman), *The United States Army in the Korean War*, 1:675–708.

82. FEC, *IS*, 28 October 1950, RG 260.

83. MacArthur estimated at Wake that there were 300,000 troops in Manchuria, 100,000 to 125,000 along the Yalu, only 50,000 to 60,000 of which could be moved into Korea.

84. Quoted in U.S. Department of the Army, *United States Army in the Korean War*, 3:233–34.

85. Major General C. V. R. Schuyler to Major General Robinson E. Duff, 31 October 1950, quoted in ibid., 3:234.

86. U.S. Department of the Army, *United States Army in the Korean War*, 3:234.

87. Ibid., 3:237–39.

88. Clubb to Rusk, 1 November 1950, *FR, 1950*, 7:1023–25.

89. Barrett to Rusk, 3 November 1950, ibid., 7:1030.

90. Wilkinson to Acheson, 3 November 1950, ibid., 7:1034–35.

91. *FR, 1950*, 7:1058n.

92. Draft Memorandum by Davies, Clubb to Rusk, 7 November 1950, *FR, 1950*, 7:1078–93.

93. Draft Memorandum by Davies, 7 November 1950, ibid., 7:1079.

94. Clubb to Rusk, 7 November 1950, ibid., 7:1090.

95. Ibid., 7:1091.

96. Ibid., 7:1088–89.

97. Memorandum by the Central Intelligence Agency, 8 November 1950, *FR, 1950*, 7:1103.

98. Ibid., 7:1102.

99. Joint Chiefs to Marshall, 9 November 1950, *FR, 1950*, 7:1117–21.

100. Memorandum of Conversation, by Jessup, 21 November 1950, ibid., 7:1205; Acheson, *Present*, p. 467.

101. MacArthur to the Joint Chiefs, 9 November 1950, *FR, 1950*, 7:1108.

102. Ibid., 7:1110.

103. Truman, *Memoirs*, 2:379.

104. MacArthur's most recent biographer, William Manchester, is correct on this point, but not on much else regarding the November crisis. See Manchester, *American Caesar*, pp. 590–610.

105. Edward Barrett to F. H. Russell, 13 November 1950, Box 92, *GE*.

106. Acheson, *Present*, p. 468.

107. Austin to Acheson, 11 October 1950, *FR, 1950*, 6:528.

108. Memorandum of Conversation, by Allison, ibid., 6:534–36.

109. *FR, 1950*, 6:573n. The vote was 53 to 0 with 5 abstentions.

110. Memorandum of Conversation, by Rusk, 13 November 1950, *FR, 1950*, 7:1141–42. See also *FR, 1950*, 7:1124n.

111. Henderson to Acheson, 16 November 1950, ibid., 7:1167–68.

112. Emmerson to Rusk, 20 November 1950, ibid., 7:1197–98.

113. *DSB*, 23 (27 November, 4 December 1950):853, 889.

114. U.S. General Services Administration, *Public Papers of the Presidents: Harry S. Truman, 1950*, p. 711.

115. Chapin to Acheson, Austin to Acheson, 14 November 1950, *FR, 1950,*
7 : 1151, 1156–57; Stanley Woodward to Acheson, 15 November 1950, ibid., 7 : 1159–
60; Memorandum of Conversation, by Johnson, 16 November 1950, ibid., 7 : 1161–
62.

116. *FR, 1950,* 7 : 1127.

117. British Embassy to the Department of State, 13 November 1950, ibid.,
7 : 1138–40; Memorandum of Conversation, by Johnson, 16 November 1950, ibid.,
7 : 1161–62.

118. David M. Key to Acheson, 14 November 1950, ibid., p. 1147; Chapin to
Acheson, 14 November 1950, ibid., pp. 1151–53.

119. FEC, *IS,* 15 November 1950, RG 260; U.S. Department of the Army, *United
States Army in the Korean War,* 3 : 263–64.

120. Memorandum by Davies, 17 November 1950, *FR, 1950,* 7 : 1181–83.

121. Bolté to Collins, 20 November 1950, RG 218.

122. Memorandum of Conversation, by Jessup, 21 November 1950, *FR, 1950,*
7 : 1204–8.

123. Collins to MacArthur, 24 November 1950, ibid., 7 : 1222–24.

124. MacArthur to the Joint Chiefs, 25 November 1950, ibid., 7 : 1231–33.

125. On 17 November, for instance, MacArthur told Muccio that the Chinese had
at most thirty thousand soldiers in Korea. Memorandum of Conversation, by Muccio, 17 November 1950, ibid., 7 : 1174–75.

126. Bolté interview with the author.

127. Bolté to Collins, 20 November 1950, RG 218.


## Conclusion

1. Memorandum of Conversation, by Jessup, 3 December 1950, *FR, 1950,* 7 : 1325,
1328.

2. Robert R. Simmons, *The Strained Alliance;* Raymond Aron, *The Imperial Republic,* pp. 67–68.

3. United Nations Delegation, Minutes of the First Meeting of President Truman
and Prime Minister Atlee, 4 December 1950, *FR, 1950,* 7 : 1367.

4. For a retrospective view of the Communists during 1946, see Marshall's comments of 4 December 1950 in ibid., 7 : 1369.

5. United States Delegation, Minutes of the Second Meeting of President Truman
and Prime Minister Atlee, 5 December 1950, ibid., 7 : 1402.

6. For a revealing discussion of the international situation by Acheson, see Memorandum of Conversation, by Acheson, 14 August 1950, Box 65, *DA.*

7. On the domestic political climate, see ibid.

8. On Marshall's fear of the impact of an end to the war on American defense
policy, see interview with Frank Pace, Harry S. Truman Library, Independence, Mo.

# Bibliography

## MANUSCRIPT SOURCES

ANN ARBOR, MICH.
Bently Historical Library, University of Michigan.
  Arthur H. Vandenberg Papers.
ATHENS, GA.
Richard B. Russell Library.
  Richard B. Russell Papers.
CARLISLE, PA.
Army War College.
  Charles L. Bolté Papers.
  Omar N. Bradley Papers.
  Matthew B. Ridgway Papers.
COLUMBUS, OHIO.
Ohio Historical Society.
  John Vorys Papers.
HENNIKER, N.H.
New England College Library.
  Styles Bridges Papers.
INDEPENDENCE, MO.
Harry S. Truman Library.
  Dean G. Acheson Papers.
  Eben A. Ayers Papers.
  Clark M. Clifford Papers.
  Democratic National Committee Papers.
  George M. Elsey Papers.
  Paul G. Hoffman Papers.
  Francis P. Matthews Papers.
  John F. Melby Papers.
  Richard E. Neustadt Papers.
  Frank Pace Papers.
  Theodore M. Tannenwald Papers.
  Harry S. Truman Papers.
  James E. Webb Papers.
NEW YORK, N.Y.
Nicholas M. Butler Library, Columbia University.
  Wellington Koo Papers.
NORFOLK, VA.
Douglas A. MacArthur Memorial Library.
  Douglas A. MacArthur Papers.
PHILADELPHIA, PA.
University of Pennsylvania Library.
  William R. Mathews Papers.
PRINCETON, N.J.
Princeton University Libraries.
  John Foster Dulles Papers.
  James Forrestal Papers.
  George F. Kennan Papers.
  Livingston Merchant Papers.
  H. Alexander Smith Papers.
  Whiting Willauer Papers.

STANFORD, CALIF.
Hoover Institution of War, Revolution, and Peace.
  Joseph W. Ballantine Papers.
  David D. Barrett Papers.
  Alonzo Bland Calder Papers.
  Charles M. Cooke Papers.
  Eugene H. Dooman Papers.
  Paul W. Frillman Papers.
  M. Preston Goodfellow Papers.
  Randall Gould Papers.
  Robert Allen Griffin Papers.
  Maxwell W. Hamilton Papers.
  Stanley K. Hornbeck Papers.
  Joseph E. Jacobs Papers.
  Roger D. Lapham Papers.
  Milton E. Miles Papers.
  L. B. Moody Papers.
  Ernest B. Price Papers.
  Hubert G. Schenck Papers.
  Bruce M. Smith Papers.
  T. V. Soong Papers.
  Oliver J. Todd Papers.
  United States Mediation in China Collection.
  Ivan D. Yeaton Papers.
  Arthur N. Young Papers.
SUITLAND, MD.
Federal Records Center.
  Record Group 260, "Records of the Occupation of Japan."
  Record Group 332, "Records of the U.S. Theaters of War, World War II."
WASHINGTON, D.C.
Library of Congress.
  Joseph and Stewart Alsop Papers.
  Claire Lee Chennault Papers (on microfilm).
  Tom Connally Papers.
  Theodore F. Green Papers.
  Philip C. Jessup Papers.
  Robert P. Patterson Papers.
  Carl Spaatz Papers.
  Robert A. Taft Papers.
National Archives.
  Record Group 46, "Records of the Foreign Relations Committee of the United States Senate."
  Record Group 51, "Records of the Bureau of the Budget, 1947–49."
  Record Group 59, "Records of the Department of State, 1946–49."
  Record Group 94, "Records of the Adjutant General's Office."
  Record Group 218, "Records of the Plans and Operations Division, United States Army, 1946–49."
  Record Group 319, "Records of the Joint Chiefs of Staff."
  Record Group 335, "Records of the Office of the Secretary of the Army."
  Record Group 428, "General Records of the Department of the Navy, 1947–   ."
Naval Archives, Washington Navy Yard.
  Oscar C. Badger Papers.
  William D. Leahy Papers.
  Central Security-Classified Records of the Offices of the Secretary of the Navy/Chief of Naval Operations.
  Navy Plans Division Files.

## UNITED STATES GOVERNMENT PUBLICATIONS

U.S. Congress. *Conference Report 1655: Foreign Assistance Act of 1948.* 80th Cong., 2d sess., 2 April 1948.
———. *Congressional Record.* 1947–50.
———. *Substance of Statements Made at Wake Island Conference on October 15, 1950, Compiled from Notes Kept by the Conferees from Washington.* 1951.
———. House. Appropriations Committee. *Third Supplemental Appropriations Bill for 1948.* 80th Cong., 1st sess., 4 December 1947.
———. House. Armed Services Committee. *Military Establishment Appropriations Bill for 1950.* 4 vols. 81st Cong., 1st sess., 1949.
———. House. Armed Services Committee. *United States–Vietnam Relations, 1945–1967.* Vol. 8. 1971.
———. House. Foreign Affairs Committee. *Assistance to Greece and Turkey. Hearings on S. 938.* 80th Cong., 1st sess., 24–31 March 1947.
———. House. Foreign Affairs Committee. *Background Information on Korea.* 81st Cong., 2d sess., 1950.
———. House. Foreign Affairs Committee. *Korean Aid. Hearings on S. 938.* 81st Cong., 1st sess., 8–23 June 1949.
———. House. Foreign Affairs Committee. *Military Assistance Act of 1949.* 81st Cong., 1st sess., 1949.
———. House. Foreign Affairs Committee. *United States Foreign Policy for a Postwar Recovery Program. Hearings on H.R. 4579 and 4840.* 80th Cong., 2d sess., 17 December 1947–10 March 1948.
———. Senate. Appropriations Committee. *Appropriations for the Departments of State, Justice, Commerce, and the Judiciary for the Fiscal Year Ending June 30, 1952.* 82d Cong., 1st sess., 28 February 1951–6 June 1951.
———. Senate. Appropriations Committee. *Military Establishment Appropriations Bill for 1948.* 80th Cong., 1st sess., 17 February–29 April 1947.
———. Senate. Appropriations Committee. *Third Supplemental Appropriations Bill for 1948. Hearings on H.R. 4748.* 80th Cong., 1st sess., 17 December 1947.
———. Senate. Foreign Relations Committee. *Economic Assistance to China and Korea: 1949–1950. Hearings held in Executive Session on S. 2319 and S. 2845.* 81st Cong., 11 March 1949–31 January 1950. Historical Series, 1974.
———. Senate. Foreign Relations Committee. *Foreign Relief Assistance Act of 1948.* 80th Cong., 2d sess., 9 February–7 April 1948. Historical Series, 1973.
———. Senate. Foreign Relations Committee. *Interim Aid for Europe.* 81st Cong., 1st sess., 10–14 November 1947.
———. Senate. Foreign Relations Committee. *Nomination of Philip C. Jessup.* 81st Cong., 1st sess., 27 September–18 October 1951.
———. Senate. Foreign Relations Committee. *Reviews of the World Situation.* 81st Cong., 1st and 2d sess., 19 May 1949–22 December 1950. Historical Series, 1974.
———. Senate. Foreign Relations Committee. *Senate Report 1026: Aid to China.* 80th Cong., 2d sess., 25 March 1948.
———. Senate. Foreign Relations Committee. *State Department Employee Loyalty Investigation.* 81st Cong., 2d sess., 8 March–28 June 1950.
———. Senate. Foreign Relations Committee. *The United States and Communist China in 1949 and 1950: The Question of Rapprochement and Recognition.* 93d Cong., 1st sess., 1973.
———. Senate. Foreign Relations and Armed Services Committees. *Military Assistance Program. Hearings on S. 2388.* 81st Cong., 1st sess., 8–19 August 1949.
———. Senate. Foreign Relations and Armed Services Committees. *Military Situation in the Far East.* 82d Cong., 1st sess., 3–31 May 1951.
———. Senate. Judiciary Committee. *Institute of Pacific Relations.* 82d Cong., 1st and 2d sess., 25 July–7 August 1952.
———. Senate. Judiciary Committee. *Morgenthau Diary.* Vol. 2. 1965.
U.S. Department of the Army. *Military Advisers in Korea: KMAG in Peace and War,* by Robert K. Sawyer. 1962.

———. *The United States Army in the Korean War.* Vol. 1, *South to the Naktong, North to the Yalu,* by Roy E. Appleman. Vol. 3, *Policy and Direction: The First Year,* by James F. Schnabel. 1961–72.

———. Supreme Commander, Allied Powers, Japan. *South Korean Interim Government Activities.* Vols. 23–35. 1947–48.

———. Supreme Commander, Allied Powers, Japan. *Summation of Non-Military Activities in Japan and Korea, 1945–1946.* Vols. 1–5. 1945–46.

———. Supreme Commander, Allied Powers, Japan. *Summation of U.S. Army Military Government Activities in Korea.* Vols. 6–22. 1946–47.

U.S. Department of the Navy. *History of United States Naval Operations: Korea,* by James A. Field, Jr. 1962.

U.S. Department of State. *American Foreign Policy, 1950–1955: Basic Documents.* 1957.

———. *Biographic Register of the Department of State.* 1947–51.

———. *Department of State Bulletin.* Vols. 12–23. 1945–50.

———. *Economic Aid to the Republic of Korea, ECA Recovery Program to Fiscal Year 1950.* 1949.

———. *Foreign Relations of the United States, 1942.* Vol. 1, *The British Commonwealth, The Far East.* 1960.

———. *Foreign Relations of the United States: Conferences at Cairo and Tehran 1943.* 1961.

———. *Foreign Relations of the United States, 1944.* Vol. 5, *The Near East, South Asia, Africa, The Far East.* 1965.

———. *Foreign Relations of the United States, 1945.* Vol. 6, *The British Commonwealth, The Far East.* 1969.

———. *Foreign Relations of the United States, 1945: The Conference of Berlin (The Potsdam Conference).* 2 vols. 1957.

———. *Foreign Relations of the United States: Conferences at Malta and Yalta 1945.* 1955.

———. *Foreign Relations of the United States, 1946.* Vol. 8, *The Far East.* Vols. 9 and 10, *The Far East, China.* 1971–72.

———. *Foreign Relations of the United States, 1947.* Vol. 6, *The Far East.* Vol. 7, *The Far East, China.* 1972.

———. *Foreign Relations of the United States, 1948.* Vol. 6, *The Far East and Australasia.* Vol. 7, *The Far East, China.* Vol. VIII, *The Far East, China.* 1974.

———. *Foreign Relations of the United States, 1949.* Vol. 2, *The United Nations, The Western Hemisphere.* Vol. 7, *The Far East and Australasia.* Vols. 8 and 9, *The Far East, China.* 1974–78.

———. *Foreign Relations of the United States, 1950.* Vol. 1, *National Security.* Vol. 2, *The United Nations, The Western Hemisphere.* Vol. 6, *East Asia and the Pacific.* 1976–77.

———. *Korea, 1945–1948.* 1948.

———. *Korea's Independence.* 1947.

———. *Moscow Meeting of Foreign Ministers, December 16–26, 1945.* 1946.

———. *North Korea: A Case Study in the Techniques of Takeover.* 1961.

———. *United States Policy in the Korean Conflict.* 1951.

———. *United States Policy in the Korean Crisis.* 1950.

———. *United States Relations with China with Special Reference to the Period 1944–1949.* 1949.

U.S. General Services Administration. *Public Papers of the Presidents of the United States: Harry S. Truman, 1947–50.* 1963–65.

U.S. Joint Chiefs of Staff. *The History of the Joint Chiefs of Staff.* Vol. 1, *The Joint Chiefs of Staff and National Policy, 1945–1947,* by James F. Schnabel. Vol. 2, *The Joint Chiefs of Staff and National Policy, 1947–1949,* by Kenneth W. Condit. Vol. 3, *The Joint Chiefs of Staff and National Policy, The Korean War,* by James F. Schnabel and Robert J. Watson. Wilmington, Del.: Michael Glazier, 1979.

**UNITED NATIONS PUBLICATIONS**

United Nations. *Official Records*. 1947–50.


**NEWSPAPERS**

*New York Times*, 1947–50.


**INTERVIEWS AND PERSONAL CORRESPONDENCE**

Roy E. Appleman, 6 August 1974.
Charles L. Bolté, 20 October 1973.
Niles Bond, 30 July 1977.
W. Walton Butterworth, 16 November 1971.
Clark Clifford, 30 July 1977 (by telephone).
O. Edmund Clubb, 16 March 1977.
J. Lawton Collins, 21 July 1974.
John B. Coulter, 26 December 1973.
George M. Elsey, 23 July 1974.
Philip C. Jessup, 6 June 1972.
Marx Leva, 30 July 1974.
John J. Muccio, 27 December 1973.
Paul H. Nitze, 9 January 1975.
John H. Ohly, 4 August 1975.
William O. Reeder, 21 October 1973.
Matthew B. Ridgway, 26 November 1971.
Dean Rusk, 24 July 1972 (also letter, 12 September 1978).
William Sebald (letter, 8 September 1977).
Raymond Thurston, 4 May 1978.
Thomas B. Timberman, 30 December 1973 and 13 August 1974.
James E. Webb, 7 August 1974.


**ORAL HISTORIES**

INDEPENDENCE, MO.
Harry S. Truman Library.
  Robert W. Barnett.
  Robert K. E. Bruce.
  Laurence E. Bunker.
  John Cabot.
  O. Edmund Clubb.
  William H. Draper.
  George M. Elsey.
  Gordon Gray.

Loy W. Henderson.
John D. Hickerson.
Paul G. Hoffman.
U. Alexis Johnson.
John Wesley Jones.
Jack K. McFall.
Edwin W. Martin.
H. Freeman Matthews.
John J. Muccio.

Charles Murphy.
Frank Pace.
Arthur R. Ringwalt.
Francis J. Russell.
Philip C. Sprouse.
Richard Strout.
John L. Sullivan.
Walter Trohan.
Arthur N. Young.


**BOOKS AND ARTICLES**

Acheson, Dean G. *Morning and Noon*. Boston: Houghton Mifflin, 1965.
———. *Present at the Creation: My Years in the State Department*. New York: W. W. Norton, 1969.
———. *Sketches from Life of Men I Have Known*. New York: Harper and Brothers, 1959.

Allen, Richard C. *Korea's Syngman Rhee*. Rutland, Vt.: Charles E. Tuttle, 1960.
Allison, John M. *Ambassador from the Prairie, or Allison Wonderland*. Boston: Houghton Mifflin, 1973.
Almond, Gabriel A. *The American People and Foreign Policy*. New York: Frederick A. Praeger, 1950.
Arkes, Hadley. *Bureaucracy, the Marshall Plan, and the National Interest*. Princeton: Princeton University Press, 1972.
Aron, Raymond. *The Imperial Republic: The United States and the World, 1945– 1973*. Translated from the French by Frank Jellinek. Englewood Cliffs, N.J.: Prentice-Hall, 1974.
Bachrack, Stanley D. *The Committee of One Million: 'China Lobby' Politics, 1953– 1971*. New York: Columbia University Press, 1976.
Baldwin, Frank, ed. *Without Parallel: The American-Korean Relationship since 1945*. New York: Random House, 1973.
Barber, Joseph, ed. *American Policy toward China: A Report on the Views of Leading Citizens in Twenty-three Cities*. New York: Council on Foreign Relations, 1950.
Barnet, Richard. *Intervention and Revolution: The United States in the Third World*. New York: World Publishing Co., 1968.
Barnett, A. Doak. *China on the Eve of Communist Takeover*. New York: Frederick A. Praeger, 1963.
Beal, John Robinson. *Marshall in China*. New York: Doubleday, 1970.
Bell, Coral. *Negotiations from Strength*. New York: Alfred A. Knopf, 1963.
Beloff, Max. *Soviet Policy in the Far East, 1944–1951*. London: Oxford University Press, 1953.
Berger, Carl. *The Korean Knot*. Philadelphia: University of Pennsylvania Press, 1957.
Berkes, Ross N., and Bedi, Mohinder S. *The Diplomacy of India*. London: Oxford University Press, 1953.
Bodde, Derke. *Peking Diary*. New York: Schuman, 1950.
Bohlen, Charles E. *Witness to History, 1929–1969*. New York: W. W. Norton, 1973.
Borg, Dorothy, and Heinrichs, Waldo, eds. *Uncertain Years: Chinese-American Relations, 1947–1950*. New York: Columbia University Press, 1980.
Buhite, Russell D. *Patrick J. Hurley and American Foreign Policy*. Ithaca: Cornell University Press, 1973.
————. "Major Interests: American Policy toward China, Taiwan, and Korea, 1945– 1950." *Pacific Historical Review* 47 (August 1978):425–51.
Bullitt, William C. "Report on China." *Life* 23 (13 October 1947):35–37 and 139–54.
Bundy, McGeorge, ed. *The Pattern of Responsibility*. Boston: Houghton Mifflin, 1952.
Cagle, Malcolm W., and Manson, Frank A. *The Sea War in Korea*. Annapolis, Md.: U.S. Naval Institute, 1957.
Caldwell, John C., in collaboration with Frost, Lesley. *The Korea Story*. Chicago: Henry Regnery, 1952.
Caridi, Ronald J. *The Korean War and American Politics: The Republican Party as a Case Study*. Philadelphia: University of Pennsylvania Press, 1968.
Chang, Carsun. *Third Force in China*. New York: Record Press, 1952.
Chassin, Lionel Max. *The Communist Conquest of China: A History of the Civil War, 1945–1949*. Translated from the French by Timothy Osato and Louis Gelas. Cambridge: Harvard University Press, 1965.
Chennault, Claire Lee. "Hold 'Em! Harass 'Em! Hamstring 'Em!—The Chennault Plan." *Reader's Digest* 55 (October 1949):25–28.
————. "Last Call for China." *Life* 27 (11 July 1949):36.
————. *Way of a Fighter*. New York: G. P. Putnam's Sons, 1949.
Chiang Kai-shek. *China's Destiny and Chinese Economic Theory*. Edited and translated from the Chinese by Philip J. Jaffe. New York: Roy Publishers, 1947.
Cho, Soon Sung. *Korea in World Politics, 1940–1950*. Los Angeles: University of California Press, 1967.

Clubb, O. Edmund. *China and Russia: The Great Game*. New York: Columbia University Press, 1971.
──────. *The Witness and I*. New York: Columbia University, 1974.
Cohen, Warren J. *America's Response to China*. New York: John Wiley & Sons, 1971.
──────. "The Development of Chinese Communist Attitudes toward the United States." *Orbis* 11 (Summer 1967):551–69.
──────, ed. "Ambassador Philip D. Sprouse on the Question of Recognition of the People's Republic of China in 1949 and 1950." *Diplomatic History* 2 (Spring 1978):213–17.
Collins, J. Lawton. *War in Peacetime: The History and Lessons of Korea*. Boston: Houghton Mifflin, 1969.
Connally, Tom. *My Name Is Tom Connally*. New York: Thomas Y. Crowell, 1954.
Crabb, Jr., Cecil V. *Bipartisan Foreign Policy: Myth or Reality?* White Plains, N.Y.: Row, Peterson, and Company, 1957.
Davies, Jr., John Paton. *Dragon by the Tail: American, British, Japanese, and Russian Encounters with China and One Another*. New York: W. W. Norton, 1972.
Dayal, Shiv. *India's Role in the Korean Question*. Delhi: S. Chand, 1959.
Dedijer, Vladimir. *Tito*. New York: Simon and Schuster, 1953.
Democratic People's Republic of Korea. *Facts Tell*. Pyongyang: Foreign Languages Publishing House, 1960.
Detzer, David. *Thunder of the Captains*. New York: Thomas Y. Crowell, 1977.
Djilas, Milovan. *Conversations with Stalin*. New York: Harcourt, Brace, and World, 1963.
Djonovich, Dusan J., ed. *United Nations Resolutions*. Series 1, vols. 1–3. Dobbs Ferry, N.Y.: Oceanu Publications, 1973.
Doenecke, Justus D. *Not to the Swift: The Old Isolationists in the Cold War Era*. Lewisburg, Pa.: Bucknell University Press, 1979.
Douglass, Bruce, and Terrill, Ross, eds. *China and Ourselves: Explorations and Revisions by a New Generation*. Boston: Bacon Press, 1969.
Dulles, Foster Rhea. *American Policy toward Communist China: The Historical Record, 1949–1969*. New York: Thomas Y. Crowell, 1972.
Dulles, John Foster. *War or Peace?* New York: Macmillan, 1950.
Duncan, David Douglas. *This is War*. New York: Harper and Brothers, 1951.
Emmerson, John K. *The Japanese Thread: A Life in the United States Foreign Service*. New York: Holt, Rinehart, and Winston, 1978.
Fairbank, John King. *The United States and China*, 2d ed. New York: Viking Press, 1967.
Farnsworth, David N. *The Senate Committee on Foreign Relations*. Urbana, Ill.: University of Illinois Press, 1961.
Feis, Herbert. *The China Tangle*. Princeton: Princeton University Press, 1953.
Feraru, Arthur N. "Public Opinion Polls on China," *Far Eastern Survey* 20 (12 July 1950):130–32.
Fetzer, James Alan. "Senator Vandenberg and the American Commitment to China." *The Historian* 36 (February 1974):283–303.
Freeland, Richard M. *The Truman Doctrine and the Origins of McCarthyism: Foreign Policy, Domestic Politics, and Internal Security, 1946–1948*. New York: Alfred A. Knopf, 1971.
Friedman, Edward, and Selden, Mark, eds. *America's Asia*. New York: Random House, 1969.
Futrell, Robert. *The United States Air Force in Korea, 1950–1953*. New York: Duell, Sloan, and Pearce, 1961.
Gaddis, John Lewis. *The United States and the Origins of the Cold War, 1941–1947*. New York: Columbia University Press, 1972.
──────. "Was the Truman Doctrine a Real Turning Point?" *Foreign Affairs* 52 (January 1974):386–402.
Gati, Charles, ed. *Caging the Bear: Containment and the Cold War*. New York: Bobbs-Merrill, 1974.

Gayn, Mark J. *Japan Diary*. New York: W. Sloane Associates, 1948.

George, Alexander L., and Smoke, Richard. *Deterrence in American Foreign Policy: Theory and Practice*. New York: Columbia University Press, 1974.

Gittings, John. *The World and China, 1922–1972*. New York: Harper & Row, 1974.

Goodrich, Leland. *Korea: A Study of U.S. Policy in the United Nations*. New York: Council on Foreign Relations, 1956.

Gordenker, Leon. *The United Nations and the Peaceful Unification of Korea: The Politics of Field Operations, 1947–1950*. The Hague: Martinus Nijhoff, 1959.

Graebner, Norman A. *The New Isolationism*. New York: Ronald Press, 1956.

Grey, Jr., Arthur L. "The Thirty-eighth Parallel." *Foreign Affairs* 29 (April 1951): 482–87.

Griffith, Robert. *The Politics of Fear: Joseph R. McCarthy and the Senate*. Lexington, Ky.: University of Kentucky Press, 1970.

Gunther, John. *The Riddle of MacArthur*. New York: Harper, 1951.

Gupta, Karunker. "How Did the Korean War Begin?" *China Quarterly* 8 (October–December 1972): 699–716.

Halberstam, David. *The Best and the Brightest*. New York: Random House, 1972.

Halle, Louis J. *The Cold War As History*. New York: Harper & Row, 1967.

Hamby, Alonzo L. *Beyond the New Deal: Harry S. Truman and American Liberalism*. New York: Columbia University Press, 1973.

Harper, Alan D. *The Politics of Loyalty: The White House on the Communist Issue, 1946–1952*. Westport, Conn.: Greenwood Publishing Corp., 1969.

Harriman, W. Averell. *America and Russia in a Changing World*. Garden City, N.Y.: Doubleday, 1971.

Hartmann, Susan. *Truman and the 80th Congress*. Columbia, Mo.: University of Missouri Press, 1971.

Hawes, Grace. *The Marshall Plan for China: The Economic Cooperation Administration, 1948–1949*. Cambridge: Schenkman, 1977.

Haynes, Richard F. *The Awesome Power: Harry S. Truman as Commander in Chief*. Baton Rouge, La.: Louisiana State University Press, 1973.

Heller, Frances, ed. *The Korean War: A 25-Year Perspective*. Lawrence, Kansas: The Regents Press of Kansas, 1978.

Henderson, Gregory. *Korea: The Politics of the Vortex*. Cambridge: Harvard University Press, 1968.

Higgins, Marguerite. *War in Korea*. Garden City, N.Y.: Doubleday, 1951.

Higgins, Trumbull. *Korea and the Fall of MacArthur*. New York: Oxford University Press, 1960.

Hitchcock, Wilbur W. "North Korea Jumps the Gun." *Current History* 20 (March 1951): 136–44.

Hohenberg, John. *Between Two Worlds: Policy, Press, and Public Opinion in Asian-American Relations*. New York: Praeger, 1967.

Hsueh, Chun-tu, ed. *Dimensions of China's Foreign Relations*. New York: Praeger, 1977.

Iriye, Akira. *Across the Pacific: An Inner History of American-East Asian Relations*. New York: Harcourt, Brace, and World, 1967.

———. *The Cold War in Asia: A Historical Introduction*. Englewood Cliffs, N.J.: Prentice-Hall, 1974.

James, D. Clayton. *The Years of MacArthur*. 2 vols. Boston: Houghton Mifflin, 1970–72.

Jervis, Robert. *Perception and Misperception in International Politics*. Princeton: Princeton University Press, 1976.

Kahn, Jr., E. J. *The China Hands: America's Foreign Service Officers and What Befell Them*. New York: Viking Press, 1975.

Kalinov, Kyril. "How Russia Built the North Korean Army." *The Reporter* 3 (26 September 1950): 4–8.

Keeley, Joseph C. *The China Lobby Man: The Story of Alfred Kohlberg*. New Rochelle, N.Y.: Arlington House, 1969.

Kennan, George F. *Memoirs, 1925–1950*. Boston: Little, Brown, 1967.

————. *Memoirs, 1950–1963*. Boston: Little, Brown, 1972.

Kennedy, Edgar. *Mission to Korea*. London: D. Versohoyle, 1952.

Khrushchev, Nikita. *Khrushchev Remembers*. Edited by Edward Crankshaw and translated from the Russian by Strobe Talbott. Boston: Little, Brown, 1979.

————. *Khrushchev Remembers: The Last Testament*. Edited and translated from the Russian by Strobe Talbott. Boston: Little, Brown, 1974.

Kiernan, Jr., Frank A. *The Fluke that Saved Formosa*. Cambridge: MIT Press, 1954.

Kim Chum-kon. *The Korean War*. Seoul: Kwangmyong Publishing Co., 1973.

Kim, Joungwon A. *Divided Korea: The Politics of Development, 1945–1972*. Cambridge: Harvard University Press, 1975.

King, O. H. P. *Tail of the Paper Tiger*. Caldwell, Idaho: Caxton, 1961.

Kirkendall, Richard. *The Truman Period as a Research Field: A Reappraisal, 1972*. Columbia, Mo.: University of Missouri Press, 1974.

Koen, Ross Y. *The China Lobby in American Politics*. New York: Harper & Row, 1974.

Koh, Byung Chul. *The Foreign Policy of North Korea*. New York: Frederick A. Praeger, 1969.

Kolko, Joyce and Gabriel. *The Limits of Power: The World and United States Foreign Policy, 1945–1954*. New York: Harper & Row, 1972.

Kolodjiez, Edward A. *The Uncommon Defense and Congress, 1945–1963*. Columbus, Ohio: Ohio State University Press, 1966.

Kundra, J. C. *Indian Foreign Policy, 1947–1954*. Groningen, Holland: J. B. Walters, 1955.

Larson, David L. *United States Foreign Policy Toward Yugoslavia, 1943–1963*. Washington, D.C.: University Press of America, 1979.

Leary, Jr., William M. "Portrait of a Cold Warrior: Whiting Willauer and Civil Air Transport." *Modern Asian Studies* 5 (1971):373–88.

————. "Aircraft and Anti-Communists: CAT in Action, 1949–1952." *China Quarterly* 52 (October–December 1972):654–69.

Levine, Steven I. "A New Look at American Mediation in the Chinese Civil War: The Marshall Mission in Manchuria." *Diplomatic History* 3 (Fall 1979): 349–75.

Lie, Trygve. *In the Cause of Peace*. New York: Macmillan, 1954.

Liu, F. F. *A Military History of Modern China*. Port Washington, N.Y.: Kennikat Press, 1972.

MacArthur, Douglas A. *Reminiscences*. New York: McGraw Hill, 1964.

McCune, George, in collaboration with Grey, Jr., Arthur L. *Korea Today*. Cambridge: Harvard University Press, 1950.

McLellan, David S. *Dean Acheson: The State Department Years*. New York: Dodd, Mead, 1976.

Manchester, William. *American Caesar: Douglas MacArthur, 1880–1964*. Boston: Little, Brown, 1978.

Mao Tse-tung. *Selected Works of Mao Tse-tung*. Vol. IV. Peking: Foreign Language Press, 1961.

————. *On People's Democratic Dictatorship*. Peking: Foreign Language Press, 1952.

Marks, John D., and Marchetti, Victor. *The CIA and the Cult of Intelligence*. New York: Alfred A. Knopf, 1974.

Matray, James I. "An End to Indifference: America's Korea Policy During World War II." *Diplomatic History* 2 (Spring 1978):181–96.

————. "Truman's Plan for Victory: National Self-Determination and the Thirty-Eighth Parallel Decision in Korea." *Journal of American History* 66 (September 1979): 314–33.

May, Ernest R. *"Lessons of the Past": The Use and Misuse of History in American Foreign Policy*. New York: Oxford University Press, 1973.

————. *The Truman Administration and China, 1945–1949.* New York: J. P. Lippincott, 1975.

————, and Thomson, James C., eds. *American-East Asian Relations.* Cambridge: Harvard University Press, 1972.

May, Gary. *China Scapegoat: The Diplomatic Ordeal of John Carter Vincent.* Washington, D.C.: New Republic Books, 1979.

Meade, E. Grant. *American Military Government in Korea.* New York: King's Crown Press, 1951.

Melby, John F. *The Mandate Of Heaven: Record of a Civil War, China, 1945–1949.* Toronto: Toronto University Press, 1968.

Miller, Merle. *Plain Speaking: An Oral Biography of Harry S. Truman.* New York: Berkeley Publishing Corp., 1973.

Millis, Walter, ed. *The Forrestal Diaries.* New York: Viking Press, 1951.

Nagai, Yonosuke, and Iriye, Akira, eds. *The Origins of the Cold War in Asia.* New York: Columbia University Press, 1977.

Nam, Koon Woo. *The North Korean Communist Leadership, 1945–1965: A Study of Factionalism and Political Consolidation.* University, Ala.: University of Alabama Press, 1974.

Neumann, William L. *After Victory: Churchill, Roosevelt, Stalin, and the Making of the Peace.* New York: Harper & Row, 1967.

Neustadt, Richard E. *Presidential Power: The Politics of Leadership.* New York: John Wiley and Sons, 1960.

Newman, Robert. *Recognition of Communist China?* New York: Macmillan, 1961.

Noble, Harold Joyce. *Embassy at War.* Edited by Frank Baldwin. Seattle: University of Washington Press, 1975.

Nourse, Edwin G. "What Effect Will Armament Spending Have on the Business Outlook?" *U.S. News and World Report* 25 (10 December 1948): 40–46.

Oliver, Robert T. *Syngman Rhee: The Man behind the Myth.* New York: Dodd, Mead, and Co., 1954.

————. *Why War Came to Korea.* New York: Fordham University Press, 1950.

Osgood, Robert. *Limited War.* Chicago: University of Chicago Press, 1957.

Paige, Glenn D. *The Korean Decision.* New York: Free Press, 1968.

————. *The Korean People's Democratic Republic.* Stanford: Hoover Institution Press, 1966.

Panikkar, K. M. *In Two Chinas.* London: Allen and Unwin, 1950.

Pelz, Stephen. "When the Kitchen Gets Hot, Pass the Buck," *Reviews in American History* (December 1978): 548–55.

Phillips, Cabell. *The Truman Presidency: The History of a Triumphant Succession.* Baltimore: Penguin Books, 1969.

Pogue, Forrest. *George C. Marshall.* 3 vols. New York: Viking Press, 1963–1973.

Purifoy, Lewis McCarroll. *Harry Truman's China Policy: McCarthyism and the Diplomacy of Hysteria, 1947–1951.* New York: Franklin Watts, 1976.

Rankin, Karl Lott. *China Assignment.* Seattle: University of Washington Press, 1964.

Rees, David. *Korea: The Limited War.* Baltimore: Penguin Books, 1964.

Reston, James. "Secretary Acheson: A First Year Audit." *New York Times Magazine* 99 (22 January 1950): 7–9, 35–38.

Ridgway, Matthew B. *The Korean War.* New York: Doubleday, 1967.

Riggs, Robert E. *Politics in the United Nations: A Study of United States Influence in the General Assembly.* Urbana, Ill.: University of Illinois Press, 1958.

Robinson, Frank M., and Kemp, Earl, eds. *Report of the U.S. Senate Hearings—The Truth About Vietnam.* San Diego: Greenleaf Classics, 1966.

Roper, Elmo. *You and Your Leaders.* New York: William Morrow, 1957.

Rose, Lisle A. *Roots of Tragedy: The United States and the Struggle for Asia, 1945–1953.* Westport, Conn.: Greenwood Publishing Corp., 1976.

Rovere, Richard H., and Schlesinger, Jr., Arthur M. *The MacArthur Controversy and American Foreign Policy.* New York: Noonday Press, 1965.

Salisbury, Harrison E. *War between Russia and China*. New York: W. W. Norton, 1969.

Scalapino, Robert A., and Lee, Chong-Sik. *Communism in Korea*. Vol. 1. Los Angeles: University of California Press, 1972.

Schaller, Michael. *The U.S. Crusade in China, 1938–1945*. New York: Columbia University Press, 1979.

Schell, Jonathan. *The Time of Illusion*. New York: Alfred A. Knopf, 1976.

Schilling, Warner, ed. *Strategy, Politics, and Defense Budgets*. New York: Columbia University Press, 1962.

Schlesinger, Jr., Arthur M. *The Imperial Presidency*. New York: Popular Library, 1973.

Schonberger, Howard B. "The General and the Presidency: Douglas MacArthur and the Election of 1948." *Wisconsin Magazine of History* 57 (Spring 1974):201–19.

Schulman, Marshall D. *Stalin's Foreign Policy Reappraised*. Cambridge: Harvard University Press, 1963.

Sebald, William. *With MacArthur in Japan*. New York: W. W. Norton, 1965.

Service, John S. *The Amerasia Papers: Some Problems in the History of U.S. China Relations*. Berkeley: University of California Press, 1971.

Sheridan, James. *China in Disintegration: The Republican Era in Chinese History, 1912–1949*. New York: Free Press, 1975.

Sherwood, Robert E. *Roosevelt and Hopkins: An Intimate History*. New York: Harper & Row, 1948.

Shewmaker, Kenneth E. *Americans and the Chinese Communists, 1927–1945*. Ithaca: Cornell University Press, 1971.

Simmons, Robert R. *The Strained Alliance: Peking, Pyongyang, Moscow, and the Politics of the Korean Civil War*. New York: Free Press, 1975.

Smith, Beverly. "The White House Story: Why We Went to War in Korea." *Saturday Evening Post* 224 (10 November 1951):22–23 and 76–88.

Smith, Gaddis. *Dean Acheson*. New York: Cooper Square, 1972.

———. "Mr. Acheson Answers Some Questions." *New York Times Book Review* 119 (12 October 1969):2, 30–31.

Spanier, John W. *The Truman-MacArthur Controversy and the Korean War*. New York: W. W. Norton, 1965.

Stairs, Denis. *The Diplomacy of Constraint: Canada, the Korean War, and the United States*. Toronto: University of Toronto Press, 1974.

Steele, A. T. *The American People and China*. New York: McGraw-Hill, 1966.

Stein, Harold, ed. *American Civil-Military Relations*. Birmingham, Ala.: University of Alabama Press, 1963.

Stein, Herbert. *The Fiscal Revolution in America*. Chicago: University of Chicago Press, 1969.

Stone, I. F. *The Hidden History of the Korean War*. New York: Monthly Review Press, 1952.

Stuart, John Leighton. *Fifty Years in China*. New York: Random House, 1954.

Stueck, William. "Cold War Revisionism and the Origins of the Korean Conflict: The Kolko Thesis." *Pacific Historical Review* 42 (November 1973):537–60.

———. "The Soviet Union and the Origins of the Korean War." *World Politics* 28 (July 1976):622–35.

Suh, Dae-sook. *The Korean Communist Movement, 1918–1948*. Princeton: Princeton University Press, 1967.

Sulzberger, C. L. *A Long Row of Candles: Memoirs and Diaries, 1934–1954*. New York: Macmillan, 1969.

Swanberg, W. A. *Luce and His Empire*. New York: Charles Scribner's Sons, 1972.

Thorne, Christopher. *Allies of a Kind: The United States, Britain, and the War Against Japan, 1941–1945*. New York: Oxford University Press, 1978.

Thornton, Richard. *China: the Struggle for Power, 1917–1972*. Bloomington, Ind.: University of Indiana Press, 1973.

Topping, Seymour. *Journey between Two Chinas*. New York: Harper & Row, 1972.

Tozer, Warren. "Last Bridge to China: The Shanghai Power Company, the Truman Administration, and the Chinese Communists." *Diplomatic History* 1 (Winter 1977):64–78.

Truman, Harry S. *Memoirs*. 2 vols. Vol. 1, *Year of Decision*. Vol. 2, *Years of Trial and Hope*. Garden City, N.Y.: Doubleday, 1955–56.

Truman, Margaret. *Harry S. Truman*. New York: William Morrow, 1972.

Tsou, Tang. *America's Failure in China, 1941–1950*. Chicago: University of Chicago Press, 1963.

Tuchman, Barbara W. *Stilwell and the American Experience in China, 1911–1945*. New York: Macmillan, 1970.

Tucker, Nancy Bernkopf. "An Unlikely Peace: American Missionaries and the Chinese Communists, 1948–1950." *Pacific Historical Review* 45 (February 1976):97–116.

Ulam, Adam B. *Expansion and Coexistence: The History of Soviet Foreign Policy, 1917–1967*. New York: Praeger, 1968.

———. *The Rivals: America and Russia Since World War II*. New York: Viking Press, 1971.

Vandenberg, Jr., Arthur S. *The Private Papers of Senator Vandenberg*. Boston: Little, Brown, 1952.

Van Slyke, Lyman P., ed. *The Chinese Communist Movement*. Stanford: Stanford University Press, 1968.

Varg, Paul A. *The Closing of the Door: Sino-American Relations, 1936–1946*. East Lansing, Mich.: Michigan State University Press, 1973.

Wedemeyer, Albert C. *Wedemeyer Reports*. New York: Henry Holt, 1958.

Westerfield, H. Bradford. *Foreign Policy and Party Politics: Pearl Harbor to Korea*. New Haven: Yale University Press, 1955.

Whiting, Allen S. *China Crosses the Yalu: The Decision to Enter the Korean War*. New York: Macmillan, 1960.

Whitney, Courtney. *MacArthur: His Rendezvous with History*. New York: Alfred A. Knopf, 1956.

Willoughby, Charles A., and Chamberlain, John. *MacArthur, 1941–1951*. New York: McGraw-Hill, 1955.

Wiltz, John Edward. "The MacArthur Hearings of 1951: The Secret Testimony." *Military Affairs* 39 (December 1975):166–73.

———. "Truman and MacArthur: The Wake Island Meeting." *Military Affairs* 42 (December 1978):168–75.

Yergin, Daniel. *Shattered Peace: The Origins of the Cold War and the National Security State*. Boston: Houghton Mifflin, 1977.

## UNPUBLISHED SECONDARY WORKS

Dobbs, Charles M. "American Foreign Policy, the Cold War, and Korea, 1945–1950." Ph.D. dissertation, Indiana University, 1978.

Eggleston, Noel Clinton. "The Roots of Commitment: United States Policy Toward Vietnam, 1945–1950." Ph.D. dissertation, University of Georgia, 1977.

Far Eastern Command. "History of United States Army Forces in Korea." 3 vols. Washington, D.C.: Office of the Chief of Military History, United States Army, 1948.

Fetzer, James Alan. "Congress and China, 1941–1950." Ph.D. dissertation, Michigan State University, 1969.

Flint, Roy K. "The Tragic Flaw: MacArthur, the Joint Chiefs, and the Korean War." Ph.D. dissertation, Duke University, 1975.

Goodno, Floyd Russel. "Walter H. Judd: Spokesman for China in the United States House of Representatives." D.Ed. dissertation, Oklahoma State University, 1970.

Kang, Han Mu. "The United States Military Government in Korea, 1945–1948: An

Analysis and Evaluation of Its Policy." Ph.D. dissertation, University of Cincinnati, 1970.

Kotch, John Barry. "United States Security Policy toward Korea, 1945–1953: The Origins and Evolution of American Involvement and the Emergence of a National Security Commitment." Ph.D. dissertation, Columbia University 1976.

Leary, Jr., William M. "Smith of New Jersey: A Biography of H. Alexander Smith." Ph.D. dissertation, Princeton University, 1966.

Matray, James I. "The Reluctant Crusade: American Foreign Policy in Korea, 1941–1950." Ph.D. dissertation, University of Virginia, 1977.

Mauck, Kenneth R. "The Formation of American Foreign Policy in Korea, 1945–1953." Ph.D. dissertation, University of Oklahoma, 1979.

Merrill, John. "Internal Welfare in Korea, 1948–1950: The Local Setting of the Korean War." Unpublished paper delivered at a workshop on Korean-American relations, 1945–53, University of Washington, Seattle, March 1978.

Morris, William George. "The Korean Trusteeship, 1941–1947: The United States, Russia, and the Cold War." Ph.D. dissertation, University of Texas at Austin, 1975.

Paul, Mark. "Diplomacy Delayed: The Atomic Bomb and the Division of Korea." Unpublished paper delivered at a workshop on Korean-American relations, 1945–53, University of Washington, Seattle, March 1978.

Reardon-Anderson, James Byron. "The Foreign Policy of Self-Reliance: Chinese Communist Policy toward the Great Powers, 1944–1946." Ph.D. dissertation, Columbia University, 1976.

Roche, III, George C. "Public Opinion and the China Policy of the United States, 1941–1950." Ph.D. dissertation, University of Colorado, 1956.

Stueck, William. "American Policy toward China and Korea, 1947–1950." Ph.D. dissertation, Brown University, 1977.

———. "Domestic Politics, Far Eastern Strategy, and the Early Months of the Korean War." M.A. thesis, Queens College, 1971.

Tsuan, Tai-hsun. "An Explanation of the Change in U.S. Policy toward China in 1950." Ph.D. dissertation, University of Pennsylvania. 1969.

# Index

Acheson, Dean G. (secretary of state): and Chinese intervention in Korea, 3–4, 244–46, 248–50, 254–55; and Communist China, 4, 112, 121, 122–24, 132, 133–34, 146, 230–31; on U.S. objectives in China, 18; on aid to Nationalist China, 44, 57, 130, 275 (n. 9), 277 (nn. 57, 61), 280 (n. 156), 282 (n. 231); and domestic politics, 65–66, 113–17, 144–46, 246, 257; on aid to Western Europe, 82; influence with Truman, 113, 141, 236, 250; becomes secretary of state, 113; background and personality of, 113–15; on Taiwan policy, 118–19, 137–43, 149–52, 211, 221, 246; as Europe-firster, 123, 162, 236; on containment in Asia, 130; and Indochina, 130, 147–49, 152; and *China White Paper*, 130–31, and Cold War and China, 137; tensions with Johnson, 141, 236, 250; National Press Club speech of, 143, 147, 151, 153, 161; and Japanese peace treaty, 145, 147; and negotiations from strength, 149; and Communist victory in South Korea, 153; on U.S. troop withdrawal from Korea, 154, 158; and aid to South Korea, 159, 161, 289 (n. 67); fears Communist moves, 169; and outbreak of war in Korea, 177–79, 183, 185, 186, 187, 192, 195, 197; and negotiations during Korean War, 199–202, 209, 221, 232–34; on crossing 38th parallel, 204, 235; and Marshall, 236; and Wake Island meeting, 238–39; relations with Pentagon, 250, 253; on containment in Korea, 253; and Nitze, 294 (n. 229)
Ahalt, Colonel Henry, 183
Air power: popularity of in U.S., 108
Allen, Robert S., 53
Allison, John M. (director, Division of Northeast Asian Affairs): and Korea policy, 87; replaced by Bishop, 105; and crossing 38th parallel, 203–5, 233–35
Alsop, Joseph: on aid to Nationalist China, 39, 264 (n. 23)
Alsop, Stewart: supports Chennault plan, 128
*Amerasia* affair, 43, 145

American China Policy Association, 16, 53, 127
Amtorg Trading Corporation, 135
Arnold, Major General A. V., 23, 262 (n. 63)
Arthur, William, 127
Atlee, Clement (British prime minister), 255
Austin, Warren R. (U.S. ambassador to the United Nations), 202, 208, 209, 214, 215, 233
Australia, 95–97, 159, 180, 183
Azerbaijan, 88

Badger, Vice-Admiral Oscar C., 60, 63–64, 66, 67, 137, 268 (n. 170)
Ball, Joseph (senator), 44
Bao Dai (emperor of Vietnam), 130, 149, 196
Barkley, Alben W. (vice-president), 116–17
Barr, Major General David, 64, 66
Barrett, Edward (assistant secretary of state for public affairs), 243
Belgium, 180
Benninghoff, H. Merrell, 23
Berkey, Admiral Russell S., 139
Berlin, Germany, 100, 106, 115, 128, 169
Bipartisanship, 42–43, 113–15, 129, 130, 142, 145–46
Bishop, Max W. (director, Division of Northeast Asian Affairs), 105–6, 110, 154, 157–58
Blandford, John, 40
Bloom, Sol (congressman), 70, 116–17
Bohlen, Charles E. (minister at Paris), 36
Bolté, Major General Charles L., 138, 167, 182, 249–50, 285 (n. 37)
Bond, Niles W. (assistant chief, Division of Northeast Asian Affairs), 105–6, 157
Boxer Rebellion, 136
Bradley, General Omar N.: on Korea policy, 99, 156; on Taiwan policy, 142, 198, 213; on planning for war, 155–56; visits Tokyo, 161, 169; compared to MacArthur, 207; and Inchon landing, 225; at Wake Island, 238–39; and Chinese intervention in Korea, 242, 245; becomes a chairman of JCS, 281 (n. 167)

Brannan, Charles (secretary of agriculture), 184
Brewster, Owen (senator), 44
Bridges, Styles (senator): advocates aid to Chiang, 42–43, 53, 58, 61, 63, 68, 115; position in Senate, 43, 55; attacks Vincent nomination, 43; cultivated by Acheson, 145; supports Truman on Korea, 180
Bromfield, Louis, 63
Bruce, David L. K. (U.S. ambassador to France), 148
Budenz, Louis, 145
Bullitt, William C., 53, 60, 63, 65, 116
Burma, 134, 138
Butterworth, W. Walton (assistant secretary of state for the Far East): background and personality of, 48–49, 73, 150, 234–35; and U.S. China policy, 49, 52–53, 69, 70, 117–18, 122, 261 (n. 35), 265 (n. 72), 276 (n. 42); and U.S. Korea policy, 87, 98–99, 100, 106, 154, 158, 272 (n. 53); fight over nomination of, 128–29; on Taiwan policy, 142; replaced by Rusk, 146
Byrd, Harry F. (senator), 81, 129
Byrnes, James F. (secretary of state), 11, 23, 24, 36, 51, 113

Cabot, John M. (U.S. consul general at Shanghai), 124–25, 136
Cairo Conference, 20, 246
Cambodia, 147
Canada, 95–97, 180–81, 183
Cannon, Clarence (congressman), 70
Case, Everett, 131
Chamberlin, Major General S. J., 78
Chambers, Whittaker, 143–44
Cheju Island, 104
Chen Cheng, 119
Chennault, Major General Claire L., 42, 49, 60, 126–31, 131–37, 139, 189, 278 (n. 90)
Chen Yi, General, 212
Chiang Kai-shek, Generalissimo, 41, 43, 45, 46, 47, 66, 67, 71, 133, 266–67 (n. 113), 267 (n. 119); in U.S. politics, 3, 42, 44, 52, 77, 143, 146; U.S. aid to, 5, 9, 11–13, 16, 18–19, 58–67, 111, 126, 196–97, 212, 251, 254–55, 256; nature of government of, 5, 18, 28, 57–58, 140; on Yalta accords, 11; and use of force, 11, 15–16; relations with Russia, 15, 48; ideology of, 17–18; Marshall view of, 33, 39; U.S. inability to influence, 38, 65; prospects of, 47, 116, 124; meets with Wedemeyer, 48; American

perception of, 54–55, 247; distrusts Fu, 64; and Badger plan, 64–65; defended by Forrestal, 64–65; reassessed by Stuart, 69; compared with Rhee, 77, 108, 158, 164, 191; importance of Korea to, 87; resigns, 115; in Roots plan, 117–18; Chen loyalty to, 119; rule of on Taiwan, 137, 140; possible removal of, 151; offers U.S. support in Korea, 183, 184; meeting with MacArthur, 210–11; unleashing of, 216. *See also* Nationalist China
China: and Russia, 4, 71, 78, 117, 118, 137, 142; and Japanese-American conflict, 9; Japanese aggression against, 9, 11; U.S. policy toward, 9–10, 31–33, 133; U.S. expertise on, 17, 149; compared with Korea, 19, 28–30, 32, 75, 81, 91, 92, 93–95, 101, 109–10, 154, 159, 161, 169, 191; State and Defense departments clash over, 38–41, 44–46, 50–52, 56; U.S. marines in, 40; Vincent warns against investment in, 43; importance to U.S. of, 44–46, 94; problems of contrasted to Europe, 52; compared with Greece, 56–57; chaos in, 72–73; failure of U.S. to coordinate policies in, 107; Roots plan for, 117; trade of, 120, 126; resistance to Communists in, 134; and U.S. Asian specialists, 162; MacArthur on, 189; alleges U.S. aggression against, 221; possible expansion of Korean War into, 253. *See also* Communist China; Nationalist China
China Aid Act, 58–59, 61–67, 70, 136, 146, 280 (n. 156), 282 (n. 202)
China bloc, 52–54, 57, 65, 120, 123, 126–31, 136, 146, 214, 217, 266–67 (n. 113). *See also* United States Congress
China Emergency Committee, 127, 128
China lobby. *See* Allen, Robert S.; Arthur, William; Chennault, Claire; China bloc; Kohlberg, Alfred
*China White Paper*, 130–31
Chinese Civil War, 55, 59, 66–67, 74, 152, 210, 215
Cho, Soon Sung, 6
Cho Man-Sik, 98
Chou En-lai: breaks talks with Nationalists, 13; offers to visit Washington, 14; approaches U.S., 121–22, 124; anti-American speeches of, 125; letter to U.S. from, 132; and outbreak of war in Korea, 181; message from to U.N. on Korea, 208–9; and Taiwan issue, 213; on Chinese Communist intervention

in Korea, 231; on Korean War, 242
Church, Major General John H., 182
Civil Air Transport Company, 127
Clark, Lewis (minister-counselor to U.S. embassy in China), 69, 128–29
Clubb, O. Edmund (director, Office of Chinese Affairs), 291 (n. 128), 292 (n. 156); background of, 17; lauds Fu, 63–64; supports Lapham proposal, 70; and talks with Communists, 68, 123–24, 126, 132; and Chou overture, 122; departs from Peking, 133; on Ward affair, 135; on splits within Communist China, 135; on Sino-Soviet relations, 150; on crossing 38th parallel, 231, 234–35; and Chinese intervention in Korea, 242–43
Coalition Committee in Korea, 26
Cold War, 6, 7, 74, 75
Collins, General J. Lawton: orders proposals on aid to China, 138; on U.S. Taiwan policy, 139, 140–41; and Korean War, 183, 203, 204, 206–7, 223, 225, 226, 239, 242; and U.S. military preparedness, 281 (n. 167)
Columbia Broadcasting System, 203, 208
Committee to Defend America by Aiding Anti-Communist China, 128, 132
Communiqué No. 5, 82
Communist China: and U.S., 3–5, 13–14, 15, 37, 44–45, 67, 68, 70–72, 110–12, 120–26, 131–37, 138, 146–52, 173–75, 178–79, 211–12, 253–55, 257, 260 (n. 17), 270 (n. 208), 278 (n. 83), 279 (n. 136); intervenes in Korea, 3–5, 173–74, 190, 241–46, 249, 251, 253, 254–55; and Nationalists, 11–12, 13, 68, 119; and Russia, 15–16, 28, 49, 56–57, 71–72, 135, 146–52, 196, 206, 207, 220–21, 230, 253–54, 255; advance of on mainland, 39, 63, 106, 161, 186, 255, 259–60 (n. 13), 260 (n. 4); U.S. concern about advance of, 44–45; viewed by State Department, 48; viewed by Wedemeyer, 48, 51; Sprouse on, 51; and possible hostilities with U.S. at Tsingtao, 67; possible involvement of in Korea, 107, 167, 203, 205–6, 208–9, 219–21, 228–32, 237, 238, 289 (n. 67); and Taiwan, 119, 138, 139, 150–51, 178–79, 211–12, 213, 216, 291 (n. 116); internal divisions, 121, 135–36; possible entry of into U.N., 146, 178, 181, 199–201, 253; and Indochina, 147–48; aid to North Korea, 153, 275 (n. 148); armies of in Manchuria, 157,

216; intervention of in Korea, 173–74, 190; and outbreak of war in Korea, 181, 182, 184, 186; and British and Indian peace initiatives, 199–201; shells Quemoy, 212, 216; American bombing of, 216; U.S. assurance to, 217; relations with India, 233–34; and U.S. operations near, 235–36; and possible negotiations on Korea, 248; recognizes Ho, 255. *See also* People's Republic of China
Communists-in-government issue, 3, 143–46, 217–18
Connally, Tom (senator), 70, 114, 116–17, 123, 129, 133, 146, 153, 161, 179
Cooke, Admiral Charles M., 39, 40, 49, 60
Cooper, John Sherman, 145
Coplon, Judith, 144, 280 (n. 150)
Council on Foreign Relations, 143
Crane, Burton, 149
Credibility, U.S.: concern for, 6–8, 255; in China, 28, 57, 94, 133; in Korea, 28, 31, 75, 94, 101, 169, 173–75, 186–88, 191, 228, 231, 240, 248; in Europe and Asia, 152. *See also* Prestige, U.S.
Cuba: supports U.S. in Korea, 181
Czechoslovakia, 60, 100, 266–67 (n. 113)

Davies, John Paton, 74, 122–24, 220–21, 243, 249, 251, 294 (n. 229)
Dean, Major General William F., 97
Democratic party, U.S.: and China issue, 54, 65–66; controls both houses, 107, 131; and bipartisanship, 114; and Communists-in-government issue, 143–46, 218; attacked by Republicans, 194, 256; and congressional election, 217, 246; and Wake Island meeting, 238
Democratic People's Republic of Korea, 103, 237, 262 (n. 65). *See also* North Korea
Denfeld, Admiral Louis, 281 (n. 167)
Deterrence, 159–71
Detzer, David, 187
Dewey, Thomas E., 54, 62–63, 66, 180
Ditmanson, Marcy, 68
Domino theory, 111
Donaldson, Jesse, 104–5
Douglas, Helen Gahagan (congresswoman), 156
Doyle, Rear Admiral James H., 225
Draper, William H. (under secretary of the army), 100
Dulles, John Foster (secretary of state), 4, 91, 145–46, 149–51, 161–62, 188,

201, 217, 246–47, 290–91 (n. 101)
Durdin, Tillman, 277 (n. 79)

Eastern Europe, 15, 21, 160
Eaton, Charles (congressman), 63, 116–17, 141
Economic Cooperation Administration, 61, 63, 70
Ecuador, 181
Eisenhower, General Dwight D., 75, 77, 188
Eisenhower administration, 4–5
Egypt, 202, 288
El Salvador, 95
Emmerson, John K., 220–21
Ethnocentrism, U.S.: 6, 17, 29, 73–74, 91–92, 254–55
European Recovery Program. *See also* Marshall Plan
Europe-first strategy of U.S., 6, 19, 82, 154–55
Export-Import Bank, U.S., 12, 14, 41, 43, 46

Fairbank, John King, 17–18, 55
Feis, Herbert, 203–5
Ferguson, Homer (senator), 44
Flying Tigers, 42, 127–28
Formosa. *See* Taiwan
Forrestal, James (secretary of defense), 39–40, 41, 64–65, 100, 137, 155
*Fortune* (magazine), 16
Fosdick, Raymond, 131
Foster, William C., 166
Fourteenth Air Force Association, 127
France, 95–97, 130, 147–49, 169, 180, 196, 221, 245, 249
Frankfurter, Felix (Supreme Court justice), 131
French Union, 130
Fuchs, Klaus, 144
Fugh, Philip, 122, 125
Fulbright, J. William (senator), 114, 278 (n. 96)
Fulton, James G. (congressman), 44, 70
Fu Tso-yi, General, 63–64, 66

Gaddis, John Lewis, 4
Gallup poll, 60, 131, 132, 143
George, Alexander L., 153
Germany, 15, 76, 85, 173, 232, 243, 245
Goodfellow, Colonel M. Preston, 77
Goodrich, Leland, 88
Goodwin, William J., 127
G. P. Putnam's Sons, 127
Gray, Gordon (secretary of the army), 138
Great Britain: and trusteeship in Korea,

20, 24; and guardianship over Manchuria, 51; ends aid to Greece and Turkey, 80; and Korea, 96, 180, 227, 231, 233, 245, 249; and recognition of Communist China, 132, 135, 136; peace initiative of, 198–200; and Taiwan issue, 214, 221, 246
Greece: U.S. and the civil war in, 15; U.S. aid to, 41, 44, 50, 59, 61, 62, 67, 80–81, 148; compared with China, 56–57; strategic importance of, 94; priority of over Korea, 168; possible attack on, 169; British withdrawal from, 250–60 (n. 13); and Yugoslavia, 278 (n. 83)
Green, Theodore (senator): on Korea, 166
Griffin, Robert Allen (deputy director, ECA Mission, China), 268 (n. 176)
Griffith, Robert, 145, 218
Gromyko, Andrei (Soviet ambassador to the U.N.), 90–91
Gruenther, Major General Alfred M., 138, 140
Guardianship, 50–52
Gubichev, Valentin, 135, 280 (n. 150)
Gullion, Edmund (U.S. chargé in Vietnam), 148

Hainan Island, 141
Hall, Lieutenant General G. P., 99
Harriman, Averell (assistant to the president), 185, 211–13, 215, 238
Hawaii, 159
Hearst, William R., 278 (n. 90)
Hearst newspaper chain, 77, 128, 217
Hébert, F. Edward (congressman), 128
Henderson, Loy W. (U.S. ambassador to India), 229
Hickenlooper, Bourke B. (senator), 218
Hickerson, John W. (assistant secretary of state for U.N. Affairs), 179
Hilldring, Major General John H., 80
Hiss, Alger, 143–44
Hiss, Donald, 144
Hitler, Adolf, 7, 19
Ho Chi Minh (president of North Vietnam), 130, 147, 149, 255
Hodge, Lieutenant General John R.: background and personality, 22–23, 262 (nn. 62, 63, 73); occupation policies of, 23, 24, 26–27, 29, 76; and Rhee, 27, 75–76, 77, 89, 97–98, 99, 102, 271 (n. 37); visit of to U.S., 79; relationship with Jacobs, 87; replaced by Muccio, 102; on possible attack from north, 164
Hoffman, Paul G. (director, Economic

Cooperation Administration), 70–71
Hoover, Herbert, 141
Hornbeck, Stanley K., 116
Huang Hua, 121–26
Hurley, Patrick J. (U.S. ambassador to China), 13–14, 17, 43

Inchon landing, 223–31, 240–41, 246
India, 148; as member of UNTCOK, 95, 97; on recognition of Communist China, 132; and Korean War, 180, 183, 193, 198–203, 207, 209, 220, 230, 233–34, 238, 239, 248, 288 (n. 33); and Taiwan, 221
Indochina: U.S. concern regarding, 111, 130, 147–49, 162, 169; U.S. aid to, 148, 196, 282 (n. 231); and outbreak of war in Korea, 173, 178–79, 181, 197
Indonesia, 138, 148
Iran, 15, 67, 88, 168, 169, 259 (n. 13)
Italy, 180

Jackson, S. H., 96–98, 103
Jacobs, Joseph E. (political adviser to American army forces in Korea), 83, 87–89, 91
Jaffe, Philip, 43
Japan, 37, 178, 195, 199, 207, 210; and Korea, 9, 19–20, 22, 76, 78, 93, 106; and China, 19, 147; U.S. position in, 76, 85–87, 94, 105, 108, 109, 154, 155, 156, 158, 159–60, 161, 162, 170, 180, 182, 185, 188, 190, 191, 253, 257, 283 (n. 242); and peace treaty with U.S., 111, 145–46, 147, 232; and Taiwan, 118, 139, 141; and Indochina, 148
*Jen Min Jih Pao*, 181, 208, 211
Jessup, Philip C. (U.S. ambassador at large), 96, 130, 131, 136, 144, 161, 163, 208, 272 (n. 52)
Johnson, Louis A. (secretary of defense), 213; becomes secretary of defense, 137; and China, 137; and military spending, 139–40, 158; and Acheson, 141; and Japanese peace treaty, 145, 147; and Taiwan, 151, 211–12, 215–16; visits Tokyo, 161, 169; and State-Defense relations, 162; and beginning of Korean War, 179, 195, 197; fired, 216, 236, 293 (n. 196); compared with Marshall, 236, 250, 253, 257; personality of, 281 (n. 192); and Korea, 285 (n. 37)
Johnson, Lyndon B., 5
Johnson, U. Alexis (assistant director, Division of Northeast Asian Affairs), 231, 234–35
Joint Commission on Korea, 24, 25, 82–85, 88–89, 91, 93

Joint Korean-American Conference, 26
Joy, Admiral Turner, 139
Judd, Walter (congressman): and China, 16, 42, 44, 52–53, 55, 58–59, 62, 63, 115, 129, 260 (n. 29); and Korea, 156–57

Kao Kang, 135, 280 (n. 149)
Kefauver, Estes (senator), 128
Kennan, George F. (counselor, U.S. State Department), 53, 70, 142, 154, 177, 200–201, 203–5, 220, 235
Kennedy, John F., 5
Keon, Michael, 121
Khrushchev, Nikita, 109, 161, 232
Kim, Joungwon A., 105
Kim Il-sung (North Korean premier), 92, 97, 103, 109, 161, 170, 191
Kim Koo, 76, 91, 98
Kimm Kiu-sic, 97, 98
Kim Tu-bong, 97
Kirk, Alan G. (U.S. ambassador to the Soviet Union), 132, 231
Knowland, William F. (senator), 65, 115–16, 120, 127–28, 129, 139, 141, 166, 180, 269 (n. 179)
Kohlberg, Alfred, 16, 53
Korea: and United Nations, 3, 78, 81, 84, 88–98, 101–3, 105, 151, 159, 177–78, 179, 180–81, 193–94, 199–200, 203–4, 205–6, 207–9, 219–20, 223, 227–28, 231, 233–34, 248–49; compared with China, 6, 9–10, 28–30, 32, 75, 81, 92, 93–94, 109–10, 161, 169, 191; conditions in, 6, 19, 22–28, 75–76, 85–88, 92–93, 97, 98, 101–5, 112, 153, 157, 163–71; division of, 6, 22, 89–91, 95–98, 102–3; and World War II, 9, 21; strategic importance of, 9, 20, 29, 49, 78, 86–87, 94, 106, 110, 154–56, 169; Soviet-American negotiations on, 15, 20, 21–22, 23–25, 80–81, 82–83, 89, 91, 93, 101–2, 227–28, 232–34; and trusteeship, 19–20, 24, 83; People's Republic in, 19; provisional government of, 19; and vacuum in Northeast Asia, 20. *See also* Credibility, U.S.: in Korea; Korean War; North Korea; South Korea
Korea Democratic party, 105
Korean War: Chinese intervention in, 3–5, 241, 243–46, 253, 254–55; and Taiwan, 4, 198–202, 207–17, 221, 246–47; impact of on U.S., 3–5, 206, 254–55, 257–58, 259–60 (n. 13); outbreak of, 4, 173, 177–85, 254; reasons for U.S. intervention in, 173, 185–90; crossing of 38th parallel in by U.S.,

174, 228, 231, 232–36, 255; process of
U.S. intervention in, 177–85; possible
Chinese intervention in, 181, 183,
185–86, 190, 205, 219–21, 228–31,
232, 237; possible Soviet intervention
in, 181, 185–86, 190, 192, 205–6, 219–
21, 228–31, 232; compared with Vietnam War, 190–91; evaluation of U.S.
intervention in, 190–95; settlement
of linked to Taiwan issue, 198–201;
possibility of ending, 198–203, 208–9,
232; and Communists-in-government
issue, 217–18; U.S. public support for,
217. *See also* India: and Korean War;
Korea; North Korea; South Korea
Ku Chu-tung, 69
Kung, H. H., 12
Kuomintang, 73. *See also* Chiang Kai-
shek; Nationalist China
Kuomintang Revolutionary Committee,
69
Kurile Islands, 106
Kwangsi, 139

Lang Wei-hsu, 63–64
Laos, 147
Lapham, Roger D. (director, U.S. Eco-
nomic Cooperation Administration,
China), 63, 70–72, 270 (n. 210)
Lattimore, Owen: attacked by McCar-
thy, 144–45
Leahy, Admiral William, 265 (n. 62)
Lehman, Herbert (senator), 145
Li Chi-shen, Marshal, 69, 269 (n. 198)
Lie, Trygve (secretary-general of the
United Nations), 193, 214, 233
*Life* (magazine), 16, 53, 128
Limb, Ben C., 77
Li Tsung-jen (president, Nationalist
China), 64, 69, 117, 119
Liu Shao-chi, 121
Lodge, Henry Cabot (senator), 70, 141,
218
Lodge, John Davis (congressman), 129,
156
Lovett, Robert A. (under secretary of
state), 65, 70, 84, 85, 87, 100, 106, 113,
114, 116
Lucas, Major General John P., 39, 264 (n.
23)
Lucas, Scott (senator), 185
Luce, Henry, 16
Luce press, 60
Ludden, Raymond P. (counselor at U.S.
embassy in China), 17
Lyuh Woon-hyung, 23, 26, 92

MacArthur, General Douglas: on Chinese intervention in Korea, 3, 243–46,
249–50; and Nationalist China, 39,
40; and Korea before June 1950, 78,
99, 102, 109, 154, 159–62, 166, 169,
174–75; concern for Japan, 154; and
beginning of Korean War, 178, 180,
182, 183–84, 187, 188–90, 195, 197,
209–10; and Taiwan, 137, 139, 140,
150, 151, 197–98, 281 (n. 187); background and personality of, 188–89,
206–7; on uniting Korea, 203, 206; influence of with JCS, 206–7, 240–41,
245, 249–50; and VFW letter, 213,
215–17, 225, 238, 257; and crossing
38th parallel, 210, 231; and Inchon
landing, 223–27; and campaign in
North Korea, 235–36, 237, 238, 239,
240–41, 248–51; meeting with Truman, 238–40, 241, 297 (n. 83); and negotiations in Korea, 254; independence of, 256–57
McCarran, Patrick (senator), 116, 126–
27, 218
McCarthy, Joseph R. (senator), 3, 144–
46, 217–18
McConaughy, Walter P. (U.S. consul at
Shanghai), 136, 150
McCormack, John W. (congressman),
180
McCormick newspaper chain, 77, 217
McKee, Frederick C., 127, 129
Mackenzie King, W. L. (Canadian prime
minister), 96
Malaya, 118, 141
Malik, Jacob A. (Soviet delegate to the
U.N. Security Council), 181, 202, 209,
211, 215
Manchuria, 49, 50, 66, 107; Communist
gains in, 44, 58, 90, 121, 154, 157, 260
(n. 4); possible trusteeship over, 50–
52; Russian position in, 71–72, 78,
119, 120, 136, 148, 230; importance of
Korea to, 86–87; Nationalist collapse
in, 115; Communist troop movements
toward, 216, 229; U.S. activity near,
235–36, 238, 239–41, 254; as base for
Chinese intervention in Korean War,
237, 243; possible U.S. action in, 248;
U.S. aid to Nationalists in, 260 (n.
17)
Manhattan Project, 144
Mansfield, Mike (senator), 63
Mao Tse-tung, 55, 73, 132, 133–34; re-
nounces cease-fire with Nationalists,
13; and U.S., 14, 15–16, 71–72, 124–25,
251, 254; and Russia, 71–72, 112, 119,
124–25, 135–36, 251, 253, 254; position of in China, 117–18, 130, 251; and

Korean War, 161, 170, 181, 229, 237, 248

Marcantonio, Vito (congressman), 180

Marshall, General George C., 42; testimony of at MacArthur hearings, 4; and mission to China, 5, 13–14; and U.S. China policy, 11, 16, 33–34, 36–41, 46–47, 51–58, 62, 66–69, 115, 127, 128, 132, 254, 264 (n. 18); backs Stilwell, 14; prescription for reform in China, 17; background of in China, 33; doubts about Chiang, 33; as leader of State Department, 36, 263 (nn. 4, 5); relationship with Truman, 36, 236; and U.S. Korea policy, 79, 80, 82, 87, 98–99; on aid to Western Europe, 82; retires as secretary of state, 106, 110; and Korean War, 175, 236, 239, 250, 253, 257; becomes secretary of defense, 236; compared with Johnson, 236, 250, 253, 257

Marshall mission to China, 5, 13, 14–15, 35, 66

Marshall Plan, 58–60, 68, 72, 101, 116, 120, 217, 256

Martin, Joseph W. (speaker of the U.S. House of Representatives), 53, 59

Martin, William McChesney (director, Export-Import Bank), 41

Mathews, William R., 167

Matthews, Francis B. (secretary of the navy), 216

Melby, John F. (U.S. consul at Nanking), 48, 265 (n. 72)

Menon, K. P. S., 97

Merchant, Livingston T. (deputy assistant secretary of state for Far Eastern affairs), 119, 231, 234

Middle East, 108, 148, 160

Molotov, V. M. (Soviet foreign minister), 82, 84, 87

Montreux Convention, 15

Morse, Wayne L. (senator), 114

Moscow agreement on Korea, 23–24, 82–84, 88

Muccio, John J. (U.S. ambassador to South Korea): as U.S. representative in Korea, 102; background of, 104, 274 (n. 124); and Rhee, 104–5, 163, 164; on military balance in Korea, 107, 165–70; and U.S. withdrawal from Korea, 158; on possible North Korean attack, 165; and Korean War, 177–78, 195, 204

Mughir, Yasin, 97–98, 103

Murphy, Charles (assistant to the president), 238

Mutual Defense Assistance Program, 130, 134, 165, 168

Nationalist China, 69, 71, 266–67 (n. 113), 267 (n. 119); U.S. frustration with, 5, 12, 17–18, 41, 54–57, 64–65; united front with Communists, 11; military strength of, 11–12; treaty with Soviet Union, 12; purges Communists, 13; in U.S. politics, 16, 42–44, 46–47, 52–63, 65–67, 70, 115–17, 120, 127–31, 143, 146; impact on of Sino-Japanese war, 18; and Korean trusteeship, 20, 24; U.S. aid to, 31, 37–38, 52–53, 58–67, 116–17, 120, 124, 126, 129–30, 131, 136, 138, 150–51, 152, 210–11, 230, 247, 248, 251, 260 (nn. 5 and 17); MacArthur urges support for, 39, 189, 210–11; decline of, 44–45, 58, 63, 65–66, 115; assessed by Wedemeyer, 48; and guardianship over Manchuria, 51; reasons for defeat of, 66–67; rumors of peace talks with Communists, 68; and U.N., 95, 159, 178, 209; recognizes South Korea, 102; Chiang resigns from, 115; headed by Li, 117; and Taiwan, 118–20, 139, 140–41, 149, 212; negotiates with Communists, 119; U.S. treaties with, 121, 136; continued U.S. recognition of, 122; blockade of Shanghai, 126, 133; implications of U.S. failure to abandon, 133–34; air force of, 138; compared with South Korea, 158, 163, 178; and outbreak of war in Korea, 181, 183; and Communist Chinese intervention in Korea, 229

National Opinion Research Center, 217

Nehru, Jawaharlal, 132, 200

Netherlands, 180, 183, 231

New Deal, 77

*New York Times*, 54, 60, 126, 128, 133, 143, 149, 167

New Zealand, 183

Nimitz, Admiral Chester, 40, 57

Nitze, Paul H. (director, Policy Planning Staff), 153, 177, 203–5, 236, 294 (n. 229)

Norstad, Major General Lauris, 38–39, 78

North Atlantic Treaty, 72

North Atlantic Treaty Organization, 114, 123, 134, 158, 168, 173, 191, 236, 245, 256

Northeastern People's Government (of China), 135

North Korea, 110, 201; Chinese intervention in, 3, 241, 247–50; land reform in, 27; and Russia, 29, 78, 84, 157; communism in, 78, 92; military strength of, 88–89, 99–100, 101, 107,

109, 156–58, 165–69, 240, 242, 243–
44, 285 (n. 32), 289 (n. 67); invites
South Koreans to conference, 97; possible U.S. negotiations with, 102;
conditions in compared with south,
103–4; possible U.S. warning to, 108;
possible attack by on South Korea,
153, 158, 164–65, 167, 168–69, Soviet
withdrawal from, 154; attacks South
Korea, 159, 161, 169, 170–71, 173, 177–
98 passim, 204, 222, 232, 255–56, 289
(n. 70), 290 (n. 86); activities of in
South Korea, 163; U.N. operations in,
174, 228, 234, 235–36, 239–41, 244–
46, 249; possible U.N. action in, 203–
9; possible participation of in U.N.,
190, 208–9; possible Soviet or Chinese intervention in, 219–21, 228–31;
military defeat of, 223, 225–26, 228,
232; possible election in, 233; U.N.
establishment of government in, 237.
*See also* Korea; Korean War
North Vietnam, 190
Norway, 181, 228
NSC 8, 99–100, 105–6
NSC 68, 148–49, 160, 173, 259–60 (n.
13)
NSC 81, 219–20

Okinawa, 139, 140, 154, 158, 182
Oliver, Robert T., 77

Pace, Frank (secretary of the army), 183
Pacific pact, 158
Pak Hon-yong, 92
Pakistan, 148, 180
Palestine, 95, 116
Pandit, Vijaya Lakshmi (Indian ambassa-
dor to U.S.), 200
Panikkar, K. M. (Indian ambassador to
Communist China), 199–200, 229,
231, 248
Patterson, George S., 96–98
Patterson, Robert P. (secretary of war),
39, 40, 41, 76, 78, 79–80, 117, 264 (n.
23)
Paul-Boncour, Jean-Louis, 97–98
Pauley, Edwin W., 29
Peffer, Nathaniel, 55
Penfield, James K. (deputy director, Of-
fice of Far Eastern Affairs), 17, 36–37,
47
People's Assembly of North Korea, 103
People's Liberation Army in Korea, 103–
4
People's Republic of China, 131–37, 208.
*See also* Communist China
Pescadores, 118, 137, 141

Petersen, Howard C. (under secretary of
war), 79–80
Philippines, 95, 102, 118, 134, 139, 140,
148, 160, 173, 178, 181, 182, 185, 190,
196, 197, 210
Point Four, 217
Poland, 248
*Pravda*, 147
Prestige, U.S.: 86, 87, 94, 101, 140, 158,
244–45. *See also* Credibility, U.S.
Price, Ernest B., 269 (n. 194)
Princeton-Yenching Foundation, 116
Pyrenees, 160

Quemoy, 212, 216

Radhakrishnan, Sarvepalli (Indian am-
bassador to the Soviet Union), 199
Rankin, Karl Lott (U.S. minister to Tai-
wan), 293 (n. 174)
Rau, Sir Benegal (Indian delegate to the
U.N.), 202, 233
Reardon-Anderson, James, 72
Rees, David, 241
Reischauer, Edwin O., 132
Republic of China. *See* Nationalist
China
Republic of Korea, 177, 179, 191, 194,
203, 214, 241; created, 102; recognized
by foreign powers, 102; problems of,
103–5; National Assembly of, 104–5,
161–62, 167, 170; prospects for, 107;
U.S. commitment to, 158–59; defeat
of U.S. aid bill for, 161; U.S. relationship with, 185; MacArthur on, 189;
operations of in North Korea, 219; inclusion of North in, 220; and possible
government over all Korea, 237–38.
*See also* South Korea
Republican party, 14, 72; seeks to undermine Democrats, 3; and election of
1952, 4; China bloc in, 43; and U.S.
China policy, 54, 62, 65–66, 114, 186,
194, 214, 256; attacks Democratic
spending, 76–77; embitterment of,
114; loses control of Congress, 131;
and Communists-in-government issue, 143–46, 217–18; and 1950 elections, 246; in Congress, 283 (n. 236)
Reston, James, 54, 115, 133, 211, 227
Rhee, Syngman, 272 (nn. 76, 77), 273 (n.
81), 273–74 (n. 109), 290 (n. 86); and
U.S. occupation, 25, 27, 75–77, 272
(nn. 37, 38); and trusteeship, 27; trip
of to U.S., 75, 77; background of in
U.S., 77; opposes Joint Commission,
83, 85; and U.S. move to U.N. (1947),
89, 91; U.S. alternatives to, 91–92; and

police activities in South Korea, 96; and elections in south, 97, 98, 101; and meeting with northern leaders, 97; elected president of Republic of Korea, 102; regime of, 103–5, 157, 187, 191; pleads for retention of U.S. troops, 105; U.S. aid to, 107–9, 110, 111, 169; belligerence of toward North Korea, 157, 164, 170–71; demands U.S. support, 158; U.S. dissatisfaction with, 162–64; and Communist guerrillas, 168; and beginning of Korean War, 179, 181, 186, 195; on unifying Korea, 203; and crossing 38th parallel, 234; possible control of all Korea, 237–38

Rice, Edward E. (assistant chief, Division of Chinese Affairs), 36–37

Ringwalt, Arthur R. (chief, Division of Chinese Affairs), 36–37, 38, 43

Roberts, Brigadier General William L., 157, 164, 166–69, 189

Robertson, Walter S. (U.S. commissioner in China), 39

Roosevelt, Eleanor, 77

Roosevelt, Franklin D., 12, 13–14, 19–20, 21, 36, 53, 113

Roots, John, 117, 127

Rosinger, Lawrence, 55

Royall, Kenneth (secretary of the army), 61

Rusk, Dean (assistant secretary of state for Far Eastern Affairs), 231, 294 (n. 229); as secretary of state, 5; and Korea, 87, 169–71, 272 (n. 52); characterizes Acheson, 123; sees Chennault, 128; replaces Butterworth, 146; background and personality of, 150, 234–35; on Taiwan policy, 150–51, 247; and beginnings of Korean War, 179, 183; on crossing 38th parallel, 205, 233–35; rejects approach to India, 220–21; at Wake Island, 238, 239; on MacArthur, 286 (n. 62)

Russell, Richard B. (senator), 129

Russia, 9, 22. *See also* Soviet Union

Ryukyus, 118

Sachs, Alexander, 153

Sakhalin Island, 106, 262 (n. 51)

Schell, Jonathan, 6–7

Schnabel, James F., 164–65

Scripps-Howard chain, 60

Sebald, William J. (U.S. political adviser for Japan), 211

Selective Service Act, 180

Sentner, David P., 278 (n. 90)

Service, John Stewart (second secretary to U.S. embassy in China), 13, 43, 145

Sevareid, Eric, 208, 230

Shanghai Power Company, 125

Sherman, Admiral Forrest P., 40, 225, 226, 281 (n. 167)

Short, Dewey (congressman), 184

Sinkiang, 119, 120

Sino-Japanese War, 18

Sino-Soviet Treaty of Friendship, Alliance, and Mutual Assistance (1950), 135

Sino-Soviet Treaty of Friendship and Alliance (1945), 12, 71–72

Smith, Gaddis, 7, 143, 192

Smith, H. Alexander (senator), 65, 70, 115–17, 129, 130, 139, 142, 166, 180, 184, 217, 269, (n. 179), 275 (n. 9), 276 (n. 18)

Smith, Major General Oliver P., 225

Smith, Walter Bedell (U.S. ambassador to the Soviet Union), 87

Smoke, Richard, 153

Snyder, John W. (secretary of the treasury), 184

Soong, T. V. (Nationalist Chinese foreign minister), 12, 49

South Korea, 203; conditions in, 6, 24, 26, 27, 75–76, 85–89, 92, 98, 102, 162–64, 170; U.S. action is contrasted with Soviet action in North Korea, 29; creation of republic in, 31; U.S. aid to, 79, 100–101, 157, 159, 161, 168–70, 178, 278 (n. 96), 280 (n. 156); U.S. position in, 79, 93–95, 110, 156, 171; U.S. plans for, 80–81; possible creation of independent government in, 85, 89–91, 92, 93; military strength of, 88, 89, 99–100, 103–4, 108–9, 156–58, 165–69, 220–21, 239, 285 (n. 32), 288 (n. 69); representation of in U.S. plan in U.N., 90; prospect of maintaining U.S. position in, 93–95, 102, 156; elections in, 97–98, 101, 170, 273 (n. 101), 273–74, (n. 109); compared with Nationalist China, 91, 163, 178; and NSC 8, 99–100, 105–6; U.S. withdrawal of troops from, 100, 106–7, 153–59, 253; U.S. defense of related to security of Japan, 106; possible U.S. guarantee to, 108; and U.S. defense perimeter, 153; intelligence operations of, 164; and beginning of Korean War, 177–98 passim, 289 (n. 70); possible participation of in U.N., 208–9; troops of cross 38th parallel, 223, 228; and unification of peninsula, 234, 245; first contact with Chinese soldiers, 241; behavior of toward north, 290 (n. 86)

South Korean Interim Legislative Assembly, 26, 27, 76, 80–81, 97, 272 (n. 76)
South Korean National Assembly, 102, 187, 237
South Vietnam, 190
Soviet Union, 44–45, 96, 248, 273 (n. 84), 289 (n. 67); relations with China, 4, 12, 15–16, 28, 50, 56–57, 71–72, 118, 119, 120, 121, 122, 124–26, 135, 137, 146–52, 196, 206; U.S. fear of, 7; gains of at Yalta, 11; and Manchuria, 15, 28, 38, 51; tensions with U.S., 15; and Korean trusteeship, 20, 24; and ideological differences with U.S., 21; enters war against Japan, 21; occupation of North Korea, 21, 22–23, 92; accepts 38th parallel dividing line in Korea, 22; U.S. negotiations with on Korea, 25, 27–28, 83–84, 272, (nn. 69, 77), 273 (n. 82); confrontation of with U.S. in Korea, 29; role in China and Korea compared, 29–30; refuses to cooperate with U.N. in Korea, 31, 90–91, 96, 107; possible domination of Northeast Asia, 49, 78; capacity of to dominate China, 71; position of on Korea, 85, 88–89; possible impact of domination of Korea by, 20, 29, 86, 106; attitude of toward U.N., 88; troop strength of in North Korea, 88; possibility for dominating Korea, 92; as military threat to Japan, 93; withdraws troops from North Korea, 105, 154; possible U.S. warning to on Korea, 108; as model for China, 117; explodes atomic bomb, 131, 148, 186, 255, 259–60 (n. 13); and Ward affair, 135; and Indochina, 147, 255; and U.S. position in Japan, 147; growing power of in Asia, 154; and possible U.S. war with, 155, 160, 197, 216, 253, 289 (n. 66); concludes arms pact with North Korea, 157; and beginning of Korean War, 161, 170, 174, 178–79, 181, 185–86, 192, 193; possible intervention in Korean War, 174, 203, 205–6, 219–21, 228–32; roles in Korea, Vietnam, and China compared, 190–91; on possible end to Korean War, 199–202, 208–9, 227–28, 232, 233, 243, 296 (n. 40); and military activity near, 235–36, 238, 239–41; and Chinese intervention in Korea, 237
Sprouse, Philip D. (chief, Division of Chinese Affairs), 49, 50, 57–58, 124, 128
Staggers, John S., 77
Stalin, Joseph, 20, 22, 109, 112, 126, 161, 170, 174, 200, 232
Stassen, Harold (governor of Minnesota), 132
Steelman, John R. (presidential assistant), 63
Stilwell, General Joseph W., 14, 17, 33, 39, 46
Stone, Donald C. (budget director), 117
Strong, Robert C. (U.S. first secretary at Taipei), 293 (n. 174)
Strout, Richard L., 180
Stuart, John Leighton (U.S. ambassador to China), 11, 260 (n. 29), 293 (n. 174); background and personality of, 16, 49, 64, 73; and U.S. China policy, 37, 49, 64, 68, 69, 121–26, 128; on Communist attitude toward U.S., 71; view of China, 73
Sun Li-jen (commander in chief, Chinese army training headquarters), 119
Supreme People's Assembly of North Korea, 103
Sweden, 248
Symington, W. Stuart (secretary of the air force), 155
Syria, 95–97
Szechwan, 139

Taber, John (congressman), 61, 70
Taegu, South Korea, 104
Taft, Robert A. (senator), 65, 141, 180, 194, 269 (n. 178)
Taiwan, 139, 216, 257; U.S. policy toward, 4–5, 111, 119, 131, 136, 137–43, 149–51, 173–74, 178–79, 181, 187, 196–98, 198–202, 209–17, 221–22, 227, 246–47, 251, 253, 260 (n. 14); strategic importance of, 118, 140; possible autonomy of, 119, 142–43; MacArthur concern about, 139, 140, 151, 188–89, 210–13, 215–16; as issue in American politics, 141–43, 161, 216–17, 247
Tang Tsou, 6, 66
Teheran conference, 20
Thailand, 134, 138
Tibet, 138, 233–34
Timberman, Brigadier General Thomas B., 156, 182, 264 (n. 23), 285 (n. 37)
*Time* (magazine), 16, 53, 143
Titoism, 111–12, 148, 149
Topping, Seymour, 126
Truman, Harry S., 130, 291 (n. 119); low popularity of, 4; clashes with MacArthur, 3; and China, 14, 38, 41, 63, 70, 122–24, 146, 281 (n. 160); appoints Marshall to mediate in China, 14; and

Korea before June 1950, 21, 29, 96, 100, 102, 154, 159, 161; view of Marshall, 33, 36, 263 (nn. 4, 5); attitude toward formulation of foreign policy, 33, 36; universalistic rhetoric of, 44; and domestic politics on China issue, 52, 116–17, 131, 214, 257; Wedemeyer's report to, 50–52; and internal divisions on China policy, 56; victory of over Dewey, 66; and military spending, 76–77, 108, 155, 232; proposes increase in armed forces, 100; starts full term, 110; and Acheson, 113, 114, 141; and Webb, 113; announces Soviet explosion of atomic device, 131; and NSC 68, 149; and Taiwan, 140–41, 142, 150–51, 197–98, 211, 215–17, 247; and Dulles, 145; and Korean War, 173, 177–87, 193–95, 197–98, 204, 216, 232, 236, 238–39, 243, 245, 251, 290 (nn. 92, 94); and Indian peace initiative, 200; fires Johnson, 216; vetoes internal security bill, 218; meeting with MacArthur, 236, 238–39; and Congress, 283 (n. 236); and tax cuts, 275 (n. 149)

Truman administration: and Communist China, 3–5, 65, 134–35, 137, 201, 254; and Communists-in-government issue, 3, 143–46, 217–18; and Nationalist China, 5, 11–19, 28–29, 31, 37–38, 40, 52, 54–67 passim, 119–20, 133–34, 140, 150–51, 184, 197, 211–17, 247, 254; concern for credibility abroad, 6–8, 28–30, 94, 173, 174, 186–87, 255; and domestic politics on China policy, 16, 42–43, 54, 65–66, 69, 115, 120, 126–31, 142–43, 145–46, 255–56, 266–67 (n. 113); divisions within on China, 38–41, 44–46, 51–52, 56, 60–61, 111, 119, 140–41, 142, 151, 215–16, 221, 251, 256; plans aid to Western Europe, 53–54, 82; unpreparedness of to implement foreign policies, 67, 107–8, 155–56; foreign policy offensive of, 75; divisions within on Korea, 78–81, 100, 105–6, 107–8, 158, 162, 169, 175, 204–6, 219–20, 256; Korea policy emerges within, 78–81; and aid to South Korea, 81–82, 107, 156–58; submits Korean issue to U.N., 84; reappraises Korea policy, 84–88; prepares to withdraw troops from Korea, 95; China and Korea policies of compared, 107, 109, 219–22, 280 (n. 156); options of in Korea, 107–9; reappraises East Asian policy, 111–12; relations with Congress, 114, 131;

impact of domestic politics on, 123; and Taiwan, 142–43, 209–17, 247; and Indochina, 147–49, 282 (n. 231); flirts with containment in Asia, 152; and failure of to protect U.S. position in Korea, 159–71, 251, 253; and beginning of Korean War, 173, 177–98 passim; and crossing 38th parallel, 174, 208–9, 219–21, 228, 231–36; and British and Indian peace initiatives, 198–203, 207; and MacArthur, 210–17, 244–46, 247, 256–57; and negotiations on Korea, 227–28, 232–34; and U.N. campaign in North Korea, 236–38, 241; arrogance and insecurity of, 257–58

Truman Doctrine, 44, 259–60 (n. 13)

Trusteeship: for Korea, 19–20, 23–24, 75–76, 79; for Manchuria, 50–52; for Taiwan, 139, 215

Turkey, 15, 41, 44, 50, 57, 59, 61, 62, 67, 80–81, 94, 168, 169, 180

Tydings, Millard E. (senator), 145, 218

Ukraine, 95

Ulam, Alan, 109, 233

United Nations, 23, 81, 162, 174–75, 190, 193, 199–203, 205–6, 208–9, 219, 221, 223, 227–28, 232–33, 237, 238–42, 243, 248–50, 251; and Korea before 1950, 31, 84, 86–87, 88–95, 100, 101, 105, 153, 159, 162; and possible trusteeship over Manchuria, 50; and Taiwan, 119, 139, 142, 151, 211, 214–16; and China's seat in, 173, 178, 199–201, 227; proceedings in, 236. *See also* United Nations Commission on Korea; United Nations General Assembly; United Nations Relief and Rehabilitation Administration; United Nations Security Council; United Nations Temporary Commission on Korea

United Nations Commission on Korea, 159, 177, 220

United Nations General Assembly, 103, 107; and Korea, 31, 77, 84, 88–91, 93, 95, 96–97, 98–99, 101, 105, 154, 159, 227, 231, 233, 238; U.S. domination of, 88, 90; First Committee of, 90–91, 227, 233, 247; Interim Committee of consulted by UNTCOK, 96–97; and Taiwan, 142, 215, 221, 246–47

United Nations Relief and Rehabilitation Administration, 14–15, 43

United Nations Security Council, 208; and Iranian crisis, 88; possible admission of Communist China to, 146; and

Korean War, 177–81, 193, 199–200, 202–3, 208–9, 220–21, 227, 248–49; and Taiwan, 213–16, 221, 247, 248
United Nations Temporary Commission on Korea (UNTCOK), 90–91, 95–98, 102–3, 107
United States Air Force, 76, 138, 151, 155–56, 158, 160, 178–79, 181, 185
United States Army: and China policy, 38–39, 46, 51, 62, 138; budget of, 76, 86, 93, 160; and Korea, 86, 99, 105, 182, 183, 184, 187–88; weakness of, 108, 140; on Taiwan, 139; on planning for war, 155–56, 160; relations with other services, 155–56. *See also* United States Army Plans and Operations Division
United States Army Advisory Group in China, 11, 39, 52, 61–62, 64, 264 (n. 18)
United States Army Plans and Operations Division: and China policy, 38, 51, 61, 89, 138; and Korea policy, 78, 86–87, 99, 167
United States Bureau of the Budget: and aid to China, 60–61, 76–77, 79, 85, 113, 117, 159
United States Central Intelligence Agency, 99–100; 151–52, 164–65, 243–44
United States Central Intelligence Group, 27–28
United States Communist party, 143
United States Congress, 63, 107, 132, 266–67 (n. 113); and China, 31, 41, 42–43, 52–54, 58–63, 67, 120, 130, 146, 282 (n. 231); and State Department, 47, 113–15; and defense spending, 57, 76–77, 85, 100, 149, 155, 232; and foreign aid, 75, 217; and Korea before June 1950, 77, 80–82, 99, 101, 107, 159, 166, 168; passes Greek-Turkish aid bill, 81; pressure of to lower taxes, 107–8; and creation of NATO, 114; passes MDAP, 130, 138; trends in, 130; Truman administration position in, 131; and Hiss case, 144; and beginning of Korean War, 179–80, 184–85, 194–95, 197; presidential message to on Korean War, 202, 214; and unleashing of Chiang, 216; and Taiwan, 247. *See also* United States House of Representatives; United States Senate
United States Defense Department, 124; relations with State, 111, 162, 250, 294 (n. 223); and aid to South Korea, 112, 169; and Indochina, 148, 150–51; and Taiwan policy, 150–51, 212; financial pressures on, 155; and Johnson take-

over, 158; and beginning of Korean War, 178, 183; on crossing 38th parallel, 205–6, 207; on campaign in North Korea, 235–36, 240–41; Johnson and Marshall as heads of, 257
United States Far Eastern Command, 151, 164–65, 169, 178, 196–97, 225, 226, 237, 241, 283 (n. 242)
United States Foreign Military Assistance Coordinating Committee, 169
United States House of Representatives: and China policy, 42, 44, 52–53, 59, 61, 63, 129; and aid to Korea, 161, 280 (n. 156); and beginning of Korean War, 179; overrides Truman veto, 218; and foreign aid, 283 (n. 236). *See also* United States House of Representatives Foreign Affairs Committee
United States House of Representatives Appropriations Committee, 61
United States House of Representatives Foreign Affairs Committee: on China policy, 42, 44, 59, 60, 129, 141; on Korea, 156–57
United States House of Representatives Military Affairs Committee, 52
United States Joint Chiefs of Staff, 204; and China, 40–41, 45–46, 57, 60–61, 64, 67, 240–41, 243–46, 250, 265 (n. 55), 281 (n. 167); conflicts of with State Department, 60–61, 251, 256; and Korea before June 1950, 86, 106, 154–55, 156–58, 162, 167–68, 169, 206; and Taiwan policy, 118, 119, 137–39, 140–41, 142, 146, 150–51, 197–98, 212, 215; oppose Japanese peace treaty, 145, 147; and Indochina, 148; military strategy of, 154–55; relationship of with MacArthur, 162, 207, 240–41, 245–46, 249–50, 256; and Korean War, 175, 182, 187–88, 190, 197–98, 219–22, 225–27, 236, 240–41, 243–46, 250, 254
United States Joint Committee on Foreign Economic Cooperation, 127
United States Joint Munitions Allocation Committee, 138
United States Joint Strategic Survey Committee, 137, 138, 204
United States Justice Department, 144
United States Korean Military Advisory Group, 159, 160, 165, 166–67
United States National Security Council: and Korea, 99–100, 106, 154, 156, 158, 165, 180, 182, 204, 244, 248; on aid to Chiang, 116–17; projected paper of on Asian policy, 137–38; and Taiwan, 139, 141, 212; and Indochina, 147;

approves NSC 68, 148; creation of, 274 (n. 115)

United States Naval Advisory Group: and China, 40, 264 (n. 18)

United States Navy: and China policy, 39–40, 46, 138, 264 (n. 18); budget of, 76, 160; and Taiwan, 151; relations with other services, 155–56; and Korea, 158; ships of visit Korea, 161; in Korean War, 178–79, 181, 184, 185, 196

*U.S. News and World Report*, 215

United States Office of Strategic Services, 152

United States Provisional Army Advisory Group in Korea, 108

*United States Relations with China, 1943–1949*, 130–31

United States Senate, 42–44, 53, 59, 61, 63, 65, 123, 129, 130, 145, 179, 218. *See also* United States Senate Appropriations Committee; United States Senate Armed Services Committee; United States Senate Foreign Relations Committee; United States Senate Judiciary Committee

United States Senate Appropriations Committee, 43, 53, 61, 166

United States Senate Armed Services Committee, 127, 129

United States Senate Foreign Relations Committee, 81, 116, 129; and China policy, 42–43, 59, 129; partisan controversy over, 114; leadership of, 114; and recognition of Communist China, 123; Acheson testimony before, 132, 149; and Taiwan, 139, 142, 149–50; and Communists-in-government issue, 144–45; and Truman administration, 145–46

United States Senate Judiciary Committee, 218

United States Seventh Fleet, 139, 173–74, 178–79, 185, 196, 209–10, 216

United States State Department, 41, 43, 131; and Communists-in-government issue, 3, 143–46, 217; and Nationalist China, 17, 36–38, 45–46, 51–52, 54–55, 56, 61–72, 118, 119–20, 122, 267 (n. 119); and Korea before June 1950, 20, 21, 25–26, 27, 75, 79, 80–81, 85, 87, 90–93, 93–95, 98–101, 104, 105–8, 112, 154, 157–58, 159–71, 272 (n. 69); and Communist China, 37–38, 45, 48, 70–74, 117–18, 119–24, 132, 133–34, 135, 230–31, 280 (n. 150), 281 (n. 160); clashes of with military, 45–46, 60–61, 111, 250, 256, 294 (n. 223); suspicions toward in Congress and mili-

tary, 47; and U.S. credibility, 57, 152, 255; impact of refusal of to educate public on China, 60; impact of domestic pressures on, 67; retirement of Marshall and Lovett from, 106; moves toward containment in Asia, 111; personnel changes in, 113; relations with legislative branch, 113–15; and Taiwan, 118–19, 140, 141, 150–51, 198, 210–13, 215, 217, 246–47, 290–91 (n. 101); reorganization of, 128; and *China White Paper*, 130–31; desires contingency fund for China area, 130; on Indochina, 130, 147–51; and study group on China, 131; conference on Asian policy, 132; consultations with Senate Foreign Relations Committee, 146; relations with Defense, 162; and Korean War, 173, 177–86, 193, 197–98, 201, 203–6, 209, 235–36, 240–41, 242–46, 248–50, 254, 290–91 (n. 101); and MacArthur, 257, 286 (n. 62)

United States State Department's Division of Chinese Affairs, 36, 124

United States State Department's Division of Northeast Asian Affairs: and Korea policy, 87, 105–6, 154, 157–58, 203–5, 220, 231, 234–35

United States State Department's Office of Far Eastern Affairs, 23, 116; China experts in, 17; impact of, 36; and China policy, 37, 42, 46, 58; Vincent's transfer from, 43; suspicion of, 47; Butterworth leadership of, 52, 128–29; and Korea policy, 78–79, 154, 157–59, 234–35

United States State Department's Policy Planning Staff: and China policy, 53, 73, 74, 87, 153, 203–5, 206, 220, 249

United States State-War-Navy Coordinating Committee, 25, 40, 85

United States War Department, 38, 46, 75–82, 85–86, 264 (n. 18)

Vandenberg, Arthur H. (senator), 49, 55; on aid to China, 53, 58, 129–30, 264–65 (n. 46), 266 (nn. 97, 105), 268 (n. 156); personality of, 42; influence of in Senate, 42–43; guides interim aid bill through Congress, 53–54; legislative skills of, 59; defends commitment to Korea, 81; wants no more foreign aid proposals, 81; view of Acheson, 114; and Fulbright appointment, 114; relations with Lovett, 114; and Smith, 116; at meeting on China issue, 116–17; on Butterworth nomination, 129; uncertain health of, 130;

on Taiwan, 141–42, 281 (n. 79); presses Truman administration, 145
Vandenberg, General Hoyt: concern of for Taiwan, 138, 203, 204, 206–7, 223, 281 (n. 167)
Veterans of Foreign Wars, 213, 215, 225, 238, 257
Vietminh, 111
Vietnam, 5, 147, 149
Vincent, John Carter (director, Office of Far Eastern Affairs), 17, 36–37, 41, 43, 58, 78–81
Vishinsky, Andrei (Soviet foreign minister), 227
Voorhees, Tracy S. (under secretary of the army), 140
Vorys, John (congressman), 42, 53, 55, 59, 70, 129, 156

Wake Island, 236, 238–39
Ward, Angus (U.S. consul general at Mukden), 122, 125, 133, 135
*Way of a Fighter*, 127
Webb, James E. (under secretary of state), 76, 113, 117, 122, 195, 231
Wedemeyer, Lieutenant General Albert C., 58; replaces Stilwell, 14; supports Chiang, 14; mission of to China, 46–52, 82, 87; background and personality of, 47; testimony in Congress of, 53, 60; proposals of on China rejected, 57; on aid to Chiang, 61–63; report on Korea, 86–87; and U.S. China policy, 268 (n. 148)
Westerfield, H. Bradford, 65, 114
Western Europe, 131, 145; and relationship to China, 52, 55–57, 123; and U.S. aid to, 53–54, 58–59, 82, 93, 120, 128–29, 159, 217, 256; importance of, 94, 108; and recognition of Communist China, 121, 122, 125, 132; connec-

tion of to U.S. policy in Indochina, 148; and U.S. Asia policy, 151–52; in U.S. war plans, 156–60; and outbreak of war in Korea, 187; attitude of toward Korea and Vietnam, 190–91; and Sino-American clash, 234; U.S. leadership in, 253; possible Soviet attack on, 289 (n. 66)
Wherry, Kenneth (senator), 44, 115, 184, 194, 216–17
Wiley, Alexander (senator), 63
Wilkinson, James R. (U.S. consul general at Hong Kong), 229–30, 243
Williams, Jay, 77
Willoughby, General Charles A., 164–65, 241–42, 249
Wilson, Woodrow, 290 (n. 94)
*World Culture*, 209
World War I, 92
World War II, 39, 92, 103, 118, 130, 139, 144, 153, 174, 188, 190, 195, 196, 199; Sino-American relations during, 12–14, 16, 18; lessons of to Nationalist China, 16, 18; lessons of to U.S., 18, 19, 20–21, 28, 251; U.S. demobilization following, 67; U.S. influence in China during, 109
Wright, Colonel W. H. Sterling, 167, 177, 189
Wu, K. C. (mayor of Shanghai), 119, 140

Yalta accords: on Manchuria, 11, 20, 48, 66, 71–72, 262 (n. 51)
Yen Hsi-shan, General, 64
Yim, Louise, 77
Yosu rebellion, 104, 163
Yugoslavia, 126, 136, 148, 177, 181, 202–3, 278 (n. 83)
Yu Han-mou, 69
Yunnan, 128